T0211014

Communications
in Computer and Information Science 692

Commenced Publication in 2007
Founding and Former Series Editors:
Alfredo Cuzzocrea, Xiaoyong Du, Orhun Kara, Ting Liu, Dominik Ślęzak,
and Xiaokang Yang

More information about this series at http://www.springer.com/series/7899

Slimane Hammoudi · Luís Ferreira Pires
Bran Selic · Philippe Desfray (Eds.)

Model-Driven Engineering and Software Development

4th International Conference, MODELSWARD 2016
Rome, Italy, February 19–21, 2016
Revised Selected Papers

 Springer

Editors
Slimane Hammoudi
Université d'Angers/ESEO
Angers
France

Luís Ferreira Pires
Faculty of EEMCS
University of Twente
Enschede
The Netherlands

Bran Selic
Malina Software Corp.
Nepean, ON
Canada

Philippe Desfray
SOFTEAM
Paris
France

ISSN 1865-0929 ISSN 1865-0937 (electronic)
Communications in Computer and Information Science
ISBN 978-3-319-66301-2 ISBN 978-3-319-66302-9 (eBook)
DOI 10.1007/978-3-319-66302-9

Library of Congress Control Number: 2017952392

Printed on acid-free paper

This Springer imprint is published by Springer Nature
The registered company is Springer International Publishing AG
The registered company address is: Gewerbestrasse 11, 6330 Cham, Switzerland

Preface

The present book contains extended and revised versions of selected papers from the fourth International Conference on Model-Driven Engineering and Software Development (MODELSWARD 2016), held in Rome, Italy during February 19–21, 2016.

MODELSWARD received 118 paper submissions from 38 countries, of which 14% have been included in this book. The papers were selected by the event chairs, and this selection was based on a number of criteria that included the evaluation and comments provided by the Program Committee members, the session chairs' assessment, and also the program chairs' global view of all papers included in the technical program. The authors of selected papers were then invited to submit a revised and extended version of their papers, which had to contain at least 30% additional material.

The purpose of the International Conference on Model-Driven Engineering and Software Development is to provide a platform for researchers, engineers, academics, as well as industrial professionals from all over the world to present their research results and development activities in using models and model-driven engineering techniques for software development. We are confident that the papers included in this volume will strongly contribute to the understanding of some current research trends in model-driven engineering and software development, including:

– models syntax and semantics;
– theories and tooling for model verification;
– combined use of ontologies and metamodeling;
– software development automation/code generation;
– application of MDE to different areas, like web services, learning, IoT security, and industrial real-time systems.

We would like to thank all the authors for their contributions and also express our gratitude to the reviewers, who have helped to ensure the quality of this publication.

February 2017

Slimane Hammoudi
Luís Ferreira Pires
Bran Selic
Philippe Desfray

Organization

Conference Co-chairs

Bran Selic	Malina Software Corp., Canada
Philippe Desfray	SOFTEAM, France

Program Co-chairs

Slimane Hammoudi	ESEO, MODESTE, France
Luis Ferreira Pires	University of Twente, The Netherlands

Program Committee

Silvia Abrahão	Universitat Politecnica de Valencia, Spain
Achilleas P. Achilleos	University of Cyprus, Cyprus
Hamideh Afsarmanesh	University of Amsterdam, The Netherlands
Guglielmo De Angelis	CNR - IASI, Italy
Keijiro Araki	Kyushu University, Japan
Marco Autili	University of L'Aquila, Italy
Elarbi Badidi	United Arab Emirates University, UAE
Luca Berardinelli	Vienna University of Technology, Austria
Alexandre Bergel	University of Chile, Santiago, Chile
Antonia Bertolino	Italian National Research Council - CNR, Italy
Lorenzo Bettini	Università di Firenze, Italy
Paolo Bocciarelli	University of Rome Tor Vergata, Italy
Jan Bosch	Chalmers University of Technology, Sweden
Jean-Pierre Bourey	Ecole Centrale de Lille, France
Mark van den Brand	Eindhoven University of Technology, The Netherlands
Antonio Brogi	Università di Pisa, Italy
Achim D. Brucker	SAP Research, Germany
Bernd Bruegge	Technische Universität München, Germany
Philipp Brune	University of Applied Sciences Neu-Ulm, Germany
Christian Bunse	University of Applied Sciences Stralsund, Germany
Dumitru Burdescu	University of Craiova, Romania
Juan Manuel Gonzalez Calleros	Universidad Autónoma de Puebla, Mexico
W.k. Chan	City University of Hong Kong, Hong Kong
Hassan Charaf	BME, Hungary
Yuting Chen	Shanghai Jiaotong University, China
Dickson Chiu	The University of Hong Kong, Hong Kong
Antonio Cicchetti	Malardalen University, Sweden
Tony Clark	Sheffield Hallam University, UK

Bernard Coulette	Université Toulouse Jean Jaurès, France
Kevin Daimi	University of Detroit Mercy, USA
Andrea D'Ambrogio	Università di Roma "Tor Vergata", Italy
Florian Daniel	University of Trento, Italy
Leonidas Deligiannidis	Wentworth Institute of Technology, USA
Birgit Demuth	TU Dresden, Germany
Giovanni Denaro	University of Milano-Bicocca, Italy
Enrico Denti	Università di Bologna, Italy
Zinovy Diskin	McMaster University and University of Waterloo, Canada
Dimitris Dranidis	CITY College, Int. Faculty of the University of Sheffield, Greece
Schahram Dustdar	Vienna University of Technology, Austria
Sophie Ebersold	IRIT, France
Holger Eichelberger	Universität Hildesheim, Germany
Maria Jose Escalona	University of Seville, Spain
Rik Eshuis	Eindhoven University of Technology, The Netherlands
Angelina Espinoza	Universidad Autónoma Metropolitana, Iztapalapa (UAM-I), Spain
Vladimir Estivill-Castro	Griffith University, Australia
Anne Etien	CRIStAL, University Lille 1 - Inria - CNRS, France
Dirk Fahland	Eindhoven University of Technology, Netherlands
João Faria	FEUP - Faculty of Engineering of the University of Porto, Portugal
Gianluigi Ferrari	University of Parma, Italy
Stephan Flake	Redknee Germany OS GmbH, Germany
Piero Fraternali	Politecnico di Milano, Italy
Jicheng Fu	University of Central Oklahoma, USA
Carlo A. Furia	ETH Zurich, Switzerland
Paola Giannini	University of Piemonte Orientale, Italy
Cesar Gonzalez-Perez	Institute of Heritage Sciences (Incipit), Spanish National Research Council (CSIC), Spain
Carmine Gravino	University of Salerno, Italy
Klaus Havelund	NASA/Jet Propulsion Laboratory, USA
Brian Henderson-Sellers	University of Technology, Sydney, Australia
Jose R. Hilera	University of Alcala, Spain
Bernhard Hoisl	WU Vienna, Austria
Pavel Hruby	DXC Technology, Denmark
Marianne Huchard	CNRS and Université de Montpellier, France
Javier Gonzalez Huerta	Blekinge Institute of Technology, Sweden
Emilio Insfran	Universitat Politècnica de València, Spain
Stefan Jablonski	University of Bayreuth, Germany
George Kakarontzas	Technological Educational Institute of Thessaly, Greece
Teemu Kanstren	VTT, Finland
Georgia Kapitsaki	University of Cyprus, Cyprus

Jacek Kesik	Lublin University of Technology, Poland
In-Young Ko	Korea Advanced Institute of Science and Technology, South Korea
Jun Kong	North Dakota State University, USA
Jochen Kuester	University of Applied Sciences in Bielefeld, Germany
Uirá Kulesza	Federal University of Rio Grande do Norte (UFRN), Brazil
Anna-Lena Lamprecht	Lero - The Irish Software Research Centre, Ireland
Philip Langer	EclipseSource Services GmbH, Austria
Lior Limonad	IBM, Israel
Claudia Linnhoff-Popien	Ludwig-Maximilians-Universität Munich, Germany
Dongxi Liu	CSIRO, Australia
Francesca Lonetti	National Research Council (CNR) Pisa, Italy
Roberto Lopez-Herrejon	École de Technologie Supérieure, Canada
Der-Chyuan Lou	Chang Gung University, Taiwan
Frederic Mallet	Université Nice Sophia Antipolis, France
Eda Marchetti	ISTI-CNR, Italy
Beatriz Marin	Universidad Diego Portales, Chile
Steve McKeever	Uppsala University, Sweden
Stephen Mellor	Freeter, UK
Dragan Milicev	University of Belgrade, Serbia
Dugki Min	Konkuk University, South Korea
Valérie Monfort	LAMIH Valenciennes UMR CNRS 8201, France
Andrzej Niesler	Wroclaw University of Economics, Poland
Halit Oguztüzün	Middle East Technical University, Turkey
Olaf Owe	University of Oslo, Norway
Gordon Pace	University of Malta, Malta
Alexander Petrenko	ISPRAS, Russian Federation
Rob Pettit	The Aerospace Corp., USA
Elke Pulvermueller	University of Osnabrueck, Germany
Iris Reinhartz-Berger	University of Haifa, Israel
Wolfgang Reisig	Humboldt-Universität zu Berlin, Germany
Colette Rolland	Université Paris 1 Panthéon-Sorbonne, France
Jose Raul Romero	University of Cordoba, Spain
Gustavo Rossi	Lifia, Argentina
Davide Di Ruscio	University of L'Aquila, Italy
Houari Sahraoui	Université de Montreal, Canada
Rick Salay	University of Toronto, Canada
Comai Sara	Politecnico di Milano, Italy
Anthony Savidis	Institute of Computer Science, FORTH, Greece
Jean-Guy Schneider	Swinburne University of Technology, Australia
Martina Seidl	Johannes Kepler University Linz, Austria
Peter Sestoft	IT University of Copenhagen, Denmark
Marten van Sinderen	University of Twente, The Netherlands
John Slaby	Raytheon, USA
Stefan Sobernig	WU Vienna, Austria

Arnor Solberg	Sintef, Norway
Richard Soley	Object Management Group, Inc., USA
Stéphane Somé	University of Ottawa, Canada
Jean-Sébastier Sottet	Luxembourg Institute for Science and Technology, Luxembourg
Ioannis Stamelos	Aristotle University of Thessaloniki, Greece
James Steel	University of Queensland, Australia
Alin Stefanescu	University of Pitesti, Romania
Arnon Sturm	Ben-Gurion University of the Negev, Israel
Hiroki Suguri	Miyagi University, Japan
Eugene Syriani	University of Montreal, Canada
Massimo Tivoli	University of L'Aquila, Italy
Andreas Tolk	MITRE Corporation, USA
Mario Trapp	Fraunhofer IESE, Germany
Salvador Trujillo	Ikerlan, Spain
Naoyasu Ubayashi	Kyushu University, Japan
Sabrina Uhrig	Universität Bayreuth, Germany
Andreas Ulrich	Siemens AG, Germany
Gianluigi Viscusi	EPFL Lausanne, Switzerland
Shuai Wang	Simula Research Lab, Norway
Christiane Gresse von Wangenheim	UFSC - Federal University of Santa Catarina, Brazil
Viacheslav Wolfengagen	Institute JurInfoR, Russian Federation
Amiram Yehudai	Tel Aviv University, Israel
Tao Yue	Simula Research Lab, Norway
Gefei Zhang	Hochschule für Technik und Wirtschaft Berlin, Germany
Chunying Zhao	Western Illinois University, USA
Haiyan Zhao	Peking University, China
Kamil Zyla	Lublin University of Technology, Poland

Additional Reviewers

Michele Amoretti	University of Parma, Italy
Onder Babur	Eindhoven University of Technology, The Netherlands
Anne-Lise Courbis	École des Mines d'Alès, France
Yanja Dajsuren	TU/e, The Netherlands
Adel Ferdjoukh	University of Montpellier, France
Yannis Lilis	Institute of Computer Science, FORTH, Greece
Hong Lu	Software Engineer Institute, China
Jacopo Soldani	Università di Pisa, Italy
Yannis Valsamakis	Institute of Computer Science, FORTH, Greece
Sylvain Vauttier	LGI2P, France

Invited Speakers

Manfred Broy	Technische Universität München, Germany
Paola Inverardi	Università dell'Aquila, Italy
Lionel Briand	Université du Luxembourg, Luxembourg

Contents

Applications and Software Development

Modeling Languages, Tools and Architectures

Survey on the Applicability of Textual Notations for the Unified Modeling Language

Stephan Seifermann$^{(\boxtimes)}$ and Henning Groenda

FZI Research Center for Information Technology, Software Engineering,
Haid-und-Neu-Str. 10-14, Karlsruhe, Germany
{seifermann,groenda}@fzi.de

Abstract. The Unified Modeling Language (UML) is the most commonly used software description language. Today, textual notations for UML aim for a compact representation that is suitable for developers. Many textual notations exist but their applicability in engineering teams varies because a standardized textual notation is missing. Evaluating notations in order to find a suitable one is cumbersome and guidelines found in surveys do not report on applicability. This survey identifies textual notations for UML that can be used instead of or in combination with graphical notations, e.g. by collaborating teams or in different contexts. Additionally, it rates the notation's applicability with respect to UML coverage, user editing experience, and applicability focused on engineering teams. Our results facilitate the otherwise unclear selection of a notation tailored for specific scenarios and enables trade-off decisions. We identified and characterized 21 known notations and 12 notations that were not covered in previous surveys. We used 20 categories to characterize the notations. Our findings show that a single notation does not cover more than 3 UML diagram types (mean 2.6), supports all surveyed state of the art editing features (only one notation supports all), and fits into existing tool chains.

Keywords: UML · Textual notation · Survey · Editing experience

1 Introduction

The Unified Modeling Language (UML) has become the de-facto standard for describing software systems. The specification defines a graphical but no textual notation for fully representing the model. Researchers such as Spinellis [1] argue that textual notations provide compact and intuitive alternatives. For instance, Erb represents UML activity diagram-like service behavior specifications textually in a developer-friendly way and more compact than graphics.

The absence of a standard leads to many textual notations that do not fully cover UML modeling partially but focus on supporting documentation, being compact, or serving as input for code generation. They largely differ in syntax, UML coverage, user editing experience, and applicability in engineering teams.

© Springer International Publishing AG 2017
S. Hammoudi et al. (Eds): MODELSWARD 2016, CCIS 692, pp. 3–24, 2017.
DOI: 10.1007/978-3-319-66302-9_1

The latest surveys covering textual UML notations were performed by Luque, et al. [2–4]. The former two [2,3] focus on the accessibility of UML for blind students in e-learning and classrooms, respectively. The latter [4] surveyed tools for use-case and class diagrams used in industry at 20 companies in the state of Sao Paolo (Brazil). All surveys target notations used in practice. The literature studies rely on existing studies on the accessibility domain but do not search for scientifically published notations. The survey of Mazanec and Macek [5] focuses on textual notations in general but is a few years old and covers few notations. It does not represent the current development state and available variety of notations and modeling environments. The surveys illustrate the variety of specialized textual notations but do not analyze the editing experience in an objective way. The editing experience is, however, crucial for engineering teams and is hard to survey. The latter degrades the selection quality because it limits the amount of notations to be tested because of time constraints.

The contribution of this survey is the identification and classification of textual UML notations including the user experience. Engineering teams can use the classification for identifying appropriate notations for their usage scenarios. The classification scheme is tailored to support this selection. This survey examines usability of notations with respect to their syntax, editors, and modeling environment. Usability in realistic scenarios is determined by covered diagram types, supported data formats for information exchanges such as XMI, and synchronization approaches with other notations. It additionally evaluates whether non-necessary parts of the notation can be omitted. This support for sketching models eases low-overhead discussion and brainstorming. For instance, the UML specification allows to omit the types of the class attributes.

This survey extends the trade-off selection discussion and includes two additional notations with respect to our previously published survey [6]. The two new notations stem from the latest survey from Luque et al. [2] that we became aware of in the meantime. This adds two new notations that we reviewed with the same 20 categories covering applicability in engineering teams. Considering that survey, we identified 12 notations not covered in surveys of other authors. We rewrote and extended the discussion to identify drawbacks of the notations that limit applicability. This allows practitioners to focus their notation evaluations on critical aspects. Tool vendors can identify unique features. Researchers can develop approaches on how to make notations more applicable.

The remainder of this survey is structured as follows: Sect. 2 describes the survey's review method by defining objectives and the review protocol consisting of three phases. Section 3 describes the classification scheme based on the defined objectives. Section 4 presents the extended analysis results in terms of classified textual notations. Section 5 covers our new extensive discussion of the findings and discusses the validity of the results. Finally, Sect. 6 concludes the paper.

2   Review Method

The review process follows the guidelines of Kitchenham and Charters [7] for structured literature reviews (SLR) in software engineering based on the guidelines in the field of medical research. Their guidelines cover the planning, conduction, and writing of reviews. Planning involves defining research objectives and creating a review protocol describing the activities in each review step.

The following sections describe our implementation of the SLR and mapping to the proposed method. The results of our search activities are documented and available for reproducibility at http://cooperate-project.de/CCIS2016.

2.1 Objectives

Our objectives are to determine each notation's (O1) coverage of the UML, (O2) user editing experience and (O3) applicability in an engineering team. The reasoning requires an analysis of the textual notations and of the modeling environments. Section 3 presents the detailed classification scheme based on the objectives and instructions on information extraction from literature.

2.2 Review Protocol

Figure 1 shows an overview of our review protocol. We distinguish three phases during the conduction: classic SLR, Quality Assurance and Complement.

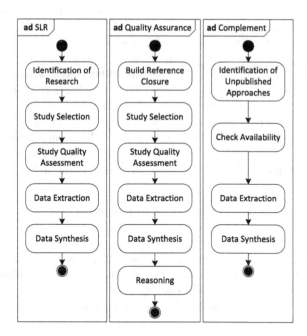

Fig. 1. The three phases of the review conduction process used in this survey.

The classic *SLR* follows the guidelines of review conduction by Kitchenham, et al. [7]. We extend the SLR with two additional phases in order to increase the quality of the results and to take notations into account that are mainly used in (industrial) practice: The *Quality Assurance* phase focuses on incoming and outgoing literature references as suggested by the Snowballing search approach [8]. In contrast to the original proposal, we use Snowballing only to cross-check our SLR search strategy. The *Complement* phase focuses on textual notations that are available in practice but are not scientifically published.

2.3 Phase 1: SLR

Reviews according to [7] consist of the five activities marked as *SLR* in Fig. 1.

The *Identification of Research* describes the search strategy for collecting literature. We chose a keyword-based search approach using the search engines ACM Digital Library, IEEExplorer, CiteSeer, ScienceDirect, SpringerLink and Google Scholar. These search engines cover relevant journals and are suggested by Kitchenham and Charters for the software engineering domain. We did not include EI Compendex and Inspec as we could not query these search engines without subscriptions. Their focus is on high-qualitative entries and metadata and they do not belong to a not-covered established publishing authority. We are confident that the selected search engines and their metadata are sufficient.

We defined a set of keywords T for identifying textual notations and another one U for identifying the usage of UML. Table 1 presents both sets as variations of our original terms *textual notation,* and *UML*. They are based on commonly used terminology in the modeling domain. A search query is given by $\vee_{t_i} \wedge \vee_{u_i}$ with $t_i \in T \wedge u_i \in U$. The query enforces the exact matching of keywords. It considers abstracts and titles because this restricts the search to literature that focuses on textual notations for UML. Google Scholar has API restrictions that limit queries on abstracts to papers that have been released at most one year ago. This restriction does not apply to our title-based search. We restrict ScienceDirect queries to computer science papers. We implemented a search on the SpringLink results enabling keyword identification in the abstract. After collecting the results of all search engines, we merge them and filter duplicates.

Table 1. Keyword groups used in search queries.

Group	Keywords
Textual T	CTS, textual modeling, textual modelling, text-based modeling, text-based modelling, textual notation, text-based notation, textual UML, text-based UML, textual syntax
UML U	UML, unified modeling language, unified modelling language

Study Selection covers a rough screening based on titles and abstracts to allow spending more time on relevant literature. We focus on textual notations for graphical parts of the UML specification [9, p. 683]. We exclude all textual notations only extending UML or its elements rather than expressing UML itself.

We exclude all notations that are not related to UML. We exclude notations not intended for human usage such as data transfer containers, e.g. XMI serialization [10]. We include (a) primary papers describing a single textual notation, and (b) secondary survey-like papers including their references as primary sources.

The *Study Quality Assessment* considers title, abstract, and the content of the full paper. We decide on in-/exclusion of the remaining papers in this step.

Data Extraction is the process of determining the information required to judge about the fulfillment of the objectives. Section 3 shows the analyzed features of the notations, their hierarchy, and individual decision basis in detail. We reason on the modeling environment based on information found directly in literature, implemented prototypes, prototype websites, and source code. We identify prototypes, their website, and the source code by: (a) following links in the papers, (b) mining the website of the institute or company of the authors, (c) and searching for the name of the notation (full name and abbreviation if used) via the Google search engine and on Githuband visit the first one hundred search results. Data extraction takes place for the declared primary editor. If there is more than one prototype, we use the declared primary editor and an IDE-integrated editor. We assume the latter to profit from advanced accessibility features of the IDE. If there are editors for several IDEs, we decide in favor of the Eclipse-based one because Eclipse is open source, highly extensible, and offers many accessibility features[1].

Data Synthesis summarizes the information. We show and summarize the analysis results according to the classification given in Sect. 3.

2.4   Phase 2: Quality Assurance

The Quality Assurance phase is based on the Snowballing approach [8] of Wohlin for literature identification. Wohlin suggests starting with an initial set of relevant literature and including relevant forward and backward references. We do not use Snowballing as primary source for relevant literature because its quality heavily depends on the initial literature set as described by Wohlin. Instead, we accept the overhead of a prior SLR phase with broad search terms and use Snowballing to verify the quality of our SLR phase as described below.

Build Reference Closure determines the completeness of results from the SLR phase. We collect all directly referenced and referencing literature for the analyzed papers. We derive the referenced literature from the references section of the paper. We use Google Scholar to determine incoming references.

The *Study Selection* and *Study Quality Assessment* from phase SLR are applied to identify additional notations.

We perform *Data Extraction* on selected papers as in the SLR phase and add the notation to our database.

Data Synthesis summarizes the information as carried out in the SLR phase.

---

[1] https://wiki.eclipse.org/Accessibility.

Reasoning addresses why newly identified notations have been missed in the SLR phase. Section 5 presents the results. This phase is different from Wohlin's Snowballing approach and allows verifying the quality of our SLR phase.

2.5   Phase 3: Complement

Identification of Unpublished Approaches focuses on textual notations that are available in practice but are not scientifically published. We use the Google search engine to identify the top 5 pages for 'UML textual notation', 'UML textual notations', 'UML textual notations list'. We mine the resulting websites to identify new approaches. We follow the links from the identified websites looking for notations or comparisons of notations.

Additionally, we search for unrecognized scientific surveys or notation comparisons. We perform a full-text search via Google Scholar with the names of the three most popular non-scientific notations. We assume that recent surveys including non-scientific notations cover them and thereby will be included in the search results. We determine a notation's popularity by querying Google with the name of the notation and comparing the announced results with the amount of other notations. We only included notations that claim to relate to the UML.

In *Check Availability*, we filter all potential notations with dead links.

We perform *Data Extraction* for new notations, analyze the information, and add the notation to our database.

Data Synthesis summarizes the information as carried out in the SLR phase.

3   Classification

This section presents the classification and information extraction goals derived from the three objectives presented in Sect. 2.1. The objectives cover aspects of what can be edited based on the textual notation definition (O1, O2) as well as how it can be edited based on modeling environments (O2, O3). We use feature modeling to represent the evaluation classes, their hierarchy, and possible values. The resulting overview is depicted in Fig. 2. The features themselves and how their values are evaluated for the notations are presented in the following.

Each *Textual Notation* is defined by a Language (O1, O2) and an optional Implementation (O2, O3) in a modeling environment.

The *Implementation* is optional and covers all aspects with respect to a modeling environment for a notation. It can have Recent Activity (O3), a License (O3), and can support Change Propagation (O2, O3) between different notations, data Format Exchange (O2), and Editor (O2) features.

We divide the classification of the implementation into two parts for a better overview: integration aspects, and the editor itself. The former covers the features relevant for integrating an implementation into a tool chain. The latter covers the editing experience of the editors.

The following subsections will cover the language, integration, and the editor in that order.

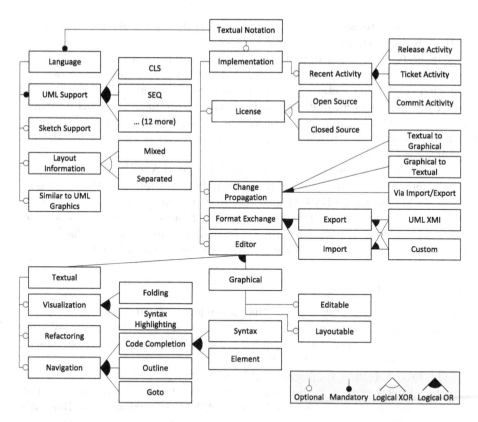

Fig. 2. Feature model for analyzed characteristics and their hierarchy.

3.1 Language

The mandatory *Language* definition describes the language's syntax. It consists of UML Support (O1) for diagram types, can have Sketch Support (O2), integrated Layout Information (O2), and be Similar to UML Graphics (O2).

UML Support is mandatory and describes the supported UML diagram types. At least one type has to be supported. A type is supported if the documentation states it to be supported or the modeling environment allows the creation of a corresponding type. The considered diagram types are based on the UML specification [9, p. 682]. The abbreviations are based on the official abbreviations from [9, p. 682], or self-made if there is no official one: Activity Diagram (ACT), Class Diagram (CLS), Communication Diagram (COM), Component Diagram (CMP), Composite Structure Diagram (COS), Deployment Diagram (DEP), Interaction Overview Diagram (INT), Object Diagram (OBJ), Package Diagram (PKG), Profile Diagram (PRO), Sequence Diagram (SEQ), State Machine Diagram (STM), Timing Diagram (TIM), and Use Case Diagram (UC).

Sketch Support is optional and can ease the notation's usage during discussions. Discussions benefit from quick interaction. Formal full-fledged modeling can extend the interaction time. There is support if only mandatory elements of UML's abstract syntax are required.

Layout Information is optional and states if the textual model can contain graphical layout information. This information allows to improve graphical presentations of textual statements. The information is irrelevant to describe the model itself. The interpretation is difficult as only graphic notations illustrate graphical positions. The information can be either *Mixed* with model elements or kept *Separated*. It is marked as *Mixed* if at least one element has mandatory layout information.

Similar to UML Graphics is optional and denotes if ASCII art memes graphical elements such as arrows in the textual notation. For instance, the characters <>--> are similar to the UML graphical representation for an aggregation. This can work well for people knowing the graphical representation but has adverse effects when typing or for people using accessibility tools like Braille displays. A notation is marked as similar if there is at least one ASCII art mapping.

3.2 Integration

The integration covers all features that are relevant for integrating an implementation into a tool chain. Such a decision is based on the costs, extensibility, support, maintainability and compatibility to existing tools. The following features cover these aspects in more detail.

The *Recent Activity* is optional and indicates the support status. In contrast to a maintained project, a discontinued project will not receive bugfixes and might be incompatible to recent software such as new versions of an IDE. We determine three activity dates that allow judging project activity. One of them has to be identifiable: *Release Activity* relates to the date of the last release. A release can be a proper release, snapshot, or nightly build. *Ticket Activity* is determined by the date of the most recently closed ticket. *Commit Activity* is given if we can determine the most recent commit.

The *License* is optional and can be crucial for using and maintaining the modeling environment. Open Source licenses allow own bug fixing and the development of extensions and adaptations. The individual requirements for a license depend heavily on the usage context of the modeling environment. An expert review is required to check for a notation of interest if it applies to the own use case. We therefore differentiate solely between Open Source and Closed Source licenses. We rely on the list of the Open Source Initiative [11]. If the license is listed on their website, we treat the project as open source. All other licenses are considered *Closed Source*.

Change Propagation can be supported and addresses transferring changes from one notation into another. The modification in the modeling environment for a textual notation can therefore result in an according change in a graphical notation of the same content. This targets a consistent view of the content and allows different team members to work with different notations during discussion. This can mean updates in real-time for close collaboration or based on exporting and importing models in different environments. We consider the three cases:

Textual to Graphical, Graphical to Textual, and Via Import/Export propagation. *Textual to Graphical* and *Graphical to Textual* apply if the modeling environment includes a textual and a graphical editor. We consider it supported if changes in one editor are reflected in the other one. *Via Import/Export* applies if there is an import or export functionality and notations can be updated sequentially. It is marked if it provides import and export function for UML models in the standardized XMI data format.

Data *Format Exchange* is optional and allows integrating the modeling results into other tools or existing tool chains. We only consider fully-automated exchange procedures provided by the implementation itself. We do not consider other procedures such as the error-prone manual translation between notations or tools that is usually done by assistants. A modeling environment can support the *Import* or *Export* of a different set of data formats. This feature can have the value *UML XMI* as standardized UML data exchange and can list *Custom* formats supported by the tools. The values are selected based on the documentation or file extensions provided in the editing environment.

3.3 Editor

Editor categorizes properties related to user input, interaction, and presentation. They can be Textual (O2), Graphical (O2) or both. An editor is considered textual if it contains only text and no graphical elements. Text coloring may be used. This ensures that textual editors are accessible by accessibility techniques such as screen readers. Otherwise, it is treated as Graphical.

Textual editors address several features to increase user experience and accessibility. A textual editor can support Visualization (O2), Refactoring (O2) of the model, and user Navigation (O2) within the model. Previous surveys did not focus on the editing experience in detail. Therefore, we selected the features according to our objectives.

A *Visualization* is optional and allows focused presentation of content by means of information hiding. It can support Folding (O2), and Syntax Highlighting (O2).

Folding (un)hides selected partitions of the model, eases comprehension for complex models and focused presentation. It is selected if there is at least one partition in a model that can be hidden or shown based on the editor's UI.

Syntax Highlighting highlights keywords or important structural parts of the model. It eases comprehension and identifying the structure of models. It is selected if colors or text formats highlight at least one keyword of the language.

Refactoring is optional and addresses batch changes to the model. For instance, all occurrences of a model element can be replaced with another one in one single step instead of using a manual search and replace approach. This feature exists if there is at least one supported refactoring.

Navigation is optional and addresses navigation to model elements and providing an overview to users. There can be support for Code Completion (O2), overviews on model elements by Outline (O2), and model element navigation by Goto (O2). Navigation is selected if at least one of its child features is selected.

Code Completion is optional and provides completion of a language's syntax or referenced model elements. It can provide hints on keywords of the Syntax or model Elements allowed at the current position. It aids users in specifying correct models and speeds up changes. We consider two types of values: *Syntax*-based and *Element*-based completion. They are selected if there is at least one corresponding code completion feature in the editor.

Outline is optional and provides an overview of the elements in a model. This can include their hierarchical structure. It is selected if there is at least a list of all top-level elements in a model depicted in the editor.

Goto is optional and allows direct navigation or jumps to specific model elements. This eases comprehension and look-up of elements. It is selected if there is navigation or jump support for at least one element type. It is included if it is directly in the textual notation and excluded if its only in the Outline.

Graphical editors are optional and allow displaying and editing graphical version of the models. There are many advanced graphical UML editors available based on the formal UML specification. [12] gives a good overview in his survey of interoperability of UML tools. [13] illustrates the features of various UML tools. There are many comparisons between few selected tools such as IBM Rational Software Architect, MagicDraw, and Papyrus in [14] or between Rational Rose, ArgoUML, MagicDraw, and Enterprise Architect in [15]. This survey focuses on the synchronization aspect with textual languages and their editors (O3). Our categories show if the editor is mainly a pure static presentation of the model or allows interactions. We distinguish for Graphical editors if their content is Editable (O2) and Persistable (O2). This feature is selected if there is a graphical presentation of the model in the modeling environment.

Editable is optional and denotes if the graphical content can be modified, e.g. a user can rename elements. This feature is selected if at least some elements in the graphical editor can be modified.

Layoutable is optional and denotes if modifications to the graphical layout, e.g. the position of model elements, can be done. Users can structure the graphical representation in this way. This feature is selected if elements can be moved.

4   Analysis Results

This chapter presents the analysis results for all notations. Tables 2 and 3 provide an overview and show the determined characteristics for all notations. The following paragraphs provide short notation descriptions. They point out features or provide comments, which are not already covered by the overview.

Alf [16] has been specified by the OMG and is the UML action language. It is based on Foundational UML (fUML). There is no official editor implementation.

Alloy [17] is a model finder and solver based on the Z notation [18] instead of UML. The author compares it to UML in Sects. 4.1 and 6.4 and states that "Alloy is similar to OCL, the Object *Constraint* Language (OCL) of UML"[2].

---

[2] http://alloy.mit.edu/alloy/faq.html.

Table 2. Language and textual editor implementation characteristics of analyzed textual UML notations. Characteristics are: not extractable (-), given ($\checkmark$), or not given ($\times$). Layout information is: mixed (m) or separated (s).

Notation	UML Support	Sketch Support	Layout Information	Graph. Similarity	Syntax Highlighting	Folding	Compl. (Syntax)	Compl. (Element)	Outline	Goto	Refactoring
Alf	CLS, ACT, PKG	$\checkmark$	$\times$	$\times$	-	-	-	-	-	-	-
Alloy	$\times$	$\times$	$\times$	$\times$	$\checkmark$	$\times$	$\times$	$\times$	$\times$	$\times$	$\times$
AUML	SEQ	$\times$	$\times$	$\times$	$\checkmark$	$\times$	$\times$	$\times$	$\times$	$\times$	$\times$
AWMo	CLS	$\times$	$\times$	$\times$	-	-	-	-	-	-	-
blockdiag: seqdiag, actdiag	SEQ, ACT	$\checkmark$	m	$\checkmark$	-	-	-	-	-	-	-
Clafer	CLS, OBJ	$\times$	$\times$	$\times$	$\checkmark$	$\times$	$\times$	$\times$	$\times$	$\times$	$\times$
cwknc	SEQ	$\times$	$\times$	$\times$	$\checkmark$	$\times$	$\times$	$\times$	$\times$	$\times$	$\times$
Dcharts	STM	$\checkmark$	$\times$	$\times$	-	-	-	-	-	-	-
Earl Grey	CLS, SEQ, STM	$\times$	$\times$	$\times$	$\checkmark$	$\checkmark$	$\checkmark$	$\checkmark$	$\checkmark$	$\checkmark$	$\checkmark$
EventStudio	SEQ, STM, UC	$\times$	s	$\checkmark$	$\checkmark$	$\times$	$\times$	$\times$	$\times$	$\times$	$\times$
Finite State Machine Diagram Editor	STM	$\checkmark$	$\times$	$\times$	$\checkmark$	$\times$	$\times$	$\times$	$\times$	$\times$	$\times$
HUTN	all	$\checkmark$	$\times$	$\times$	-	-	-	-	-	-	-
IOM/T	SEQ	$\times$	$\times$	$\times$	-	-	-	-	-	-	-
js-sequence-diagrams	SEQ	$\checkmark$	m	$\checkmark$	-	-	-	-	-	-	-
MetaUML	CLS, STM, ACT, UC, CMP, PKG	$\checkmark$	m	$\times$	-	-	-	-	-	-	-
modsl	CLS, COM	$\checkmark$	$\times$	$\times$	$\checkmark$	$\checkmark$	$\checkmark$	$\times$	$\checkmark$	$\checkmark$	$\checkmark$
Nomnoml	CLS, OBJ, STM, UC, PKG	$\checkmark$	m	$\checkmark$	-	-	-	-	-	-	-
pgf-umlcd	CLS	$\checkmark$	m	$\times$	$\checkmark$	$\times$	$\times$	$\times$	$\times$	$\times$	$\times$
pgf-umlsd	SEQ	$\checkmark$	m	$\times$	$\checkmark$	$\times$	$\times$	$\times$	$\times$	$\times$	$\times$
PlantUML	CLS, OBJ, SEQ, STM, ACT, UC, CMP, DEP	$\checkmark$	m	$\checkmark$	-	-	-	-	-	-	-
Quick Sequence Diagram Editor	SEQ	$\checkmark$	$\times$	$\times$	-	-	-	-	-	-	-
TCD	CLS	$\checkmark$	$\times$	$\checkmark$	-	-	-	-	-	-	-
TextUML	CLS, STM	$\times$	$\times$	$\times$	$\checkmark$	$\times$	$\checkmark$	$\times$	$\checkmark$	$\times$	$\times$
tUML	CLS, STM, COS	$\times$	$\times$	$\times$	$\checkmark$	$\checkmark$	$\times$	$\times$	$\checkmark$	$\checkmark$	$\times$
txtUML	CLS, STM, ACT	$\times$	$\times$	$\times$	$\checkmark$	$\checkmark$	$\times$	$\times$	$\checkmark$	$\checkmark$	$\times$
UML/P	CLS, OBJ, SEQ, STM, ACT	$\checkmark$	s	$\checkmark$	$\checkmark$	$\checkmark$	$\checkmark$	$\times$	$\checkmark$	$\checkmark$	$\times$
UMLet	CLS, OBJ, UC, PKG	$\checkmark$	m	$\times$	$\checkmark$	$\times$	$\times$	$\times$	$\times$	$\times$	$\times$
UMLGraph	CLS, SEQ	$\checkmark$	m	$\times$	-	-	-	-	-	-	-
uml-sequence-diagram-dsl-txl	SEQ	$\checkmark$	m	$\checkmark$	$\checkmark$	$\checkmark$	$\checkmark$	$\times$	$\checkmark$	$\checkmark$	$\times$
Umple	CLS, STM, COS	$\checkmark$	s	$\checkmark$	$\checkmark$	$\times$	$\times$	$\times$	$\times$	$\times$	$\times$
USE	CLS	$\times$	s	$\times$	$\checkmark$	$\times$	$\times$	$\times$	$\times$	$\times$	$\times$
WebSequenceDiagrams	SEQ	$\checkmark$	m	$\checkmark$	-	-	-	-	-	-	-
yUML	CLS, ACT, UC	$\checkmark$	$\times$	$\checkmark$	-	-	-	-	-	-	-

Table 3. Implementation characteristics (without textual editor) of analyzed textual UML notations. Characteristics are: not extractable (-), given (✓), or not given (×). The License is: open (*O*) or closed (*C*) source.

Notation	Recent Activity	License	Change Propag.	Graph. Editor Editable	Layoutable	Format Exchange Export	Import
Alf	-	-	-	-	-	-	-
Alloy	2015	O	×	×	✓	dot, xml	als
AUML	2014	-	T2G	-	-	png	×
AWMo	2013	C	T2G,G2T	-	-	×	×
blockdiag: seqdiag, actdiag	2015	O	T2G	-	-	png, svg, pdf	×
Clafer	2015	O	×	-	-	own, Python Z3, Choco JS, alf, dot	×
cwknc	2013	O	T2G	-	-	png	×
Dcharts	-	-	-	-	-	-	-
Earl Grey	2012	O	×	-	-	×	×
EventStudio	2016	C	T2G	-	-	pdf, emf, xml, html	×
Finite State Machine Diagram Editor	2015	O	T2G,G2T	✓	×	own	own
HUTN	-	-	-	-	-	-	-
IOM/T	-	-	-	-	-	-	-
js-sequence-diagrams	2015	O	T2G	-	-	svg	×
MetaUML	2015	O	T2G	-	-	×	×
modsl	2009	O	T2G	-	-	png, jpg	×
Nomnoml	2015	C	T2G	-	-	png	×
pgf-umlcd	2015	O	T2G	-	-	×	×
pgf-umlsd	2015	O	T2G	-	-	×	×
PlantUML	2015	O	T2G	-	-	uml, svg, eps, txt, html	×
Quick Sequence Diagram Editor	2015	O	×	-	-	pdf, (e)ps, svg, swf, emf, gif, jpg	×
TCD	-	-	IE	-	-	uml	uml
TextUML	2015	O	×	-	-	uml	×
tUML	-	-	T2G,IE	×	×	uml	uml
txtUML	2015	-	T2G	-	-	uml	×
UML/P	-	C	T2G	✓	×	×	×
UMLet	2015	O	×	✓	✓	bmp, eps, gif, jpg, pdf, png	uxf
UMLGraph	2014	O	T2G	-	-	png, svg, emf, ps, gif, jpg, fig	×
uml-sequence-diagram-dsl-txl	2009	×	T2G	-	-	xml, Code	×
Umple	2015	O	T2G,G2T	✓	✓	uml, tuml, uxf, als, use, emf, code, yUML	×
USE	2015	O	T2G	✓	×	pdf	×
WebSequenceDiagrams	-	×	T2G	-	-	×	×
yUML	-	-	T2G	-	-	png, pdf, jpg, json, svg	×

It provides a graphical and textual notation but no support for any UML diagrams. It has a MIT license and does not provide access to source code.

AUML [19] is an extension to UML SEQ diagrams. Winikoff defined a textual notation for AUML that has been included in the Prometheus Design Tool[3]. It provides a PNG export but no mechanism to import or export a model.

Ckwnc [20] is a web editor that allows specifying UML SEQ diagrams with a programming language-like syntax. Users can export graphics.

Clafer [21] is a modeling language for CLS diagrams and constraints. The online tool[4] provides no graphical view but offers a GraphViz export.

DCharts [22] specifies a meta-model in AToM (see footnote 3)[5] and a graphical and textual notation. The textual notation is the leading one and the graphical implemented only partially [22, p. 35]. No tool or files could be found actually implementing the theoretical concept. We could not find an advanced textual editor with collaboration features for the self-defined language. The publication claims that there is a transformation from the meta-model to UML state charts.

Earl Grey [5] is a proof of concept for an accessible textual notation. The Eclipse implementation creates a model during editing but there is no export.

EventStudio [23] is a commercial tool suite for modeling object and message flows. It supports SEQ, STM, and UC diagrams and can generate images. The images, however, do not correspond to the official UML graphical syntax.

HUTN [24] is an OMG standard for text-based representation of MOF-based meta-models, which covers the UML meta-model. Humans can use it easier than XMI. There is no official reference implementation of an editor.

IOM/T [25] allows specifying protocols for agent communication. It covers AUML [19] sequence diagrams partially, which we consider as SEQ support. The notation seems to consist of two papers, the latest in 2007.

MetaUML [26] is a DSL leveraging TeX in the background. It creates graphics in UML style but no UML models.

modsl[6] is a text to diagram sketch tool based on Java code specifications. The proposed default editing environment is Eclipse. It creates graphics in UML style but no UML models.

pgf-umlcd[7] and pgf-umlsd[8] are both based on PGF/TikZ. They leverage TeX interpreters. This has a major influence on its syntax and structure. They create graphics in UML style but no UML models.

PlantUML [27] is a textual notation to diagram tool. CLS diagrams can be exported as UML files for the StarUML and ArgoUML tools. Imports and synchronization mechanisms are not available. There are various standalone and integrated editor implementations.

---

[3] https://sites.google.com/site/rmitagents/software/prometheusPDT.
[4] http://t3-necsis.cs.uwaterloo.ca:8094.
[5] http://atom3.cs.mcgill.ca/.
[6] https://code.google.com/p/modsl/.
[7] https://github.com/xuyuan/pgf-umlcd.
[8] https://code.google.com/p/pgf-umlsd.

Quick Sequence Diagram Editor[9] is a text to diagram sketch tool written in Java. It creates graphics in UML style but no UML models.

TCD [28] is an ASCII-art converter for CLS diagrams. It provides conversions from and to UML XMI representations. The implementation is not available.

TextUML [29] exports standard UML models but does not provide a graphical view. Services such as Cloudfier[10] use it as alternative for graphical modeling.

tUML [30] focusses on modeling for validation and verification purposes. The mentioned prototype is not available.

txtUML [31] uses regular Java syntax for modeling. Java Annotations provide additional information. There is no dedicated textual or graphical editor but a Papyrus model can be exported.

UML/P [32] is a textual notation claiming to merge programming and modeling by enriching UML models with Java expressions. The Eclipse plugin provides textual and graphical editors but no import or export.

UMLet[11] [33] is a graphical UML sketch tool. It provides graphical UML shapes. A selected shape is shown in a textual view, which allows to modify the element. The textual view covers only the selected element. It create graphics in UML style but no UML models.

UMLGraph [1] uses Java source files and customized JavaDoc comments to create diagrams. It creates graphics in UML style but no UML models.

uml-sequence-diagram-dsl-txl[12] is a command-line based text to diagram sketch tool written in the transformation language TXL. The Eclipse IDE plugin was not available. The table lists the mentioned features of the guide[13]. It creates graphics in UML style but no UML models.

Umple [34] is a model-to-code generator with textual notations. UML elements not relevant for code generation such as aggregations are omitted. The online tool synchronizes the textual and graphical notation.

USE [21] aims for specifying systems with including OCL constraints. The official tool does not provide an editor but textual and graphical views.

AWMo [35][14] is a Web application targeting the collaboration of blind and sighted users. The Web tool does not work, there is no included documentation. The characteristics have been determined based on the source code, available presentations and the paper. They define their own simplistic meta-model inspired by CLS diagrams for their proof of concept. Collaboration is realized via store and load mechanism, which maps to Import and Export in the table.

blockdiag[15] has the subprojects seqdiag[16] and actdiag[17]. Both are written in Python and convert textual diagram descriptions to graphics. The syntax is

---

[9] http://sdedit.sourceforge.net/.

[10] http://doc.cloudfier.com/creating/language/.

[11] www.umlet.com.

[12] http://www.macroexpand.org/doku.php.

[13] http://www.txl.ca/eclipse/TXLPluginGuide.pdf.

[14] http://garapa.intermidia.icmc.usp.br:3000/awmo/.

[15] http://blockdiag.com/en/.

[16] https://bitbucket.org/blockdiag/seqdiag.

[17] http://blockdiag.com/en/actdiag/index.html.

Graphviz's DOT format. The code and release activities are taken from seqdiag only being representative. It creates graphics in UML style but no UML models.

Finite State Machine Diagram Editor and Source Code Generator[18] has an own XML Schema Definition, which defines their textual language called FsmML. Conforming XML documents can be Imported and Exported. Links to model elements are realized via String matching.

js-sequence-diagrams[19] is a text to diagram sketch tool written in Java Script. It is inspired by the commercial WebSequenceDiagram. It parses plain text and can report basic parsing errors. Its shared with an own license title as simplified BSD. It creates graphics in UML style but no UML models.

nomnoml[20] is a text to diagram sketch tool written in Java Script. The syntax is oriented at the graphical UML shapes. It creates graphics in UML style but no UML models.

WebSequenceDiagrams[21] is a text to diagram sketch tool written in Java Script. It creates graphics in UML style but no UML models. A free alternative is js-sequence-diagrams.

yUML [36] is a text to diagram sketch tool. It creates graphics in UML style but no UML models.

5   Discussion of Findings

This section discusses the results of the survey presented in the previous section. We use the results to reason about the applicability in engineering teams and especially identify open points and potential improvements. Additionally, we discuss threats to validity. Section 5.1 focuses on the UML coverage of the found notations. The quality of the provided user editing experience is covered in Sects. 5.2 and 5.3 illustrates the issues of using the notations in engineering teams. Threats to internal and external validity are discussed in Sect. 5.4.

5.1   UML Coverage

The benefit of a high coverage of UML diagram types is a wide range of applicable scenarios. This stems from an increased probability that a diagram type required for a scenario is supported by a notation. The results of our survey with respect to the UML coverage are shown in Fig. 3. We discovered that most notations (14 out of 31) only support a single diagram type. This prohibits modeling different aspects of a system such as structure and behavior in a single model. Relations between elements describing different aspects are hard to express. The conceptional HUTN notation supports all diagram types but provides no implementation. In summary, only six notations support four or more diagram types and are, therefore, not restricted to specific application scenarios.

---

[18] http://www.stateforge.com/.

[19] https://bramp.github.io/js-sequence-diagrams/.

[20] https://github.com/skanaar/nomnoml.

[21] https://www.websequencediagrams.com/.

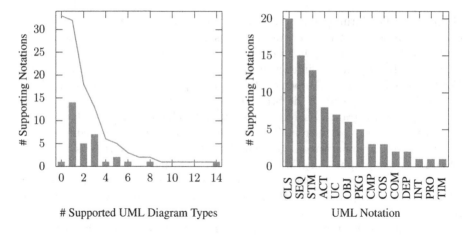

Fig. 3. UML coverage of the surveyed notations.

We found that the most supported diagram types are class (20) and sequence diagrams (15) as well as state machines (13). Only few notations support other diagram types as shown in Fig. 3. No implementation exists for TIM, PRO, and INT diagrams. The focus of the notations is in line with research on graphical UML usage: Dobing and Parsons [37] as well as Erickson and Siau [38] already identified the class diagram as most commonly used diagram. Both consider sequence diagrams and state machines to be in the top five used diagram types. Reggio et al. [39] achieved similar results and stress that practitioners only use small subsets of the UML elements. As a consequence, vendors of textual notations tailor their notations to support the commonly used UML diagram types and elements in order to facilitate usage. Potential users of the notation have, nevertheless, to carefully check if it supports the elements required for the envisioned usage scenario.

5.2   User Editing Experience

Even if using state of the art editors increases efficiency when working with textual representations, only about half of the notations (18 of 33) provide specialized editors. The support for specific features is visualized in Fig. 4.

Basic Features. All implementations support syntax highlighting. Around a third of the implementations provide navigation support including outlines and goto links. The same amount provides view customization such as folding. This most probably stems from textual editing frameworks such as Xtext[22] generating these features automatically and without additional effort.

---

[22] https://eclipse.org/Xtext.

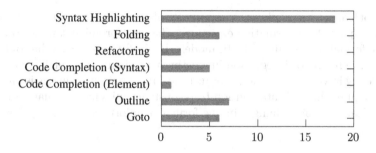

Fig. 4. Amount of notations that support specific textual editor features.

Large Model Handling. Most editors, however, lack features required for working with more complex models as given within industrial contexts. We consider code completion and refactorings to be such features because they free the user from knowing the whole model in order to finish their modeling tasks. The support for code completion is twofold: About 25% of the implementations support code completion for syntactical elements such as keywords but lack support for code completion for elements. Therefore, a user has to remember all usable elements or has to look them up. Only one surveyed editor supports code completion for elements. Only two editors support refactorings such as renaming of elements. The results indicate that the models created with most of the surveyed notations have a limited maintainability: Refactorings ease restructuring or fixing typos but the majority of editors do not support them. Finding applicable elements becomes cumbersome without advanced code completion. Therefore, most notations should be used for small to medium sized models or for simple models without complex relationships between elements.

Coupling with Graphical Notation. Seven implementations include a graphical editor to visualize the modeled UML diagram and five implementations allow editing it. In contrast, 22 implementations provide the export of graphics. This indicates that graphical representations are still in the focus but mostly for documentation purposes.

5.3   Applicability in Engineering Teams

Active development is crucial to get bug fixes and helps when it comes to upgrading the editing environment. About half of our surveyed notations had recent activity in 2015 and later, which means they are actively developed. Unfortunately, only two-thirds of the notations provide a clear license statement, which is crucial for using a notation and its implementation in professional contexts.

The integration in existing tool chains mainly depends on supported import and export formats. Two-thirds (22) of the surveyed implementations provide exports in various formats and only five implementations support imports. Roundtrip engineering, however, requires both features and usage of well-structured formats. Only 8 out of 22 notations provide well-structured formats for exports.

Four out of five notations allow the import of well-structured formats. The remainder uses graphics for information exchange. The most prominent well-structured exchange format are serialized UML models. Basically, this means that only four notations are ready for integration in existing tool chains that enable collaborative modeling in various notations, for instance. Information exchange is only partial and requires human intervention to reconstruct missing information including graphical positions, changes in one format or information not expressible in graphics.

5.4   Threats to Validity

We address four common threats to internal validity: incomplete selection, inconsistent measurements, biased experimenter, and incomplete information.

We addressed *incomplete selection* with two additional phases that check the completeness of search results. During the survey, we found a total of 33 textual UML notations. Two notations originate from including the latest survey of Luque et al. [2] in this extended version. These notations are not published scientifically and therefore did not originate from the first two phases that focus scientific notations. In addition, they are not popular enough to be listed in the very first Google search results that we used to find industrial notations. We would, however, have found the survey of Luque et al. in earlier phases if it had been published at the time we conducted our literature study.

We found half of the remaining 31 notations in the SLR phase. In the Quality Assurance phase, we found four new papers and three new notations. The first phase did not reveal three of these papers [17, 25, 40] because their main contribution was not about a textual UML notation. Therefore, they did not clearly indicate that they also cover a textual UML notation in their title or abstract. The remaining paper [31] is not indexed by the search engines that we used. The major new result of the completion phase was the textual UML tool list [41] provided by Jordi Cabot, a professor with research interests in model-driven software engineering at the ICREA research institute. We found eleven new notations compared to the previous phase. We did not find ten of them in earlier phases because of their scientific focus. The found notations of the third phase have not been scientifically published. The remaining notation [35] did use the term *textual language*, which we consider to broad for our research subject. Nevertheless, we consider the keywords of the SLR phase and the whole notation finding process to be successful and appropriate.

The Complement phase did not include an extensive search strategy because we focus on scientifically published notations in this survey. We complement previous intensive search strategies with the most common notations used in industry. To achieve this, we imitate the common search strategy that covers the very first popular results only. We included all notations of previous surveys [3–5] in the analysis. In total, we found 12 new notations compared to previous surveys: Alloy, AUML, Clafer, Dcharts, IOM/T, pgf-umlcd, pgf-umlsd, TCD, tUML, txtUML, UML/P, and uml-sequence-diagram-dsl-txl.

We addressed *inconsistent measurements* and *biased experimenter* with a rigorous review protocol and instructions for the characteristics extraction. The characteristics for the notations can be determined in an objective way. Mazanec et al. [5], however, used subjective characteristics such as *readability* or *simplicity* and did not mention how they have been determined.

We addressed *incomplete information* by using multiple information sources. We characterized all 33 notations by extracting information from the papers, and mining websites and source code (if possible). The former is the standard approach during a SLR but the two latter allow filling the gaps left by the scientific papers. Especially, the project's activity and editor features are most commonly not covered by publications. Only Alf, Dcharts, HUTN, IOM/T, and TCD did not provide sufficient information to determine these characteristics.

The external validity requires generalizable results. The survey results are applicable for scenarios that cover collaborative UML editing with textual notations in general because the characteristics do not focus on a specific scenario. This is a benefit over the previous surveys [2–4] that focused on teaching UML to visually impaired people or focused on specific UML diagram types in industry. The fuzzy characteristics in [5] lead to a limited generalization and applicability.

6   Conclusions

The Unified Modeling Language (UML) is the most commonly used modeling language. Its specification defines a graphical but no complete textual notation. Many specialized textual notations evolved but they are incompatible and highly fragmented with respect to UML coverage, editing experience, and applicability in engineering teams. There is no notation that clearly dominates the other notations in every aspect. Therefore, practitioners have to select a notation per usage scenario and do many trade-off decisions. This survey facilitates the selection of notations by providing a comprehensive list of 33 UML notations and their 20 characteristics related to applicability. The characteristics do not focus on a specific application domain but provide objective selection criteria.

The review method used in the survey produces reproducible and reliable results. We applied a classic systematic literature review in order to identify scientifically published approaches. In the second phase, we used snowballing to build a reference closure in order to find publications not covered by the keyword-based search from the first phase and to validate the keywords. In a third phase, we used Google searches to find not-scientifically published notations and complement our existing results. This approach is beneficial because we identified about half of the notations in the latter two phases.

The major insights we gained by analyzing our results are: (a) Users have to know the UML diagram types they require in their scenearios because most notations only support a single diagram type and there is no single implemented notation that supports all types. (b) Using the surveyed notations for complex UML models degrades the maintainability because almost all implementing tools do not provide editing support for complex tasks such as refactoring models or referencing existing elements. (c) Teams can integrate the textual notation in existing tool chains mostly by using imports and exports of UML models but only few notations provide this feature. We could, however, not find a single notation that is applicable without restrictions and clearly dominates all other notations. Instead, many notations simply focus on graphics generation for documentation purposes and do not allow modeling and processing of the modeled information. A scenario-specific selection process is still necessary.

Practitioners, tools vendors, and researchers can benefit from this survey: Practitioners can focus on evaluating important characteristics of notations instead of struggling with finding notations and extracting the information with respect to UML coverage, editing experience, and applicability in engineering teams. Even if the survey does not cover all relevant aspects, it provides a considerable foundation for preselecting notations. This lowers the evaluation effort, allows to evaluate more notations within given time constraints, and therefore enables better selections.

Tool vendors for notations can identify seldom supported features and either advertise their support for these features or can try to integrate them in order to increase their market share.

Researchers can identify seldom supported features and can investigate the reason for the bad coverage. For instance, if tool vendors worry about the complexity of their notation when including further diagram types, researchers can develop approaches for integrating views in textual modeling frameworks.

We identified two tasks as future work: First, we see a need for notations that target proper UML modeling. This means a considerable UML diagram type coverage as well as support for import and export of standard UML models. Engineering teams cannot integrate other tools into their existing environments. Second, we need a systematic comparison and rating approach for the supported UML elements. This requires a definition of the UML elements usually contained in a UML diagram type and a set of sample models for elements. If the notation cannot represent the model, it does not support the corresponding element. We plan to develop guidelines and example models for assessing the UML coverage of UML notations.

Acknowledgements. This work is funded by the German Federal Ministry of Labour and Social Affairs under grant 01KM141108.

References

1. Spinellis, D.: On the declarative specification of models. IEEE Softw. **20**, 94–96 (2003)
2. Luque, L., Brandão, L., Tori, R., Brandão, A.: On the inclusion of blind people in UML e-learning activities. In: RBIE 2015, vol. 23, p. 18 (2015)
3. Luque, L., Brandão, L.O., Tori, R., Brandão, A.A.F.: Are you seeing this? what is available and how can we include blind students in virtual UML learning activities. In: SBIE 2014 (2014)

4. Luque, L., Veriscimo, E.S., Pereira, G.C., Filgueiras, L.V.L.: Can we work together? on the inclusion of blind people in UML model-based tasks. In: Langdon, P.M., Lazar, J., Heylighen, A., Dong, H. (eds.) Inclusive Designing, pp. 223–233. Springer, Cham (2014). doi:10.1007/978-3-319-05095-9_20

5. Mazanec, M., Macek, O.: On general-purpose textual modeling languages. In: DATESO 2012, pp. 1–12 (2012)

6. Seifermann, S., Groenda, H.: Survey on textual notations for the unified modeling language. In: MODELSWARD 2016, pp. 28–39. SciTePress (2016)

7. Kitchenham, B., Charters, S.: Guidelines for performing systematic literature reviews in software engineering (version 2.3). EBSE Technical report, EBSE-2007-01, Keele University (2007)

8. Wohlin, C.: Guidelines for snowballing in systematic literature studies and a replication in software engineering. In: EASE 2014, pp. 38:1–38:10. ACM (2014)

9. OMG: Unified Modeling Language (UML) - Version 2.5. (2015). http://www.omg.org/spec/UML/2.5/PDF

10. OMG: XML Metadata Interchange (XMI) - Version 2.5.1. (2015). http://www.omg.org/spec/XMI/2.5.1/PDF

11. Open Source Initiative: Licenses by name (2015). http://opensource.org/licenses/alphabetical. Accessed 04 Aug 2015

12. Kern, H.: Study of interoperability between meta-modeling tools. In: FedCSIS 2014, pp. 1629–1637 (2014)

13. Wikipedia: List of unified modeling language tools (2015). https://en.wikipedia.org/wiki/List_of_Unified_Modeling_Language_tools. Accessed 04 Aug 2015

14. Safdar, S.A., Iqbal, M.Z., Khan, M.U.: Empirical evaluation of UML modeling tools–a controlled experiment. In: Taentzer, G., Bordeleau, F. (eds.) ECMFA 2015. LNCS, vol. 9153, pp. 33–44. Springer, Cham (2015). doi:10.1007/978-3-319-21151-0_3

15. Khaled, L.: A comparison between UML tools. In: ICECS 2009, pp. 111–114 (2009)

16. OMG: Action language for foundational UML (ALF). PDF (2013). http://www.omg.org/spec/ALF/1.0.1/

17. Jackson, D.: Alloy: a lightweight object modelling notation. ACM TOSEM **11**, 256–290 (2002)

18. Information technology - z formal specification notation - syntax, type system and semantics. Standard, International Organization for Standardization (2002)

19. Winikoff, M.: Towards making agent UML practical: a textual notation and a tool. In: NASA/DoD Conference on Evolvable Hardware, pp. 401–412 (2005)

20. Walton, D.: CKWNC - UML sequence diagram editor (2013). http://www.ckwnc.com

21. Zayan, D.O.: Model evolution: comparative study between clafer and textual UML (2012). http://gsd.uwaterloo.ca/sites/default/files/Model%20Evolution;%20Clafer%20versus%20Textual%20UML.pdf. Project Report

22. Feng, H.: DCharts, a formalism for modeling and simulation based design of reactive software systems. Master's thesis, School of Computer Science, McGill University, Montreal, Canada (2004)

23. EventHelix: Eventstudio system designer 6 (2016). https://www.eventhelix.com/EventStudio

24. Vieritz, H., Schilberg, D., Jeschke, S.: Access to UML diagrams with the HUTN. In: Jeschke, S., Isenhardt, I., Hees, F., Henning, K. (eds.) Automation, Communication and Cybernetics in Science and Engineering 2013/2014, pp. 751–755. Springer, Cham (2014). doi:10.1007/978-3-319-08816-7_58

25. Doi, T., Yoshioka, N., Tahara, Y., Honiden, S.: Bridging the gap between AUML and implementation using IOM/T. In: Bordini, R.H., Dastani, M., Dix, J., Fallah Seghrouchni, A. (eds.) ProMAS 2004. LNCS (LNAI), vol. 3346, pp. 147–162. Springer, Heidelberg (2005). doi:10.1007/978-3-540-32260-3_8
26. Gheorghies, O.: MetaUml - GitHub (2015). https://github.com/ogheorghies/MetaUML. Accessed 14 Aug 2015
27. Roques, A.: PlantUml: Open-source tool that uses simple textual descriptions to draw UML diagrams (2015). http://plantuml.com/. Accessed 14 Aug 2015
28. Washizaki, H., Akimoto, M., Hasebe, A., Kubo, A., Fukazawa, Y.: TCD: a text-based UML class diagram notation and its model converters. In: Kim, T., Kim, H.-K., Khan, M.K., Kiumi, A., Fang, W., Ślęzak, D. (eds.) ASEA 2010. CCIS, vol. 117, pp. 296–302. Springer, Heidelberg (2010). doi:10.1007/978-3-642-17578-7_29
29. Chaves, R.: TextUml toolkit (2015). http://abstratt.github.io/textuml/readme.html. Accessed 14 Aug 2015
30. Jouault, F., Delatour, J.: Towards fixing sketchy UML models by leveraging textual notations: application to real-time embedded systems. In: OCL 2014, pp. 73–82 (2014)
31. Dévai, G., Kovács, G.F., An, Á.: Textual, executable, translatable UML. In: OCL 2014, pp. 3–12 (2014)
32. Grönniger, H., Krahn, H., Rumpe, B., Schindler, M., Völkel, S.: Text-based modeling. CoRR abs/1409.6623 (2014)
33. Auer, M., Tschurtschenthaler, T., Biffl, S.: A flyweight UML modelling tool for software development in heterogeneous environments. In: EUROMICRO 2003, pp. 267–272. IEEE (2003)
34. Lethbridge, T.: Umple: an open-source tool for easy-to-use modeling, analysis, and code generation. In: MoDELS 2014 (2014)
35. Nero Grillo, F., Mattos Fortes, R.P.: Tests with blind programmers using AWMo: an accessible web modeling tool. In: Stephanidis, C., Antona, M. (eds.) UAHCI 2014. LNCS, vol. 8513, pp. 104–113. Springer, Cham (2014). doi:10.1007/978-3-319-07437-5_11
36. Harris, T.: Create UML diagrams online in seconds, no special tools needed (2015). http://yuml.me. Accessed 14 Aug 2015
37. Dobing, B., Parsons, J.: How UML is used. Commun. ACM **49**, 109–113 (2006)
38. Erickson, J., Siau, K.: Can UML be simplified? practitioner use of UML in separate domains. In: EMMSAD 2007, pp. 89–98 (2007)
39. Reggio, G., Leotta, M., Ricca, F., Clerissi, D.: What are the used UML diagram constructs? a document and tool analysis study covering activity and use case diagrams. In: MODELSWARD 2014, pp. 66–83 (2014)
40. He, Y.: Comparison of the modeling languages alloy and UML. In: SERP 2006, pp. 671–677 (2006)
41. Cabot, J.: Modeling languages - UML tools (2015). https://modeling-languages.com/uml-tools. Accessed 04 Aug 2015

Using Workflows to Automate Activities in MDE Tools

Miguel Andrés Gamboa and Eugene Syriani[(✉)]

Université de Montréal, Montreal, Canada
{gamboagm,syriani}@iro.umontreal.ca

Abstract. Model-driven engineering (MDE) enables to generate software tools by systematically modeling and transforming this models. However, the usability of these tools is far from efficient. Common MDE activities, such as creating a domain-specific language, are non-trivial and often require repetitive tasks. This results in unnecessary increases of development time. The goal of this paper is to increase the productivity of modelers in their every day activities by automating the tasks they perform in current MDE tools. We propose an MDE-based solution where the user defines a reusable workflow that can be parametrized at run-time and executed. Our solution works for frameworks that support two level metamodeling as well as deep metamodeling. We implemented our solution in the MDE tool AToMPM. We also performed an empirical evaluation of our approach and showed that we reduce both mechanical and thinking efforts of the user. The ideas and concepts of this paper were introduced at the MODELSWARD conference [1] and are extended in this paper.

1 Introduction

Model-Driven Engineering (MDE) has been advocating faster software development times through the help of automation [2]. MDE technologies combine domain-specific languages (DSL), transformation engines and code generators to produce various software artifacts. Although some studies report success stories of MDE [3], some of the less satisfactory results include the presence of a plethora of MDE tools. Each tool defines its own development and usage process, which is a burden on the user who needs to adapt himself to every tool. To be successful, MDE needs tools that are not only well adapted to the tasks to perform, but also tools that increase the productivity of modelers in their day-to-day activities.

Modeling tools and frameworks, such as AToMPM [4], EMF [5], GME [6], and MetaEdit+ [7], provide many functionalities, such as DSL creation, model editing, or model transformations. Although based on common foundational principles, the process for performing these tasks differs greatly depending on the tool used. For example, to create a DSL in AToMPM [8], the language designer has to load the class diagram formalism and graphically build the metamodel. He generates the abstract syntax of the DSL from that metamodel by loading the compiler toolbar. Then he has to load the concrete syntax formalism and assign a concrete syntax to each individual class and association from the metamodel

© Springer International Publishing AG 2017
S. Hammoudi et al. (Eds): MODELSWARD 2016, CCIS 692, pp. 25–45, 2017.
DOI: 10.1007/978-3-319-66302-9_2

by drawing shapes. He then generates the domain-specific modeling environment by loading the compiler toolbar. In contrast, the steps are different to create a DSL in EMFText [9]. The language designer first creates a new project by specifying the project settings in the wizard dialog. He then creates an Ecore diagram file and graphically builds the metamodel. He then needs to create a generator model from the metamodel file. To define the concrete syntax, he creates a file specifying the textual grammar. Once completed, he executes the generators to create the domain-specific environment that needs to be launched as a separate Eclipse instance initiated from the generated Java code.

Many of these activities involve repetitive tasks and a lot of user interactions with the user interface of the MDE tool. These are non-trivial activities. They involve long sequences of tasks, often repetitive tasks. Additionally, they require context-dependent decisions leading to a lot of user interactions with the user interface of the MDE tool. The processes to follow are complex for all users, whether they are language engineers (i.e., MDE savvy) or domain-specific modelers (i.e., end-users). They require heavy mental loads and tasks that are error-prone. In the end, users are spending more time on development than necessary. It is therefore mandatory to try to automate MDE tasks and processes as much as possible, thus decreasing the accidental complexity of the tools used and letting the user focus on the essential complexities of the domain problem.

To solve this issue, tools can implement automated workflows for each MDE activity that involves a complex process or repetitive tasks. Many of the tools already partially support this with the help of wizards [5] or scripts [10]. However, even these wizards become quite complex offering too many options that the user has to manually input each time he wants to repeat an activity, as in Eclipse based tools. There are also several languages to define processes, such as SPEM [11], but do not support their execution (or *enactment*) natively. Other executable process languages like BPEL [12] are too complex for the tasks we want to achieve in modeling tools. Workflow languages, such as UML activity diagrams, can be enacted [13], but the execution relies on programming individual actions which hampers porting a process from one tool to another.

We therefore propose to define a DSL, inspired from activity diagrams, that fits exactly the purpose of designing workflows for common tasks in MDE tools. The tasks encompass simple operations, such as opening, closing or saving models, and more complex tasks, such as generating the artifacts for a DSL. We noted that several tasks occur in different workflows, especially common operations e.g., open and close. Therefore we opted for a reuse mechanism, where the user defines workflows that can be parametrized at run-time to minimize the number of workflows to create. Since our solution follows the MDE paradigm, the execution of workflows is entirely modeled through model transformation. Ultimately, users spend less time performing the activity by focusing on essential model management tasks rather than wasting time interacting with the tool. The ideas and concepts of this paper were introduced at the MODELSWARD conference [1] and are extended in this paper.

The paper is organized as follows. In Sect. 2, we describe the details of our solution and discuss how we solved challenges we faced. In Sect. 3, we report on the improved implementation of our approach in AToMPM. Specifically in Sect. 4, we discuss how model refactoring is automated. In Sect. 5, we perform a preliminary empirical evaluation of the impact our approach has on improving the user productivity in AToMPM. Finally, we discuss related work in Sect. 6 and conclude in Sect. 7.

2   Design of a Reusable Workflow Language

We propose an MDE-based solution where the user defines workflows that can be parametrized at run-time and executed. In this section, we describe a DSL that is adaptable to a specific modeling tool. We also describe the general process of how to design reusable workflows to semi-automate MDE activities. Furthermore, we discuss how to enact workflows using model transformation.

2.1   Language for Semi-automated Workflows

We model the DSL for defining activities that can be performed in MDE tools. A workflow is composed of tasks, to define concrete actions to be performed, and control nodes, to define the flow of tasks. The metamodel in Fig. 1 resembles that of a simplification of UML activity diagrams since, semantically, an instance of this metamodel is to be interpreted similarly to the control flow in UML activity diagrams. Additional well-formedness constraints are not depicted in the figure e.g., a cycle between tasks must involve an iteration node, there must be exactly one initial and one final node.

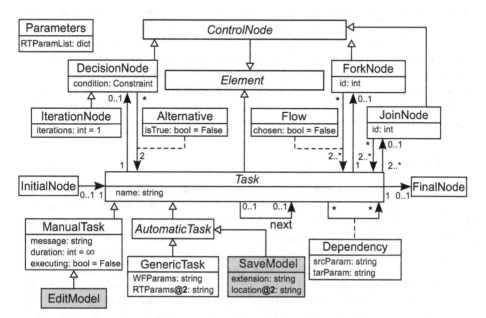

Fig. 1. Generic metamodel of workflows for modeling tools.

There are different kinds of tasks in an MDE tool. As for any modern software, there are tasks specific to the user interface, such as opening, closing, and saving models or windows. There are also tasks that are specific to models, such as editing (CRUD operations) models, constraints, or transformations. There are also tasks that are specific to the particular modeling tool used, such as loading or executing a transformation, generating code from a model, or synthesizing a domain-specific environment from a DSL. Furthermore, we want to automate users' activities as much as possible, therefore most of the tasks are automatic: they do not require human interaction. For example, loading a formalism to create a metamodel is (e.g., Ecore in EMF or Class Diagrams in AToMPM) is a task that can be automated, since the location of that formalism is known. Shaded classes in Fig. 1 (`SaveModel` and `EditModel`) are examples of tasks that may vary from one MDE tool to another. Otherwise, this is a generic metamodel implementable in any MDE tool.

Nevertheless, some tasks are hard, even impossible, to automate and thus must remain manual. These are typically tasks specific to a particular model, such as deciding what new element to add in the model. A message is specified to guide the user during manual tasks. A maximum duration can also be specified to limit the time spent on a manual task.

A workflow conforming to this metamodel starts from the initial node and terminates at the final node. Tasks can be sequenced one after the other. A decision node can be placed to provide alternative flows (one true and one false) depending on a Boolean condition evaluated at run-time. Repetitions are possible with an iteration node. This node repeats the flow along the true alternative as long as the condition is satisfied. A common condition is to limit the number of iterations: e.g., `self.iterations <= 2`. The cycle ends when either the specified number of iterations is reached or a terminating condition is satisfied. Fork and join nodes provide non-determinism when the order of execution of tasks is not relevant. Fork node is a control node that splits a flow into multiple concurrent flows and join node is a control node that synchronizes multiple flows. These correspond to the common basic control flow patterns for workflows [14]. Although not supported in our current implementation, tasks may be executed concurrently, except if the concurrent tasks are manual.

2.2   Parameters

One issue that may slow down the development time of users using workflows, is that many tasks require parameters. For example, the task `SaveModel` requires the location of where to save the model (path and name) and the extension to be used. The extension is generally known from the context of the workflow. For example, a generic model ends with `.ecore` in EMF and `.model` in AToMPM, but a domain-specific model may have a specific extension in EMF. The designer of the workflow can thus set the value of this attribute at design-time. However, the location of the model is generally unknown to the workflow designer because it is a decision often left at the discretion of the domain user. We therefore distinguish between workflow parameters that are fixed for all executions of the workflows and run-time parameters that are specific to individual executions of the workflow.

Within the same workflow, several tasks may share the same parameters. Workflow parameters are specified once per workflow. However, run-time parameters must be manually specified each time the workflow is executed. Therefore, a `Dependency` link can be specified between different tasks that share the same run-time parameters. A dependency link specifies which attribute from the target task gets its value from an attribute in the source task. For example, the location of the `SaveModel` task is the same as the location of the `OpenModel` when saving a model we just opened and modified.

2.3   Activities as Workflows

To set the values of run-time parameters, we need an intermediate model of workflows that is an instance of the metamodel presented, but where some parameters are left for further assignment. As explained in [15], the commonly used technique of two-level metamodeling does not allow us to represent this need.

An attractive solution is to apply techniques from deep metamodeling [16], and in particular, the approach defining metamodels with potency [17]. We assign a potency of 2 to attributes representing run-time parameters and a potency of 1 to those representing workflow parameters, as depicted in Fig. 1. This way, the workflow designer only needs to create one workflow for saving models with the extension set to e.g., `.model` and the user can execute the workflow only caring of the location where to save the model and not bother what the right extension is. In this setup, an instance of the workflow metamodel in Fig. 1 is a workflow. A workflow is itself the metamodel of its instantiation at run-time. The *enactment* of a workflow therefore consists in providing the run-time parameters to a workflow and executing it. These definitions are consistent with what the Workflow Management Coalition specifies [18].

2.4   Workflow Enactment by Model Transformation

In this section, we describe how workflows are instantiated with run-time parameters and executed.

Deep Instantiation. The issue with the above solution is that not many modeling frameworks (e.g., AToMPM[1] and EMF) support deep metamodeling with potency like metadepth [20] or Melanee [21] do. Therefore, we propose a workaround to enact workflows by emulating deep metamodeling with potency for tools that do not natively support it. The solution is to add a `Parameters` class to the metamodel that is instantiated once per workflow enactment. Its

---

[1] In [19], the authors proposed a deep metamodeling solution for the Modelverse of AToMPM, but no usable implementation was available at the time of writing this paper.

attributes are populated dynamically for the enactment. They consist of all the run-time parameters of every task in the workflow. The parameter object is used to generate a wizard prompting for all run-time parameters needed in the tasks of a workflow.

Once a workflow has been created by the workflow designer, a user can enact the workflow. He creates a parameter object to specify run-time parameters and executes the workflow. We have modeled the enactment of workflows by model transformation. Figure 2 depicts the transformation in MoTif [22], a rule-based graph transformation language in AToMPM. Rules are defined with a pre-condition pattern on the left and a post-condition pattern on the right. Constraints `Const` and actions `Act` on attributes are specified in Python. A scheduling structure controls the order of execution of rules. Figure 2 shows the two-step transformation that retrieves all run-time parameters of the workflow. The transformation on the left of the figure populates all attribute fields of the parameter object (the icon with two gears) by visiting each task in the workflow model. The first rule makes sure a depended run-time parameter is not added to the parameter list of the parameter object. For each parameter, we store the task type, its task name (in case multiple instances of the same task type are in the workflow), and the name of the parameter. We make use of the `setAttr` and `getAttr` functions that allows us to get and set attribute values using the attribute name as a string. This information is then used to render a wizard prompting for their corresponding values to the user. Once the user enters all parameters, the transformation on the right of the figure copies the values entered in the source run-time parameters to the target run-time parameters. This makes sure that all run-time parameters of all tasks are set. Note that the transformations uses FRules to make sure that each task is visited exactly once, which is why no negative application condition is needed.

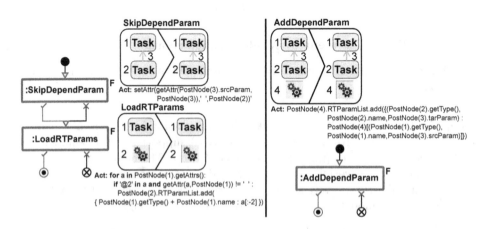

Fig. 2. Transformation for loading run-time parameters in MoTif.

Execution. With all run-time parameters set, there are two ways to execute the workflow. One is to transform the workflow into a model transformation that gets executed, as done in [23]. In this case, a higher-order transformation takes as input the workflow and parameter object, generates a rule for each task, and schedules the rules according to the order of the tasks in the workflow. This is possible in MoTif since rules and scheduling are specified in separate models. Although this approach has the advantage to reuse built-in execution mechanisms from the MDE tool, a new transformation must be generated for each workflow and, in particular, if the designer makes changes to the workflow model.

In this work, we have implemented an alternative solution: we define the operational semantics of a workflow and execute it as a simulation. Figure 3 illustrates the overall structure of this transformation and Fig. 4 depicts some of the rules. The process starts from the element (task or control node) marked with the initial node. The rule `GetInitialElement` is responsible for this and specifies only a pre-condition. The general idea is that then, each task to process each element in the order of the workflow by advancing the `current` pointer called pivot in MoTif, with the rule `GetNextElement`. The simulation ends when the final node is reached, satisfying the rule `IsFinalElement`. Executing an automatic task, such as save model depicted in rule `ExecuteSaveModel`, is performed by calling the corresponding API operation of the MDE tool with the corresponding run-time parameters. We assume that the MDE tool offers an API for interact-

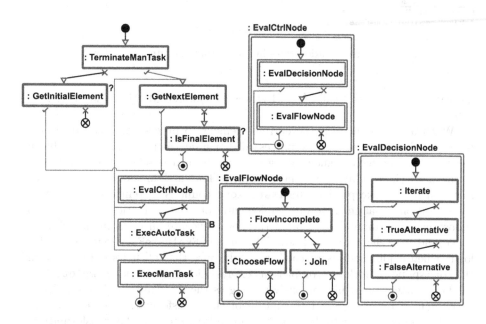

Fig. 3. Control structure of the transformation in MoTif that executes a workflow.

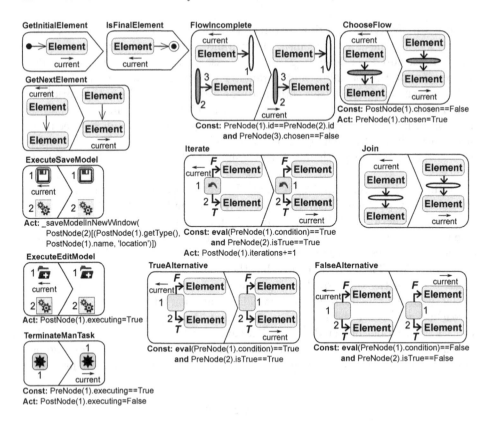

Fig. 4. Transformation rules in MoTif that execute a workflow.

ing with it programmatically (e.g., Python API for AToMPM and Java API for EMF).

When a control node is the current element to process, we need to decide on which element is next to be processed. For a decision node, if the condition is true, then the next element along the true branch is selected. Otherwise, it is the next element along the false branch. This assignment is the same for iteration nodes, except that the `iterations` count is incremented as long as the condition is satisfied. In our implementation, the semantics of a fork is to choose non-deterministically one of the flows, execute all tasks in that flow in order, and then choose another flow. The rules in `EvaluateFlowNode` ensure this logic: when a join node is reached, we make sure that all flows outgoing from the corresponding fork are complete as expressed by rule `FlowIncomplete`.

This process runs autonomously as long as there are automatic tasks. However, manual tasks require interruption of the transformation in real-time so that the user can complete the task at hand and then resume the transformation. Automating such a process requires to be able to pause and resume the transformation from the rules being executed. Although some transformation languages support real-time interruption [24], most do not. Therefore, as depicted in Fig. 3, we extend the logic to handle manual tasks separately. If the next task to execute is manual, the corresponding rule simply flags the task as executing, as rule `ExecuteEditModel` shows, and the transformation terminates. The user notifies the MDE tool that his manual task is complete by restarting the transformation. Consequently, the transformation executes the first rule `TerminateManTask` which resumes the execution from the task that was last marked as executing. The `executing` attribute for manual tasks allows the workflow model to keep track of the last manual task executed after the transformation is stopped.

2.5   Extensions and Exceptions

The approach presented here is evolution safe. MDE tools evolve with new features added. If a new feature is available via the API and is needed in an workflow, then there are only two steps the designer is required to perform to support that feature. He shall add a new sub-class of automatic or manual task in the metamodel of Fig. 1 and add a rule under `ExecAutoTask` or `ExecManTask` in Fig. 3 that calls the appropriate API function to perform the operation. `ExecAutoTask` (respectively `ExecManTask`) is a BRule that contains all the rules to execute automatic (respectively manual) tasks. BRules execute at most one of their inner rules unless none of them are applicable. The modularity of this design reduces significantly the effort of workflow designers who wish to provide additional tasks available via new features of the MDE tool.

Although it is common to explicitly model exceptional cases in workflows [25, 26], we have decided not to do that at the workflow model level. Exceptions can only occur if a task execution fails because the user is constrained to do exactly what the workflow allows as next action. In this version of our implementation, if an exception occurs, the workflow execution stops at the failing task in the workflow, as depicted by the circled crosses in Fig. 3. The user must then manually recover from the error and restart the execution of the workflow. Nevertheless, run-time parameters are retained.

3   Implementation in AToMPM

We implemented a prototype in the MDE tool AToMPM [4], since it offers a graphical concrete syntax for DSLs, which is best suited for workflow languages, and a backdoor API to programmatically interact with the tool in headless mode. Nevertheless, our approach can be implemented in any MDE tool as long as it offers an accessible API to perform operations that their user interface allows to. We implemented the workflow DSL following the metamodel in Fig. 1. Figure 5 shows the graphical representation used for each task, each control node, and parameter object.

We analyzed several processes and noted the user interactions needed to perform each task, e.g., creation of DSL. We had to decide on what level of granularity we want to present tasks. One option is to go to the level of mouse movements

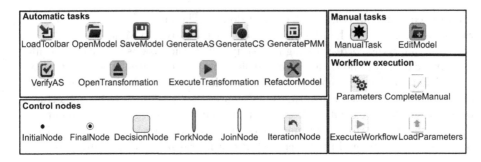

Fig. 5. Concrete syntax of the workflow DSL in AToMPM.

(graphically moving objects), clicks (selections), and keystrokes (textual editing). Although this would enable us to model nearly any user interaction AToMPM allows for, this would make the workflows very verbose and complex for designers. We therefore opted for tasks to represent core functionalities instead. Subsequently, the most common tasks we noted are opening models, loading toolbars and formalisms, saving models, generating concrete and abstract syntax of DSLs, as listed in Fig. 5. All these operations can be automated, since they require a location as run-time parameter. SaveModel also has a workflow parameter for the extension of the model file. Additionally, a task to edit models is needed, but cannot be automated since it is up to the user to create or edit the model.

3.1 Process

Our prototype is to be used as follows. The designer defines workflows by creating instances of the workflow DSL. A user (a language engineer in this example) then selects which workflow he desires to enact. To set the run-time parameters, he pushes the LoadParameters button. This creates an instance of the parameter object and pops up a dialog prompting for all required parameters, following the transformation from Fig. 2. Upon pushing ExecuteWorkflow button, the simulation (presented in Fig. 3) executes the workflow autonomously. When a manual task is reached, a new AToMPM window is opened with all necessary toolbars pre-loaded. A message describing the manual task to perform is displayed to the user and the simulation stops. After the user completes the task, he pushes the CompleteManual button. Then, the window closes and the simulation restarts.

3.2 Example Workflow for Creating a DSL

Figure 6 shows the workflow that specifies how to create a DSL and generate a modeling environment for it in AToMPM. The first task is LoadToolbar. Its location parameter is already predefined with the class diagram toolbar, since this is the standard formalism with which one creates a metamodel in AToMPM. The following task is EditModel. In this manual task, the user creates the metamodel of the DSL using class diagrams. Once this is complete, the workflow restarts executing from that task and proceeds with `SaveModel`. This task requires a run-time parameter to specify the location of where the metamodel is saved. The user sets the value in the popup dialog wizard. Now that the metamodel is created, a fork node proposes two flows: one for creating the concrete syntax of the DSL and one to generate the abstract syntax from the metamodel. Recall that the simulation chooses one flow and then the other in no specific order. Suppose the former flow is chosen. Then, a `LoadToolbar` task is executed to load the concrete syntax toolbar, the standard formalism in AToMPM. This is followed by an `EditModel` so the user can manually create the shapes of each element of the metamodel. Once this is complete, the workflow restarts and proceeds with a `SaveModel` task. Recall that the location is a run-time parameter to save the concerte syntax model with a predefined extension. In the popup dialog, we distinguish between different task with their type, and in this case their name (1 and 2). The following task in this flow is `GenerateCS`. It takes as run-time parameter the location of where the generated artifact must be output. Specifically, the name used will be also the name of the toolbar that will be used to create a model with this DSL. Therefore, the location of the generated concrete syntax is the same as the location of the concrete syntax model the user created manually. The dependency link prevents the user from having to duplicate parameter values in the wizard. When the join node is reached, the simulation notices that the second flow was not executed yet. Therefore the next task to be executed is `GenerateAS`. Its location parameter uses the same value of the location attribute of `SaveModel` 1, as depicted by the dependency link between these two tasks. When the join node is reached again, this time all flows were executed and proceeds with the final task `LoadToolbar` 3. As stated before, its location parameter use the same value of the location attribute of `SaveModel` 2. The simulation ends on a new window open with the new DSL loaded, ready for the user to create his domain-specific model.

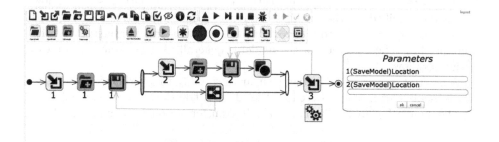

Fig. 6. Workflow to create a DSL.

4   Automating Refactoring Tasks

Refactoring is common operation on modeling artifacts that improves the structure of a model while preserving its external behavior [27]. In MDE, refactoring is either done manually on a model or through the application of a model transformation [28]. There exists several techniques to perform refactoring on generic or domain-specific models [29], and even a catalog of refactoring patterns on metamodels [30].

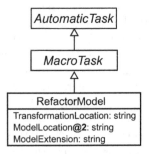

Fig. 7. Generic metamodel of Refactoring Model.

Refactoring is an activity that can be automated in our workflow system. By default, this can be done through a manual task. However, we also support automating this task for the user. To do so, we extend the metamodel of Fig. 1 with the concept of a `MacroTask` as depicted in Fig. 7. A macro task is an implicit workflow of other tasks. For example, as illustrated in Fig. 8, `RefactorModel` is decomposed into opening the model to refactor, loading the transformation that implements the refactoring, and executing that transformation on the model. For the `RefactorModel` task, the location of the transformation is a workflow parameter specified by the workflow designer. Additionally, this task requires the location of the model to refactor, but this is a run-time parameter that the user specifies. The extension of the model is generally known from the context of the workflow.

A macro task serves as syntactic sugar to simplify the workflow of the user. The semantics of a macro task is modeled by a transformation executed during the simulation in Fig. 3. The implicit transformation that is executed for

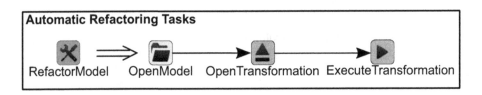

Fig. 8. Generic metamodel of Refactoring Model.

`RefactorModel` can be defined on the meta-metamodel level (e.g., class diagram in AToMPM or Ecore in EMF) so that it is syntactically applicable on any given model. The burden is on the user who needs to define a meaningful transformation that can be applied on the desired model. For example, if the model is a metamodel, then a refactoring can add a unicity constraint. If the model is a concrete syntax assignment, then a refactoring can create a default concrete syntax to every class of the metamodel.

5   Evaluation of the Improvement of MDE Activities

5.1   Research Question

The goal of the experiment is to determine whether the productivity of the user is increased when performing complex or repetitive tasks. Thus, our research question is "is the time for mechanical and cognitive efforts of the user reduced when automating activities with workflows?" Therefore, we conduct the experiment to verify that these efforts are reduced when using our approach versus when not.

5.2   Metrics

The total time T spent by a user to perform one activity is one way to quantify the effort the user produces. T is mainly made up of the mechanical time T_m (hand movements) and cognitive effort time T_t (thinking time) of the user, thus $T = T_m + T_t$, assuming there are no interruptions or distractions.

Since AToMPM only presents a web-based graphical user interface and most interactions are performed with a mouse, we can apply Fitts Law [31] to measure the time of mouse movements $t_{FL} = a + b \times log_2(1 + D/S)$. D is the distance from a given cursor position to the position of a widget to reach (e.g., button, text field) and S is the smallest value of the width or height of the widget. We denote T_{FL} as the sum of all the t_{FL} for each useful mouse movement to perform one activity.

Another useful metric we noted for the mechanical effort is the number of clicks c needed to complete the activity. Relying on empirical data from an online benchmark [32], the average time to click reactively is 258 ms. Thus we denote $T_c = 258 \times c$ the time spent clicking during an activity.

Therefore a rough estimate of the time spent on mouse actions in an activity is $T_m = T_{FL} + T_c$ for every straight line distance D between two clicks and the size S of the widget at every even click.

Delays between mechanical actions is a rough estimate of the time the user spent thinking during the activity. Hence, we deduce the thinking time $T_t = T - T_m$.

Finally, we measure the complexity N of a task by the number of automatic tasks it requires the user to perform.

These metrics are far from accurate, but serve at least as a preliminary evaluation of our approach to discard the null hypothesis: T_m, T_c and T_t are smaller for performing an MDE activity in AToMPM using workflows than without workflows.

5.3   Experimental Setup

We performed all experiments on a 15.6" laptop monitor with a resolution of 1920×1080. The machine was an ArchLinux virtual machine using 2 cores and 4 GB of RAM, running on Windows 10 quad-core computer at 2.4 GHz with 16 GB of RAM. Given this performance, we neglected the computation time of AToMPM triggered by each click. To keep a fair comparison, the experiments using the workflow did not take into account the mouse activity and time spent during manual tasks. This is the time after the simulation terminates and before the notification from the `CompleteManual` button is received.

5.4   Data Collection

To calculate t using Fitts law, the coefficients a and b must be determined empirically. For that, we recorded the straight line distances between meaningful clicks (e.g., center of canvas to toolbar button) as well as different sizes of clickable elements (e.g., model elements on the canvas) in AToMPM. We recorded 12 distances ranging from 79 to 1027 pixels and 5 sizes ranging from 20 to 305 pixels. We then placed on an empty screen a point and a rectangle of sizes and at distances that correspond to these measurements. We measured the time it took to click on the initial point and move the cursor as fast as possible to click inside the opposite rectangle. This data collection was performed by the first author who is an expert in AToMPM. We repeated each of the 57 cases 20 times (excluding those where $D \leq S$). The maximum variation in the same case was less than 9%. We determined by regression analysis the values $a = 166.75$ and $b = 155.93$ with correlation $R^2 = .9106$ with a median and average margin of error of 8%.

In our prototype, we implemented the five most common tasks in AToMPM shown in Fig. 5. There is an infinite number of possible combinations of these tasks because tasks can be repeated and the order matters. Therefore, we reduced the number of cases to only meaningful combinations of tasks in AToMPM. We identified 4 meaningful for activities with one task (compiling the concrete syntax requires a model to be opened), 9 for activities with two tasks (e.g., open then save model), 13 for activities with three tasks, 4 for activities with four tasks, 5 for activities with five tasks, 3 for activities with six tasks, and 3 for activities with seven tasks. Hence we ran our experiments on 38 distinct activities varying up to seven automatic tasks.

The most complex activity we evaluated is for the creation of a DSL in AToMPM modeled with the workflow in Fig. 6, consisting of seven automatic tasks. The workflow starts by loading the `Class Diagram` formalism. It lets the user manually create the appropriate class diagram model to define the metamodel. When the user completes that task, the metamodel is saved (location provided at run-time) and the abstract syntax is generated. Then the `ConcreteSyntax` formalism is loaded and the user creates the shapes for links and icons. When the user completes that task, the concrete syntax model is saved (name provided at run-time) and the `GenerateCS` task generates the code for the new DSL environment. Finally, the new formalism is loaded in a new window showing the new generated DSL environment to the user. Note that in this situation, the first `LoadToolbar` object does not require a run-time parameter, but a workflow parameter for the location of the `Class Diagram` formalism. We therefore suggest to create two classes in the metamodel for the same task when we want to give the option to set either run-time or workflow parameters depending on the context.

5.5 Results

The two plots in Fig. 9 report the time performances for each case. We aggregated the times by the number of tasks because there was very few variability between activities with the same number of tasks: the highest coefficient of variability 20% was obtained for activities with three tasks since this was the most populous set, while all the others remained under 5%. Both plots confirm that the use of workflows does reduce the time to perform the activity, as the complexity of the activity increases.

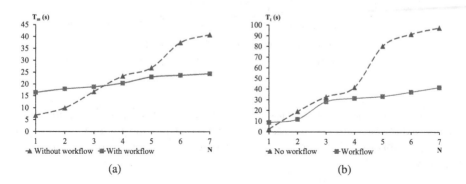

Fig. 9. Mechanical (a) and cognitive (b) efforts with respect to the number of tasks in a workflow.

The results obtained correspond to what one would expect when adding automation in a development process. The mechanical effort is greater when using workflows for simple activities that have up to three tasks. However, after that point, the mechanical effort remains almost identical as the number of tasks increases. This behavior, depicted in Fig. 9(a), is due to the overhead to open the appropriate workflow and set all run-time parameters. The reason why T_m plateaus after $N = 5$ is that the only mechanical effort needed is to specify additional run-time parameters. However, this is done by typing the values with the keyboard which we haven't taken into account in this experiment. When performing the experiments, we noted that the slowest task performed manually was for loading toolbars.

Figure 9(b) reports on the non-mechanical effort needed by the user to perform each activity. We note a trend similar to the mechanical effort. However, the flip point where less effort is needed when using workflows occurs as early as activities with more than one task. The cognitive effort increases linearly for activities with more than three tasks. An interesting result is that, when not using workflows, the cognitive effort is always greater than the mechanical effort for $N > 1$ and that gap keeps on increasing as there are more tasks. On the contrary, when using workflows, the mechanical effort is greater for activities with up to two tasks, but when the cognitive effort is greater for $N > 2$, the gap remains almost identical. When performing the experiments, we noted that most of the time was spent searching on the screen to select toolbars to load, even for an expert user who knows exactly their locations.

To complement this information, Table 1 details each metric for the most complex activities we evaluated. It shows that, although using workflows improves all the metrics, the cognitive time is the most improved component.

Table 1. Time measurements in seconds and improvements when using workflows for $N = 7$ tasks.

	T	T_{FL}	T_c	T_m	T_t
No workflow	138	29	11	41	98
Workflow	66	18	6	24	42
Improvement	52%	38%	45%	41%	57%

We conclude that our hypothesis is verified and answer our research question: for the extent of the experiments we conducted, the time for mechanical and cognitive efforts of the user is reduced when automating activities with our approach by half.

5.6 Threats to Validity

There are several threats to the construct validity of this preliminary evaluation. First, the metrics we used are not sufficient to assess the complete mechanical effort. Keystrokes can also be taken into account since there is an effort needed to set the values of run-time parameters. However, the length of the string of each depends on the file paths of the host machines and the operating system used. We discarded this metric for its lack of generalization. Further mechanical metrics could be used such as eye movements, but we lacked the proper hardware to perform eye-tracking experiments. We further mitigated these threats by using Fitts Law to achieve an objective measure of time mouse movements.

We measured cognitive effort by considering it as all non-mechanical effort, which is not a completely true statement. Otherwise, this would have required more fine grained measurements of brain activity. We also did not include the time and effort for manual tasks, which may have a negative influence on the results if they take longer than the automatic tasks. The data collection was performed by only one person, but this was only necessary to calculate t since all other metrics are obtained using Fitts Law, without needing to perform the activities. This threat only affects the absolute time, but does not affect the improvement ratio.

With respect to threats internal validity, the selection and configuration of the tools for time measurements has a weak influence on the results. We calibrated the parameters based on a pilot experiment and our experience. However, this should not strongly affect the time because we took care of configuring the tools in a way that corresponds to the empirical data from an online benchmark. We also pre-processed inconsistent times (e.g., clicks outside target) in order to eliminate false positives. Nevertheless, this only reduces the chances that we can answer our research question positively.

As far as threats to external validity are concerned, the activities were obviously not sampled randomly from all possible MDE tools activities, but we relied on our knowledge in MDE tools. Hence, the set of activities is not completely representative. The results of this study can only be generalized to the extent of AToMPM. Nevertheless, all five tasks we considered are part of the most common activities in the majority of MDE tools, such as EMF. We further mitigated this threat by including tasks with different complexity (i.e., Open Model vs Compile Abstract Syntax) and focusing on their meaningful combinations.

6 Related Work

A lot of work can be found in the literature on workflow definition and enactment [33–35]. In [36], the authors proposed a textual DSL for workflow definition that supports sequencing and iteration. It is not meant to be enacted, but serves as specification for subsequent code generators. Workflow enactment has been particularly applied in process modeling.

Various techniques exist to service the execution of workflows, such as distributing the execution on the cloud [37,38]. However, none of these approaches models workflow enactment explicitly as we did using model transformation.

We proposed a model transformation as a novel workaround for tools that do not support deep instantiation of metamodels. An alternative is to define metamodels following the Type-Object pattern [39] where both types and instances are explicitly modeled in the metamodel. This is similar to the notion of clabject [40] which generalizes this approach.

From an implementation point of view, the closest work to ours automates transformation chains in AToMPM [23]. They developed a formalism transformation graph (FTG) that specifies a megamodel indicating the transformations between languages and a process model (PM) that specifies the control and data flow to schedule the order of execution of model transformations. The execution of an FTG+PM instance is modeled as a higher-order transformation that converts the FTG+PM model into a model transformation instance, whereas our approach executes workflows by simulation. The authors also distinguish automatic actions from manual ones, but the latter are not modeled in the transformation.

Similarly to FTG+PM, Wires [41] supports the specification and execution of model transformation workflows. Wires is graphical executable language for ATL transformations that provides mechanisms to create model transformations chains. Kepler [42] is a tool to create and execute scientific workflows. Since it is based on the Ptolemy II multi-paradigm simulation system, a coordinator must be hand-written in Java to define the semantics of the workflow, unlike our approach that makes use of model transformation.

In our approach, activities essentially encapsulate model management tasks. The Epsilon language suite [43] can be used to perform model management tasks such as CRUD operations, transformations, comparisons, merging, validation, refactoring, evolution, and code generation. To combine and integrate these different tasks into workflows, the user defines Ant scripts. In our approach, users define workflows in a DSL specific to the features the MDE tool provides. As such, it reduces accidental complexity imposed by Ant and is accessible to a broader set of users that do not know Ant. One particular language is the Epsilon Wizard Language (EWL) [44] whose purpose is to refactor, refine, and update models. EWL allows users to define wizards that serve as encapsulation of EOL scripts, the action language in Epsilon. Wizards are similar to activities in our case. EWL provide feedback that can drive the execution of a model management operation using a context-independent user input. It is a command line user input interface. In our approach, the user-input method is a popup dialog with several parameters. Their approach has a more fine-grained wizard selection process, since a wizard can have a guard that must be satisfied in order to execute it. Nevertheless, EWL does not support the explicit modeling of manual tasks. EWL is especially designed for refactoring models automatically. These model refactorings are applied on model elements that are explicitly selected by the user. Typical supported refactoring patterns include adding the stereotypes, attributes and operations. EWL has constructs specifically to refactor model elements. In our approach, workflows rely on a model transformation to express the modification to the model. Therefore the user only needs to specify the model, and not individual model elements.

7   Conclusion

In this paper, we presented a model-based environment for automating daily activities of language engineers and domain-specific modelers. Designers define workflow templates conforming to a DSL to increase the productivity of users. Users enact workflows to perform tasks automatically. Our framework also supports the integration of manual tasks. The execution of workflows is entirely modeled as a model transformation, making it reusable and portable on various MDE tools. Preliminary results of our prototype indicate that, using workflows, users reduce cognitive and mechanical effort to perform common activities in the MDE tool AToMPM.

We are integrating more features of AToMPM in our prototype to allow designers define workflows for nearly any interaction process the tool can do. As future work, we plan to implement this approach in other MDE frameworks, such as EMF, in order to further generalize the reusability aspect of the metamodel of activities and their enactment by model transformation.

References

1. Gamboa, M.A., Syriani, E.: Automating activities in MDE tools. In: Model-Driven Engineering and Software Development, SciTePress, pp. 123–133 (2016)
2. Schmidt, D.C.: Model-driven engineering. IEEE Comput. **39**, 25–31 (2006)
3. Whittle, J., Hutchinson, J., Rouncefield, M.: The state of practice in model-driven engineering. IEEE Softw. **31**, 79–85 (2014)
4. Syriani, E., Vangheluwe, H., Mannadiar, R., Hansen, C., Van Mierlo, S., Ergin, H.: AToMPM: a web-based modeling environment. In: Invited Talks, Demonstration Session, Poster Session, and ACM Student Research Competition, MODELS 2013, vol. 1115, pp. 21–25. CEUR-WS.org (2013)
5. Steinberg, D., Budinsky, F., Paternostro, M., Merks, E.: EMF: Eclipse Modeling Framework, 2nd edn. Addison Wesley Professional, Boston (2008)
6. Ledeczi, A., Maroti, M., Bakay, A., Karsai, G., Garrett, J., Thomason, C., Nordstrom, G., Sprinkle, J., Volgyesi, P.: The generic modeling environment. In: Workshop on Intelligent Signal Processing, WISP 2001, vol. 17 (2001)
7. Kelly, S., Lyytinen, K., Rossi, M.: MetaEdit+ a fully configurable multi-user and multi-tool CASE and CAME environment. In: Constantopoulos, P., Mylopoulos, J., Vassiliou, Y. (eds.) CAiSE 1996. LNCS, vol. 1080, pp. 1–21. Springer, Heidelberg (1996). doi:10.1007/3-540-61292-0_1
8. AToMPM tutorial (2013). http://www.slideshare.net/eugenesyriani/atompm-introductory-tutorial. Accessed 07 Aug 2015
9. EMFText screencast (2014). http://www.emftext.org/index.php/EMFText_Getting_Started_Screencast. Accessed 07 Aug 2015
10. JetBrains MPS (2015). https://www.jetbrains.com/mps/ Accessed 07 Aug 2015
11. OMG: Software & Systems Process Engineering Metamodel specification 2.0 edn. (2008)
12. OASIS: Web Services Business Process Execution Language, 2nd edn. (2007)
13. Syriani, E., Ergin, H.: Operational semantics of UML activity diagram: an application in project management. In: RE 2012 Workshops, pp. 1–8. IEEE (2012)
14. Russell, N., van der Aalst, W., ter Hofstede, A., Mulyar, N.: Workflow Control-Flow Patterns: A Revised View. Technical report BPM-06-22, BPM Center (2006)
15. Gonzalez Perez, C., Henderson Sellers, B.: Metamodelling for Software Engineering. Wiley Publishing, Hoboken (2008)
16. Lara, J.D., Guerra, E., Cuadrado, J.S.: When and how to use multilevel modelling. ACM Trans. Softw. Eng. Methodol. **24**, 1–46 (2014)
17. Atkinson, C., Kühne, T.: The essence of multilevel metamodeling. In: Gogolla, M., Kobryn, C. (eds.) UML 2001. LNCS, vol. 2185, pp. 19–33. Springer, Heidelberg (2001). doi:10.1007/3-540-45441-1_3

18. WMC: Terminology and glossary. Technical report, WFMC-TC-1011, Workflow Management Coalition (1999)
19. Van Mierlo, S., Barroca, B., Vangheluwe, H., Syriani, E., Kühne, T.: Multi-level modelling in the modelverse. In: Workshop on Multi-Level Modelling, MULTI 2014, vol. 1286, pp. 83–92. CEUR-WS.org (2014)
20. Lara, J., Guerra, E.: Deep meta-modelling with METADEPTH. In: Vitek, J. (ed.) TOOLS 2010. LNCS, vol. 6141, pp. 1–20. Springer, Heidelberg (2010). doi:10.1007/978-3-642-13953-6_1
21. Atkinson, C., Gerbig, R.: Melanie: multi-level modeling and ontology engineering environment. In: International Master Class on Model-Driven Engineering: Modeling Wizards, MW 2012, pp. 7:1–7:2. ACM (2012)
22. Syriani, E., Vangheluwe, H.: A modular timed model transformation language. J. Softw. Syst. Model. **12**, 387–414 (2011)
23. Lúcio, L., Mustafiz, S., Denil, J., Vangheluwe, H., Jukss, M.: FTG+PM: an integrated framework for investigating model transformation chains. In: Khendek, F., Toeroe, M., Gherbi, A., Reed, R. (eds.) SDL 2013. LNCS, vol. 7916, pp. 182–202. Springer, Heidelberg (2013). doi:10.1007/978-3-642-38911-5_11
24. Syriani, E., Vangheluwe, H.: Programmed graph rewriting with time for simulation-based design. In: Vallecillo, A., Gray, J., Pierantonio, A. (eds.) ICMT 2008. LNCS, vol. 5063, pp. 91–106. Springer, Heidelberg (2008). doi:10.1007/978-3-540-69927-9_7
25. Russell, N., Aalst, W., Hofstede, A.: Workflow exception patterns. In: Dubois, E., Pohl, K. (eds.) CAiSE 2006. LNCS, vol. 4001, pp. 288–302. Springer, Heidelberg (2006). doi:10.1007/11767138_20
26. Syriani, E., Kienzle, J., Vangheluwe, H.: Exceptional transformations. In: Tratt, L., Gogolla, M. (eds.) ICMT 2010. LNCS, vol. 6142, pp. 199–214. Springer, Heidelberg (2010). doi:10.1007/978-3-642-13688-7_14
27. von Pilgrim, J., Ulke, B., Thies, A., Steimann, F.: Model/code co-refactoring: an MDE approach. In: Automated Software Engineering, pp. 682–687. IEEE (2013)
28. Mens, T.: On the use of graph transformations for model refactoring. In: Lämmel, R., Saraiva, J., Visser, J. (eds.) GTTSE 2005. LNCS, vol. 4143, pp. 219–257. Springer, Heidelberg (2006). doi:10.1007/11877028_7
29. Zhang, J., Lin, Y., Gray, J.: Generic and domain-specific model refactoring using a model transformation engine. In: Beydeda, S., Book, M., Gruhn, V. (eds.) Model-Driven Software Development, pp. 199–217. Springer, Heidelberg (2005)
30. Metamodel refactoring catalog (2016). http://www.metamodelrefactoring.org/?page_id=584. Accessed 19 May 2016
31. MacKenzie, I.S.: Fitts' law as a research and design tool in human-computer interaction. Hum.-Comput. Interact. **7**, 91–139 (1992)
32. Benchmark, H.: (2015). http://www.humanbenchmark.com/tests/reactiontime/statistics
33. WMC: Process Definition Interface - XML Process Definition Language 2.00. Technical report, WFMC-TC-1025, Workflow Management Coalition (2005)
34. Mahmud, M., Abdullah, S., Hosain, S.: GWDL: a graphical workflow definition language for business workflows. In: Gaol, F. (ed.) Recent Progress in Data Engineering and Internet Technology. LNEE, vol. 156, pp. 205–210. Springer, Heidelberg (2013). doi:10.1007/978-3-642-28807-4_29
35. Russell, N., Aalst, W.M.P., Hofstede, A.H.M., Edmond, D.: Workflow resource patterns: identification, representation and tool support. In: Pastor, O., Falcão e Cunha, J. (eds.) CAiSE 2005. LNCS, vol. 3520, pp. 216–232. Springer, Heidelberg (2005). doi:10.1007/11431855_16

36. Jacob, F., Gray, J., Wynne, A., Liu, Y., Baker, N.: Domain-specific languages for composing signature discovery workflows. In: Workshop on Domain-Specific Modeling, pp. 61–64. ACM (2012)
37. Alajrami, S., Romanovsky, A., Watson, P., Roth, A.: Towards cloud-based software process modelling and enactment. In: Model-Driven Engineering on and for the Cloud, CloudMDE 14, vol. 1242, pp. 6–15 (2014)
38. Martin, D., Wutke, D., Leymann, F.: A novel approach to decentralized workflow enactment. In: Enterprise Distributed Object Computing, pp. 127–136. IEEE (2008)
39. Johnson, R., Woolf, B.: The type object pattern. In: EuroPLoP (1996)
40. Atkinson, C.: Meta-modelling for distributed object environments. In: Enterprise Distributed Object Computing Workshop, pp. 90–101. IEEE (1997)
41. Rivera, J.E., Ruiz Gonzalez, D., Lopez Romero, F., Bautista, J., Vallecillo, A.: Orchestrating ATL model transformations. In: Proceedings of MtATL, vol. 9, pp. 34–46 (2009)
42. Ludäscher, B., Altintas, I., Berkley, C., Higgins, D., Jaeger, E., Jones, M., Lee, E.A., Tao, J., Zhao, Y.: Scientific workflow management and the kepler system: research articles. Concurrency Comput.: Pract. Exp. Workflow Grid Syst. **18**, 1039–1065 (2006)
43. Kolovos, D.S., Paige, R.F., Polack, F.A.C.: Novel features in languages of the epsilon model management platform. In: Modeling in Software Engineering, pp. 69–73. ACM (2008)
44. Kolovos, D.S., Paige, R.F., Polac, F.A., Rose, L.M.: Update Transformations in the Small with the Epsilon Wizard Language. J. Object Technol. **6**, 53–69 (2007)

Schedulability Analysis of Pre-runtime and Runtime Scheduling Algorithm of an Industrial Real Time System

Stefano Pepi[✉] and Alessandro Fantechi[✉]

DINFO, University of Florence, Via S. Marta 3, Florence, Italy
{stefano.pepi,alessandro.fantechi}@unifi.it

Abstract. The configuration of a complex, generic, real-time application into a specifically customized signalling embedded application has an important impact on time to market, deployment costs and safety guarantees for a railway signalling manufacturer. In this paper we focus on the aspect of real-time schedulability analysis, that takes an important portion of the time dedicated to configuration in this kind of systems. We propose an approach based on rigorous modelling of the scheduling algorithms, aimed at substituting possibly unreliable and costly empirical tuning. In order to comply with the needs of our industrial partners, we have resorted to the use of variants of Petri Nets with associated available tools: Timed Petri Nets (TPN) and Coloured Petri Nets (CPN), supported by open source tools, respectively *TINA* and *CPN Tools 4.0* have been exploited for the modelling of the pre-runtime and the run-time scheduling algorithms implemented in the industrial platform. The comparison of models produced with the two tools has concluded that the Coloured Petri Nets are more suited to the adopted schedulability analysis approach, for both scheduling algorithms.

Keywords: Petri Nets · Timed Petri Nets · Coloured Petri Nets · Real Time Systems · Scheduling algorithm · Modelling · Formal verification · Railway signalling

1 Introduction

Real-Time Systems (RTS) are those computer-based systems where correct operation does not only depend on the correctness of the results obtained, but also on the time at which the results are produced [21].

The interest for real-time systems is motivated by many applications that require that computations satisfy given time constraints, in domains such as automotive, avionics, communications, railway signalling etc.

The most important property of a RTS is *predictability*. Predictability is the ability to determine in advance if the computation will be completed within the time constraints required. Predictability depends on several factors, ranging from the architectural characteristics of the physical machine, to the mechanisms

© Springer International Publishing AG 2017
S. Hammoudi et al. (Eds): MODELSWARD 2016, CCIS 692, pp. 46–69, 2017.
DOI: 10.1007/978-3-319-66302-9_3

of the core, up to the programming language. Predictability can be measured as the percentage of processes for which the constrains are guaranteed.

In this article we report the experience made in collaboration with our industrial partner, a railway signalling manufacturing company, in the implementation of a generic real-time platform based on a proprietary microkernel Real Time Operating System; in particular we present a method for schedulability analysis.

With the recent expansion of markets to Asia and Africa, the company has experienced a growing need for a versatile system that can be configurable for each different application. The transition from a traditional "main loop"-based system to a general purpose platform has allowed low-cost configuration, simply by changing the application inside and the hardware to interact with. With the same Hw/Sw platform both *ground* and *on-board* systems can be built, either for urban (like metro) or main line applications, meeting the signalling regulations of different countries.

Experience has however shown that guaranteeing predictability for the different customizations of the platform takes a considerable portion of the customization effort, if based only on testing every time the newly customized software on the platform.

We have therefore considered the possibility of building a generic model of the scheduling algorithms employed in the platform, that is going to be instantiated on the temporal constraints and tasks numbers of the different specific applications (that is, customizations), in order to support the validation of predictability by means of proper model simulation tools.

Basing on the wide literature about modelling real-time systems with Petri Nets (see, for example, [3,5,10,11]) and on the availability of related tools, we have chosen to experiment two Petri Nets dialects for the modelling of the scheduling algorithms, in order to predict schedulability of the set of tasks governing a new specific application. Both Timed Petri Nets (TPN) and Coloured Petri Nets (CPN) have been evaluated for this purpose, together with their support tools, favouring at the end the adoption of Coloured Petri Nets.

Due to the limited time available to conduct the experiments, in order to satisfy stringent temporal requirements from our industrial partner, we have chosen not to investigate other temporal modelling formalisms, such as timed automata [2]. The results obtained by these experiments were however judged sufficiently satisfactory to consider the adoption of the technique inside the development process of our industrial partner.

This paper is structured as follows: the next section introduces the industrial context that has motivated our work on modelling scheduling algorithms; in Sect. 3 we present the background of the modelling method, namely the two considered variants of Petri Nets, while in the next two sections we present the models of the pre-runtime and runtime scheduling policies. Section 6 compares the models obtained with the two Petri Nets variants, and Sect. 7 draws some conclusions.

2 Scheduling in Safety-Related RT Applications

A real-time process is characterized by a fixed time limit, which is called *deadline*. A result produced after its deadline is not only late, but can be harmful to the environment in which the system operates. Depending on the consequences of a missed deadline, real-time processes are divided into two types:

- *Soft real-time*: if producing the results after its deadline has still some utility for the system, although causing a performance degradation, that is, the violation of the deadline does not affect the proper functioning of the system;
- *Hard real-time*: if producing the results after its deadline may cause catastrophic consequences on the system under control.

To meet real-time requirements, scheduling plays an important role. Depending on the assumption done on the processes and on the type of hardware architecture that supports the application, the scheduling algorithms for real-time systems can be classified according to the following orthogonal characteristics:

- *Uniprocessor* vs. *Multiprocessor*
- *Preemptive* vs. *No preemptive*
- *Static* vs. *Dynamic*
- *Pre-runtime (offline)* vs. *Runtime (online)*
- *Best-Effort* vs. *Guaranteed*

For what concerns the fourth characteristic, in pre-runtime scheduling all decisions are taken before the process activation on the basis of information known a priori. The schedule is stored in a table which will be integrated into a run-time kernel. The kernel has one component called *dispatcher* which takes tasks from the table and loads them onto the processing elements, according to specified timing constraints. The *Runtime* category represents instead those algorithms in which the scheduling decisions are made at runtime on all currently active processes. The ordering of tasks is then recalculated for each new activation.

In our case the platform is able to manage both these two types of scheduling. In fact according to the type of field application it is possible to enable one or the other algorithm. The choice is made based on the level of safety that the system must ensure.

CENELEC EN50128 is the standard that specifies the procedures and the technical requirements for the development of programmable electronic devices to be used in railway control and signalling protection [7]. This standard is part of a family, and it refers only to the software components and to their interaction with the whole system. The basic concept of the standard is the *SIL* (Safety Integrity Level). Integrity levels characterize software modules and functions according to their criticality, and range is defined from 0 to 4, where 0 is the lowest level, which refers to software functions for which a failure has no safety effects and 4 is the maximum level, for which a software failure can have severe effects on the safety of system, resulting in possible loss of human life.

The pre-runtime scheduling algorithm is used for those application that are classified at SIL 4, since it gives the possibility to fully demonstrate predictability, which is a must in a safety-critical environment. Indeed, with pre-runtime scheduling it is possible to exhibit to an assessor the analyses conducted on the considered set of tasks in order to establish that tasks, with the a priori fixed execution order, do not miss their deadlines. On the other hand, with run-time scheduling algorithms, evidences provided simply by running tests can be not convincing about their coverage of all possible cases, due to possible different run-time scheduling choices. For this reason the run-time scheduling is used for applications of lower SIL.

Indeed, the present paper aims to show a method to strengthen the analysis on pre-runtime and runtime scheduling to a high level of confidence. In particular, we present a method that can be used to verify the pre-runtime schedulability of a task set that contains only periodic tasks with time and priority constrains. The method can be used also to simulate the behaviour of a runtime scheduler with a given taskset, in order to improve confidence on their run-time schedulability.

The motivations for this approach come also from the high variability of installations of the same signalling system at different locations or controlling different stations or lines. Indeed, in railway signalling systems, a distinction is often done between *generic applications* and *specific applications* (as in the already cited CENELEC EN50128 [7] guidelines): generic software is software which can be used for a variety of installations purely by the provision of application-specific data and/or algorithms. A specific application is defined as a generic application plus configuration data, or plus specific algorithms, that instantiate the generic application for a specific purpose.

While the platform is part of a generic application, and hence it is validated once for all, for each specific application the satisfaction of real-time constraints must be verified from scratch.

Indeed, quite often in everyday work it is necessary to revise the schedule of some systems, and all this is routinely done in an empirical way. It is clear that each specific application has a different way to interact with the platform and especially with its resources, such as, for example, input/output drivers for different hardware. It is for this reason that the schedule of real-time tasks should be revised at any new specific application.

The adopted empirical approach includes actions to be taken when configuring the platform for a new specific application, such as: get a new schedule configuration offline and test it on the target. It rarely happens that the first test is successful.

The estimated effort required for the identification and testing of a new scheduling configuration can be summarized with the following parameters:

- **Offline Identification Time:** time needed in order to design the new schedule, it is usually about 30 min (not necessary for runtime scheduling).
- **Flashing Time:** the time needed to load the scheduling on the target, 15 min.
- **Startup Time:** start-up time of the platform, 1.5 min.

- **Running Time:** time during which the system must run without exhibiting timing problems, 30 min/1 h.
- **Attempts:** average number of attempts to get the scheduling, 3.

Summing all the times shown above we get that for each test scheduling, the whole process easily reaches 8 h, which means an entire working day. This process can be automated by a tool that, given a task set and a number of constraints, is able to produce a feasible scheduling. This would mean a huge saving in terms of man hours used to refine the scheduling. Moreover, an empirical evaluation of schedulability of a given dataset does not guarantee that the deadlines are met in any case, putting in danger the overall safety of the system. Using a rigorous approach to the analysis of the schedulability will improve hence the conformance, of a specific application, to safety guidelines.

3   Proposed Method

The rigorous approach we propose is based on the use of Petri Nets to build a model of the scheduling algorithm. A Petri Net [17–19] is a mathematical representation of a distributed discrete system. As a modelling language, it describes the structure of a distributed system as a bipartite graph with annotations. A Petri Net consists of places, transitions and directed arcs. There may be arcs between places and transitions but not between places and places or transitions and transitions.

The places can hold a certain number of tokens and the distribution of tokens on all the places of the network it's named marking. Transitions act on input tokens according to a rule, that is named *firing rule*.

A transition is enabled if you can fire it, that is, if there are tokens in every input place. When a transition fires, it consumes tokens from its input places and places a token in each of its output places.

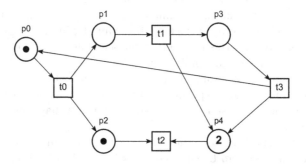

Fig. 1. Representation of an ordinary Petri Net.

Figure 1 shows an example of an ordinary Petri Net. The execution of Petri Nets is nondeterministic, that is, if there are more transitions enabled at the same time any of them can fire. Since taking a transition is not predictable in advance, Petri Nets are well suited for modelling the concurrent behavior of distributed systems.

Formally we can define a Petri Net as a tuple $PN = (P, T, F, W, M_0)$ where:

- P is a finite set of *places*;
- T is a finite set of *transition*;
- $F \subseteq (PxT) \cup (TxP)$ is a set of *arcs*;
- $W : F \to \mathbb{N}$ represents the weight of the flow relation F.
- $M_0 : P \to \mathbb{N}$ is the initial marking vector, which represents the initial state of system.
- $P \cap T = \emptyset$ and $P \cup T \neq \emptyset$.

3.1   TPN

A Timed Petri Net is a Petri Net extended with time. In Timed Petri Nets, the transitions fire in "real-time", i.e., there is a (deterministic or random) firing time associated with each transition, the tokens are removed from input places at the beginning of firing, and are deposited into output places when the firing terminates. Formally we can define a Timed Petri Net [20] as a tuple $TPN = (PN, I)$ where:

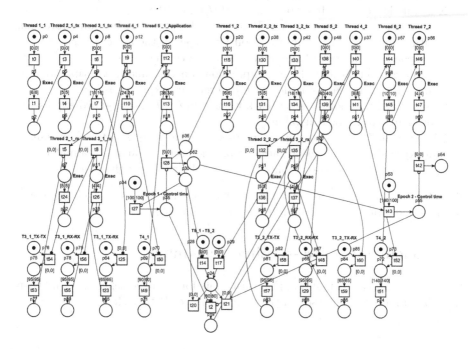

Fig. 2. Timed Petri Net model for a fixed scheduler.

- PN is a standard Petri Net;
- $I : T \rightarrow \mathbb{N} \times \mathbb{N}$ is a function that maps each transition to a bounded static interval
- $P \cap T = \emptyset$ and $P \cup T \neq \emptyset$.

3.2 CPN

An ordinary PN has no types and no modules, only one kind of tokens and the net is flat. With *Coloured Petri Nets* (CPNs) it is possible, instead, to use data types and complex data manipulation. In fact each token has attached a data value called the *token colour* of a given data type: the type defines the range of values that the attributes can assume and the operations applicable in the same way of a variable type in any programming language. The types can be basic types or structured types, the latter defined by the user. The token colour values can be inspected and modified by the occurring transitions.

Formally we can define a Coloured Petri Net as a tuple $CPN = (P, T, F, \Sigma, C, N, E, G, I)$ where:

- P is a finite set of *places*;
- T is a finite set of *transition*;
- $F \subseteq (PxT) \cup (TxP)$ is a set of *arcs*;
- Σ is a set of data types (colour domains).
- C is a colour function. It maps places in P into colours in Σ.
- N is a node function. It maps A into $(PxT) \cup (TxP)$.
- E is an arc expression function. It maps each arc $a \in A$ into an expression e with values in Σ. The input and output types of the arc expressions must correspond to the type of the nodes the arc is connected to.
  The node function and the arc expression function allows multiple arcs to connect the same pair of nodes with different arc expressions.
- G is a guard function. It maps each transition $t \in T$ into a guard expression g, evaluated to a boolean value.
- I is an initialization function. It maps each place $p \in P$ into an initialization expression i. The initialization expression must evaluate to a multiset of tokens with a colour corresponding to the colour $C(p)$ of the place p.

With CPNs it is possible to build a hierarchical description, so that a large model can be easily obtained by combining a set of submodels.

4   Modelling the Pre-runtime Scheduling

We provide now the taskset and the constraints for the fixed scheduler, and then the related models, expressed in the two variants of Petri Nets.

4.1   Taskset and Constraints Specification

In our system the application is decomposed into a set of tasks $\tau_i : i = 1, ...n$ and for this paper we only consider periodic tasks, and we assume that non-periodic tasks are carried out by a periodic server, or processed in the background [6]. The temporal model mostly used in real-time scheduling theory is an extension of the model of Liu and Layland [16] where each task τ_i is characterized by the following parameters:

- R_i: first release time of τ_i;
- C_i: run time of τ_i, which is its worst case execution time (WCET);
- D_i: relative deadline of τ_i, the maximum time elapsed between the release of an instance of τ_i and its completion;
- P_i: release period of τ_i.

In the following we use as a running example the case of a real signalling application, an interlocking system. An *interlocking* system is the safety-critical system that controls the movement of trains in a station and between adjacent stations. The interlocking monitors the status of the objects in the railway yard (e.g., points, switches, track circuits) and allows or denies the routing of trains in accordance with the railway safety and operational regulations that are generic for the region or country where the interlocking is located. The instantiation of these rules on a station topology is stored in the part of the system named control table that is specific for the station where the system resides. We refer to [9] for a review on the vast literature on formal modelling of interlocking systems. In this context, we are interested instead to focus on the characteristics of the task set of this application, consisting of 7 threads which have the following goal:

- T_1 is in charge of operating on the Ethernet channel;
- T_2 is one of the most important thread and it is in charge of the safety of the system;
- T_3 implements a protocol stack for the receipt and transmission of messages;
- T_4 is in charge of copying the value received in the input of the Business Logic and preparing the output for the transmission.
- T_5 is the application thread that contains the logic of the system.
- T_6 is a diagnostic thread;
- T_7 is a USB driver used for logging data in a key.

The scheduler operates by dividing processor time into epochs. Within each epoch, every task can execute up to its time slice. In this case, the scheduler has two epochs of 100 ms and the taskset have the following constraints:

- The total time of scheduling cycle is 200 ms.
- Each epoch needs to last exactly 100 ms.
- The first execution of T_3 in the first and second epoch must terminate within 95 ms.
- The second execution of T_3 in the first and second epoch must terminate within 95 ms.

- The second execution of T_3 in the first and second epoch must execute at least 65 ms after the first one.
- T_4 in the first epoch must terminate within 90 ms and in the second epoch in 140 ms.
- The total processor time assigned to T_5 in the two epochs must be of at least 90 ms.

The taskset used in our example is defined in the Tables 1 and 2 with the relative scheduling order and parameters.

Table 1. TaskSet in first epoch.

Epoch1	R_i	C_i	D_i
T_1	0	6	6
T_2	6	5	11
T_3	11	16	27
T_2	27	5	32
T_3	32	4	36
T_4	36	24	60
T_5	60	40	100

Table 2. TaskSet in second epoch.

Epoch2	R_i	C_i	D_i
T_1	0	6	6
T_2	6	5	11
T_3	11	16	27
T_2	27	5	32
T_3	32	4	36
T_5	36	40	76
T_4	76	8	84
T_6	84	10	94
T_7	94	6	100

The constraints and parameters given for the taskset are the basis on which a model of the scheduling algorithm can be built. We resorted to the use of Petri Nets, that result quite intuitive in the modelling of scheduling algorithms [5,10,15,23]. In order to represent time, we have investigated the use of both Timed Petri Nets (TPN) [20] and Coloured Petri Nets (CPN) [13]. In the following we illustrate the two kinds of models by means of this running example, giving a comparison between the two modelling approaches.

4.2   Presentation of Fixed Scheduler Models

In Fig. 2 the model generated with the tool TINA [4,22] for a fixed scheduler [1,3,11] is reported. As we can see the representation with TPN is a little bit chaotic and representing larger sets of tasks could be very difficult. Looking at the model we can underline some diagram parts which are used for the verification of constraints [23]:

- **Check for the Total Time**

  The network used to control the time of each epoch consists of two transitions and respectively five and three places. Taking into consideration the network (a) in Fig. 3, the transition t27 counts the total time available for the execution in the epoch. When the available time expires, the token content in place p34 is moved to place p35 inhibiting the passage of the token coming from the last running thread to places p36, p62 and p30.

  If this happens it means that the execution time has not respected the constraints for this epoch. If, instead, the execution ends before the deadline, the transition t28 will not be inhibited by place p35 and will allow tokens to go in places p36, p62 and p30, establishing the positive conclusion of the first epoch and the start of the second one.

- **Check Constraints on T_3**

  The network in Fig. 4 models the various checks on the execution times for T_3. For example the last block checks that between the first execution of T_3 in the first epoch and the second execution in the second epoch, at least 65 ms have expired. The transition t25 is enabled when the task is running and, if the task completes before the time set in the transition t23, scheduling can continue. Otherwise, if the task does not complete within the specified time, the inhibitor arc starting from p65 does not allow the scheduler to continue.

- **Checking the Scheduled Time between Two Epochs**

  The network in Fig. 5 monitors the execution time of a task between the two epochs. The transitions t14 and t17 are enabled when the task is run in both the first and the second period. This starts the timer of transition t2. If the task completes before the time set in the transition, the scheduling can continue. Otherwise, if the task does not complete within the specified time, the inhibitor arc starting from p19 does not allow the scheduler to continue.

The simulation of this model by means of the TINA tool ends either with a token at place p54, which means that the hypothesized schedule is correct, or by stopping as soon as an error is generated, with a different marking.

We show now the corresponding model described as a CPN. In Fig. 6 the model of the running example generated with CPN tools 4.0 [8,14] is reported. As we can see the representation with CPN is more compact than the one seen with TPN, for example by using only one place we can represent all the tasks of the set. The tasks are represented as a list of objects, and each one is represented by a token having as colour two attributes: a string that contains the name and one integer that represents the WCET C_i of the task.

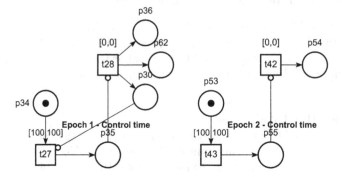

Fig. 3. Diagram of epoch control block.

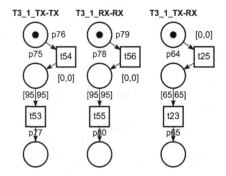

Fig. 4. Diagram of block for the verification of constraints on task T_3.

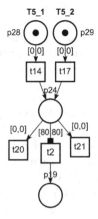

Fig. 5. Check block for the scheduled time between two epochs for task T_5.

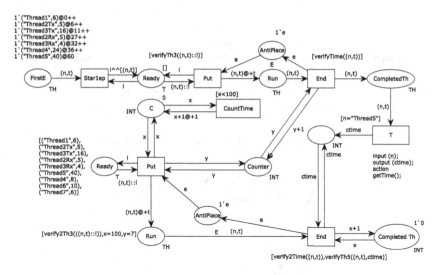

Fig. 6. Coloured Petri Net model for a fixed scheduler.

Inhibitor arcs are not provided by CPNs (as supported by CPNTools); since they are extensively used in our modelling, we have used a pattern that allows to simulate their behaviour: the *Antiplace* pattern, natively provided by CPNTools. This is exemplified in Fig. 7, where the execution of a thread at a certain time is achieved by simulating an inhibitor arc on place Run by using the Antiplace pattern () initialized with a token: when a thread is executed, the token is removed from Antiplace, so that the transition Put is not enabled until the thread finishes executing (so the token spends in place Run a time equal to its value C_i, represented by the variable t), and then it enables the transition End; at this point a token is put back in Antiplace, allowing the next thread to run. In Fig. 6 the Antiplace pattern is used in the modelling of both the first epoch (top Antiplace) and of the second (bottom Antiplace).

The second epoch performs its scheduling after 100 time units have elapsed. Time is not inherently modelled in CPNs as is in Timed Petri Nets. Hence a time-passing simulating pattern has been used; the pattern shown in Fig. 8 implements a timer that increments by 1 at each simulation step, till the simulated time has reached 100, in which case the transition CountTime is disabled. The Timer pattern has been used in Fig. 6 to start the second epoch at time 100. The place C containing a token value 100 allows threads to run, as long as the other constraints on the transition Put are respected; in particular the threads of the first portion of the schedule (first epoch) must have all finished running.

Due to the absence of the built-in timing mechanisms of TPNs, verification of the constraints on the execution time of the thread need to be explicitly realized by means of some functions listed on the transitions. On the first and second transitions named "Put", for example, we can find respectively the functions called *[verifyTh3 ()]* and *[verify2Th3 ()]*. These two functions implement the

58   S. Pepi and A. Fantechi

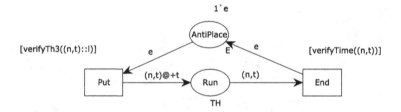

Fig. 7. Antiplace pattern used to simulate an inhibitor arc.

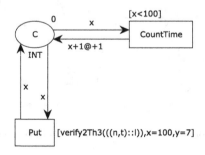

Fig. 8. Timer pattern.

constraint that between the two executions of T_3 cannot elapse less than 65 ms. The functions are defined as follows:

```
fun verifyTh3((n,t)::l) =
  if n="Thread3" andalso
     intTime() > 65
  then false else true
fun verify2Th3(((n,t)::l)) =
  if n="Thread3" andalso
     (intTime()-100) > 65
  then false else true
```

The function checks if the token in input to the transition represents the task 3, and verifies that the current simulation time (obtained with the function *intTime()*) is less than 65 units. If the constraint is not respected, the transition is not enabled.

On the transition "End" we can find a function named *[verifyTime()]* that checks all the other constraints (the function is similar to the one above).

An exception is the constraint on T_5 that is represented by function *[verifyTh5ctime()]* placed as guard on the same transition. The modelling of this last constraint, specific for task T_5, requires to save in a variable the time at which the token of the T_5 exits from the "Run" place in the first epoch. This has been achieved through the transition "T" with label pattern *input, output, action* where we take a variable in input (variable *n*) and by the action (*getTime()* function) we generate an output (variable *ctime*). This transition is enabled only for T_5 as we can see from the guard on the arch. So the variable that we have obtained has be used in the function:

```
fun verifyTh5 ((n, t), ctime)=
  if  n = "Thread5" andalso
      (intTime () - ctime) >= 90
  {then false else true}
```

Similarly to the modelling done with TPN, also the simulation of the CPN model by means of the CPN Tools 4.0 stops if one of the constraint is not satisfied, so the user is able to understand where the problem is located.

5   Modelling the Runtime Scheduling

As previously said, the platform also implements a runtime (on-line) scheduling algorithm: a round robin scheduling with priority levels, deadlines, a preemption mechanism and a donation mechanism. Runtime scheduling is used for applications of the platform that do not require stringent hard real-time requirements. Although scheduling predictability in these applications is less urgent, we have applied the same modelling framework used for the pre-runtime algorithm to this case: having a certain level of predictability at a low cost can anyway avoid annoying (although not safety-critical) software bugs due to poor scheduling performances, that could anyway increase software maintenance costs.

Also in this case we have used both TPNs and CPNs in order to complete the comparison of the two modelling frameworks also in this other case. The following sections provide the generated models with Petri Nets for three variants of the Round Robin algorithm, namely with FIFO queue, with prioritized FIFO queue, and adding preemption. The experiments are conducted on a reduced taskset of three tasks, starting from the simpler variant, by inserting then various functions incrementally.

5.1   Round Robin with FIFO Queue

The first variant considered is a round robin without priority, without preemption but with the introduction of a FIFO queue for arriving tasks. Figure 9 shows the diagram of execution time for this variant, assuming the following taskset data:

- The first process arrives at time 20 and has a duration of 8 time units,
- The second arrives at time 25 and has a duration of 12 time units,
- The third arrives at time 20 and has a duration of 16 time units.

The time slice assigned to each task at run time is 4 time units. In the Timed Petri net of Fig. 10 a FIFO queue for the management of the processes during their arrival and their displacement has been introduced in the *WAIT* places. Three FIFO queues have actually been implemented (highlighted by a box), one for each task, given the impossibility to use only one for all the tasks, due to the fact that in TPN it is not possible to distinguish tokens representing different tasks.

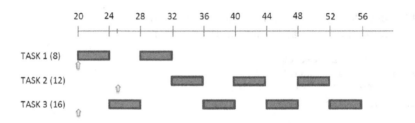

Fig. 9. Temporal schema of a RR with three tasks with FIFO queue.

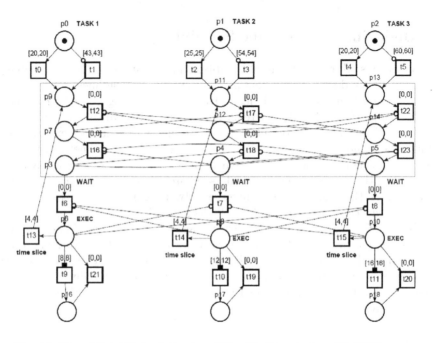

Fig. 10. Timed Petri Net relative to a RR with three tasks with FIFO queue.

Each queue is formed by three places and two transitions. The places are used to store the position of the task in the queue and transitions allow the progress of the task in the queue, moving the token. To simulate the correct order of tasks in the queue, inhibitors arcs have been used, which inhibit the passage of the token to the next place if the other queues already contain a token in a place of the same level.

The same round robin variant was modelled with CPNs and the result is shown in Fig. 11. The tasks are represented by tokens of type *Sting*int* defined as: *colset T = product STRING*INT timed;*, where the string is the task identifier and the integer represents the time slice. The FIFO queue in this case can be programmed as a single token having as type a list structure: the management

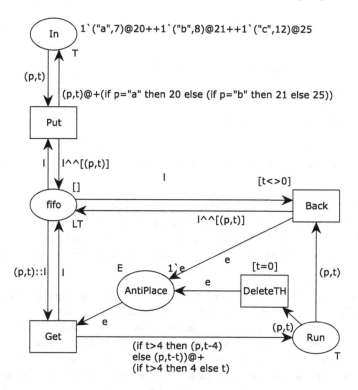

Fig. 11. Coloured Petri Net relative to a RR with FIFO queue, and three tasks.

of the queue is represented by the place *fifo*, which takes token type LT defined as: *colset LT = list T timed* or rather an object list of type *T*.

Tokens have an initial timestamp representing their time of arrival. They are put in the list by the concatenation function $l\,\hat{}\,\hat{}\,[(p, t)]$, where l is the token associate to the place *FIFO*. If there are no tokens in the place *Run*, the transition *Get* is enabled, the element at the head of the FIFO is extracted by the function $(p,\ t)::l$, and the updated list is sent back to the place *FIFO*. Before being added to *Run* every input token receives a timestamp, and the time slice value is decremented. If the remaining time is less than the timeslice, it receives a timestamp value equal to the remaining time, and the integer value of the token, represented by the variable t, is brought to 0. In this way, once elapsed the timestamp, the token will not be placed back in the queue but will be eliminated through the transition *DeleteTh*.

5.2   Round Robin with Priority FIFO Queue

Figure 12 shows the timing diagram of a Round Robin scheduling with FIFO queues to which priority has been added. Similarly to the previous example, there are three processes:

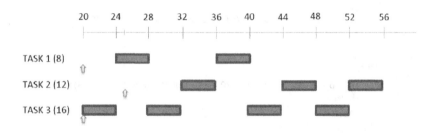

Fig. 12. Temporal schema of a RR with three tasks with FIFO queue and priority.

- The first arrives at time 20 and has a duration of 8 time units,
- The second arrives at time 25 and has a length of 12 time units,
- The third arrives at 20 and has a duration of 16 time units.
- The second and third process have equal priority and greater than the first one.

The quantum of CPU time assigned to each of them at run time is 4 time units.

The Timed Petri Net of Fig. 13 is the model of the round robin variant with priority and FIFO queue. The boxes show queues formed by nine places arranged in three rows and connected together with instant transitions. This is a generalization of the previous modelling of a single queue for the three tasks case, where in principle the three tasks can have three different priority levels: the priority levels are represented by the three columns in each box. The task priority is expressed by including a link to the first place of the queue related to the actual task priority: If the arc is connected with the first (last) vertical row of places, the process will have the lowest (highest) priority. In the case under consideration, the first task has a lower priority than the other two tasks, that have equal priority. Notice that only one of the columns is connected, so the other two are useless, but this design is maintained for easy modification of tasks'priorirty. As for the simple FIFO queue of Fig. 10, inhibitor arcs are used to enforce the correct priority and FIFO policy.

The corresponding CPN model for this case is shown in Fig. 14. The model must then insert the thread into a ready queue based on their order of arrival and an integer value representing the priority of the thread. A token that has a priority value higher than those already present in the queue will be inserted in the head, and then perform first. Hence the management of the priority and FIFO policy is implemented through a data structure instead of the convolutes net layout of the TPN case. The structure of the model is virtually unchanged compared to the case without priority, the differences are basically two, namely the label on the arcs in input to the place that represent the tail and a different type to define the task. In this model, threads are represented by token type *colset T = product STRING*INT*INT timed* where last INT value is associated to the task priority. In the previous model the insertion was performed by concatenation function and the token was placed at the tail of the queue. In the version with priorities a check on the value that represents the priority is needed

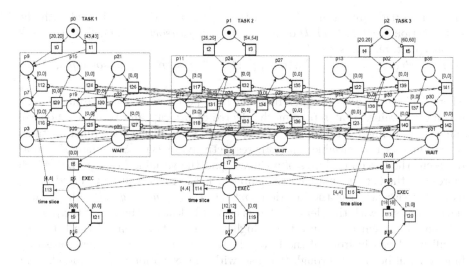

Fig. 13. Timed Petri Net relative to a RR with three tasks with FIFO queue and priority.

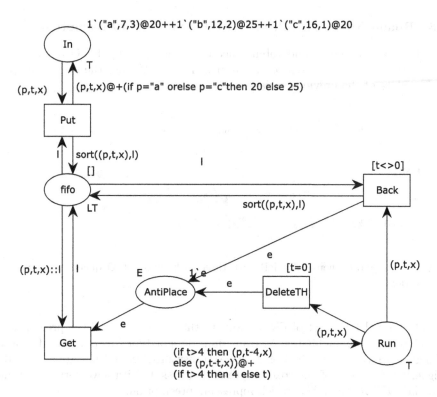

Fig. 14. Coloured Petri Net relative to RR scheduling model with with FIFO queue and priority.

in order to determine the location in the queue, and this is achieved with the sort function $sort((p, t, x), l)$ defined as follow: $funsort((p, t, x), []) = [(p, t, x)]|$
$$sort((p, t, x), ((m, s, q) :: l)) =$$
$$if\,higher\,Pr(x, q)then(p, t, x) :: (m, s, q) :: l \qquad else(m, s, q) :: (sort((p, t, x), l));$$

where $higherPr(x,q)$ is another function that performs a comparison between two integer values that represent the degree of priority and returns a boolean value, thus defined: $fun\,higher\,Pr(x, y) = (x > y);$. The $sort()$ function takes as parameters the variables (p, t, x), respectively, of type $String, int, int$ that represent the three attributes of a thread, and the variable l of type LT, which represents the list. If l matches the empty list, the token will be inserted in the list, otherwise, will run the function $sort\ ((p, t, x), ((m, s, q) :: l));$ that makes the comparison with the element that is currently leading the list. If the priority value of the token to be inserted is higher than that in front of the list, then it will be placed in front of the latter. Instead, if the value is lower, the $sort()$ function will be called through that list, with the exception of the head element in the head, recursively until it finds a token with a lower priority or the list is empty.

5.3   Round Robin with Priority FIFO Queue and Preemption

The last variant is a round robin scheduling with priority FIFO queues and preemption, whose time schema is given in Fig. 15. We use the same example taskset data of the previous variant.

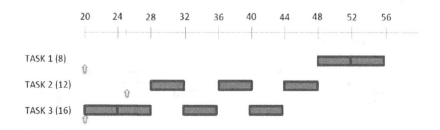

Fig. 15. Temporal schema of a RR with three tasks with FIFO queue, priority and preemption.

The Timed Petri Net of Fig. 16 adds to the previous model the preemption technique: the box highlights the transitions designed for this purpose. If a task of higher priority arrives in *WAIT* place, transitions *t28* and *t43* are activated, triggering the move of the token representing task 1, with lower priority, from the place *EXEC* to *WAIT*, which represents preemption.

The model of this variant by means of CPNs is shown in Fig. 17. Compared to Sect. 5.2 a transition *CheckPr* and a place called *Count* have been added.

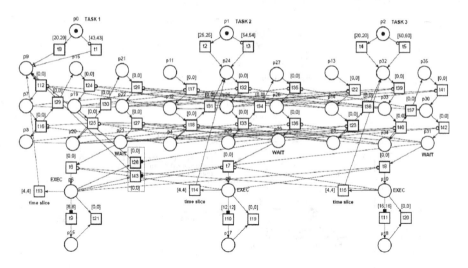

Fig. 16. Timed Petri Net modelling a RR with FIFO queue, priority and preemption, with three tasks.

The place is used to simulate the continuous flowing of time, with time increasing of a time until at each simulation step. Indeed, the model of Sect. 5.2 advances the time at each simulation step of the amount of time needed to reach a change of system status, while preemption requires to check the status of the tasks at any simulation step. When the integer token contained in *Count* reaches four (the value attributed to the timeslice), it enables the transition *Back in Run* and the token is queued by the *sort()* function. For every unit of time, through the transition *CheckPr* a comparison is made between the priority of the running threads and that of the thread at the top of the queue. If the priority of the latter is lower, the token currently in Run will decrease the execution time of 1 and its timestamp will be incremented by 1. The transition *CheckPr* remains enabled as long as the executing thread will have an execution time greater than 0 or until it will have spent the whole time slice. In case a token is in the *Run* place and a token with higher priority arrives in the queue, the time counting is stopped and the replacement is done instantly, by inserting the token with the higher priority in *Run* and inserting the other in the queue via the *sort()* function. The verification of the priority value is executed, via inscriptions on the arcs, by the function *higherPr(x, y)* defined earlier. The same function is used to determine the value of the timestamp on the token in *Run* and *Count*, and to decrease or not the execution time of the thread. If in fact the function returns true, it means that they will be replaced, and the value of the token *t* in execution will not be decreased.

66   S. Pepi and A. Fantechi

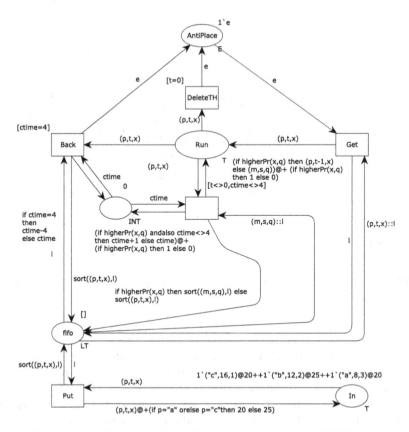

Fig. 17. Coloured Petri Net relative to RR scheduling model with FIFO queue, priority and preemption.

6 Comparison Between TPN and CPN

The experiments have allowed a comparison between the two Petri Nets dialects and related supporting tools, in particular enlightening the following points:

The TPN model is difficult to read, and the addition of further tasks would result in a huge increase of the places and transitions number, making it more and more unreadable. This increase is due to the following reasons:

– Any place can hold a single token and the execution of a thread must be reproduced a number of times equal to the number of modelled processes; indeed in TPNs it is not possible to express an attribute that differentiates the identity of a token.
– Time management for each thread is left to time constraints on the transitions themselves.
– It is not possible to create aggregate objects: a FIFO queue, for example, can be realized only through checks by inhibitors arcs with a number of places

that depends on how many threads should be modelled (the number of places to represent the queue is equal to n^2 where n is the number of threads).

- With the inclusion of the priority, it is noted that for each thread nine places and seven transitions with inhibitor arcs between them are needed for three thread. In this case we have a cubic relation of the net size to the number of threads, although optimizations can be done by loosing flexibility of the approach.

The CPNs instead can represent a queue using a single place that contains a token of type list. Time management is shifted to the token colour using an integer and a timestamp. This allows a large number of tasks to be represented by simply adding tokens to the initial marking, leaving the structure of the model unaffected.

As cons the CPN Tools software does not support the inhibitors arcs, so it was necessary to simulate them through the Antiplace pattern. The increase of the size due to the use of this pattern is however only locally additive, and the absence of replicated instances of inhibitor arcs typical of TPN models allows for containing the usage of the pattern to a few units.

CPNs do not natively support time, so time constraints (modelled in TPN through places and transitions) have to be expressed in auxiliary functions, but this in the end simplifies the model.

With TINA and TPNs the management of time during simulation allows to easily understand the global state of the system. The time is increased at any simulation step of a time unit. In CPNTools and CPNs if there are no transitions enabled at the current time, the simulated time count is increased in one step, up to the time at which at least one transition is activated. In one case we had to enforce simulation of step by step time advance by means of a specific Timer mechanism.

CPNs however resulted to be more advantageous in terms of time spent in model design or in changes, mainly for two reasons:

1. constraints can be simply modelled by a guard on the transition, expressed by a function written in pseudo code, which is easier to express;
2. populating the model with new tasks does not require to draw new graphic elements but just add an entry to the related place;

We have experienced that the time spent in CPN modelling is at the end less than half that spent in TPN modelling.

7 Conclusions

We have applied the two modelling options sketched above to different scheduling algorithms, a fixed one and a Round Robin, and different sets of tasks as well. The quite straightforward conclusion is that the CPN modelling is more advantageous in terms of size and readability of the model, and in terms of adaptability of the model to different task sets.

It is indeed easier with CPN to instantiate the same model, for the same scheduling algorithms, on a different set of tasks, and this is what is important in the daily application of this modelling framework. Since essentially only the taskset data need to be changed for a new, or modified, specific application, the overall time to analyse a new taskset, summing up the time to produce a model of the schedule of a new specific application, to run a simulation and to analyse the simulation, is about two hours with a TPN modelling and about one hour with the CPN modelling. Anyway, this time compares with the much longer time (eight hours) needed by the previously used empirical approach, and therefore is convenient in both cases.

Even if some rework is needed in case of a negative response of the simulation, the information returned by the simulation helps understanding where the problem lies, indicating the solution to the problem. Usually one rework cycle is at most needed, so the overall cost is anyway reduced.

For this reason we have not considered convenient to investigate solutions based on counterexample generated by a model checker [12], able to provide automatically the taskset parameters satisfying the scheduling requirements.

The low cost of the simulation based solution has an obvious positive impact on the costs of the process of instantiating a generic application to a new specific application for marketing a new product or variant.

Regarding the Round Robin runtime scheduling algorithm, we have shown the modelling, with the two Petri Net variants, for a taskset of three tasks. It is already evident from the presented models that for real application tasksets, such as one that we have addressed, containing 16 tasks, with 32 priority levels, the TPN model cannot be feasible, while the CPN model is an easy extension of the one presented.

The design process based on this modelling approach is currently under experimentation by our industrial partner, with the aim of introducing it in the routine customization process. An help for this introduction could come from providing tools to support an easier instantiation of the generic models into specific ones, so that the use of CPN is transparent to the final user who only sees the simulation results. This objective requires also a facility to explain the reasons of a negative response without showing the underlying CPN model. This is considered as future work.

Although motivated by specific needs of a railway signalling company, we believe that this approach can be ported to other domain as well, as soon as configurable real-time applications have to be designed on top of available real-time scheduling algorithms.

Acknowledgements. We wish to thank Marco Bartolozzi, Daniele Marchetti and Luca Santi for their contribution to the conducted modelling experiments.

References

1. van der Aalst, W.M.P.: Petri net based scheduling. Oper. Res. Spektrum **18**, 219–229 (1996). Springer

2. Alur, R., Dill, D.: The theory of timed automata. In: Bakker, J.W., Huizing, C., Roever, W.P., Rozenberg, G. (eds.) REX 1991. LNCS, vol. 600, pp. 45–73. Springer, Heidelberg (1992). doi:10.1007/BFb0031987

3. Barreto, R., Cavalcante, S., Maciel, P.: A time Petri Net approach for finding preruntime schedules in embedded hard real-time systems. In: Proceedings of Distributed Computing Systems Workshops, pp. 846–851. IEEE (2004)

4. Berthomieu, B., Vernadat, F.: Time petri nets analysis with TINA. In: Quantitative Evaluation of Systems, pp. 123–124. IEEE (2006)

5. Berthomieu, B., Diaz, M.: Modeling and verification of time dependent system using time petri nets. IEEE Trans. Softw. Eng. 17(3), 259–273 (1991). IEEE

6. Buttazzo, G.: Hard Real-Time Computing System, 3rd edn. Springer, New York (2011)

7. Cenelec: Cenelec EN 50128:2011. In: Railway Applications - Communications, Signalling and Processing Systems - Software for Railway Control and Protection Systems (2011)

8. CPNTools (2015). http://cpntools.org/

9. Fantechi, A.: Twenty-five years of formal methods and railways: what next? In: Counsell, S., Núñez, M. (eds.) SEFM 2013. LNCS, vol. 8368, pp. 167–183. Springer, Cham (2014). doi:10.1007/978-3-319-05032-4_13

10. Felder, M., Mandrioli, D., Morzenti, A.: Proving properties of real-time systems through logical specifications and petri net models. IEEE Trans. Softw. Eng. 20(2), 127–141 (1994)

11. Grolleau, E., Choquet-Geniet, A.: Off-line computation of real-time schedules using Petri Nets. Discrete Event Dyn. Syst. 12(3), 311–333 (2002). Springer

12. Gardey, G., Lime, D., Magnin, M., Roux, O.H.: Romeo: a tool for analyzing time petri nets. In: Etessami, K., Rajamani, S.K. (eds.) CAV 2005. LNCS, vol. 3576, pp. 418–423. Springer, Heidelberg (2005). doi:10.1007/11513988_41

13. Jensen, K.: Coloured petri nets. In: Brauer, W., Reisig, W., Rozenberg, G. (eds.) ACPN 1986. LNCS, vol. 254. Springer, Heidelberg (1987)

14. Jensen, K., Kristensen, L.M., Wells, L.: Coloured petri nets and CPN tools for modelling and validation of concurrent systems. Int. J. Softw. Tools Technol. Transf. 9(3), 213–254 (2007). Springer

15. Leveson, N.G., Stolzy, J.L.: Safety analysis using Petri Nets. IEEE Trans. Softw. Eng. 13(3), 386–397 (1987)

16. Liu, C.L., Layland, J.W.: Scheduling algorithms for multiprogramming in a hard-real-time environment. J. ACM 20(1), 46–61 (1973). ACM

17. Murata, T.: Petri nets: properties, analysis and applications. Proc. IEEE 77(4), 541–580 (1989). IEEE

18. Peterson, J.L.: Petri Net Theory and the Modeling of Systems. Prentice Hall PTR, Upper Saddle River (1981)

19. Petri, C.A.: Kommunikation mit automaten. Ph.D. thesis. Universitat Hamburg (1962)

20. Ramchandani, C.: Analysis of asynchronous concurrent systems by Timed Petri Nets. Massachusetts Institute of Technology (1974)

21. Stankovic, J.: Misconceptions about real-time computing. IEEE Comput. 21, 10–19 (1988). IEEE

22. TINA (2015). http://projects.laas.fr/tina/

23. Tsai, J., Yang, S.J., Chang, Y.-H.: Timing constraint Petri Nets and their application to schedulability analysis of real-time system specifications. IEEE Trans. Softw. Eng. 21(1), 32–49 (1995). IEEE

Cognitive Feedback and Behavioral Feedforward Automation Perspectives for Modeling and Validation in a Learning Context

Gayane Sedrakyan[✉] and Monique Snoeck

Department of Decision Sciences and Information Management,
Research Center for Management Informatics, KU Leuven, Leuven, Belgium
{gayane.sedrakyan,monique.snoeck}@kuleuven.be

Abstract. State-of-the-art technologies have made it possible to provide a learner with immediate computer-assisted feedback by delivering *a feedback targeting cognitive aspects of learning*, (e.g. reflecting on a result, explaining a concept, i.e. improving understanding). Fast advancement of technology has recently generated increased interest for previously non-feasible approaches for providing *feedback based on learning behavior observations* by exploiting different traces of learning processes stored in information systems. Such learner behavior data makes it possible to observe different aspects of learning processes in which feedback needs of learners (e.g. difficulties, engagement issues, inefficient learning processes, etc.) based on individual learning trajectories can be traced. By identifying problems earlier in a learning process it is possible to deliver individualized feedback helping learners to take control of their own learning, i.e. to become self-regulated learners, and teachers to understand individual feedback needs and/or adapt their teaching strategies. In this work we (i) propose cognitive computer-assisted feedback mechanisms using a combination of MDE based simulation augmented with automated feedback, and (ii) discuss perspectives for behavioral feedback, i.e. feedforward, that can be based on learning process analytics in the context of learning conceptual modeling. Aggregated results of our previous studies assessing the effectiveness of the proposed cognitive feedback method with respect to improved understanding on different dimensions of knowledge, as well as feasibility of behavioral feedforward automation based on learners behavior patterns, are presented. Despite our focus on conceptual modeling and specific diagrams, the principles of the approach presented in this work can be used to support educational feedback automation for a broader spectrum of diagram types beyond the scope of conceptual modeling.

Keywords: Conceptual modeling · Model driven development · Simulation · Simulation feedback · Rapid prototyping · Model testing/validation · Feedback automation · Learning process analytics · Smart learning environments

S. Hammoudi et al. (Eds): MODELSWARD 2016, CCIS 692, pp. 70–92, 2017.
DOI: 10.1007/978-3-319-66302-9_4

1   Introduction

During a learning process feedback can be provided in a variety of types (e.g., verification of response accuracy, explanation of the correct answer, hints, worked examples, etc.), in a variety of forms (verbal/written text, graphics, audio, video, animation, simulation, etc.), at various times (e.g., immediately following an answer, at the end of a module, etc.) [1], by different people (e.g. teacher, peer, self,...) [2]. The role of feedback in linking learners' past and future work, and helping them to create a progressive developmental trajectory, means that *timeliness* should be central to any discussion of feedback [3]. Research has shown that the sooner students receive feedback the more effective it is for their learning [4]. Usually feedback is not available during a learning task completion process but is given after a certain learning task has been completed, thus having the form of *outcome feedback*. Outcome feedback is a minimal form of external guidance, stating if an achieved solution/answer is correct or not and why. In feedback research the effectiveness of more informative types of *feedback that can guide a learning process* is highlighted [1, 5, 6]. Different theories have attempted to explain the *process of how people learn*. Even though psychologists and educators are not in complete agreement, most do agree that learning may be explained by a combination of two basic approaches: *cognitive theories*, i.e. *constructivism*, that view the learning process as a step by step knowledge construction process, and *behavioral theories, i.e. behaviorism*, in which learning is defined as a change of the behavior of a learner by reinforcing some aspect of his/her behavior. In the context of feedback research these approaches translate into two major forms: (1) explanations that are targeting at improving cognitive dimensions of knowledge (e.g. understanding), and (2) guidance that intend influencing a learner's behavior, e.g. engaging in a specific type of activity that is believed to be related to a successful learning path. As learning is multifaceted these approaches are often combined. For instance, in theories on *(self-)regulation of learning* that are closely intertwined with research on feedback and improved learning outcomes, learners are no longer viewed as repositories for information but rather they are proactive and active processors of information acting as *constructors of their own knowledge by reinforcing themselves for goal-directed behavior*. Self-regulated learning is defined as the ability of a learner to monitor and evaluate own progress with respect to self-improvement needs in the process of knowledge construction [7].

State-of-the-art technologies have made it possible to provide a learner with immediate computer-assisted feedback in the context of different learning tasks, by delivering *a feedback targeting cognitive aspects of learning*, (e.g. reflecting on a result, explaining a concept, i.e. improving understanding). Fast advancement of technology has recently generated increased interest for previously non-feasible approaches for providing *feedback based on learning behavior observations* by exploiting different traces of learning processes stored in information systems (IS). Such learner behavior data makes it possible to observe different aspects of learning processes in which feedback needs of learners (e.g. difficulties, engagement issues, etc.) based on individual learning trajectories can be traced. By identifying problems earlier in a learning process it is possible to deliver individualized feedback helping learners to take control of their own learning, i.e. to become self-regulated learners, and teachers to understand individual feedback needs and/or adapt their teaching strategies.

In this paper we present computer assisted feedback perspectives for learning conceptual modeling. We first review the general feedback needs of novices based on the challenges of learning/teaching found in the literature. Subsequently, we aim proposing computer-assisted feedback perspectives with respect to: (1) *cognitive aspects of learning processes* (concept understanding) that can address the identified challenges ("what" aspect that allows comparing current vs. good performance, i.e. what is achieved vs, what is expected), and (2) *behavioral aspects of learning* by grounding the idea of feedback on learning process analytics, more specifically by identifying learning behavior paths that can be indicative for better/worse learning outcomes ("how" aspect in terms of "how a good performance is achieved").

The proposed approach of feedback is based on the definitions of **process-oriented cognitive feedback and behavioral feedforward** by [8] in which the term process-oriented in the context of feedback refers to **immediate** feedback needs during a task completion (e.g. problem solving) process, that a learner can either be aware (learner knows whenever s/he needs a feedback) or unaware (learner does not realize that s/he needs a correction) of. We refer here to computer-assisted feedback possibilities that can be achieved before a teacher feedback can be available. Subsequently our research aims are defined as follows:

RA1:   Exploring process-oriented (immediate) feedback mechanisms for addressing the learning/teaching challenges from the perspective of *cognitive aspects* of learning.

RA2:   Exploring process-oriented (immediate) feedback perspectives based on *behavioral characteristics* of novices' learning processes that, in addition to being directed to a learner, can also help a teacher to observe learning processes and based on identified inefficient processes to also rethink/adapt instructional materials/processes.

The cognitive feedback is achieved by a combination of MDE-based simulation and automated feedback. The implications for behavioral feedforward perspectives are further discussed based on the findings of our previous research proposing adopting process analytics view on learning modeling [8–10].

2   Reviewing Cognitive Feedback Needs Through the Prism of Learning Challenges

While experienced requirements engineers and business analysts manage to mentally picture the prospective system in their mind when transforming requirements into formal conceptual models, such ability to truly understand the consequences of modeling choices can only be achieved through extensive **experience**. However, the tacit knowledge experts have developed over time is difficult to transfer to junior analysts. While teaching such knowledge and skills to junior analysts is already a challenging task considering that system analysis is by nature an **inexact field of science**, transferring the academic knowledge and skills to real world businesses is yet another concern as the classroom and real world situations are not identical. In their early career the error-prone problem-solving patterns of juniors lead to incomplete, inaccurate, ambiguous, and/or incorrect specifications [11, 12]. When detected later in the engineering process such requirements and modeling errors can be expensive and time-consuming to resolve. This significant gap between the knowledge and skills of novices and experts triggers the question of *how analysis and modeling skills can be trained to facilitate the fast progression of novice analysts into advanced levels of expertise*. Amongst the factors affecting modeling process quality and learning outcomes of novices are:

- *Lack of Comprehension Methodologies: Understandability* (a model's ability to be easily understood) has been extensively evaluated in the literature both for static and dynamic aspects of modeling pointing out to comprehension difficulties both by practitioners and juniors due to the lack of comprehension methodologies [13];
- *The Cognitive Aspects of Modeling*: Studies on comparing model quality checking approaches of novices and experts indicate the poorly adapted cognitive schemata of novice modelers to identify relevant triggers for verifying the quality of models [11];
- *The Complexity of Modeling Tools*: being too "noisy" with various concepts, which can result in misusing concepts and creation of unintended models [13, 14] thus making them less effective in supporting a teaching process [15];
- *Lack of Understanding of Domain Requirements*: Students have a hard time for achieving a thorough understanding of a set of given requirements. Absence of intensive trial and error rehearsals in the classroom [11] and the lack of possibilities to interview stakeholders in a requirements gathering process are considered the major source of limitation in novices modeling experience;
- *The Lack of Validation Procedures and Tool Support*: In addition, the lack of established validation procedures [16] makes the conceptual modeling for novices very difficult to learn.
- Additionally, several researchers correlated novices learning achievements in modeling with the *lack of technical insights* considering the absence of technical components (such as computer-assisted learning) from education as a major contributing factor to the lack of preparedness of their skills [17]. Furthermore, there are aspects that cannot be obtained through reading and lecturing alone, e.g. the *dynamic representation of a system*.

3   Simulation as a Cognitive Feedback

Cognitive feedback gives information to learners about their success or failure concerning the task at hand provided through prompts, cues, questions, etc. that helps learners reflect on the quality of the problem solving processes and solutions so that they construct more effective cognitive schemas to improve future performance. Cognitive feedback targets at improved understanding of intermediate solutions of a learner allowing improving a problem solving process and its outcomes [18]. Simulation is known to be an excellent technique allowing understanding complex structures and behaviors and has been successfully used in a variety of learning domains, such as science education [19], mining engineering [20], aerospace engineering [21], biological engineering [22], etc. Among key education benefits of simulation is the ability to provide *feedback* and *deliberate practice* [23]. The interventions of simulation in a learning process can be described as an ability to produce **externally observable outcomes** that can trigger **internal feedback** engaging **self-regulatory learning** mechanisms of learning (e.g. *self-assessing of own performance with respect to the expected performance* in terms of capability of achieving a satisfactory quality of a prospective system, *identifying needs for improvement* and *adapting* in terms of engaging in further trial/error activities for adapting a model of a prospective system that served an input for simulation). The externally observable outcomes in the form of simulation serve as a *cognitive feedback* in terms of improving understanding of a problem by reflecting on intermediate solutions of learners during a learning process and as such are also *learning process oriented*. Simulation is also known to allow *skill acquisition that accompany knowledge*. Some skills follow from conceptual knowledge whereas others involve intricate activities to develop, i.e. **experience** [24]. Thanks to realistic scenarios and equipment, simulation allows for expertise training through *deliberate, repetitive and evidence-based practice* (e.g. retraining till one can master the procedure or skill) [23] that is also coupled with cognitive feedback. Achieving cognitive process-oriented feedback through simulation requires:

- designing and building an simulation instrument,
- ensuring its support for the intended goal as a cognitive feedback,
- ensuring its support for the intended goal as a process-oriented feedback.

In the context of conceptual modeling learning achievements can be measured by the capability of producing physical models with high **semantic quality**, i.e. the level to which the statements in a model reflect the real world in a valid and complete way [25]. In order to check a model for validity, a person needs to read and **understand the model** and compare his/her understanding of the model with his/her understanding of the given domain description. On the knowledge side, this requires an appropriate level of *modeling knowledge, modeling language knowledge* (e.g. understanding the modeling concepts, graphical notation) and *domain knowledge* among others [26]. To our knowledge, no research can be found in the context of courses that use simulation of object-oriented multi-view conceptual models (i.e. combining structural and behavioral aspects), nor empirically proven learning benefits have been reported for a certain simulation tool. The reason is that the existing standards for simulation technologies also introduce a number of shortcomings. The major disadvantages include:

- simulation is too complex and time consuming to achieve by novice modelers whose technical expertise is limited.
- it is sometimes difficult to interpret the simulation results.

Among different *types of simulation* (symbolic or graphical animation, execution, prototyping), the **method of prototyping** is capable of achieving the **most concrete form of a prospective system**. Semantic prototyping method and tool was introduced by [27] with the goal to improve conceptual model comprehensibility however aiming at facilitating communication with stakeholders rather than a support for learning.

Among the variety of forms of prototypes in this research we refer to the definition of a prototype as "fully *functional* to prove a concept" [28]. This goal is achieved through the creation of an experimental full-scale working exemplar of a model that illustrates the typical qualities of the prospective system based on the design of its model. Prototyping is also thought of as a type of design language [29]. The learning context of prototyping as a design language includes testing of a function of a prototype with the purpose to identify potential issues concerned with *problem understanding with respect to its design* [28]. We will therefore use the terms "simulated model" and "prototype" interchangeably.

3.1 MDE-Based Simulation for Conceptual Modeling: CodeGen

We followed the principles of *Design Science in Information Systems research* which proposes two main guidelines 1. *building* and 2. *(re)evaluating novel artefacts* to help understanding and solving knowledge problems [30]. In this work we refer to simulation of a conceptual model as a process of generating prototype applications using a conceptual model as input. The Model-driven architecture (MDA) is the collection of current OMG standards for model-driven engineering (MDE), enabling, among others, code generation. MDA allows designing *platform independent models (PIM)* as the main representation of a system-to-be that have a sufficient level of completeness to generate other models or code from them; MDE focuses on *transformation(s)* (mappings) from platform independent to platform specific models or code, a process that may pass through a number of mappings before a software artefact can be generated. However, existing MDA/MDE solutions require extensive training due to the large set of skills required for using accepted standard MDA/MDE technologies, such as Unified Modeling Language (UML). As stated in [31]: "The technical complexity of UML has been held responsible for modeling adoption issues. Few expert modelers can rapidly evolve an application from requirements to code. Many of today's modelers are casual in their approach; MDA, however, requires increased rigor and training in UML modeling". Among the other fundamental deficiencies of UML is that it is unclear how to combine interactive, structural and behavioral aspects together in a single model [32]. The same holds true for the OMG's MOF and XMI standards which are used to store, transport and exchange models between tools, that are also associated with issues like semantic mismatches, version incompatibilities (XMI/UML/MOF), human-readability, etc., e.g. [33–36]. The new standards providing key technology for expressing application domains in a platform independent manner that are in addition executable include executable UML (xUML), foundational UML (fUML) - an executable UML standard that specifies precise semantics for an executable subset of UML, and Action language for fUML (Alf) - an executable UML standard that specifies a textual action language with fUML semantics. These however do not bring the MDE any closer to the novice modelers or simplify it such as making model validation by means of rapid prototyping easily feasible for business domain experts who lack technical expertise. Still a very detailed diagramming with fUML is required and a solid knowledge of both fUML and Alf is required to make further transformation of UML to code. Thus, the practical utility of MDE is still limited by the fact that:

- UML lacks a methodology to achieve a right design within a short time to be further processed with an MDA/MDE approach.
- MDE model-to-model and model-to-code transformations are hard to write, trace/debug, maintain and reuse.

In this research to achieve an in-house prototyping solution, i.e. designed and implemented rather than relying on third party code generation tools [8], we rely on the MERODE methodology [37], as the benefits models designed in MERODE specific JMermaid environment include:

- Starting from a high-level PIM (close to a Computational Independent Model (CIM)) allows removing or hiding details irrelevant for a conceptual modeling view.
- It relies on a *domain specific language* and proprietary MERODE modeling environment that uses a restricted part of UML adapted to conceptual modeling goals.
- It provides a framework for *combining structural and behavioral views* into a single model using two prominent UML diagrams – 1. a class diagram, 2. statecharts, and a CRUD-matrix based collaboration view called Object-Event Table (OET) that defines how statecharts interact (see Fig. 1).

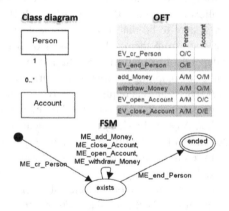

Fig. 1. Modeling views within MERODE modeling environment: class diagram, Object-Event Table (OET) and a Finite State Machine (FSM) [38].

- It allows achieving *executable PIM* that have a sufficient level of abstraction, while being sufficiently complete to enable applying transformation(s) from platform independent to platform specific models or code.

In the learning context of prototyping-based teaching, this research builds on, and tackles the issues of the experiences from the first iteration of conceptual model prototyping. The first version of the prototyping environment was achieved by means of the AndroMDA open source code generation tool combining its existing XMI-based cartridges and a MERODE-specific cartridge that provides an XMI transformation from a model designed in a MERODE environment and specifies a functionality of generated prototypes such as basic interface consisting of buttons, corresponding input windows they trigger and event handling mechanisms that ensure the functionality [39].

The tool already demonstrated certain positive effects in a learning context (with student evaluations of the usefulness of the tool from two academic years resulting on average 3.46 and 3.7 in the range of 5-point Likert scale). However, despite its merits, a number of usability issues negatively impacted the intended utility in the learning context, among them being time-consuming in terms of requiring multiple steps to achieve and launch a generated prototype, and issues with the intuitiveness of the user interfaces to support easy navigation and testing, e.g. it was not clear how the prototype links to a model, making it difficult to apply the method in a teaching/learning context. As a result, the evaluation survey revealed that the majority of students seemed to be reluctant in using the tool in their learning process resulting mostly in the "didn't use" answers while assessing the tool. In this paper an in-house prototyping method is introduced based on a *template-based transformation* [8] going straight from model to code (i.e. a model-to-text transformation) allowing to generate a prototype with a *single click* [8, 38, 40]. Such instant prototype production serves as a quick simulation technique that raises the usability as it lowers the required skill-set for its use and allows verifying the conformance of conceptual designs and the description of the domain in a fast and easy way. By enabling a fully functional output the method also serves as a rapid prototyping and simulation instrument. This allows assessing the generated prototype (simulation results) with respect to the expected outcome. In case of a semantic mismatch the desired outcome can be achieved through a trial and error correction process by means of modification, regeneration and verification loops.

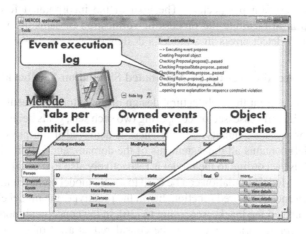

Fig. 2. The main GUI of the prototype application [38].

Such an approach yields additional benefits such as better support for process-oriented assistance allowing developing modeling competences by engaging a learner in a "trial and error learning process" [41], test the incrementally modified (growing) prototypes and letting him/her check the semantic conformance of a model with the domain description. In addition, user interfaces were adapted to support maximally intuitive user experience. A user interacts with the generated application through the graphical user interface (GUI) which offers basic functionality like triggering the creating and ending of objects, and triggering other business events. Figure 2 shows the main interface of a generated prototype.

3.2 Enhancing Simulation with Feedback to Facilitate Interpretation of Simulation Results

It is known that simulation accompanied with feedback can result in better learning outcomes [17, 18, 22, 42]. More commonly, human instructors provide feedback for simulations usually with a post-simulation debriefing [46]. However, feedback automation methods that can guide a learning process with simulation are to our knowledge absent. In this research we present a feedback automation method that embeds a feedback generation mechanism into a simulation of a model thus allowing achieving feedback-enabled simulation. We make use of *negative corrective feedback* [47, 48] based on two type of formats: (1) *textual explanations* of the causes for the errors (execution failures as a result of constraint violations) that explain the involved modeling constructs and their implications with respect to execution outcomes [49] and (2) improved transparency between a prototype and its model by means of *graphical visualization* that links the execution results to their causes in the model [49]. The inclusion of textual/visual feedback into simulation is achieved by the generation of feedback as a response to execution failures in a prototype application targeting a facilitation of interpretation of testing (simulation) results. The errors include event execution failures that result from constraint violations, which are regarded as invalid actions from the domain perspective. The goal of the incorporated feedback in the simulation loop is to facilitate the process of verification of semantic validity of the model allowing to detect errors in a model's design.

3.3 What Is needed to Set up an Automated Simulation Feedback?

In this chapter we present the architectural design of the automated feedback approach [49]. Thereto we identify assessed by comparing two such sets, goals being completeness and validity. For semantic quality, completeness is achieved if the physical represen-tation (the model) contains all the statements of the domain, and validity is achieved if what is true or false according to the model is respectively also true or false according to the domain rules. Model simulation can be used to assess model completeness by simply verifying the presence of desired functionality in the prototype. the model elements used to set up an automated feedback. According to [26], in the conceptual modeling quality framework each framework element can be considered as a set of statements. Model quality is assessed by comparing two such sets, goals being completeness and validity. For semantic quality, completeness is achieved if the physical representation (the model) contains all the statements of the domain, and validity is achieved if what is true or false according to the model is respectively also true or false according to the domain rules. Model simulation can be used to assess model completeness by simply verifying the presence of desired functionality in the prototype. Assessing the validity of the model requires verifying the truthfulness of a statement in the prototype. In other words, if something should be allowed according to domain rules, then this should be allowed according to the model as well, and if something is forbidden according to domain rules, then a corresponding constraint should be included in the model. To verify validity, a modeler needs to define test scenarios and define an oracle (desired outcome) for each scenario according to the domain rules. The results of the execution of the test scenario are compared to the oracle to determine the semantic correspondence between model and domain. While novice modelers seem at ease with using a fast prototyping approach for the verification of model completeness, we witnessed that novice modelers have difficulties in understanding why a test scenario fails and relating the cause of the failure to model constructs.

Test scenario failure finds its origins in constraint violation. For example, if a course can be attributed to at most one teacher, then assigning a second teacher to a course will result in a constraint violation and a failed test scenario. Therefore, the first step in our architectural design includes the identification of the *constraints* that are supported by a *diagram type*. Next, the typology of errors with respect to the *constraint types* are specified. We also need to identify the *diagram properties* that take part in those constraints. The *error type* can be described as a constraint violation scenario. The error type contains a reference to the violated constraint type and also encapsulates the properties that *participate* in the context of the event execution and those that *cause* the error (execution failure).

Figure 3 depicts the generic meta-model on how error types are related to the corresponding model elements. As mentioned earlier in this paper we realize our approach in the context of one specific type of models, namely, conceptual models, that combine structural and behavioral aspects of a system. The modeling approach uses a combination of a class diagram (to realize the structural aspects) and multiple interacting statecharts (to support a system's dynamics). In the class diagram, constraints are captured as cardinality constraints (mandatory one, maximum one) and referential integrity constraints (creation dependency and restricted delete). In the case of a statechart, constraints are captured as sequence constraints. For each of these constraints, a corresponding error type and explanations used for feedback can be constructed as shown in Table 1. Explanations include model properties (underlined in column "Explanation & model properties").

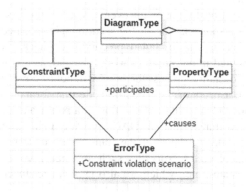

Fig. 3. Model-elements used for a feedback [49].

Table 1. Examples of model elements used to construct feedback for class diagram and statecharts [49].

Diagram	Constraint type	Error type	Explanation and model properties
Class diagram	Cardinality of minimum 1	Create-event execution failure	an *object of type A* is attempted to be *created* without choosing an *object of type B it is associated with*
	Cardinality of maximum 1	Create-event execution failure	an *object of type A* is attempted to be *created* for which an *object of type B associated with a cardinality of max 1* is chosen which already has been assigned *another instance of an object of type A*
	Referential integrity for creation dependency	Create-event execution failure	an *object* is attempted to be *created* before the *objects it refers to* were created
	Referential integrity for restricted delete	End-event execution failure	an *object* is attempted to be *ended* before its *"living" referring objects* (objects that did not reach the final state of their lifecycle) are ended
Statechart diagram	Sequence constraint	Event execution failure	an *event* is attempted to be executed for an *object* whose *state* does not enable a *transition for that event*

3.4 How the Approach Can Be Realized: Inclusion and Generation of Simulation Feedback

The feedback generation mechanism is handled by inclusion of a feedback generation package in the output of the model-to-code transformation and is illustrated by the conceptual model shown in Fig. 4. This package is responsible for 1. capturing the execution errors (failures) and mapping them with corresponding causes; 2. identifying the causing model properties as well as those being involved/affected; 3. matching the causes with relevant feedback template for a textual feedback; 4. generating feedback dialogs with the textual explanation and 5. further extending the textual explanation with its graphical visualization.

In the model-to-code transformation the event execution process is supported by the event handler which is responsible for the transaction logic specified by a model. Error messages are generated in case of failed precondition checks. The model-to-code transformation is presented in our previous work [38] and, as it is not the core subject of this paper, the transformation process therefore will not be covered in detail. We will however refer to some aspects of the model-to-code transformations that are relevant for feedback generation. This includes the notion of a parser and Data Access Objects (DAO) in the generated transformation. DAOs provide a simplified access to model properties stored in a database layer of the transformed code (e.g. key-value maps containing a collection of object properties such as a name, collections of attributes, events, dependencies, states, etc.) which are also used for feedback purposes.

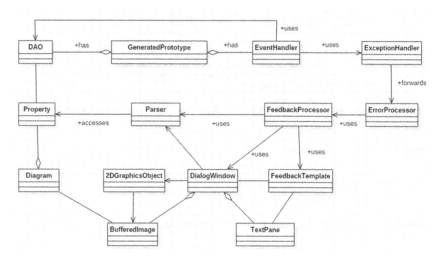

Fig. 4. Architecture of the feedback generation in the context of MDE-based simulation [49].

These properties are constructed during the transformation process using a parser and Apache Velocity Templates and are accessible in the final code. In the generated application the execution failures are implemented as exceptions. The exception handler contains the cause of the exception such as a reference to the corresponding constraint type along with the model properties involved in the constraint violation in a lightweight data-interchange format (comma separated string). The exception handler identifies the exception type and in case a model related execution failure is detected (there can be code related exceptions too) further links to the corresponding error processor responsible for model related errors. The error processor further derives the necessary properties error message data stream, converts them into appropriate formats and forwards to the feedback processor. The feedback processor uses a feedback template to provide a textual explanation on the corresponding parts of the diagram along with the properties of a diagram causing the execution failure as well as those being involved/affected. Sample textual feedback templates are presented in Figs. 5 and 6. Using the model parser the coordinates of model properties from the GUI model of a diagram are passed to a 2D graphics object. The parser is used to access any other model properties that are required to provide a hint for a possible correction scenario (e.g. if an event execution fails due to an object state, the state(s) in which the execution is allowed are used to construct a hint). The 2D graphics object is used to access the coordinate, color and font management system of the buffered image (an image with an accessible buffer of image data) of a diagram. This allows to highlight the parts of the diagram that contains the constraint that causes the error as well as to visualize the suggested hints for the correction of the error. The color scheme is consistent with the textual feedback which makes it easier to trace between the textual explanation and its graphical visualization. Sample generated textual and corresponding graphical feedback is presented in Fig. 8. The architecture of the proposed realization model also

```
feedbackText = "The FSM (statechart) of " + objectName + " puts a constraint on "
             + transitionEventName + ". The current state of " + objectName
             + " is " + objectStateName + ". In the state " + objectStateName
             + " there is no transition enabled for the business event "
             + transitionEventName + ". Look at the FSM to find which "
             + "business events are allowed in this state or find the "
             + " state(s) at which you can execute the business event "
             + transitionEventName + ".";
```

Fig. 5. Sample textual feedback template for a sequence constraint violation [49].

```
feedbackText = "You already have one instance of "
             + objectType + " and according to the " + diagramType
             + " you cannot create a second instance of "
             + objectType + " because of the cardinality constraint"
             + " of maximum 1.";
```

Fig. 6. Sample textual feedback template for a cardinality constraint violation [49].

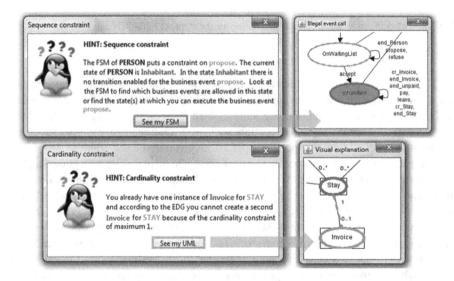

Fig. 7. Sample generated textual and graphical feedback for a UML class diagram and a finite state machine (FSM) [49].

allows the feedback generation package to be easily plugged in/out in the final output. The exception handler can serve as a (dis)connection gate (Fig. 7).

3.5   Locating Simulation Feedback in the Validation Process

In terms of positioning the proposed feedback technique with respect to the modeling and semantic validation process, the following sequence is implied (see Fig. 8): the user starts with analyzing a textual description of requirements. S/he will then transform the requirements into a conceptual model containing both the static and dynamic

Fig. 8. Positioning of the feedback in the modeling and validation process [49].

representations of a system. At any step during the modeling process the user can simulate the model by means of prototype generation. The prototype is then used to test a model in terms of its semantic conformance with the requirements. The model is revisited/refined if semantic errors are detected. The feedback is intended to facilitate the interpretation of the causes of the detected errors. Such repetitive trial/error loops will also allow to reflect on the requirements in terms of detection of ambiguous, missing or contradictory requirements.

3.6 Assessing the Effectiveness of Feedback - Enabled Simulation as Means for Process-Oriented Cognitive Feedback

An experimental study method was used to evaluate the feedback-enabled simulation with respect to learning effectiveness and usability. Six studies were conducted in the course of three academic years with participation of 201 master-level final year students from two Management Information Systems programs at KU Leuven. The effectiveness of the feedback-enabled simulation was assessed with respect to novices' comprehension of (i) structural aspects of a system represented as a class diagram [45], (ii) behavioral aspects of a system represented as multiple interacting statecharts [42], as well as understanding the interplay aspects between structural and behavioral views of a model [42] and (iii) hidden dependencies represented through inheritance hierarchies [44]. A classical pre/post-test control group experimental design was used in combination with a two-group and factorial designs [50]. During the experiments students had to validate a proposed model against given requirements by answering a set of questions (requirements reformulated as questions). The test results were scored in the range of min = 0, max = 8. The effectiveness of the proposed simulation method was measured by comparing students' test results between experimental cycles (without and with the use of simulation). A confirmatory analysis has been conducted to assess the validity of hypothesized effects. The results of the experimental studies showed a significant positive impact of the inclusion of the feedback on the semantic validation process of novices resulting in the average magnitude of effect of 2.33 out of 8 for validating the structural consistency (class diagram) [45], 4 out of 8 for validating the behavioral consistency (statecharts) and the consistency of behavioral aspects with the structural view of a system (contradicting constraints) [42], 2.33 out of 8 for validating hidden dependencies in a model represented through inheritance hierarchies [44]. This suggests that the proposed simulation method supports its intended goal as a *cognitive feedback*.

Despite a tool's benefits, **user acceptance** however can be another important factor affecting its success. In the studies we chose to control important variables dealing with user acceptance. To test and evaluate the proposed design of the feedback-enabled simulation with respect to its subjective perceptions of usability by users (perceived easiness of use, perceived utility, preference and satisfaction) yearly evaluations were performed. Ease of use and usefulness are widespread and validated acceptance beliefs from the Technology Acceptance Model [51–53], referring to the required effort to interact with a technology and its efficiency and effectiveness respectively. We used the concept of preference as another success dimension, as proposed by [54, 55]. Preference is defined as "the positive and preferred choice for the continued use of simulation tool in the classroom". User satisfaction is another key success measure that has been defined as the feelings and attitudes that stem from aggregating all the efforts and benefits that an end user receives from using an system [56, 57]. Thereto a questionnaire was used including three questions per measurable dimension, each of which measured with a six-position Likert-type scale. Furthermore, context information about personal characteristics such as gender, previous knowledge, and the level of computer self-efficacy, was collected. Exploratory correlation analyses have been performed to study the correlation of the test results (relative advantage in score when using simulation) with user acceptance and personal characteristics. The findings from our analyses showed significant positive effects of the proposed feedback-enabled simulation on learning outcomes of novices regardless of personal characteristics and attitudes.

User acceptance of the feedback-enabled simulation tool was repeatedly evaluated in the course of several years of usage. The students found the tool useful and preferred its use (mean scores above 4.5 in six-position Likert-type scale). User satisfaction, preference, perceived usefulness and perceived ease of use were evaluated resulting respectively on average of 4.77, 4.78, 4.78 and 4.68 (with Cronbach Alpha above 0.84 and factor loadings per item above 0.86). The highest score in the anonymous evaluations was attributed by students to the incorporated feedback in the prototype (5.58 on average). Reliability and validity of the acceptance measures were assessed by factor analysis using SPSS. The findings from our analysis of acceptance variables show that, in addition, the students found the tool useful and preferred its continuous use during their learning process which suggests that the proposed simulation method supports its intended goal as a *process-oriented feedback*. In addition, the use of CodeGen [8] during a learning process allows benefiting from the advantages of simulation-based learning by providing a learner with the opportunity to practice the obtained knowledge in order to obtain experience-based skills in the domain of conceptual modeling. As opposed to paper exercises which limit the scope of model understanding to a static view of a model, the dynamic testing with simulation fosters a more thorough understanding (cfr. challenge for teaching experience). In addition, the proposed method serves as a validation instrument allowing verifying the conformance of a model with the requirements (cfr. challenge for absence of validation tools). Using the insights from the testing a learner can either refine a model or reflect on the requirements by looking for instance for conflicting or missing requirements, allowing to improve the understanding of the domain to be engineered (cfr. challenge for lack in domain knowledge).

The textual and visual feedback that is generated as a response to the errors during a testing process, allows linking the error with the causes in a model by also explaining the implications of the modeling constructs involved in the causes of the error (cfr. challenge for modeling language difficulties).

The reader is referred to [43–45, 58–61] for more details on these experimental evaluations.

4 Behavioral Feedforward Perspectives Based on Learning Process Analytics

While in the previous chapters cognitive feedback opportunities were investigated, in this chapter we discuss the perspectives for behavioral feedback based on learning process observation for modeling, i.e. feedforward opportunities that can reinforce a successful learning behavior.

Observing learning processes is however a challenging task considering the fact that learning is (meta)cognitive in nature. In order to observe learning processes several questions need to be answered:

– What is to be considered a learning process?
– What type of data is needed to observe a learning process?

In the context of this research we refer to the definition of a *cognitive activity* as "an operation that affects mental content, e.g. thinking, the cognitive operation of remembering, problem solving"; and to a *learning process* as "a composite cognitive activity that is concerned with acquisition of problem-solving abilities by which knowledge is acquired". In order to observe learning processes in the context of this research we make use of the traces produced during the *problem-solving process* of novices. We use the term "cognitive learning process" to refer to the set of modeling activities a learner performed within a modeling environment during his/her problem-solving process which are used as a proxy for the cognitive learning process [8]. During the semester students were assigned to a group project in which they were assigned the task of constructing a semantically correct conceptual model that reflects the structural and dynamic view of the given domain described in an approximately 5 page specification document based on real-world requirements. Modeling behavior data have been collected through the logging functionality of the MERODE modeling environment throughout a semester of study while students were working on their group's project. In order to observe the modeling process (how the novices created their models) interactions with the modeling tool have been logged conforming the *actor-event-target-timestamp*. As modeling manifests itself in the creation of modeling elements, in our logs we capture a modeling process as a sequence of create, edit, delete, undo, redo, and copy events. These events are further abstracted into CREATE and EDIT (grouping events edit, delete, undo, redo, copy) representations. For experimental data collection purposes the CodeGen simulation environment [8, 38, 40] was integrated within the MERODE modeling environment JMermaid allowing to, besides tracking only the modeling activities, log also simulation activities and thus observing the validation (also referred to as **self-regulation**) activities within the task completion process.

Conceptual modeling event data of 36 cases (event logs of students' group works) from 2 academic years, 28.455 events in total have been subject to a three-dimension analysis using learning process analytics and **process mining techniques** in particular: 1. data has been examined at *different abstraction levels* (activities grouped for different modeling views such as structural or behavioral, fine-grained analysis zooming into each view in isolation), further expanded by diagram type information (class diagram –EDG, statecharts –FSM, interaction view), event type information (e.g. create/edit/delete/simulate),element type (object, attribute, association, event, state, transitions, etc.), 2. contrast analysis to identify differences based on *modeling performance* (best vs. worst scoring groups), 3. *time trend analysis* by making distinction between "early" and "late" sessions allowing to capture a change of behavior over time [9, 10].

The analysis resulted in identification of learning (i.e. modeling and simulation) behavior patterns indicative for worse/better learning outcomes. These first insights from our empirical studies suggest that the learning achievements, in addition to being related to cognitive aspects of learning, can be also associated with behavioral aspects [8–10] such as:

- Pattern 1 (modeling approach): best performance being associated with a more *iterative way* of modeling manifested in more frequent switches between different model views (such as structural and behavioral) as opposed to worst performance characterized by *sequential way* of working (targeting one task/view at a time).
- Pattern 2 (validation approach): best performance being characterized by *earlier engagement* n *validation (simulation)* activities with a *broader coverage of testing* targeting both structural and behavioral views of a model as opposed to worst performance characterized by limited coverage of model testing.
- Pattern 3 (validation target): best performance being characterized by the *intention to test recent changes*, and the validation effort being positioned around the *interplay effects between views* as opposed to worst performance characterized by a *general (unstructured) test and disconnected way of testing* targeting either structural or behavioral views.
- Pattern 4 (engagement styles): best performance being associated with an *earlier and systematic engagement* in modeling activities as opposed to worst performance characterized by *deadline-oriented engagement.*
- Pattern 5 (effort distribution across time): best performance being characterized by *more effort* put in the modeling process with a *tendency to decrease* over time as opposed to worst performance associated with *less effort* in earlier stages of project with a *tendency of continuous or increased effort* presumably indicating difficulties in achieving a right solution.
- Pattern 6 (effort distribution within modeling tasks): best performance being associated with a broader coverage of transforming requirements into a model in the early stages of the modeling process and continuing to adapt the model in later sessions, as opposed to worst performance associated with partial capturing of concepts and actively expanding the model in later sessions, by also supplying irrelevant concepts not required by requirements.

The findings showed that process analytics based feedback is feasible. Such a feedback can complement cognitive content related feedback (What is wrong and why?) with a suggestive feedback targeting behavioral aspects, i.e. detecting inefficient learning processes and proposing recommendations on corrective actions (How to act?), i.e. feedforward. The findings are suggested as guidelines to improve teaching practices for multi-view conceptual modeling. The learning behavior patterns can also be used for construction of machine feedback targeting a modeling process in a learning context. However, more research is needed towards 1. identification of more generic behavior patterns, 2. automation perspectives for learning behavior pattern detection that can be used to provide advanced real time individualized guidance throughout a learning process. The reader is referred to [8–10] for more details on these empirical studies.

5 Conclusion

The results of our research both for cognitive and behavioral aspects of learning suggest that validation (i.e. self-regulation using simulation) is positively associated with learning outcomes. MDE-based feedback-enabled simulation helps to improve knowledge of modeling concepts and modeling language by improving model understanding through *reflecting on intermediate results (what is wrong ?)* during a learning process (cfr. RA1). The findings of learning process analytics learning (modeling and validation) processes of novices establish the feasibility for feedback that can *reflect on the procedural aspects of learning (how to do it the right way ?)* thus complementing a cognitive feedback (cfr. RA2). While behavioral feedback based on the learning behavior patterns presented in our research would not be mature yet, however this research can serve as a platform to guide future research in the domain of learning process analytics and learning process analytics based feedback.

Two conclusions are obtained:

1. Simulation can serve a cognitive feedback throughout a learning process, if it is instant, easy to use and is easy to interpret (i.e. enhanced with a feedback that facilitates the interpretation of simulation results) (cfr. RA1).
2. Feedback perspectives based on learning process analytics are feasible. Process analytics (and process mining techniques in particular) make it possible to detect (in)efficient behavior during learning processes thus allowing to identify and address potential feedback needs earlier *during a learning process* (e.g. during a problem solving process) as opposed to learning *process outcome feedback* (provided only after a problem has been solved and its outcome is presented for assessment).

From a theoretical perspective the results of the first part of the research contribute to improving knowledge on the *cognitive aspects* of *conceptual modeling* providing empirical support for the use of simulation in learning/teaching processes for conceptual modeling with respect to supporting *model understandability* and thus also *model validity*. The results also contribute to the research on **model-driven development** with respect to its applicability to research on *simulation* and *feedback automation*. The research is also to be situated in the domain of **simulation** with respect to (1) empirical support for the use of augmented feedback in simulation, and (2) with respect to addressing the difficulties in interpretation of simulation results. Since our approach relies on process related data captured during a learning process, this study is also to be situated in the context of *learning analytics*.

While the findings of the experiments showed a significant improvement in students' model-based validation capabilities when using feedback-enabled simulation, we still observed certain issues. One issue is related to addressing the "completeness" dimension of a model's semantic quality. Since the completeness of a model can be demonstrated through testing scenarios, and the simulation only serves as instrument to execute the scenarios, transforming requirements into test scenarios is yet an additional skill that is required to benefit from the instrument. Our observations from the experiments revealed certain difficulties among students in developing testing scenarios for verifying their models with the use of simulation resulting in either (1) Omitted simulation cycle; or (2) Partial testing with the use of prototype characterized by incomplete testing scenarios such as a test scenario limited to only a confirmatory rather than exploratory analysis of the functionality, insufficient exploration of dependencies in a model, etc. [43, 58–61]. The observations of testing patterns of students thus suggest that combining the method of feedback-enabled simulation with the teaching of high level testing knowledge and skills will result in even better learning outcomes.

The main limitation with respect to our observations and analysis of behavioral aspects of learning include the missing perspectives on (1) individual learning processes since only group level information could be derived from the logs of the project file; (2) learning activities outside the learning environment (since learning is not limited to the scope of learning environments), which however would be very challenging to obtain.

The work presented in this paper can be expanded along several directions. Since the self-regulated activities (i.e. validation with the use of simulation) of novices were found to be key to distinguishing worse/better learning approaches, automated assistance can be investigated to provide tool support for (coverage) test scenario generation that will allow checking the "completeness" of a model with respect to the requirements. While findings showed that certain behavioral patterns can indeed be associated with better/worse outcomes in terms of reaching a satisfactory model quality, further examinations are needed to evolve towards more exhaustive and generic patterns for a broader learning context [62, 63]. Analysis of the testing logs from the simulation environment will provide more insights on (in)efficient testing processes which can be used to expand the simulation feedback ("What/why is not correct?") with feedforwarding possibilities during a modeling process (e.g. "When/what/how to test?"). Since learning processes are not limited to the scope of learning environments, correlating online with offline data (e.g. reasoning, perceiving, understanding, solving, reflecting, checking, …) can be another area of future research. The simulation and simulation feedback automation method proposed in this research can be extended to support a broader context of models, diagrams. Exploring perspectives of feedback personalization by means of studies at individual rather than group level can be another area of research. Advanced feedback mechanisms, can be explored using adaptive systems and learning reinforcement algorithms that also consider physiological indicators of learners, such as cognitive load, stress levels, affective states [64, 65], etc. Ultimately, the results of our research can be inspirational beyond the scope of conceptual modeling.

References

1. Shute, V.J.: Focus on formative feedback. Rev. Educ. Res. **78**(1), 153–189 (2008)
2. Nicol, D.J., Macfarlane-Dick, D.: Formative assessment and self-regulated learning: a model and seven principles of good feedback practice. Stud. High. Educ. **31**(2), 199–218 (2006)
3. Eyers, D., Jordan, J., Hendry, K.: What are student perceptions of the timeliness of feedback? (2016). http://learning.cf.ac.uk/developing-educators/pcutl/project-reports/what-are-student-perceptions-of-the-timeliness-of-feedback/. Cited Apr 2016
4. Irons, A.: Enhancing Learning Through Formative Assessment and Feedback. Routledge (2007)
5. Narciss, S.: Feedback strategies for interactive learning tasks. In: Handbook of Research on Educational Communications and Technology, pp. 125–144 (2008)
6. Butler, D.L., Winne, P.H.: Feedback and self-regulated learning: a theoretical synthesis. Rev. Educ. Res. **65**(3), 245–281 (1995)
7. Zimmerman, B.J.: Investigating self-regulation and motivation: historical background, methodological developments, and future prospects. Am. Educ. Res. J. **45**(1), 166–183 (2008)
8. Sedrakyan, G.: Process-Oriented Feedback Perspectives Based on Feedback-Enabled Simulation and Learning Process Data Analytics. KU, Leuven (2016)
9. Sedrakyan, G., De Weerdt, J., Snoeck, M.: Process-mining enabled feedback: "tell me what I did wrong" vs. "tell me how to do it right". Comput. Hum. Behav. **57**(C), 352–376 (2016)
10. Sedrakyan, G., Snoeck, M., De Weerdt, J.: Process mining analysis of conceptual modeling behavior of novices - empirical study using JMermaid modeling and experimental logging environment. Comput. Hum. Behav. **41**(C), 486–503 (2014)
11. Schenk, K.D., Vitalari, N.P., Davis, K.S.: Differences between novice and expert systems analysts: what do we know and what do we do? J. Manage. Inf. Syst. **15**(1), 9–50 (1998)
12. Wang, W., Brooks, R.J.: Empirical investigations of conceptual modeling and the modeling process. In: Simulation Conference, pp. 762–770, Winter 2007
13. Erickson, J., Keng, S.: Can UML be simplified? practitioner use of uml in separate domains. In: Proceedings of the 12th Workshop on Exploring Modeling Methods for Systems Analysis and Design (EMMSAD 2007), held in Conjunctiun with the 19th Conference on Advanced Information Systems (CAiSE 2007), Trondheim, Norway (2007)
14. Wilmont, I., Hengeveld, S., Barendsen, E., Hoppenbrouwers, S.: Cognitive mechanisms of conceptual modelling. In: Ng, W., Storey, Veda C., Trujillo, Juan C. (eds.) ER 2013. LNCS, vol. 8217, pp. 74–87. Springer, Heidelberg (2013). doi:10.1007/978-3-642-41924-9_7
15. Siau, K., Loo, P.-P.: Identifying Difficulties in Learning Uml. Inf. Syst. Manage. **23**(3), 43–51 (2006)
16. Shanks, G., Tansley, E., Weber, R.: Using ontology to validate conceptual models. Commun. ACM **46**(10), 85–89 (2003)
17. Barjis, J., et al.: Innovative Teaching Using Simulation and Virtual Environments. Interdisc. J. Inf. Knowl. Manage. **7**, 237–255 (2012)
18. Van Merriënboer, J.J., Kirschner, P.A.: Ten Steps to Complex Learning: A Systematic Approach to Four-Component Instructional Design. Routledge (2012)
19. Rutten, N., van Joolingen, W.R., van der Veen, J.T.: The learning effects of computer simulations in science education. Comput. Educ. **58**(1), 136–153 (2012)
20. Akkoyun, O., Careddu, N.: Mine simulation for educational purposes: a case study. Comput. Appl. Eng. Educ. (2014)

21. Okutsu, M., DeLaurentis, D., Brophy, S., Lambert, J.: Teaching an aerospace engineering design course via virtual worlds: a comparative assessment of learning outcomes. Comput. Educ. **60**(1), 288–298 (2013)

22. Datta, A.K., Rakesh, V., Way, D.G.: Simulation as an integrator in an undergraduate biological engineering curriculum. Comput. Appl. Eng. Educ. **21**(4), 717–727 (2013)

23. Lateef, F.: Simulation-based learning: just like the real thing. J. Emergencies, Trauma Shock **3**(4), 348 (2010)

24. Gaba, D.M.: The future vision of simulation in healthcare. Simul. Healthc. **2**(2), 126–135 (2007)

25. Lindland, O.I., Sindre, G., Solvberg, A.: Understanding quality in conceptual modeling. IEEE Softw. **11**(2), 42–49 (1994)

26. Nelson, H.J., et al.: A conceptual modeling quality framework. Softw. Qual. J. **20**(1), 201–228 (2012)

27. Lindland, O.I., Krogstie, J.: Validating conceptual models by transformational prototyping. In: Rolland, C., Bodart, F., Cauvet, C. (eds.) CAiSE 1993. LNCS, vol. 685, pp. 165–183. Springer, Heidelberg (1993). doi:10.1007/3-540-56777-1_9

28. Hess, T.A.: Investigation of Prototype Roles in Conceptual Design Using Case Study and Protocol Study Methods. Clemson University (2012)

29. Yang, M.C.: A study of prototypes, design activity, and design outcome. Des. Stud. **26**(6), 649–669 (2005)

30. Hevner, A.R., et al.: Design science in information systems research. MIS Q. **28**(1), 75–105 (2004)

31. Borland: Keeping your business relevant with Model Driven Architecture (MDA) (2004). http://www.omg.org/mda/presentations.htm

32. Gustas, R.: Conceptual modeling and integration of static and dynamic aspects of service architectures. In: Sicilia, M.-A., Kop, C., Sartori, F. (eds.) ONTOSE 2010. LNBIP, vol. 62, pp. 17–32. Springer, Heidelberg (2010). doi:10.1007/978-3-642-16496-5_2

33. Alanen, M., Porres, I.: Model interchange using OMG standards. In: 31st EUROMICRO Conference on Software Engineering and Advanced Applications. IEEE (2005)

34. Desfray, P.: UML Profiles versus Metamodel extensions: an ongoing debate. In OMG's UML Workshops: UML in the .com Enterprise: Modeling CORBA, Components, XML/XMI and Metadata Workshop (2000)

35. Huang, S., Gohel, V., Hsu, S.: Towards interoperability of UML tools for exchanging high-fidelity diagrams. In: Proceedings of the 25th Annual ACM International Conference on Design of Communication. ACM (2007)

36. Lundell, B., Lings, B., Persson, A., Mattsson, A.: UML model interchange in heterogeneous tool environments: an analysis of adoptions of XMI 2. In: Nierstrasz, O., Whittle, J., Harel, D., Reggio, G. (eds.) MODELS 2006. LNCS, vol. 4199, pp. 619–630. Springer, Heidelberg (2006). doi:10.1007/11880240_43

37. Snoeck, M.: Enterprise Information Systems Engineering: The MERODE Approach 2014. Springer, Cham (2014)

38. Sedrakyan, G., Snoeck, M.: A PIM-to-Code requirements engineering framework. In: Proceedings of Modelsward 2013–1st International Conference on Model-driven Engineering and Software Development-Proceedings (2013)

39. Snoeck, M., et al.: Computer aided modelling exercises. Inf. Educ. **6**(1), 231–248 (2007)

40. Sedrakyan, G., Snoeck, M.: Lightweight semantic prototyper for conceptual modeling. In: Indulska, M., Purao, S. (eds.) ER 2014. LNCS, vol. 8823, pp. 298–302. Springer, Cham (2014). doi:10.1007/978-3-319-12256-4_32

41. Prather, D.C.: Trial-and-error versus errorless learning: Training, transfer, and stress. Am. J. Psychol., 377–386 (1971)

42. Sedrakyan, G., Poelmans, S., Snoeck, M.: Assessing the influence of feedback-inclusive rapid prototyping on understanding the semantics of parallel UML statecharts by novice modellers. Inf. Softw. Technol. **82**, 159–172 (2016)
43. Sedrakyan, G., Snoeck, M.: Do we need to teach testing skills in courses on requirements engineering and modelling? In: CEUR Workshop Proceedings (2014)
44. Sedrakyan, G., Snoeck, M.: Effects of simulation on novices' understanding of the concept of inheritance in conceptual modeling. In: Jeusfeld, Manfred A., Karlapalem, K. (eds.) ER 2015. LNCS, vol. 9382, pp. 327–336. Springer, Cham (2015). doi:10.1007/978-3-319-25747-1_32
45. Sedrakyan, G., Snoeck, M., Poelmans, S.: Assessing the effectiveness of feedback enabled simulation in teaching conceptual modeling. Comput. Educ. **78**, 367–382 (2014)
46. Stefanidis, D.: Optimal acquisition and assessment of proficiency on simulators in surgery. Surg. Clin. North Am. **90**(3), 475–489 (2010)
47. Ellis, R.: Corrective Feedback and Teacher Development. L2 J. **1**(1) (2009)
48. Ellis, R.: A typology of written corrective feedback types. ELT J. **63**(2), 97–107 (2009)
49. Sedrakyan, G., Snoeck, M.: Enriching model execution with feedback to support testing of semantic conformance between models and requirements: Design and evaluation of feedback automation architecture. In: Modelsward 2016 - 4th International Conference on Model-driven Engineering and Software Development, Rome, Italy (2016)
50. Trochim, W.M.: The Research Methods Knowledge Base, http://trochim.human.cornell.edu/kb/index.htm. Version 2 Aug 2000
51. Davis, F.D.: Perceived usefulness, perceived ease of use, and user acceptance of information technology. MIS Q. **13**(3), 319–340 (1989)
52. Davis, F.D., Bagozzi, R.P., Warshaw, P.R.: User acceptance of computer technology: a comparison of two theoretical models. Manage. Sci. **35**(8), 982–1003 (1989)
53. Venkatesh, V., et al.: User acceptance of information technology: toward a unified view. MIS Q. **27**(3) (2003)
54. Hsu, C.-L., Lu, H.-P.: Consumer behavior in online game communities: a motivational factor perspective. Comput. Hum. Behav. **23**(3), 1642–1659 (2007)
55. Bourgonjon, J., et al.: Students' perceptions about the use of video games in the classroom. Comput. Educ. **54**(4), 1145–1156 (2010)
56. Ives, B., Olson, M.H., Baroudi, J.J.: The measurement of user information satisfaction. Commun. ACM **26**(10), 785–793 (1983)
57. Wixom, B.H., Todd, P.A.: A theoretical integration of user satisfaction and technology acceptance. Inf. Syst. Res. **16**(1), 85–102 (2005)
58. Sedrakyan, G., Snoeck, M.: Technology-enhanced support for learning conceptual modeling. In: Bider, I., Halpin, T., Krogstie, J., Nurcan, S., Proper, E., Schmidt, R., Soffer, P., Wrycza, S. (eds.) BPMDS/EMMSAD -2012. LNBIP, vol. 113, pp. 435–449. Springer, Heidelberg (2012). doi:10.1007/978-3-642-31072-0_30
59. Snoeck, M., Sedrakyan, G.: Tutorial: boosting requirements analysis and validation skills through feedback-enabled semantic prototyping (2015)
60. Snoeck, M., Sedrakyan, G.. Tutorial: novel way of training conceptual modeling skills by means of feedback-enabled simulation (2015)
61. Sedrakyan, G., Snoeck, M.: Feedback-enabled MDA-prototyping effects on modeling knowledge, In: Enterprise, Business-Process and Information Systems Modeling, pp. 411–425. Springer (2013)
62. Sedrakyan, G., Järvelä, S., Kirschner, P.,: Conceptual framework for feedback automation and personalization for designing learning analytics dashboards. In: Conference EARLI SIG 27, Online Measures of Learning Processes (2016)

63. Sedrakyan, G., Malmberg, J., Noroozi, O., Verbert, K., Järvelä, S., and Kirschner, P.: Designing a learning analytics dashboard for feedback to support learning regulation (2017) (submitted)
64. Sedrakyan, G., Leony, D., Munoz-Merino, P. J., Delgado Kloos, K. Verbert, K.: Evaluating student-facing learning dashboards of affective states. In: 12th European Conference on Technology Enhanced Learning (ECTEL'17) - Data Driven Approaches in Digital Education, Tallinn, Estonia (2017)
65. Leony, D., Sedrakyan, G., Munoz-Merino, P. J., Delgado Kloos, K., Verbert, K.: Evaluating usability of affective state visualizations using AffectVis, an affect-aware dashboard for students. J. Res. Innovative Teach. Learn. (2017)

Automatically Testing of Multimodal Interactive Applications

Le Thanh Long[1(✉)], Nguyen Thanh Binh[2], and Ioannis Parissis[3]

[1] Department of Computing, Duy Tan University,
182 Nguyen Van Linh, Da Nang, Viet Nam
lthanhlong@gmail.com
[2] IT Faculty, The University of Danang - University of Science and Technology,
54 Nguyen Luong Bang, Da Nang, Viet Nam
ntbinh@dut.udn.vn
[3] Univ. Grenoble Alpes, LCIS, 26902 Valence, France
ioannis.parissis@grenoble-inp.fr

Abstract. Testing interactive multimodal applications is particularly important and requires a lot of effort. Automating this activity can result to significant development cost reduction and quality improvement. In this paper, we propose an approach for automating the test generation of such multimodal applications. This approach is based on the definition of a test modeling language, TTT. The objective of the TTT language is to provide a means for expressing abstract test scenarios for interactive multimodal applications, including non-deterministic choices and action occurrence probabilities that can be used to automate the test generation. Then, we built the TTTEST tool that supports to generate tests for multimodal events and to check the validity of CARE properties of this kind of applications. The approach is illustrated on a case study.

Keywords: Interactive multimodal applications · Test modeling language · CARE properties

1 Introduction

Interactive Multimodal Applications (IMA) support communication with the user through different modalities, such as voice or gesture. They have the potential to greatly improve human-computer interaction, because they can be more intuitive, natural, efficient, and robust. Multimodality brings an intuitive, natural affinity between the machine and the user, such as in virtual reality mobile application. Efficiency is obtained when the user can use equivalent modalities for the same tasks while robustness can result from the integration of redundant or complementary inputs.

The CARE properties (Complementarity, Assignment, Redundancy, and Equivalence) can be used as a measure to assess the usability of the multimodal interaction [1]. Equivalence and Assignment represent the availability and, respectively, the absence of choice between multiple modalities for performing a task while Complementarity and Redundancy express relationships between modalities. The flexibility and robustness of

S. Hammoudi et al. (Eds): MODELSWARD 2016, CCIS 692, pp. 93–113, 2017.
DOI: 10.1007/978-3-319-66302-9_5

multimodal applications result in an increasing complexity of the design, development and testing. Therefore, ensuring their correctness requires thorough validation.

Approaches based on formal specifications automating the development and the validation activities have been proposed to deal with this complexity. They adapt existing formalisms to the particular context of interactive applications. Examples of such approaches are the Formal System Modeling analysis [2], the Lotos Interactor Model (LIM) [3], the Interactive Cooperative Objects (ICO) [10] or formal methods such as B [12]. Model-based testing methods focusing on the specification of the user behavior have also been studied. For instance, the method presented in [11] relies on the specification of a finite state machine.

In [13], Maurice H. TerBeek *et al.* propose stochastic modeling and model checking to predict measures of the disruptive effects of interruptions on user behavior. The approach also provides a way to compare the resilience of different interaction techniques to the presence of external interruptions that users need to handle. In [15], P. Palanque *et al.* presents an approach for investigating in a predictive way potential disruptive effects of interruptions on task performance in a multitasking environment.

In [16], N. Kamel *et al.* propose a formal model allowing representing the input multimodal user interaction task and the CARE usability properties. Once the multimodal interaction task model is designed, the corresponding property is checked using the SMV (Symbolic Model Verifier) model-checker. They also propose an approach for checking adaptability properties of multimodal User Interfaces (UIs) for systems used in dynamic environments like mobile phones and PDAs. The approach is based on a formal description of both the multimodal interaction and the property. The SMV model-checking formal technique is used for the verification process of the property. In [17], L. Mohand-Oussaïd *et al.* present a generic approach to design output multimodal interfaces. This approach is based on a formal model, composed of two other models: semantic fission model for information decomposition process and allocation model for modalities and media allocation to composite information. An Event-B formalization has been proposed for the fission model and for allocation model. This Event-B formalization extends the generic model and supports the verification of some relevant properties such as safety or liveness.

The synchronous approach has been proposed to model and verify by model-checking some properties of interactive applications [7], but its applicability is limited to small pieces of software.

In [6], Laya Madani *et al.* present a technique of test case generation for testing CARE properties by means of a synchronous approach. According to the proposed approach, CARE properties are translated into an enhanced version of the Lustre synchronous language. An improved method presented in [8] uses Task trees and a fusion model to perform test data generation for interactive multimodal applications.

As an additional improvement to this previous research work, we have recently proposed an automatic test generation approach based on a test modeling language, TTT (Task Tree based Test). The main new feature of the TTT language is that it supports conditional probability specifications, used to express advanced operational profiles. Such conditional specifications may depend on the history of the user actions. A test generation engine makes it possible to produce test data compliant with such a description. For this, user actions are stored during the test execution.

We have extended the above work in order to take into account multimodality [5]. The TTT language is extended to specify multimodal events of IMA and CARE properties as well as to check the validity of CARE properties [5]. In this paper, we present how to automate the approach in order to test interactive multimodal applications, using the TTT language.

The paper is organized as follows: In Sect. 2, we provide the necessary background. Section 3 presents an interactive multimodal application, Memo, used as a running example. Section 4 presents the TTT language. Section 5 presents the extension of the TTT language for generating tests and checking the validity of CARE properties. Section 6 presents the test execution environment including the translation from TTT into C. A case study is presented in Sect. 7.

2   Background

2.1   Task Trees

Task trees are often used in the design of interactive software applicationsesign of interactive software applications [14] to hierarchically build task models. A well-known notation for such task models is ConcurTaskTree (CTT). CTT includes four kinds of tasks: User tasks (no interaction with the application, just an internal cognitive activity such as thinking about how to solve a problem), application tasks (application performance, such as generating the results of a query, no interaction with the user), interaction tasks (involving user actions with immediate feedback from the application, such as editing a document) and abstract tasks (tasks composed of other subtasks). A CTT abstract task is composed of subtasks connected by means of temporal operators, for example, there is an enabling operator denoted by >> which specifies that one task enables a second one when it terminates.

A CTT model is mainly intended to help designers to define interactive applications. However, it has been shown that the same notation can be also used to define test models describing the interaction between the user and the application and providing valuable information about the possible user behavior.

2.2   Finite State Machines

Finite State Machines (FSMs) are widely used to model the behavior of interactive applications. This model includes the states, the actions and the transitions presented by a state diagram [6]. When an interactive application is specified by a finite state machine, the states represent an abstraction of the operating status of interactive applications. The operations can be repeated, so the states can also be repeated. Initial state is a state that interactive applications begin to be used. Final state is the state where the interactive application ends. Inputs are the user's tasks and outputs are application tasks.

2.3   Multimodal Interaction: Care Properties

An interactive multimodal application uses at least two modalities (keyboard, speech, mouse...) for a given direction (input or output). Within a multimodal application, modalities can be used independently, but the availability of several modalities naturally raises the issue of their combined use (fusion of modalities). When talking about test data generation, we are mainly concerned with inputs, so in this paper we focus on multimodal input interaction.

The combined use of modalities is constrained by temporal constraints. It can be carried out sequentially or concurrently [1] within a Temporal Window (TW), that defines a time interval. The modalities of a set M are used concurrently if they are used at the same instant. The modalities of a set M are used sequentially within the TW, if there is at most one active modality at every instant and if all the modalities in this set are used within the TW. The concurrency and the sequencing express a constraint on the interaction space. The absence of a temporal constraint means that the duration of the TW is infinite. The CARE properties form an interesting set of relations that are relevant when characterizing multimodal applications. The Assignment implies that a single modality is assigned to a task. The Equivalence of modalities implies that the user can perform a task using a modality chosen amongst a set of modalities. The Complementarity denotes several modalities that convey complementary chunks of information. The complementary modalities must be used simultaneously or sequentially within the same TW. The Redundancy indicates that the same piece of information is conveyed by several modalities. Redundant modalities must also be used simultaneously or sequentially within the same TW.

2.4   Operational Profiles

Operational profiles [9] provide information about the effective usage of an application. In particular, they can be used to guide the test process. For the particular case of interactive applications, operational profiles can be easily defined by assigning occurrence probabilities to some of the described behaviors. In [6], the CTT notation was extended with occurrence probabilities to make possible to specify operational profiles.

2.5   Generating Test Data for IMA

Task trees are used in the design of interactive applications. To generate automatically the test data from task trees, the task tree is translated into a probabilistic finite state machine (PFSM).

It is assumed that the PFSM is simulated while the interactive application under test is executed and that inputs and outputs are exchanged between them on-the-fly. During the simulation, assuming the PFSM to be in a given state, an input is chosen according to the probabilities of the outgoing transitions of this state. The chosen input is then sent to the interactive application, the resulting application outputs are read and the next state computed, and so on.

3   The Interactive Multimodal Application Memo

The interactive application "Memo" [6] makes it possible to annotate physical locations with digital stickers ("post it"-like notes). Once a digital sticker has been set to a physical location, it can be read/carried/removed by other users. A Memo user is equipped with a GPS and a magnetometer enabling the application to compute his/her location and orientation. S/he is also wearing a head mounted semi-transparent display (HMD) enabling the fusion of computer data (the digital notes) with the real environment. Memo provides three main tasks: (1) orientation and localization of the mobile user, so that the application is able to display the visible notes according to the current position and orientation of the mobile user (2) manipulation of a note (get, set and remove a note) and (3) exiting the application. So, the mobile user can get a note and carry it while moving. S/he can set a carried note to a specific place or delete a visible or carried note.

Figure 1 shows an extended CTT for the Memo application (interaction tasks are represented by ☺🖥), that is, operators are assigned probability values. To generate test data, the task tree is translated into a PFSM (transitions are assigned probability values consistent with the extended CTT). The PFSM is simulated while the interactive application under test is executed and that inputs and outputs are exchanged between them on-the-fly. It is thus possible to describe abstract interaction scenarios as task trees, and observe the behavior of the interactive application under test. Figure 2 shows a PFSM example for the Memo application.

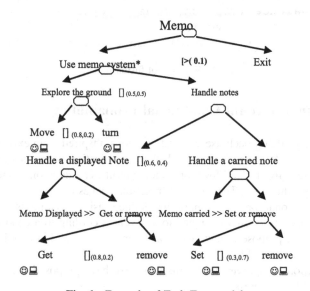

Fig. 1. Example of Task Tree model.

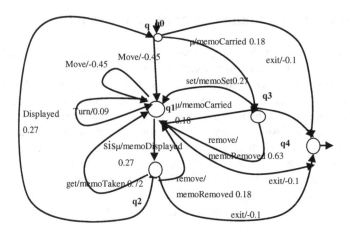

Fig. 2. FSM example for the Memo application.

Figure 3 shows a fusion model for the Memo application.

```
Tasks (get, set, remove, move, turn, exit);
Modalities (Speech(get, set, remove),
Mouse(get, set, remove),
Keyboard(get, set, remove, move, turn, exit));
Equivalence ((Speech, Mouse, Keyboard),
(get, set, remove));
Assignment ((Keyboard), (move, turn, exit));
```

Fig. 3. Example of fusion model.

4 Taking into Account Conditional Probabilities

The above presented approach uses several notations, inspired from existing modeling languages, to build test models: a model of the application behavior (a task tree), a model of the interactive tasks (FSM), operational profiles (annotations on the task tree), and modality specifications. The variety of notations makes the modeling process hard. Moreover, operational profiles cannot be defined using conditions (however, an occurrence probability is often assigned to an event according to a condition).

In Table 1, we propose a new syntax and semantics to assign conditional probabilities to CTT operators [4].

As an additional improvement to this work, we have proposed the test modeling language TTT [4] to express:

- Scenarios for interactive applications.
- Conditional probability specifications for task trees.
- The "traces" of the user actions and read-only functions on these traces.
- Expected properties of the application.

Table 1. CTT operators with conditional probabilities.

CTT operators	Notations	CTT operators with conditional probabilities
Choice	$T_1[]T_2$	$T_1[]_{(PA1,PB1|cond1),(PA2, PB2|cond2),..., (PAn, PBn|condn),(PA0,PB0)} T_2$
Independent concurrency	$T_1|||T_2$	$T_1|||_{(PA1,PB1|cond1),(PA2, PB2|cond2),..., (PAn, PBn|condn),(PA0,PB0)} T_2$
Concurrency with information exchange	$T_1|[]|T_2$	$T_2|[]|_{(PA1,PB1|cond1),(PA2, PB2|cond2),..., (PAn, PBn|condn),(PA0,PB0)} T_2$
Order independence	$T_1|=|T_2$	$T_2|=|_{(PA1,PB1|cond1),(PA2, PB2|cond2),..., (PAn, PBn|condn),(PA0,PB0)} T_2$
Deactivation	$T_1[>T_2$	$T_1[>_{(PA1|cond1),(PA2|cond2),..., (PAn|condn),(PA0)} T_2$
Suspend-resume	$T_1|>T_2$	$T_1|>_{(PA1|cond1),(PA2|cond2),..., (PAn|condn),(PA0)} T_2$
Optional tasks	$[T]$	$[T]_{(PA1|cond1),(PA2|cond2),..., (PAn|condn),(PA0)}$

The conditional probability specifications for task trees must be defined in the test model. This means that the TTT language is designed to allow the definition of variables, for example, Cond = $(X > 5)$, where X is an application input or output variable. Moreover, more complex conditions need to be expressed, for example, *Cond = F (parameter) > 5* where F is a function that can return a float value.

4.1 The TTT Language

A basic structure of a TTT model consists of a TESTCTT block and one or more FUNCTIONs. TESTCTT is defined by a set of clauses and the general form of a TESTCTT.

```
<tttmodel> ::= <testctt><function>+
<testctt> ::= <testctt_name><testctt_set>
<testctt_var><testctt_init><begin_end>
<testctt_name> ::= TESTCTT <name>
<testctt_set> ::= set <basic_type>+ ;
<testctt_var> ::= var<local_variable>+ ;
<testctt_init> ::= init<initial_state>+ ;
<begin_end> ::= begin <statement>+ end;
<function> ::= <function_name><function_var><begin_end>
<function_name> ::= FUNCTION <name> (<input>+) returns
(<output>);
<function_var> ::= var<local_variable>+;
<begin_end> ::= begin <statement>+ end;
<name> ::= <letter> | <name><letter> | <name><digit>
<letter> ::= 'A' | ... | 'Z'|'a'| ... |'z'
<digit> ::= '0' | ... | '9'
<sut_output> ::= <name>
```

```
<sut_input> ::= <name>
<basic_type> ::= <boolean> | <interger> | <enumerated>
<local_variable> ::= <variable> : <basic_type>;
<variable> ::= <name> | <variable> , <name>
<initial_state> ::= <expression>
<basic_type> ::= char| short| int| long| float| bool
```

We define the syntax for describing the CTT operators, which take into account conditional probabilities. The `ctt_operators` are used to create tasks from conditional operational profiles where the selection of the program inputs is performed with respect to probabilities specified by the testers.

```
<ctt_operator> ::= <choice> | <concurrency> |
<deact> | <sr> | <option> | <enabling> | <iteration> |
<fiteration>
```

We save all the past actions of the users and build functions on them. Functions are intended to be part of the conditions. We use an SQL-like language to update and search the data. We inherit and reduce the following SQL statements:

```
<sql_statement> ::= <create_table> | <alter_table> |
<drop_table> | <insert> | <delete> | <update>| <select>
```

4.2   Transformation Rules from CTT to Test Model by Using the TTT Language

Interactive applications are often specified by using CTT. Thus, we propose the following transformation rules in order to map tasks from CTT into statements in TTT language.

Rule 1. Interaction tasks in CTT are transformed into outputs of TESTCTT.

Rule 2. Application tasks in CTT are transformed into inputs of TESTCTT.

Rule 3. States in CTT are mapped into state variables of the TESTCTT. They are declared in the VAR clause of TESTCTT.

Rule 4. Operators with conditional probabilities in CTT are represented as predefined functions in TESTCTT.

Rule 5. Invariant properties of the application inputs are modeled with the INVAR operator.

We summarize these transformation rules in Table 2.

Table 2. Transformation rules.

Rule	CTT	Test model
1	Interaction tasks	Outputs
2	Application tasks	Inputs
3	States	State variables
4	Operators with conditional probabilities	Predefined functions
5	Invariant properties	INVAR operator

5 Taking into Account Multimodality

While testing IMA, the number of input events may increase dramatically. Indeed, each input can be produced in several modalities so the number of possible input event combinations can be much bigger than in the case of single modalities. Moreover, the fusion mechanism of IMA depends on temporal windows (TW) within which the user event occurs. For example, when two modalities are used in a redundant way, the resulting events must be combined only when they occur in the same TW.

The above observations suggest that there are two different issues when testing IMA: (1) generating tests for multimodal events, (2) checking the validity of the CARE properties. While the first issue is strictly related to test generation, the second one should be part of a test oracle. In [5], we propose to extend the TTT language to deal with both issues, as described in the following subsection.

5.1 Generating Tests for Multimodal Events

To simulate user behaviors for IMA, we use a test data generation technique based on conditional operational profiles. We add the operator modalities to the TTT language to generate tests for multimodal events. The syntax of modalities operator is the following:

```
<modalities>::=modalities (<expression-list>)
```

The tester can use $modalities(E_{M1}, E_{M2}, ..., E_{Mn}, p_1, p_2, ..., p_n, cond_1, p_{11}, p_{12}, ..., p_{13}, cond_2, p_{21}, p_{22}, ..., p_{23})$, where $i \in [1, n]$ E_{Mi} are events, p_i are probabilities; $cond_i$ are conditions; and $p_{i,j}$ ($i \in [1, n]$, $j \in [1, n]$) are conditional probabilities. The semantics of this operator are expressed as follows:

```
Input:p1, p2,…, pn, cond1, p11,p12,…,p13, cond2, p21,p22,…,p23
Output: E_M1, E_M2,…, E_Mn
Method:
{ n is a random real number in [0,1]
n= rand(1)
if (Cond1== TRUE) {
if (n<= P_11) E_M1= 1 else E_M1 = 0;
        if (n<= P_12) E_M2= 1 else E_M2 = 0;
  …
if (n<= P_1n) E_Mn= 1 else E_Mn= 0;
}
    elseif (Cond2== TRUE) {
        if (n<= P_21) E_M1= 1 else E_M1 = 0;
        if (n<= P_22) E_M2= 1 else E_M2 = 0;
  …
if (n<= P_2n) E_Mn= 1 else E_Mn= 0;
 }
    else {
        if (n<= P_1) E_M1= 1 else E_M1 = 0;
        if (n<= P_2) E_M2= 1 else E_M2 = 0;
  …
if (n<= P_n) E_Mn= 1 else E_Mn= 0;
 }
}
```

Consider the following example:
```
Modalities(speech(Remove),mouse(Remove),keyboard(Remove),
0.5,0.5,0.5,note_nb() =0,0,0,0,note_nb()>=5,0.5,0.9,0.7);
```
The events *Speech(remove), Mouse(remove)* and *Keyboard(remove)* are generated along probabilities 0.5, 0.5, 0.5 respectively. If there is no note, the user cannot remove any note, so probabilities are 0, 0, 0. But if there are more than 5 notes, the user will use other probabilities for these events. The events generated are presented in Table 3.

Table 3. Events are generated by Modalities operator.

Time	sR	mR	kR	Memo
1	0	0	0	…
2	0	0	0	Se
3	0	1	1	Tak

In Table 3, we use the abbreviation *sR*, *mR* and *kR* respectively for *speech (Remove)*, *mouse(Remove)* and *keyboard(Remove)*. At time 1, there is no note in the Memo, the user do not use any event. But at time 3 when a note is visible (Set (Se) occurred in the previous step) the user takes it (Tak) by *mouse(Remove)* and *keyboard(Remove)*.

5.2 Checking the Validity of CARE Properties

Equivalence. Let M_1, M_2 be two modalities. Let E_{M1}, E_{M2} be two expressions along M_1, M_2 respectively. Two modalities M_1, M_2 are equivalent with respect to task T, if every task $t \in T$ can be activated by E_{M1} or E_{M2}. Equivalence admits a single input event to be propagated. We add the operator *TestEquivalence(E_{M1}, E_{M2}, T, tw)* into TTT language to check the validity of the *Equivalence* property.

The syntax of *TestEquivalence* operator is the following:

<TestEquivalence> :: = TestEquivalence(<expr>,<expr>,<expr>,<expr>)

The testers can use *TestEquivalence(E_{M1}, E_{M2}, T, tw)* and the meaning of this operator is expressed as follows:

```
Input: E_M1, E_M2, T_W, T.
Output: The Equivalence of two events E_M1, E_M2.
Method:
1.begin
2. T1 <- select distinct Tout from U_ACTIONS
      where EM1= E_M1 and time between(now()-tw)and now();
3. T2 <- select distinct Tout from U_ACTIONS
      where EM2 = E_M2 and time between(now()-tw)and now();
4. if ((T == T1) and (T ==T2))
5.   IsEquivalence= True
6.   else
7. begin
8.   output("E_M1 and E_M2 are not equivalent");
9.   stop program;
10.end
11.end
```

T_1 and T_2 are two tasks corresponding to two events E_1 and E_2 in U_ACTIONS table (lines 2, 3). If task T_1 is different from task T_2, events E_1 and E_2 are not equivalent (line 8). The program under test will be stopped (line 9).

Table 4 shows an extract example of the execution trace, the result of *TestEquivalence(speech, mouse, get, 7)*.

It can be observed that when the user does *speech(get)*, *Tout* is equal to *"get"* in time 1. When the user uses the mouse to choose "get" *(mouse(get))*, *Tout* is equal to *"get"* in time 3. So event *speech(get)* is equivalent to event *mouse(get)*.

Table 4. The result of Test Equivalence.

Time	Speech(get)	Mouse(get)	Tout	TestEquivalence
1	1		get	
2				Speech(get)=Mouse(get)
3		1	get	

Redundancy-Equivalence. If there are several input events, redundancy requires the fusion process to choose one event among those of all the available modalities. Equivalence admits a single input event to be propagated. The Redundancy-Equivalence input events which are temporally close are merged and the associated output task is enabled as soon as the required inputs have been identified. The occurrence of one event of every modality in the current TW is enough to enable the output task. It is possible that several events of the same modality occur in this window. In that case, the task is computed according to the last event of each modality.

We add operator *TestRedundant_EquivalenceEarly* into TTT to test the Redundancy-Equivalence of two events E_{M1} and E_{M2} in early fusion strategies. The syntax of *TestRedundant_EquivalenceEarly* operator is the following:

```
<testRE>::= TestRedundant_EquivalenceEarly
(<expr>,<expr>,<expr>,<expr>)
```

The testers can use *TestRedundant_EquivalenceEarly(E_{M1}, E_{M2}, TaskTM1M2, tw)* and the semantics of this operator are as follows:

```
Input: E_M1, E_M2, TaskTM1M2, tw
Output: The Redundancy-Equivalence of two events E_M1,
E_M2.
Method:
1.begin
2.T_out<- select distinct Tout from U_ACTIONS
      where((EM1 = E_M1)or (EM2 =E_M2))and
      (time between(now() - tw)and now())
3.T_out_nb<- select count(Tout) from U_ACTIONS
      where((EM1 = E_M1)or(EM2 = E_M2))and
      (time between(now() - tw)and now())
4.if((Tout_nb==1)and(T_out==taskTM1M2))then
5.    output ("E_M1 and E_M2 are redundant -equivalent");
6.else
7.begin
8.    output ("E_M1, E_M2 are not redundant-equivalent");
9.    stop program;
10.end
11.end
```

T_out is the task that is generated in TW. *Tout_nb* is the number of tasks generated from the event E_{M1} or E_{M2} (line 3). The Redundancy-Equivalence property of two events E_{M1} and E_{M2} is tested by condition (line 4): *((Tout_nb == 1) and (T_out = taskTM1M2))*. If there is only one task generated in TW and *T_out* is the *taskTM1M2*, *EM1* and *EM2* are Redundant-Equivalent. Table 5 shows an extract of the execution trace resulting from *TestRedundant_EquivalenceEarly (Speech_T, Mouse_T, TaskTM1M2, 5)* with *Tw = 5*.

Table 5. The result of Test Redundant_EquivalenceEarly.

Time	E_{M1}	E_{M2}	Tout	*TESTRedundantEquivalenceEarly*
1	Speech_Task	1	Task	
2		Mouse_Task		Speech_Task, Mouse_Task are Redundant-Equivalent
3	Speech_Task			
4	Speech_Task			
5		Mouse_Task		

Complementarity(C). Let M_1, M_2 be two modalities. Let E_{M1}, E_{M2} be two expressions along M_1, M_2 respectively. Two modalities M_1, M_2 are complementary with respect to a set of Tasks *T*, if every task $t \in T$ can be activated by E_{M1} and $E_{M2}...E_{M1}$ and E_{M2} must occur in the same *TW*, i.e. *Abs((time(E_{M1}) – time(E_{M2})) < TW*.

The complementary input events which are temporally close are merged and the associated output task is enabled as soon as the required inputs have been identified. The occurrence of one event of every modality in the current TW is enough to enable the output task. It is possible that several events of the same modality occur in this window. In that case, the task is computed according to the last event of each modality.

We add operator *TestcomplementaryEarly (E_{M1}, E_{M2}, TaskTM1M2, tw)* into TTT language to test the complementary of two events E_{M1} and E_{M2}. The syntax of *TestcomplementaryEarly* operator is the following:

```
<testcom>::=TestcomplementaryEarly(<expr>,<expr>,<expr>,<
expr>)
```

The testers can use *TestcomplementaryEarly (E_{M1}, E_{M2}, TaskTM1M2, tw)* and the behavior of this operator is as follows:

```
Input: EM1, EM2, TW, T.
Output: The complementarity of two events EM1, EM2.
Method:
1.begin
2.EM1_out<- select top 1 EM1 from U_ACTIONS
      where(time between (now()-tw) and now ())
      order by time desc
3.EM2_out <- select top 1 EM2 from U_ACTIONS
      where(time between (now()-tw) and now ())
      order by time desc
4.T_out <- select distinct Tout from U_ACTIONS
5.if ((E_M1== EM1_out) and (E_M2 == EM2_out)
and(T_out ==taskTM1M2))then
6.   output ("E_M1 and E_M2 are complementary");
7.else
8.   begin
9.   output ("E_M1 and E_M2 are complementary");
10.  stop program;
11. end
12.end
```

EM1_out and *EM2_out* are the last events occurred in the TW. *T_out* is the task occurred in the TW. The Complementarity of two events E_{M1} and E_{M2} is tested by condition (line 5): $((E_{M1} == EM1\_out)$ and $(E_{M2} == EM2\_out)$ and$(T\_out == task))$. If E_{M1} and E_{M2} are last events in TW and *Tout* is the *taskTM1M2* then E_{M1} and E_{M2} are complementary. Table 6 shows an extract example of the execution trace resulting from *TestComplementaryEarly (Speech_T1, Mouse_T2, Task12, 5) with TW = 5*.

Table 6. The result of Test Complementary Early.

Time	E_{M1}	E_{M2}	Tout	*TestComplementaryEarly*
1	Speech_T1			
2		Mouse_T2		Speech_T1, Mouse_T2 are complememtary
3	Speech_T1			
4	Speech_T1			
5		Mouse_T2	TaskT12	

6 Test Execution Environment

For the purpose of testing interactive applications, we propose the test environment, called TTTEST (TTT-based Test), in Fig. 4.

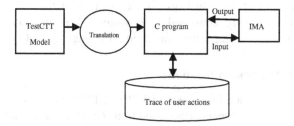

Fig. 4. The TTTEST testing environment.

The TTTEST testing environment consists of four basic components: TESTCTT model specified by TTT language, C program translated from TESTCTT models, interactive multimodal application under test, traces of the action user. The TTTEST environment activities are described as follows:

Step 1: The TESTCTT model is translated into a C program which is executed.

Step 2: The C program produces output data X from its internal state.

Step 3: Output X is translated into input data for IMA.

Step 4: IMA receives and processes input X and generates output Y.

Step 5: Program C receives Y as input data, updates internal state variable of the model and returns to Step 2.

A TESTCTT model is specified with TTT language. We translate a TESTCTT model into a C program which implements the corresponding test generator. The details of the translation are presented as follows.

6.1   Translation from TTT into C

TESTCTT model is specified by TTT language. However, instead of implementing a test generator based on TTT, we translate *TESTCTT* model into C program so that C program can be compiled in order to generate test data. To do the translation, we have built the TTTEST tool that support feature *translate*. Translation is a component of the environment *TTTEST* (Fig. 4). TESTCTT model is translated into C program, which can be executed by compiler C to generate test data. The translation from TTT into C language has four problems as follows.

The first problem is lexical substitutions. Keywords in TTT are replaced by corresponding C operators. In addition, the TTT keywords *set, function, var, init* are replaced with the null string.

The second problem of translation involves syntactic transformations. Certain constructs in TTT have equivalent constructs in C, but with differing orders of the tokens.

The third problem is translating the CTT operators and functions of TTT into equivalent C functions. These "higher-level" CTT operators constructs in TTT which must be translated down into lower-level constructs in C.

The final problem of the translation is the creation of the database connecting environment for the newly converted C program. Then we translate `insert`, `update`, `delete`, `select` statements from TTT language to C program.

6.2 Automatic Translation Solution

To implement the translation from the model TESTCTT into a C program, we use two tools Lex and Yacc. The automatic translation from *TESTCTT* model into C program is presented as Fig. 5.

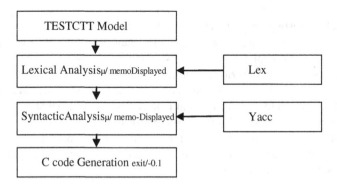

Fig. 5. Transforming TESTCTT model into C program.

Lex generates C code for a lexical analyzer, or scanner. It uses patterns that match strings in the input and converts the strings to tokens. Tokens are numerical representations of strings, and simplify processing. As Lex finds identifiers in the input stream, it enters them in a symbol table. The symbol table may also contain other information such as data type and location of the variable in memory.

The first phase in a compiler reads the input source and converts strings in the source to tokens. Using regular expressions, we can specify patterns to Lex that allow it to scan and match strings in the input. To identify the token, the lexical analyzer developed for each token a translation diagram. A translation diagram including states and denoted by circles connected the arrow next to the states. There are many translation diagrams, each diagram specifies a token group. If a translation diagram fails, the lexical analyzer translated back pointer to the initial state of this diagram, then activate the next translation diagram. If there is a failure in all the service diagram as a lexical error was detected.

Yacc generates C code for a syntax analyzer, or parser. Yacc uses grammar rules that allow it to analyze tokens from Lex and create a syntax tree. A syntax tree imposes a hierarchical structure on tokens. Yacc uses two stacks in memory: symbol stack and values stack. Symbol stack contains the terminal symbols and nonterminal symbols, perform analyzes current status. Value stack contains the corresponding values of the symbols in the symbol stack. To parse an expression, it needs to do the reverse operation. Instead of starting with a single nonterminal (start symbol) and generating an expression from a grammar, it needs to reduce an expression to a single nonterminal. This is known as bottom-upor shift-reduce parsing, and uses a stack for storing terms.

The next step, code generation, does a depth-first walk of the syntax tree to generate code. Figure 6 illustrates the file naming conventions used by Lex and Yacc. First, we need to specify all pattern matching rules for Lex and grammar rules for Yacc. To do that, we wrote a *TTT.l* for lex and a *TTT.y* for yacc.

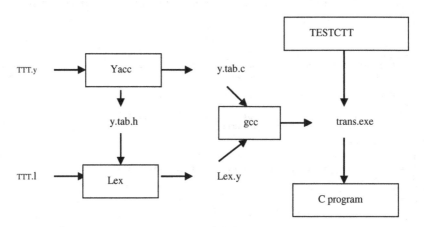

Fig. 6. Translating TESTCTT to C program with Lex/Yacc.

7 Testing the Memo Application

The TESTCTT model of Memo is built through four steps: (1) selecting a test target; (2) designing notations of activity in the model; (3) designing the state variables and selecting data types for variables; (4) writing test scripts for each activity. Figure 7 presents a part of this test model.

Based on the tool described in Sect. 4.2, TESTCTT model is transformed into a program written in C. After the translation is completed, then C program is executed to generate test data.

Table 7 shows an extract of the execution trace and the result of *TestEquivalence* (lines 40).

Table 8 shows an extract of the execution trace and the result of *TestRedundantEquivalenceEarly* (lines 41).

The test data in Table 7 is suitable to testing the equivalence properties of Memo application. The result *Speech(get) = Mouse(get)* means *Speech(get)* and *Mouse(get)* are equivalent. The test data in Table 8 is suitable to testing the Redundant-Equivalence properties of Memo application. For instance, when the user *moves* and a note appears on Memo *M_Displayed* (line 1). TESTCTT model generates input data *Speech_get* (choice between *get* or *remove* in the state q2). In lines (2, 3, 4) because of the redundancy mode, the user actions *Speech_get*, *Mouse_get* are sent through the Memo causing only one action *Get* and Memoreturns output *M_Taken* (line 2). TESTCTT model calculates and determines the

```
1.  TESTCTT Memo;
2.  VAR
3.  q0, q1, q2, q3, q4 : bool;
4.  T, Tout: char;
5.  tw : integer;
6.  begin
7.  INIT (Tout='D')
8.  do
9.  begin
10. q0=(Tout<>'D' and Tout <> 'C' and T <>'o');
11. q1=(T=='o')or(Tout=='G'and T =='g') or (Tout=='R'and T=='r')or(Tout=='S'and
    T=='s');
12. q2 = (Tout=='D');
13. q3 = (Tout=='C');
14. if (q0)
15. begin
16. T = Choice('o','',0.5, note_nb()=0,1,note_nb()>=5,0.1);
17. insert into U_ACTIONS(input) values(T);
18. end
19. if (q1)
20. begin
21. T = Choice(('o' ,'',0.5, note_nb()=0,1,note_nb()>=5,0.1);
22. insert into U_ACTIONS(input) values(T);
23. end
24. if (q2)
25. begin
26. T = choice('g' ,'r',0.8,note_nb()=0, 1, note_nb()>=5,0.1);
27. if T ='g'
28. begin
29. tw=1;
30. do
31. begin
32. Modalities(Speech_get,Mouse_get,0.3,0.7,note_nb()=0,0,0,note_nb()>=5,0.2,0.8);
33. Tout = call_Memo(T);
34. Insert into U_ACTIONS(M1,M2,input,output)values(Speech_get,Mouse_get,T,Tout);
35. Tw =tw+1;
36. end
37. while (tw<=3)
38. TestRedundantEquivalenceEarly(Speech, Mouse, get, 3)
39. end
40. else
41. begin
42.      Tw=1;
43. do
44. begin
45. Modalities(Speech_remove,Mouse_remove,0.8,0.9,note_nb()=0,0,0,
46. note_nb()>=5,0.9,0.7);
47.   Tout = call_Memo(T);
48. insert into U_ACTIONS(M1,M2,input,ouput)
49. values(Speech_remove,Mouse_remove,T,Tout);
50.   Tw=tw+1;
51. end
52. while (tw<=3)
53. TestRedundantEquivalenceEarly(Speech, Mouse, remove, 3);
54. end;
55. while (T<>'E');
56. end
57. FUNCTION note_nb() returns (note_nb: int);
58. Varget_nb, remove_nb :int;
59. begin
60. get_nb= select count(*) from U_ACTIONS where input ="g";
61. remove_nb= select count(*) from U_ACTIONS where input ="r";
62. note_nb= get_nb- remove_nb
63. end
```

Fig. 7. The test model for Memo in TTT.

Table 7. The result of *TestEquivalence*.

Time	EM1	EM2	Tout	TestEquivalence
1	Speech(get)		get	
2				
3		Mouse(get)	get	Speech(get)=Mouse(get)

Table 8. An extract of the execution trace and the result of *TestRedundantEquivalenceEarly*.

Time	E_{M1}	E_{M2}	TM1M2	Output
1	Move			M_Displayed
2	Speech_get		Get	M_Taken
3		Mouse_get		
4		Mouse_get		
5	Move			M_Display
6	Speech_remove		Remove	M_Remove
7		Mouse_remove	Remove	M_Remove

application is in state q1. In state q1, TESTCTT model generates input data *move* (choice between *move* or "-" in the state q1). When the user moves, a note appears on the Memo (*M_Display*) (line 5). The user removes this note (lines 6, 7). The user actions *Speech_remove*, *Mouse_remove* are sent through the Memo causing two actions *Remove* and Memo returns two outputs *M_Remove*. So *Mouse_remove*, *Speech_remove* are not Redundant-Equivalence, therefore the C program stops the Memo application and displays a message "*Mouse_remove* and *Speech_remove* are not Redundant-Equivalence".

8   Conclusion

Interactive multimodal applications are intuitive, natural, efficient, and robust. The flexibility and robustness of multimodal applications are increasing the complexity of the design, development and testing. Based on previous work, we have built a new modeling language TTT to test interactive applications and we have extended it to deal with multimodal applications. More precisely, TTT supports automatic test data generation for IMA as well as test oracles checking for CARE properties validity. We built the prototype TTTEST tool and conducted a first experiment on the memo application.

As future work, we plan to conduct more extensive experimental studies on other IMA.

References

1. Coutaz, J., Nigay, L., Salber, D., Blandford, A., May, J., Young, R.M.: Four easy pieces for assessing the usability of multimodal interaction: the care properties. In: INTERACT, pp. 115–120. Chapman & Hall (1995)
2. Duke, D.J., Harrison, M.D.: Abstract interaction objects. Comput. Graph. Forum **12**(3), 25–36 (1993)
3. Paternò, F., Faconti, G.: On the use of LOTOS to describe graphical interaction. In: HCI 1992: Proceedings of the Conference on People and Computers VII, pp. 155–173. Cambridge University Press, New York (1993)
4. Le, T.L., Nguyen, T.B., Parissis, I.: A new test modeling language for interactive applications based on task trees. In: Proceedings of the 4th International Symposium on Information and Communication Technology, pp. 285–293 (2013)
5. Le, T.L., Binh, N.T., Parissis, I.: Testing Multimodal Interactive Applications By Means of The TTT Language, Domain Specific Model-Based Approaches To Verification And Validation - Amaretto 2016. In: Conjunction with the 4th International Conference on Model-Driven Engineering and Software Development - MODELSWARD 2016, Rome, Italy, 19 February 2016
6. Madani, L., Parissis, I.: Automatically testing interactive applications using extendedtask trees. J. Log. Algebr. Program. **78**(6), 454–471 (2009)
7. Madani, L., Oriat, C., Parissis, I., Bouchet, J., Nigay, L.: Synchronous testing of multimodal systems: an operational profile-based approach. In: 16th International Symposium on Software Reliability Engineering (ISSRE 2005), Chicago, IL, USA, pp. 325–334, 8–11 November 2005
8. Madani, L., Parissis, I.: Automatically testing interactive multimodal systems using task trees and fusion models. In: 6th International Workshop on Automation of Software Test (AST 2011), Hawai, USA (2011)
9. Musa, J.: Operational profiles in software-reliability engineering. IEEE Softw. **10**, 14–32 (1993)
10. Palanque, P., Bastide, R.: Verification of interactive software by analysis of its formal specification. In: INTERACT 1995, Norway (1995)
11. Shehady, R.K., Siewiorek, D.P.: A method to automate user interface testing using variable finite state machines. In: FTCS 1997: Proceedings of the 27th International Symposium on Fault-Tolerant Computing (FTCS 1997), p. 80, Washington, DC, USA. IEEE Computer Society (1997)
12. Aıt-Ameur, Y., Kamel, N.: A generic formal specification of fusion of modalities in a multimodal HCI. In: Jacquart, R., (ed.) IFIP Congress Topical Sessions, pp. 415–420. Kluwer (2004)
13. TerBeek, M.H., Faconti, G.P., Massink, M., Palanque, P.A., Winckler, M.: Resilience of interaction techniques to interrupts: a formal model-based approach. In: Gross, T., Gulliksen, J., Kotzé, P., Oestreicher, L., Palanque, P., Prates, ROliveira, Winckler, M. (eds.) INTERACT 2009, Part I. LNCS, vol. 5726, pp. 494–509. Springer, Heidelberg (2009). doi:10.1007/978-3-642-03655-2_56
14. Paternò, F., Mancini, C., Meniconi, S.: ConcurTaskTrees: a diagrammatic notation for specifying task models. In: Howard, S., Hammond, J., Lindgaard, G. (eds.) Proceedings of the 6th IFIP TC 13 International Conference on Human-Computer Interaction (INTERACT 1997), Sydney, Australia, pp. 362–369. Chapman & Hall, Boca Raton (1997)

15. Palanque, P., Winckler, M., Ladry, J.-F., TerBeek, M.H., Faconti, G., Massink, M.: A formal approach supporting the comparative predictive assessment of the interruption-tolerance of interactive systems. In: Calvary, G., Graham, T.C.N., Gray, P. (eds.) Proceedings of the ACM SIGCHI Symposium on Engineering Interactive Computing Systems (EICS 2009), Pittsburgh, PA, USA, pp. 211–220. ACM Press (2009)
16. Kamel, N., AïtAmeur, Y., Selouani, S.-A., Hamam, H.: A formal model to handle the adaptability of multimodal user interfaces. In: Liang, B., Whitaker, R.M. (eds.) Proceedings of the 1st International ICST Conference on Ambient Media and Systems (AMBI-SYS 2008), Quebec, Canada (2008)
17. Mohand-Oussaïd, L., Aït-Sadoune, I., AïtAmeur, Y., Ahmed-Nacer, M.: A formal model for output multimodal HCI - an Event-B formalization. Computing **97**, 713–740 (2015)

Automated Web Service Composition
Testing as a Service

Dessislava Petrova-Antonova[1]([⊠]), Sylvia Ilieva[1,2],
and Denitsa Manova[3]

[1] Sofia University, Sofia, Bulgaria
d.petrova@fmi.uni-sofia.bg, sylvia@acad.bg
[2] IICT-BAS, Sofia, Bulgaria
[3] Rila Solutions, Sofia, Bulgaria
denitsat@rila.bg

Abstract. Cloud computing brings new business opportunities and services on infrastructure, platform and software level. It provides a new way for testing software applications known as Testing-as-a-Service (TaaS). TaaS eliminates the need of installing and maintaining testing environments on customer's side and reduces the testing cost on pay-per-use basis. Availability of on-demand testing services allows testers to provide raw cloud resources at run time, when and where needed. This paper addresses TaaS benefits by proposing a TaaS-enabled framework offering cloud-based testing services. The framework, called Testing as a Service Software Architecture (TASSA), supports testing of web service compositions described with Business Process Execution Language for Web Services (WS-BPEL). It consists of two main components: (1) TaaS functionality for fault injection and dependencies isolation of the application under test and (2) Graphical User Interface (GUI) for test case design and execution. TASSA framework could be installed on a local computer or used for building a cloud test lab on a virtual machine. Its feasibility is proved through a case study on a sample business process from wine industry.

Keywords: Cloud computing · Service-oriented architecture · Testing-as-a-Service · Web services · Web service compositions · WS-BPEL

1 Introduction

Nowadays, the cloud computing is one of the hot topics in software development. It provides a new way for building software applications known also as Software-as-a-Service (SaaS). The challenges and business opportunities that cloud computing brings affect all activities of software engineering, including software testing. A new on-demand testing model, called Testing-as-a-Service (TaaS) became available.

In general, the software testing faces various difficulties due to lack of time and testing experience, limited resources and unclearly defined requirements and testing criteria. But, the most significant difficulties could appear before beginning of the testing itself. The missing access to the hardware, different software configurations or building a test environment are examples of common problems surrounding the testing

© Springer International Publishing AG 2017
S. Hammoudi et al. (Eds): MODELSWARD 2016, CCIS 692, pp. 114–131, 2017.
DOI: 10.1007/978-3-319-66302-9_6

process of SaaS. However, with the emergence of cloud computing, the software testing gains new benefits represented by the TaaS:

- Access to virtual environments providing a variety software and hardware configurations;
- Possibility for deployment and/or usage different testing environments;
- Availability of on-demand testing services allowing testers to provide raw cloud resources at run time, when and where needed;
- Availability of multi-tenant testing services following given QoS requirements and Service Level Agreements (SLAs);
- Reduced cost of testing due to pay-per-use basis of testing services.

Following the current trends in software testing provided by TaaS, this paper proposes a methodology for testing web service compositions that can be applied in a cloud environment. It is implemented in a framework, called Testing as a Service Software Architecture (TASSA). The last three TaaS benefits listed above are available in TASSA framework by implementation of its core functionality as cloud-based testing services.

Testing web service compositions is a challenging task, since their implementation follows the Service-Oriented Architecture (SOA). Although many research efforts are focused on SOA testing in the past few years, the following difficulties still remain unsolved:

- **Distributed and Heterogeneous Nature of SOA Applications.** Implementation of SOA applications requires composition of web services that are built and deployed on heterogeneous platforms. These web services are outside organization boundaries and are hard to be tested since they are owned by different stakeholders. Furthermore, they could be unavailable for a given period of time or in the worst case could be undeployed by their provider. This in turn complicates the testing due to the needof emulation of the missing or unavailable web services. TASSA framework addresses it through support of dependency isolation and fault injection of software under test from external web services.
- **Lack of Knowledge about Testing Artefacts.** When testing traditional applications the testers rely heavily on their GUIs. However, SOA testers miss such convenience since the web services expose programming interfaces defined with Web Service Description Language (WSDL). In addition, they do not have access to the design documents and source code of the integrated software components, which often decreases the testing efficiency. Again, dependency isolation functionality of TASSA framework addresses this challenge.
- **Difficulties to Reproduce Testing Environments.** Typically, SOA solutions integrate products from different vendors following complex technical specifications and standards. That is why, it is difficult to test all software configurations and varying load on SOA infrastructure and underlying network. Thus, high technical competence is required from the testers and more attention on performance, robustness and security testing is needed. The Graphical User Interface (GUI) of TASSA framework is fully integrated with Eclipse Integrated Development Environment (IDE). Thus, end-to-end testing environment for web service compositions provided.

- **Lack of Full Automation.** Although various approaches and tools for web service composition testing have been proposed, most of them provide partial solutions covering single testing activities such as test path analysis, test case generation, web service emulation, fault injection, etc. However, in order to perform efficient testing, it is important to integrate all testing activities in a common testing environment, which is the TASSA framework case.

TASSA framework provides end-to-end testing environment for web service compositions, described with Business Process Execution Language for Web Services (WS-BPEL) that takes the benefits of the TaaS model. It consists of two main components:

- *Graphical User Interface (GUI) for test case specification and execution* that is available as a plugin for Eclipse IDE;
- *TaaS functionality for fault injection and dependencies isolation* that is available as web services deployed on a cloud infrastructure.

The rest of the papers is organized as follows. Section 2 outlines the related work. Section 3 is devoted to TASSA methodology for testing web service compositions. The architecture of TASSA framework is described in Sect. 4. Section 5 presents the implementation of the TaaS functionality for fault injection and dependencies isolation. Section 6 describes a case study of testing sample business process with TASSA framework as a proof of concept. Section 7 concludes the paper and gives directions for future work.

2 Related Work

The related work, presented in this section, covers approaches and frameworks following the TaaS concept.

An extensive overview of recently proposed approaches and tools for functional, structural and security testing of web services is presented in [16]. The authors of [17] survey the current solutions for testing web service compositions. The most work in these surveys are focused on web service signatures, namely WSDL descriptions [18–23]. However, WSDL interface does not provide a semantic information for web services and a behavioral description of them, which is important when testing web service orchestrations. In contrast, TASSA framework is focused on testing of web service compositions, described with WS-BPEL. This approach of SOA testing is adopted by several works. In order to perform control and data flow testing, the authors of [24] propose the use of model checkers for test cases generation from BPEL descriptions. Other approaches [25, 26, 28, 29] focus on analysis of test paths derived from graph models representing the composition specification. In this direction, [26] propose a graph-search based approach transforming the BPEL into an extension of a control flow graph and generating test data for each path by using constraint solvers. Other approaches, e.g. [27], propose online testing algorithms for web services composition using BPEL.

Currently, the TaaS benefits focus the attention of both industry and academic communities on building cloud-based solutions for software testing. Recently, a considerable number of definitions for TaaS were proposed. Each of them emphasizes on different TaaS perspectives. According to [1] TaaS implies two ideas: first, providing software testing as a web service that is competitive and easily accessible, and second, performing automated testing using the huge, elastic resources of cloud infrastructure. TaaS is viewed as a cloud-based service that automates the software testing in [2]. The migration of software testing to the cloud is presented from the following points of view – the characteristics of the software under test and the type of testing performed on the software. As pointed in [3] TaaS is "a new model to provide testing capabilities to end users". A more thorough definition of TaaS is provided in [4]. On one hand, TaaS is explained as a service model for software testing available on-demand. On the other hand, TaaS is described as a new business model for software testing providing cost-sharing and cost-reduction due to its pay-as-you-test abilities.

A framework of TaaS as a new model to improve the efficiency of software testing is proposed in [5]. It consists of four layers: Test Service Tenant and Contribution layer, Testing Service Bus layer, Testing Service Composite layer, and Testing Service Pool layer. The idea of the framework is similar to the one of Universal Description Discovery and Integration (UDDI) registry. Its main functionality includes registering, matching, reasoning, classifying and scheduling of testing services in order to provide TaaS-based service compositions to the end users. The authors of [30] apply similar approach by proposing a framework for collaborative testing of web services. The framework uses various test services that interoperate to complete the testing tasks. They are registered, discovered, and invoked at runtime in order to achieve testing on-the-fly with a high degree of automation. Prescriptions for implementation of TaaS strategy by the software organizations are introduced in [6].

Although there are a number of recently published research papers addressing TaaS issues, challenges, and needs, there is a very few published papers focusing on web service composition testing. In [7] requirements for web service load testing are identified and a WS-TaaS platform for such type of testing is pro-posed. The platform is based on an existing Cloud PaaS platform, called Ser-vice4All. Unfortunately, it does not support testing of web service compositions and its functionality is limited to that provided by the Apache JMeter [8]. A cloud platform for testing Service-Oriented Architecture (SOA) orchestrations, called MIDAS, is proposed in [9]. The MIDAS platform adopts SOA paradigm, so all its functionality is exposed as services deployed on a cloud infrastructure. The supported types of testing are functional testing, security testing and usage-based testing. A limitation of the MIDAS platform is that it allows testing of service interactions with SOAP messages. The test methods require specification of input models using UML-based language, called MIDAS DSL. This is a drawback of the MIDAS platform, since usually the SOA orchestrations are described with languages such as WS-BPEL, Business Process Modelling Notation (BPMN) and Windows Workflow Foundation (WWF).

There are several cloud-based commercial platforms on the market providing TaaS. SOASTA CloudTest [10] and IBM Rational Performance Tester [12] are solutions for load and performance testing. Sauce Labs is a platform for testing mobile and web applications [11]. It allows testers to create test manually or using Appium, Selenium or JavaScript unit. Oracle provides a platform covering the testing process end-to-end [13]. It automates the provisioning of so called test labs, which includes the application under test and the software tools for functional and load testing. The most powerful solution for cloud testing is provided by Parasoft [14]. Their testing platform is designed to support functional, performance, load and security testing of all the protocols and technologies that make cloud-based applications possible (HTTP/S, JMS, MQ, ESB, PoX, JDBC, RMI, Tibco, SMTP, .NET WCF, SOAP/WSDL, REST/ WADL, etc.). In addition, the behavior of dependent applications (third-party services, mainframes, database, etc.) can be emulated using Parasoft's service virtualization.

The commercial cloud-based solutions presented above are focused on building test labs mainly by installing the currently provided testing tools on cloud infrastructure. Most of them do not provide support for testing of web service compositions, which is the main purpose of TASSA framework. In addition, TASSA framework follows SOA paradigm similar to MIDAS platform and exposes its core functionality as a web services deployed on the cloud. Its GUI could be accessed from a local computer or used for building a cloud test lab on a virtual machine.

3 TASSA Methodology

TASSA methodology covers the following testing activities: (1) test template design, (2) test case generation, and (3) test case execution. Figure 1 shows the execution sequence of the methodology's steps as follows:

(1) Selection of business process to be tested.
(2) Selection of test strategy that determines how test scenarios should be generated in order to satisfy given reliability or coverage goal.
(3) Selection of test scenario.
(4) Identification of process variables and constants, which affect the execution of selected scenario.
(5) Design of test template for the scenario.
(6) Generation of test cases from the test template
    (6.1) Specification of test input containing values that satisfy the execution of the business process according to the selected scenario and are consistent with the data types defined in its XSD schema.
    (6.2) Specification of expected test output that will be used for test verdict.
    (6.3) Definition of test assertions.
(7) Execution of the test cases.
(8) Collection and assessment of test results.
(9) Test analysis and follow-up.
    Some of the partner web services of the process under test could be unavailable for a given period of time or under development. Also their execution in testing environment could require additional payments to their providers. In such situations the proposed methodology suggests simulation of the missing or unavailable web service behavior through execution of the following additional steps within step 5:
    (5.1) Identification of the invoke activities that correspond to the partner web services that should be isolated.

(5.2) Generation of appropriate data, which will replace the actual responses expected from the partner web services.

(5.3) Generation of version of the original business process in which the dependencies from the partner web services are removed.

If reliability or robustness testing should be performed the following additional steps should be executed within step 5:

(5.1) Specification of faults that will be injected in the business process in order to simulate unexpected behavior.

(5.2) Generation of version of the original business process with injected faults specified on the previous step.

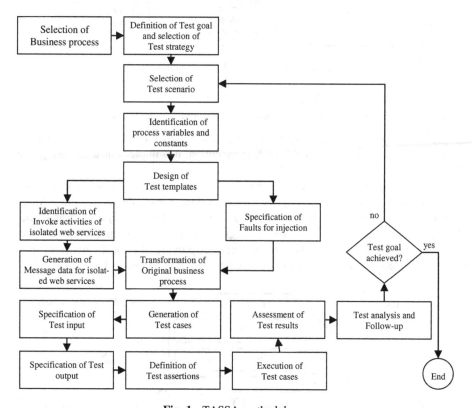

Fig. 1. TASSA methodology.

4 Architecture of TASSA Framework

TASSA is a cloud-based framework for testing web services orchestrations, described with WS-BPEL. It reduces the testing effort by providing functionality for automation and tracing of testing steps performed during test project lifecycle.

The high level architecture of TASSA framework is presented in Fig. 2. It consists of two main components:

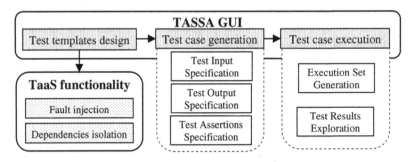

Fig. 2. Architecture of TASSA framework.

- *GUI* for test case specification and execution;
- *TaaS functionality* for fault injection and dependencies isolation.

The GUI provides functionality that is separated in three layers: Test template design; Test case generation; and Test case execution. It is implemented as a plugin for Eclipse IDE.

At test template design layer a version of the business process under test, called template, is created by transformations over original *.bpel file. Following TASSA methodology two types of transformations are supported: *Isolation of activity* and *Fault injection*. The isolation is performed through invocation of appropriate operation of *Simulate* web service, while the fault injection is provided by the *ProxyInvoke* web service. The deployment model of TASSA framework is shown in Fig. 3.

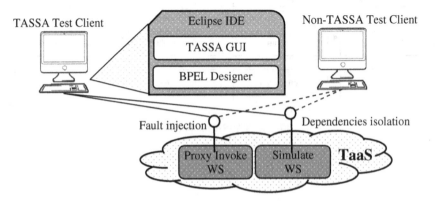

Fig. 3. Deployment model of TASSA framework.

The *Simulate* and *ProxyInvoke* web services are deployed on an application server using Amazon EC2. Thus, the time to obtain and boot a new server instances is reduced allowing capacity to be scaled quickly as the computing requirements change [15].

When a new test project is created a default read only template, called Original, is generated. It holds the original *.bpel file and all files from which its deployment and execution depend on. It can be used as a base for creation of new test templates or test cases. When a new test template is created, a folder structure is associated with it. It contains the following items:

- **Dependencies folder**, which contains all files the business process's deployment and execution depend on.
- **deploy.xml file**, which is the deployment descriptor for the Apache ODE Server;
- ***.tm file**, which represents the created test template and describes the actions, called steps, that are applied to the business process;
- ***.bpel file**, which corresponds to a transformed business process that will be used during test execution.

At the next layer, the test cases are generated automatically from the test templates. The test assertions can be specified manually by the tester in two ways:

- Defining an XPath expression over a particular business process's variable that will be evaluated during test case execution;
- Directly editing fields of particular business process's variable using provided XML editor.

The test assertions are useful in order to validate the response messages returned by the partner web services. They are stored in XML file with root element, called ListOfAssertions. Each assertion starts with Assert element that has three child elements: variable, XPath and document. The variable element of the assertion keeps the name of the business process's variable for which the test assertion is defined. The xPath element contains an XPath expression, if such is defined. If the test assertion is specified by directly editing of the business process's variable, the document element is filled with the content of that variable.

The test cases need to be added to execution set in order to be executed. The execution sets allow test cases to be grouped for simultaneous execution. The result from execution of each test case is stored in XML document, which elements are following:

- **testCaseName** – name of the test case;
- **request** – request to the business process;
- **response** – response from the business process;
- **executionTime** – duration time of the test case;
- **compareResult** – test verdict: true, if the test is passed, and false – otherwise;
- **traceEnabled** – indication for tracing ability activation;
- **activitiesPassed** – activities that have been called during BPEL process execution;
- **asserts** – test case assertions;
- **executionDate** – execution date.

5   TaaS Functionality of TASSA Framework

The TaaS features of TASSA framework are implemented by two web services. The *Simulate* web service isolates the business process from dependencies of partner web services. The *ProxyInvoke* web service provides functionality for fault injection.

5.1   Dependency Isolation

Dependency isolation provides a temporary removal of business process dependencies from one or more partner web services. This allows the tester to control the web service returned results and pre-determine the possible routines in the business process, as well as to continue testing even if a particular web service is missing. The business process's dependencies on external web services can be described as follows:

- Synchronous execution of operation provided by an external service (*Invoke* activity in the business process description);
- Asynchronous execution of operation provided by an external service (combination of Invoke and Receive activity in the business process description);
- Unforced message receipt from external service (*Pick* activity);
- Sending message to external service (resulting from an ingoing message);
- *HumanTask* activity, which requires human intervention and which affects the application through its output data (operator-entered values).

Invoke activity is modeled with following expression:

$$o = f(i_1, i_2, \ldots, i_n, R) \tag{1}$$

where f denotes the functionality of the operation provided by the external web service, $i_1 \div i_n$ are the input parameters of the operation, o is the returned result, and R is additional parameters of the activity not directly related to the operation execution.

To eliminate the dependency upon f the following modifications are necessary to isolate the business process:

- Modification of the process, where the relevant *Invoke* activity is replaced with *Assign* activity to assign the output variable o specific values set by the user;
- When isolating the process from one activity a test artifact is created – a version of the business process, in which the *Invoke* activity is replaced by an *Assign* activity.

The other dependencies are handled in a similar way – e.g. in the asynchronous mode for web service operation call (*Invoke* and *Receive*), the *Invoke* activity is replaced by the *Empty* activity (as it does not influence it) and *Receive* activity is replaced by *Assign* activity. Table 1 illustrates the replacement of the business process activities during dependencies isolation.

Table 1. Replacement of the business process activities.

Original activity	Replacement activity
Synchronous invoke	Assign
Asynchronous invoke	Empty
Receive	Assign
Reply	Empty
Pick/On alarm	Wait and On alarm branch
Pick/On message	Assign and On message branch
HumanTask	Invoke

5.2 Fault Injection

The main goal of fault injection is to simulate faults during message exchange between the business process under test and its partner web services. The possible situations that can be simulated are (1) overload of the communication channel that leads to delay of sending or receiving a message, (2) failure of the communication channel that leads to impossibility of sending or receiving a message, (3) noise in communication channel that leads to receiving a message with invalid structure, and (4) wrong business logic that leads to sending or receiving a message with invalid data.

The fault injection process consists of the following steps:

- Identification of message exchanged when the failure is simulated;
- Modification of communication channel, so that the failure expected by the tester occurs;
- Modification of an activity that corresponds to the message in order to send message to the proxy created between the message sender and receiver;
- Serialization of input arguments of the real receiver (marshalling);
- Invocation of *ProxyInvoke* web service;
- Deserialization of output arguments (unmarshalling) and sending a message to the real receiver.

Similar steps are performed for the response of the invocation. The formal representation of the process of marshalling and unmarshalling is as follows:

$$o = \text{invoke}(i_1, i_2, \ldots, i_n) \Rightarrow o = \text{Unmarshal}(\text{ProxyInvoke}(\text{Marshal}(i_1, i_2, \ldots, i_n), R)) \tag{2}$$

where i_1, i_2, ..., i_n are the real arguments of the modified *Invoke* activity, o is the original output data, *Marshal* and *Unmarshal* are the embedded BPEL functions for marshalling and unmarshalling, and *ProxyInvoke* is the call of the proxy web service with failure parameters specified by R.

The proposed approach is applicable only to invoke activities because their corresponding exchange of the messages is initiated by the business process. It is necessary condition for the realization of the approach because activities for marshalling and unmarshalling need to be placed round the initiator of the message exchange.

6   Case Study

This section presents a proof of concept of TASSA framework through a case study using a business process, called *Grapes Order*. The business process serves by wine companies while deciding to buy grapes.

6.1   Business Process Under Test

The *Grapes Order* is a synchronous business process that calls three partner web services, namely *Grape Producer North*, *Grape Producer South* and *Perform Order*. Its graphical view is shown in Fig. 4.

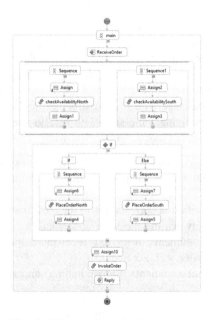

Fig. 4. Wine producer business process.

It takes as an input information about the grapes variety, the quantity and the delivery address. Then the *Grape Producer North* and *Grape Producer South* partner web services are invoked in parallel flow to check the price of the grapes. After that an order is placed in the inventory with the cheaper grape, again using one of the partner web services. Finally, *Perform Order* partner web service finalizes the order by calculating the total price and the expected delivery date.

6.2   Test Template Design

The test template includes a version of the business processes described with the BPEL language and all accompanied documents like WSDL descriptions, XSD schemas, etc. Using TASSA framework it is possible to transform the original BPEL file to isolate the business process from its external dependencies or to simulate faults. Each transformation actually produces a valid BPEL file that imitates the behavior of the initial one in testing conditions.

In order to test the business process workflow, the dependencies from the partner web services need to be removed. The *Grapes Order* business process has three partner web services and five invokes to them. At isolation an *Invoke* activity should be selected and then substitution values should be specified. As a result, the *Simulate* web service of TASSA framework transforms the BPEL file so that the partner web service invocation is removed. Figure 5 shows the BPEL code of the *Invoke* activity that calls the *checkAvailabilityNorth* operation of *Grape Producer North* partner web service, while Fig. 6 presents its transformation.

```
<bpel:invoke name="checkAvailabilityNorth"
  partnerLink="GrapeProducerNorth"
  operation="checkAvailability"
  portType="ns:GrapesProducerNorth"
  inputVariable="GrapeProducerNorthRequest"
  outputVariable="GrapeProducerNorthResponse">
</bpel:invoke>
```

Fig. 5. Original "checkAvailabilityNorth" activity.

```
<bpel:assign name="AssignIsolate1checkAvailabilityNorth">
 <bpel:copy>
  <bpel:from>
   <bpel:literal xml:space="preserve">
    <Q1:checkAvailabilityResponseElement xmlns:Q1="…" xmlns:xsi="…">
    <Q1:isAvailable>true</Q1:isAvailable>
    <Q1:Available_Quantity>1.0</Q1:Available_Quantity>
    <Q1:Price>13.4</Q1:Price>
    <Q1:Delivery_Time>48</Q1:Delivery_Time>
    </Q1:checkAvailabilityResponseElement>
   </bpel:literal>
   </bpel:from>
  <bpel:to part="parameters" variable="GrapeProducerNorthResponse"/>
 </bpel:copy>
</bpel:assign>
```

Fig. 6. Transformed "checkAvailabilityNorth" activity.

Similar transformations are performed regarding *checkAvailabilitySouth* operation of *Grape Producer South*, *PlaceOrderNorth* operation of *Perform Order* partner web service, *PlaceOrderSouth* operation of *Perform Order* partner web service and *InvokeOrder* operation of *Perform Order* partner web service.

TASSA framework supports robustness testing providing functionality for another transformation. In such case the BPEL file is transformed so that the call to a partner web service is replaced with a call to a *ProxyInvoke* web service. Thus, the fault injection is performed.

The Grapes order business process is injected with four type of faults supported by TASSA framework. The simulation of delay in the response from *Grape Producer South* web service is performed by replacement of corresponding *Invoke* activity with two *Assign* activities and one new *Invoke* activity. The first Assign activity provides configuration information to the *ProxyInvoke* web service as follows:

- **Wait interval** – an integer value that defines the delay of message in seconds;
- **Error factor** – an integer value that defines the kind of error will be injected (1 ÷ 100: insert random errors in the data, which would possible break the XML structure; 0: usually used with Wait interval to delay the message; - 1: replace the original values in the message; - 2: interrupt the communication with partner web service)
- **End point address** – an end point address of the partner web service;
- **Activity variable** – input variable of the partner web service, which invocation is injected with faults.

The second *Assign* activity copies the result from invocation of *ProxyInvoke* web service to the output variable of the partner web service, which invocation is injected with faults. The Invoke activity calls *ProxyInvoke* web service.

Similar transformations are performed regarding *Grape Producer North* and *Perform Order* partner web services.

Test templates created for the business process under test are listed in Table 2.

Table 2. Test templates (TT).

TT	Description
TT1	Original business process without any transformation
TTI1	Isolation of all partner web services
TTI2	Isolation of Perform Order partner web service
TTI3	Isolation of Grape Produces North partner web service
TTI4	Isolation of Grape Produces South partner web service
TTF1	Simulation of small delay in the response from partner web service
TTF2	Simulation of large delay in the response from partner web service
TTF3	Simulation of missing partner web service
TTF4	Simulation of low level noise in the response from partner web service
TTF5	Simulation of high level noise in the response from partner web service
TTF6	Simulation of response with wrong data from partner web service

TASSA framework also supports generation of test templates from the existing one. Thus, a rollback to the previous version of the business process under test could be performed.

6.3   Test Case Definition

Test cases created with TASSA framework are in correlation with test templates. Each test case is linked to exactly one test template. It consists of test input, expected output and assertions if any. During test case execution the BPEL file from the test template is deployed on the application server, the test input from the test case is sent as a request to the business process, its response is compared to the expected output and the assertions from the test case are checked.

Actually, many test cases could be created from the same test template. Thus, several requests with different test inputs will be send to the same version of the business process (deployed BPEL file). Using this feature of TASSA framework a set of test cases are created from the test templates described above.

Two test cases for the test templates that isolate *Grape Producer North* and *the Grape Producer South* web services are created (TCI1 and TCI2). They provide full path coverage of the business process since both True and False branches of the If activity are executed. The same test scenarios are designed when the partner web services are available and their operations are actually invoked (TC1 and TC2).

Several test cases with invalid data are also created (negative test cases):

- TCN1 – send request with zero quantity;
- TCN2 – send request with quantity over availability;
- TCN3 – send request with invalid grape type;
- TCN4 – send request with invalid quantity;
- TCN5 – send request with invalid delivery type.

In order to perform robustness testing the following test cases are defined using fault injection features of TASSA framework:

- TCF1 – simulates a small wait interval;
- TCF2 – simulates a big wait interval;
- TCF3 – simulates missing partner web service;
- TCF4 – simulates low level noise in the response from partner web service;
- TCF5 – simulates high level noise from partner web service;
- TCF6 – simulates response from partner web service with random data.

As it was already mentioned, TASSA testing framework supports specification of test assertions, namely XML assertions and XPath assertions. Figure 7 shows a sample assertion defined for the response from Perform Order partner web service.

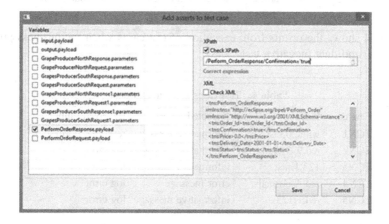

Fig. 7. GUI for writing an assertion.

XML Assertion compare the specified XML message with the received one. In many cases, especially when dynamic data such as IDs or Dates are used, it is better to check only part of the XML message. In such cases the XPath assertion is recommended to be used.

6.4   Test Case Execution

Test cases are grouped in Execution sets. The execution set is a list of test cases, which are executed in the order specified in the list. The test cases in the execution set can be logically grouped. For example all negative test could be arranged in one execution set and all tests performing isolation could be arranged in other execution set. This feature of TASSA framework is especially useful when it is applied to test cases that should be executed in proper order. For example, one may need to execute a test which adds some quantity for a given item and then to execute a test in which this item is sold. Similarly to the test templates, the test cases are reusable. Single test case can be placed in more than one execution set.

When execution sets are ready to run on the application server, for each test case the results are collected and the assertions are checked. The results are written in log files that are grouped according to the execution set they belong to.

Table 3 shows the results from execution of the test cases when partner web services are isolated and when partner web services are actually invoked and the business process receives valid test data. Using TASSA framework the isolation is performed in a way that the business process acts in the same way as when the real partner services are available and called.

Table 3. Test cases showing isolation of partner web services.

Test case	Input	Expected output	Received output
TCI1	white,1,fast	reserved, north,48 h	reserved, north,48 h
TCI2	red,2,normal	reserved, south,48 h	reserved, south,48 h
TC1	white,1,fast	reserved, north,48 h	reserved, north,48 h
TC2	red,2,normal	reserved, south,72 h	reserved, south,72 h

Table 4 shows the results from execution of test cases when the business process receives invalid data (negative test cases).

Table 4. Test cases with invalid data.

Test case	Input	Expected output	Received output
TCN1	white,0,fast	informative message	reserved, north,48 h
TCN2	red,99999,normal	informative message	log error
TCN3	123,1,fast	informative message	log error
TCN4	red,A,normal	error message	log error
TCN5	red,1,123	informative message	log error

Usually a well formed business process should catch exceptions and send proper messages when incorrect action is performed. That is why, an informative or error message is expected to be received in case of testing with invalid values. After performing the negative tests (those with invalid test data) and checking the execution logs, it was found that the business process does not catch several exceptions.

Table 5 shows the results from robustness testing of the business process. Such testing suppose that the system under test should not crash and respond with error message, overcoming violations if it is possible.

Table 5. Test cases performing robustness testing.

Test case	Failure parameter	Expected output	Received output
TCF1	Wait = 10 s	Delayed common output	Delayed common output
TCF2	Wait = 20 m	Time elapsed	Time elapsed
TCF3	Interrupt	Error message	Error message
TCF4	Noise range = 1%	Log error/common output/informative msg	Log error
TCF5	Noise range = 60%	Log error	Log error
TCF6	Random	Informative message/error output	Common output

The *Grapes Order* business process acts properly in case of small delays of the response from a partner web service. It returns an expected output with a delay specified with the wait interval parameter of the Proxy Invoke web service of the TASSA framework. In case of long message delay from partner web service, missing partner web service or noise in the communication channel the business process crashes and the server logs should be explored in order to fix the problems. Test results obtained when random invalid data is injected in the response form partner web service show differences between the expected and the received outputs. It is expected that when a random invalid data is sent, the process should respond with informative or error message. As Table 4 shows the business process accepts such data and responds with a common output. Therefore, additional fixtures should be done in the business process.

7 Conclusions

The paper presents TASSA methodology for testing web service compositions described in cloud environment. It is automated by a framework, which core functionality is implemented as web services deployed on a cloud infrastructure. A case study over a business process serving a wine company is used as a proof of concept. It shows the usefulness and benefits of the proposed solution as follows:

- Ability to test web service compositions even if partner web services are unavailable or under development through provided functionality for dependency isolation;

- Ability to perform robustness testing through provided functionality for fault injection;
- Availability of on-demand testing services allowing testers to provision raw cloud resources at run time, when and where needed;
- Reduced cost of testing due to pay-per-use basis of testing services.

The future work includes evaluation of performance and efficiency of TASSA framework in comparison with other automated testing tools as well as manual testing. Additional functionality for load testing and runtime monitoring is planned to be implemented.

Acknowledgments. The authors acknowledge the financial support by the Scientific Fund of Sofia University under agreement no. 180/13.04.2016.

References

1. Candea, G., Bucur, S., Cristian, Z.: Automated software testing as a service (TaaS). In: 2010 Proceedings of the 1st ACM Symposium on Cloud Computing, pp. 155–160 (2010)
2. Parveen, T., Tilley, S.: When to migrate software testing to the cloud? In: Third International Conference on Software Testing, Verification, and Validation Workshops (ICSTW), pp. 424–427 (2010)
3. Yu, L., Tsai, W., Chen, X., Liu, L., Zhao, Y., Tang, L., Zhao, W.: Testing as a service over cloud. In: Proceedings of the Fifth IEEE International Symposium on Service Oriented System Engineering, pp. 181–188 (2010)
4. Gao, J., Bai, X., Tsai, W.: Testing as a service (TaaS) on clouds, In: Proceedings of the Seventh IEEE International Symposium on Service-Oriented System Engineering, pp. 212–222 (2013)
5. Yu, L., Zhang, L., Xiang, H., Su, Y., Zhao, W., Zhu, J.: A framework of testing as a service. In: Proceeding of the Conference of Information System Management (2009)
6. Sathe, A., Kulkarni, R.: Study of testing as a service (TaaS) - cost effective framework for TaaS in cloud environment. Int. J. Appl. Innov. Eng. Manage. (IJAIEM) **2**(5), 239–243 (2013)
7. Yan, M., Sun, H., Wang, X., Liu, X.: Building a TaaS platform for web service load testing. In: Proceeding of the IEEE International Conference on Cluster Computing, pp. 576–579 (2012)
8. Apache JMeter. http://jmeter.apache.org/. Accessed 11 June 2015
9. Herbold, S., et al.: The MIDAS cloud platform for testing SOA applications. In: Proceedings of the IEEE 8th International Conference on Software Testing, Verification and Validation (ICST), pp. 1–8 (2015)
10. SOASTA CloudTest. https://www.soasta.com/wp-content/uploads/2015/05/CT-Data-Sheet.pdf. Accessed 12 Mar 2016
11. SOASTA CloudTest. https://saucelabs.com/downloads/one_pager_sales_sheet.pdf. Accessed 12 Mar 2016
12. IBM Rational Performance Tester. https://www.ibm.com/developerworks/cloud/library/cl-loadtest-softlayer-trs/. Accessed 14 Apr 2016
13. Oracle Testing as a Service. http://www.oracle.com/technetwork/oem/cloud-mgmt/ds-oracletesting-as-a-service-1905796.pdf. Accessed 14 Apr 2016

14. Parasoft Cloud Testing. http://www.parasoft.com/capability/cloud-testing/. Accessed 15 Oct 2015
15. Amazon EC2. http://aws.amazon.com/ec2/. Accessed 15 Apr 2016
16. Bartolini, C., Bertolino, A., Lonetti, F., Marchetti, E.: Approaches to functional, structural and security SOA testing. In: Cardellini, V., Casalicchio, E., Lucas Jaquie Cast Branco, K. R., Estrella, J.C., Monaco, F.J. (eds.) Performance and Dependability in Service Computing: Concepts, Techniques and Research Directions. IGI Global, Hershey, pp. 381–401 (2012)
17. Bucchiarone, A., Melgratti, H., Severoni, F.: Testing service composition. In: Proceedings of the 8th Argentine Symposium on Software Engineering (ASSE) (2007)
18. Bartolini, C., Bertolino, A., Marchetti, E., Polini, A.: Towards automated WSDL-based testing of web services. In: Bouguettaya, A., Krueger, I., Margaria, T. (eds.) ICSOC 2008. LNCS, vol. 5364, pp. 524–529. Springer, Heidelberg (2008). doi:10.1007/978-3-540-89652-4_41
19. Dong, W.: Testing WSDL_based web service automatically. In: Proceedings of the 2009 WRI World Congress on Software Engineering, pp. 521–525 (2009)
20. Noikajana, S., Suwannasart, T.: An improved test case generation method for Web service testing from WSDL-S and OCL with pair-wise testing technique. In: Proceeding of the 33rd Annual IEEE International Computer Software and Applications Conference, pp. 115–123 (2009)
21. Bai, X., Dong, W., Tsai, W.-T., Chen, Y.: WSDL-based automatic test case generation for Web Services testing. In: Proceedings of the IEEE International Workshop on Service-Oriented System Engineering, pp. 215–220 (2005)
22. Lopez, M., Ferreiro, H., Francisco, M.A., Castro, L.M.: Automatic generation of test models for web services using WSDL and OCL. In: Proceedings of the 11th International Conference on Service-Oriented Computing (ICSOC), pp. 483–490 (2013)
23. Masood, T., Nadeem, A., Ali, S.: An automated approach to regression testing of Web services based on WSDL operation changes. In: Proceeding of the IEEE 9th International Conference on Emerging Technologies (ICET), pp. 1–5 (2013)
24. García-Fanjul, J., Tuya, J., de la Riva, C.: Generating test cases specifications for BPEL compositions of web services using SPIN. In: International Workshop on Web Services Modelling and Testing, pp. 83–94 (2006)
25. Hou, S.-S., Zhang, L., Lan, Q., Mei, H., Sun, J.-S.: Generating effective test sequences for BPEL testing. In: Proceeding of QSIC 2009, pp. 331–340 (2009)
26. Yuan, Y., Li, Z., Sun, W.: A graph-search based approach to BPEL4WS test generation. In: Proceeding of ICSEA 2006, pp. 14–22 (2006)
27. Cao, T.-D., Felix, P., Castanet, R., Berrada, I.: Online testing framework for web services. In: Proceeding of ICST 2010, pp. 363–372 (2010)
28. Karam, M., Safa, H., Artail, H.: An abstract workflow-based framework for testing composed web services. In: Proceedings of International Conference on Computer Systems and Applications, pp. 901–908 (2007)
29. Li, Z.J., Tan, H.F., Liu, H.H., Zhu, J., Mitsumori, N.M.: Business-process-driven gray-box SOA testing. IBM Syst. J. **47**, 457–472 (2008)
30. Zhu, H., Zhang, Y.: Collaborative testing of web services. IEEE Trans. Serv. Comput. **5**(1), 116–130 (2012)

Software Testing Techniques Revisited for OWL Ontologies

Cesare Bartolini[✉]

Interdisciplinary Centre for Security, Reliability and Trust (SnT), Université du Luxembourg, Luxembourg, Luxembourg
cesare.bartolini@uni.lu

Abstract. Ontologies are an essential component of semantic knowledge bases and applications, and nowadays they are used in a plethora of domains. Despite the maturity of ontology languages, support tools and engineering techniques, the testing and validation of ontologies is a field which still lacks consolidated approaches and tools. This paper attempts at partly bridging that gap, taking a first step towards the extension of some traditional software testing techniques to ontologies expressed in a widely-used format. Mutation testing and coverage testing, revisited in the light of the peculiar features of the ontology language and structure, can can assist in designing better test suites to validate them, and overall help in the engineering and refinement of ontologies and software based on them.

Keywords: Mutation testing · Coverage testing · Ontology · OWL · Mutant generation

1 Introduction

The use of semantics in information technology is greatly enhancing the expressiveness of knowledge bases, especially with respect to information representation and retrieval. Information is classified according to domain-specific structures which describe the concepts and the relations between them, and this organization allows an efficient access to such information. Cross-domain organization is also made possible through the use of formal languages to describe the domains. Nowadays, knowledge bases structured according to description logic [1] are popular, and they can also be generated using Natural Language Processing (NLP) techniques to classify unstructured documents.

Semantic knowledge is a wide field of research and application, and it is based on a multi-layered framework of components and technologies. However, at the very basic level, there is the need to describe the domains. This result is achieved by means of *ontologies*. Ontologies are a general concept to denote the definition of a domain, describing it at various level of abstraction.

Of course, to be used in computer systems, ontologies need to be described according to some formal language. Early attempts at defining a language to

© Springer International Publishing AG 2017
S. Hammoudi et al. (Eds): MODELSWARD 2016, CCIS 692, pp. 132–153, 2017.
DOI: 10.1007/978-3-319-66302-9_7

structure knowledge resulted in the Resource Description Framework (RDF) language [2]. However, the purpose of RDF is mainly to describe resources by means of metadata, and it is too low level to provide an efficient means of describing an ontology. For that purpose, the Web Ontology Language (OWL) specification [3] has been defined.

OWL, that was developed starting from another ontology language [4] called DAML+OIL [5], is a family of abstract languages which are expressed in several different syntaxes, some of which are based on eXtensible Markup Language (XML). The primary syntax is RDF/XML, which easily maps onto RDF concepts and integrates with other XML languages.

It is widely known that there is no "right" way of defining an ontology. Its definition really depends on the domain, the desired level of abstraction, the purpose for which the ontology is intended, and a number of choices by the developer. In other words, the same domain could be represented by several totally different ontologies, which would result in different structures of the respective knowledge bases (and consequently, with different results when classifying and querying information). However, for ontology-based applications to be integrated, it is necessary that they are based on the same ontology.

Ontologies have a number of uses, primarily that of describing some domain of knowledge from a specific perspective. In this sense, they act much like a vocabulary, similarly to a database. They have found their place as the basis of knowledge representation in many application fields, from web searches to the medical and legal domains [6].

Ontologies are also used for decision support [7], therefore it is important that they are as complete as possible (within their domain and purpose), and also that they do not contain errors. Previous experiences [8] have highlighted the risks of using an incorrect ontology as a structure for a knowledge base. However, despite the acknowledged importance of the correctness of ontologies, few methodologies and tools exist for the testing and validation of ontologies.

This paper aims at partly filling this void by proposing an extension of some popular software testing techniques to the domain of OWL ontologies. Namely, this work is focused on adapting mutation testing and coverage testing to ontologies.

Mutation testing is a well-known testing method that assesses the validity of a test suite by generating *mutants*, i.e., incorrect versions of the System Under Test (SUT), by introducing single errors in the trustworthy version. The ontology-based software could then be linked to the mutants generated in this way, and run against the test suite. The mutants thus killed can provide important information about the ontology and the program using it, including coverage details and fault detection.

Coverage testing aims at evaluating what portion of the SUT is exercised by a test suite. Such knowledge can be used to determine if the test suite is fit for validating the SUT, or if additional tests need to be designed. On the other hand, coverage testing may reveal some parts of the SUT which are useless or redundant, thus suggesting some possible optimizations. This paper does not introduce a detailed approach for measuring the coverage of ontologies, but rather a preliminary idea focused mainly on classes, leaving further developments to future work.

The paper is organized as follows. Section 2 provides a survey of existing literature in ontology testing and mutation testing. Section 3 offers a high-level description of mutation testing. Section 3.1 describes the proposed methodology, explaining the various operators used for the mutation of an OWL ontology. It also contains a high-level description of the implementation of the mutation tool. Section 4 proposes a basic methodology to measure the coverage of an ontology by a test suite, with a sample application in Sect. 4.1. Section 5 shows the methodology in action, applying the mutation operators to various ontologies in different domains. Finally, Sect. 6 summarizes the results and envisions some directions for future research.

2   Related Work

Although knowledge bases and semantic applications are a very consolidated domain nowadays, it appears that there has been little attention to the validation of ontologies [9].

The World Wide Web Consortium (W3C) provides a set of test cases for evaluating the OWL ontology from a structural point of vies [10]. [11] defines an algorithm to "debug" ontologies in search of inconsistent classes. [12] offer a means of ontology validation through user-defined test cases, whereas [13] defines an approach to merge large ontologies and find inconsistencies.

A lot of research addresses metrics and benchmarks for ontologies. The work proposed by [14] defines some measures for assessing an ontology, and evaluates these measures by means of a *meta-ontology* against which the ontology under validation is compared. This work does not seem to address the semantic correctness of the ontology but mainly its structure and engineering methodology. A similar approach, but with a greater attention to semantics, is proposed by [15]. [16] defines a benchmark for the analysis of ontologies based on two different semantics, OWL Lite and OWL DL.

In [9], the authors propose a methodology and tool for testing an ontology. The methodology addresses three main perspectives: verification of the Competency Question (CQs) to which the ontology is supposed to provide an answer, verification of the inferences by means of an OWL reasoner, and provocation of errors. The last perspective differs significantly from the current work because it does not modify the ontology structure, but rather introduces test data that are inconsistent with the ontology.

A significant model-checking methodology to validate the design of an ontology is OntoClean [17]. It consists in introducing annotations in the ontology which allow to perform a consistency check.

An interesting approach is described in [18]. The authors have built a testing tool which tries to search for potential pitfalls in ontology development. The list of pitfalls has been introduced by the authors in [19]. Although different from the idea of introducing errors in the ontology, their work can provide interesting suggestions for the definition of mutation operators.

An approach that combines ontology evaluation with software engineering techniques is described by [20], which introduces a proposal to adapt unit testing to OWL ontologies. In the past, several tools have been developed for ontology unit testing, although it does not appear to be a mainstream testing approach for ontologies. Another interesting approach is presented in [21]: instances are generated from an ontology, and hypotheses are formulates on these instances. The validation of the generated hypotheses is then fed as an input to refine the ontology.

Some previous work concerning mutation testing in the OWL language can be found in [22]. The methodology does not apply to the general ontology language OWL, but rather to a specific ontology called OWL-S [23] which can be used as a semantic descriptor for web services, and it applies mutation to classes, conditions, control flows and data flows. The purpose of that paper is not to improve an ontology and its related test suite, but rather to detect errors in the web service specification. However, some of the concepts introduced in that work are similar to those introduced in the current work.

Concerning coverage testing, again, there does not appear to be any relevant work on the topic. As per mutation testing, some works exist to measure the coverage of web services in OWL-S [24], but the issue of measuring the actual coverage of an ontology appears to be unexplored so far.

3   Mutation Testing

Mutation testing is a testing technique originally proposed in [25, 26], although allegedly the initial idea can be traced back to a few years earlier [27]. It is classified either among the syntax-based testing techniques [28], or among the error-based or fault-based testing techniques [29, 30]. It is normally, but not exclusively, meant for unit testing [31].

In its essence, it is a methodology in which small parts of a software code are changed. Its main purpose is not to test the SUT proper, but the quality of its test suite. However, it has an indirect benefit on the SUT, because the detection of faults in the test suite can often also lead to detecting errors in the SUT.

According to the description provided by [28], mutation is carried out by applying a set of *mutation operators* to a *ground string*. The ground string is expressed in the grammar, and a mutation operator is "[a] rule that specifies syntactic variations of strings generated from a grammar". These operators can also be applied directly to the grammar if no ground string exists. Mutation can be used to generate both invalid strings and strings that are valid but different from the ground string. In both cases, the strings thus generated are called *mutants*.

The mutants generated from the SUT are then executed on the test suite, and the test results are compared against those of the original code. Those mutants which behave differently with respect to the test suite are *killed* by the test suite. An ideal test suite would kill n out of n generated mutants. The whole process is generally automated by means of batch scripts, because the generation of a high number of mutants and the execution of the test suite on each is a complex and tedious process which is well-suited for automatization. Mutation can be also carried out by introducing simplifications that reduce the number of mutants [32,33] to lower the complexity of the testing process.

Mutation testing has generally been applied to software code, particularly to Java [34,34]. Previous research [28,35] has identified a set of operators for mutation.

Traditional mutation testing operates at the syntax level, by introducing errors in the code. However, techniques for semantic mutation testing have also been defined [36–38], in which mutation operators affect the semantics of the code. In other words, the code is still syntactically correct, but its functionality is different from the intended one.

3.1   Mutation Testing Applied to OWL

To apply the mutation testing methodology to an ontology, some premises are in order.

First off, the mutation operators will be applied to the ontology. However, the testing can be carried out in two different ways: either by viewing the ontology as the SUT, independently of what it is used for; or when the SUT is the knowledge base or software that relies upon the ontology. Choosing either perspective has significant consequences in the testing and the test suite that is used.

The mutation proposed in this paper is a kind of semantic mutation. The syntax of an ontology is managed satisfactorily by the various parsers and editors available, so unless the SUT is a new OWL editor or parser there would be little need for a syntactic mutation testing. What is significantly more interesting is the evaluation of the ontology definition. Additionally, using OWL as the underlying specification, there is no point in working at the syntax level because OWL does not have a syntax *per se*, but can be built according to different syntaxes. In fact, the proposed methodology has been executed using the OWL/RDF, OWL/XML and Manchester [39] syntaxes with identical results.

The mutation operators have therefore been defined as a set of operations that conceptually modify the ontology. An ontology refers to *entities*, which are the main building blocks used to represent real-world objects. The ontology does not define the entities, which are defined by the domain itself. For the purposes of this work, the following entity types have been used as the ground string for mutation:

classes represent the core concepts in the ontology. A class is the abstraction which subsumes all individuals of a given type;
individuals are the real-world objects, single instances of a class;
object properties describe the relationships between individuals;
data properties are used to associate information data to classes.

In addition to entity-specific mutation operators, it is also possible to define some general operators. In particular, some static information can be added to any entity by means of *annotations*. Typical annotations include *label* and *comment*, which are part of RDF Schema (RDFS) and are language specific.

All mutation operators affect some *axiom*, which is the base expression in the ontology. Axioms are connections between entities, and some examples of axioms are:

- a *subclass* relationship between two classes;
- the belonging of an individual to a class;
- the *domain* or the *range* of an object or data property;
- association of an annotation with its entity.

3.2 Mutation Operators

This section describes the various classes of mutation operators defined for OWL mutation testing. Entities in OWL can be declared using either a human-readable Internationalized Resource Identifier (IRI), or an auto-generated one. When using the latter naming convention, which is recommended by the Protégé software, the domain-specific names must be referred to by means of label annotations. This solution is very versatile, because it does not force a naming, but an entity can have a number of names, also in different languages. However, when referring to entities using labels, the absence of a label can cause errors.

Table 1 offers an overview of all the mutation operators.

Some of the mutation operators produce identical mutants: for instance, the ORI operator, when applied to a class and to its inverse, generates two identical mutants.

Entities. Some mutation operators are general and can be applied to any entity:

ERE. Remove entity. This operator deletes the declaration of an entity from the ontology, be it a class, property, or individual. All axioms concerning the deleted entity are removed as well.

ERL. Remove label. This operator removes a label annotation from an entity.

ECL. Change label language. A label annotation is composed by the actual label and a language attribute. This operator removes the language attribute, setting it to a meaningless value.

While it is possible to also apply mutation operators to comment annotations, comments are generally not meant for processing purposes, but only to provide a description to the human user. Therefore, no mutation on comment annotations has been introduced in this work. Similarly, no mutation operators have been defined for other annotations such as *versionInfo* or *seeAlso*.

Table 1. List of mutation operators.

Entity	Operator	Effect
Any entity	ERE	Remove the entity and all its axioms
	ERL	Remove entity labels
	ECL	Change label language
Class	CAS	Add a single subclass axiom
	CRS	Remove a single subclass axiom
	CSC	Swap the class with its superclass
	CAD	Add disjoint class
	CRD	Remove disjoint class
	CAE	Add equivalent class
	CRE	Remove equivalent class
Object property	OND	Remove a property domain
	ONR	Remove a property range
	ODR	Change property domain to range
	ORD	Change property range to domain
	ODP	Assign domain to superclass
	ODC	Assign domain to subclass
	ORP	Assign range to superclass
	ORC	Assign range to subclass
	ORI	Remove inverse property
Data property	DAP	Assign property to superclass
	DAC	Assign property to subclass
	DRT	Remove data type
Individual	IAP	Assign to superclasses
	IAC	Assign to subclasses
	IRT	Remove data type

Classes. Classes are entities which describe the conceptual abstraction of real-world objects. Class relations can be described in hierarchical terms, from the general to the particular. In other words, a class can be defined as the subclass of another class, by means of an "is a" relationship. Classes can be subclasses of more than one superclass. If a class is not defined as a subclass, then it is implicitly a subclass of the top-level class, *Thing*. A class can also be the subclass of an anonymous class, i.e., a class defined "on the fly" using properties.

In addition to the mutation operators applicable to all entities, the following operators have been defined for class entities:

CAS. Add subclass axiom. This operator introduces a subclass axiom between one class and any other class of which it is not already asserted as being a subclass.

CRS. Remove subclass axiom. This operator removes a subclass axiom, thus changing the hierarchical structure of the ontology. If the class has a single superclass, then it will become a subclass of the top-level class.

CSC. Swap subclass axiom. This operator exchanges a class with one of its superclasses. Simply put, it reverses part of the hierarchical structure.

CAD. Add disjoint class. A class can be asserted as being disjoint with other classes. This operator introduces a disjointness relation between one class and another with which the former is not already disjoint.

CRD. Remove disjoint class. This operator erases a disjoint declaration, so the two classes are no longer disjoint.

CAE. Add equivalent class. A class can be asserted as being equivalent to other classes. This operator introduces an equivalence relation between one class and another to which the former is not already equivalent.

CRE. Remove equivalent class. This operator erases an equivalent declaration, so the two classes are no longer equivalent.

Object Properties. Object properties represent relations between classes which cannot be in hierarchical terms. All relations except "is a" must be defined in terms of object properties.

An object property normally has at least one *domain* and one *range*. The domain represents the classes (which can also be anonymous classes, defined for example using set operations) to which the object property applies. A range represents the possible values that the property can have. In other words, domain and ranges are limitations to the individuals to which the property can be applied and to the individuals that it can have as its values, respectively.

The following mutation operators specific to object properties have been defined:

OND. Remove domain. One domain (set of entities to which the property can apply) is removed from the object property. Since the actual domain is the intersection of all ranges, this operator actually widens the possible entities to which the property can apply.

ONR. Remove range. One range is removed from the object property. Since the actual range is the intersection of all ranges, this operator actually widens the possible values that the property can have.

ODR. Change domain to range. One of the domains of the property is changed to a range, actually restricting its possible values but increasing the classes it can apply to.

ORD. Change range to domain. One of the ranges of the property is changed to a domain.

ODP. Assign to superclass. One of the domains of the property is replaced with one of the superclasses of that domain. This operator cannot be applied to anonymous domains or to domains which are only subclass of the top-level class.

ODC. Assign to subclass. One of the domains of the property is replaced with one of the subclasses of that domain. This operator cannot be applied to anonymous domains.

ORP. Set range to superclass. One of the ranges of the property is replaced with one of the superclasses of that range. This operator cannot be applied to anonymous ranges or to range which are only subclass of the top-level class.

ORC. Set range to subclass. One of the ranges of the property is replaced with one of the subclasses of that range. This operator cannot be applied to anonymous ranges.

ORI. Remove inverse property. The property can be declared as being inverse to another one. This operator removes the inverse declaration, but it does not remove the other property.

Data Properties. Data properties are used to describe additional features of an entity. Technically, they represent a connection between entities and literals (such as XML strings and integers). Data properties have a *domain* which limits the entities it can be applied to, and a range which limits the set of possible literals it can have as values.

In addition to the general operators, the following operators have been defined for data properties:

DAP. Assign to superclass. One of the domains of the property is replaced with one of the superclasses of that domain. This operator cannot be applied to anonymous domains or to domains which are only subclass of the top-level class.

DAC. Assign to subclass. One of the domains of the property is replaced with one of the subclasses of that domain. This operator cannot be applied to anonymous domains.

DRT. Remove data range. One of the data ranges of the property is removed, and it is implicitly replaced with the top-level literal *rdfs:Literal*, actually increasing the set of possible literals that this property can have.

Individuals. Individuals represent single instances of a class (including anonymous classes). Individuals are very similar to classes, but they represent a single object and not an abstract generalization. Therefore, they can be defined as belonging to one or more classes.

The following specific operators have been defined for individuals.

IAP. Assign to superclass. One of the types of the individual is replaced with one of its superclasses. This operators can be applied only to those types which have a superclass different from the top-level class.

IAC. Assign to subclass. One of the types of the individual is replaced with one of its subclasses.

IRT. Remove type. One of the types to which the individual belongs is removed (both named and anonymous classes). If the individual is of a single type, then it becomes an individual of the top-level class.

4 Measuring the Coverage

Although not strictly related to mutation testing, coverage testing [40,41] can be used to assist in analysing the results of mutation testing.

The purpose of coverage testing is to evaluate what parts of the SUT are exercised by the test suite. However, different meanings can be attributed to the concept of coverage, each requiring its own criterion. Traditionally, coverage testing is applied to software code, which can be structured as a graph [42]. In this context, several coverage criteria have been defined and classified according to their perspective. Some of the coverage criteria, such as node coverage (also called statement coverage in some literature [40]), edge coverage [43] or path coverage [44], measure the structural coverage of a graph. Other criteria, such as the definition-usage path coverage, focus on the flow of the data within the software [45]. A detailed description of the most relevant coverage criteria is presented in [46].

When coverage testing is performed on software code, this occurs through *instrumentation*, i.e., adding extra code (either statically, or dynamically at runtime [47]) which does not change the behaviour of the software, but collects some significant information [48] which is used to measure the coverage.

The idea to evaluate the coverage of an OWL ontology does not appear to have been explored in the past. Traditional coverage testing techniques must be revisited to allow such an analysis, primarily because there is no code which can be instrumented in an ontology. An ontology is essentially a knowledge base which can be used by software tools. Additionally, the peculiar structure of the ontology calls for new coverage criteria: although ontologies can certainly be represented as a graph, there is no standard way to do so, and nodes and edges can have different meanings in different representations. As stated in Sect. 3, OWL ontologies are made up of entities, and axioms which represent relations between entities. Both these components can be too generic and abstract to offer a clear coverage criterion.

The main focus of this paper is on mutation testing, and as such it does not intend to define a complete coverage testing approach for OWL ontologies. Rather, a basic coverage testing criterion for the limited scope of analysing the mutation testing results will be proposed. For the purposes of this paper, therefore, a coverage criterion which only takes into account the classes (which are generally the most relevant entities in an ontology) has been introduced. More specifically, the criterion will measure the coverage of the named classes, excluding the anonymous classes created by means of a restriction. This criterion will be called Named Class Coverage (NCC).

Preliminarily, the concept of visiting a named class can be expressed as follows.

Definition 1. *A test suite TS **visits** a given class C_i if at least one test $T \in TS$ is based on a query which retrieves C_i.*

This definition applies both when the SUT is the ontology itself and when it is a software which makes use of the ontology. In the former perspective, a test case will directly query the ontology and retrieve some entities and axioms. In the latter perspective, a test case may or may not exercise some code segment which queries the ontology.

Given this definition, the test requirement for class coverage is

$$TR = \{\text{visits class } C_1, \ldots, \text{visits class } C_n\}, \tag{1}$$

where n is the number of named classes in the ontology.

Definition 2 *Named Class Coverage (NCC):* *TR visits every named class asserted in the ontology.*

Therefore, the coverage of an ontology by a test suite TS is the percentage of named classes that are retrieved by the queries executed by the test suite.

Measuring this amount is not straightforward, and depends on the structure of the test suite. An example of how the coverage can be measured in a specific setup is shown in the following section.

The coverage of an ontology can be used to further derive test cases. In particular, the uncovered portions of the ontology are the ones that new test cases should explore. However, given the lack of literature in the topic of ontology coverage, there is currently no means to derive new test cases based on coverage.

4.1   An Application of NCC

To show a sample application of the NCC coverage criterion, the setup used in Sect. 5.4 will be used. The SUT will be the ontology itself, and the test suite will be made up of a set of SPARQL Protocol and RDF Query Language (SPARQL) queries.

A SPARQL query operates much like a query in a relational database: it accesses the knowledge base searching for content that matches the requested pattern, and produces an output in some format. However, the query needs to be modified to measure the coverage, because:

1. on one side, the SPARQL query may access more entities (including named classes) than those that are actually produced as output;
2. on the other side, during its search, the query will access some components of the ontology (e.g., other entities) that are not included in NCC.

Therefore, from the first perspective, the outputs of the query must be widened, to include all the classes which are searched but then left out of the report. From the second perspective, the query must be purged of all those elements of the ontology (e.g., labels and object properties) that are not class entities.

This normalization process is based on the following steps:

1. remove all FILTER operations (since they remove part of the results from the output);
2. only retrieve the named classes, ignoring any anonymous class;
3. remove search patterns based on label annotations and only retrieve the class IRIs;
4. change sub-queries into separate queries. For example, the MINUS operator executes a subquery which subtracts some results from the main query. However, these results are actually processed by the query, and if they contain class entities they must be accounted for, and not subtracted, to measure the coverage.

Additional changes were made for the ease of processing:

1. replace all blank nodes with identifiers;
2. purge the output format of the query of anything that is not a class entity;
3. split queries whose result format contains more than one result into a set of queries whose output format contains just one result. The queries thus generated will be identical, but each will output only one of the results of the original query;
4. remove namespace prefixes, using only full namespaces;
5. add a DISTINCT keyword (if not already present) to the query, to ensure that no duplicates are retrieved.

After these changes, each SPARQL query simply returns a set of named class entities. The union of all the result sets from the queries (ignoring any cross-query duplicates) is the complete set of named class entities involved by the test suite. Comparing this set to the total number of class entities gives a measure of the coverage.

5   Experiments

The proposed testing methodologies have been implemented and executed on several existing ontologies. This section describes the test platform, the reference ontologies and the results of the application of the mutation and coverage testing.

5.1   Experimental Setup

The implementation of the proposed mutation testing approach was done using Eclipse 4.5 (Mars) as a development environment. The programming language used is Java (Sun Java 1.8). The setup is platform-independent and has been successfully tested on Windows 7, Ubuntu Linux 14.04 and Mac OS X 10.10 machines, both at 32 and 64 bit.

The implementation is lightweight and only requires the following libraries, managed through Maven[1]:

- OWL API[2], for general processing of the ontologies;
- JFact[3], to parse inferred axioms within the ontologies;
- Apache Jena[4], to process the SPARQL query language.

The mutation testing tool, called Mutating OWLs, is available as a public Git repository[5]. The repository also contains the test ontologies described below.

5.2   Reference Ontologies

The proposed methodology has been executed on three different ontologies.

Data Protection. The data protection ontology has been introduced in [49, 50]. The European Union is currently undergoing a reform of the protection of personal data. The main legislative document of the reform is the General Data Protection Regulation (GDPR), which was very recently approved, introducing significant changes in the duties of the controller [51]. The ontology has been defined to describe the new reform; however, it does not aim at modeling the whole domain of data protection in the European Union, but only focuses on the requirements of the data controller.

The ontology is preliminary and subject to change, especially given that the reform is very recent and it lacks interpretation yes. It is mainly made up of hierarchical relations, and contains a number of object properties that relate the duties of the controller with the corresponding rights of the data subject.

Entities in the ontology are named using an auto-generated IRI, and labels contain the human-readable names.

Passenger Rights. The second ontology used as an experimental base has been introduced in [52,53] to describe the legal framework for flight incidents. In particular, the ontology addresses the perspective of the rights of the passenger.

This ontology has a more complex structure, and is split into three files. Since the import links were actually broken, some changes had to be made to the ontology to allow the OWL API to access local files. Specifically, the ontology had to be converted from Turtle syntax [54] to an XML serialization because of some limitations of OWL API in parsing non-XML syntaxes.

The naming convention differs from the previous ontology in that the IRIs are human-readable terms in English language, and no labels are used throughout the ontology.

---

[1] https://maven.apache.org/.
[2] http://owlapi.sourceforge.net/.
[3] http://jfact.sourceforge.net/.
[4] https://jena.apache.org/.
[5] https://github.com/guerret/lu.uni.owl.mutatingowls.

Pizza. Finally, the proposed methodology has been run against the well-known pizza ontology[6], which is the one provided as a standard example for OWL and Protégé tutorials. The naming convention used in this ontology is based on English-language identifiers for the entities, but entities also feature label annotations in Portuguese.

Summary. Table 2 displays a summary of the main features of the three ontologies used.

Table 2. Summary of the test ontologies.

	Data protection	Passenger rights	Pizza
Total number of axioms	848	541	940
Classes	88	89	100
Object properties	42	26	8
Data properties	3	31	0
Individuals	16	14	5
Subclass axioms	114	83	259

5.3 Experimental Results

The mutation operators defined in Sect. 3.2 have been applied to the three test ontologies, generating mutants for each. The total number of mutants per mutation operator is displayed in Table 3.

Some considerations are offered by the very structure of the three ontologies. For example, the data protection ontology, as mentioned earlier, uses auto-generated IRIs as identifiers, and labels for descriptive purposes. The pizza ontology uses English terms as identifiers, but entities also have Portuguese labels. Finally, the passenger rights ontology does not use label annotations. For this reason, the ERL and ECL operators do not generate any mutant in the latter. Similarly, no mutant is generated by the IAP, IAC and IRT operators in the passenger rights ontology because the individuals are not assigned to any class.

The data protection ontology makes a very limited use of data properties, so very few mutants are generated from the data property entity; the same is not true for the passenger rights entity, which has a significant number of data properties but less object properties. The pizza ontology does not have any data properties at all, and few object properties. However, the classes that make up the domain and range of some of the object properties have a large number of subclasses, hence many mutants from the ODC and ORC operators.

---

[6] http://protege.stanford.edu/ontologies/pizza/pizza.owl.

Table 3. Mutants by mutation operator.

Operator	Data protection	Passenger rights	Pizza
ERE	145	67	112
ERL	145	0	95
ECL	145	0	95
CAS	7102	886	8151
CRS	114	33	255
CSC	101	33	83
CAD	7084	886	7404
CRD	18	0	753
CAE	7076	886	8134
CRE	37	0	41
OND	41	10	6
ONR	37	8	7
ODR	41	10	6
ORD	37	8	7
ODP	31	8	6
ODC	228	54	250
ORP	31	5	7
ORC	126	22	253
ORI	0	0	0
DAP	1	29	0
DAC	3	3	0
DRT	2	13	0
IAP	12	0	0
IAC	30	0	0
IRT	12	0	10

5.4 Validation

The proposed approach was validated by testing the ontologies themselves and not an application running on top of them. Specifically, the validation was performed on the data protection ontology and on the pizza ontology. For the SUT to be an ontology, the simplest approach to test it is to have a set of SPARQL queries [55] which retrieve data from the ontology.

For the most part, the queries for the data protection ontology are the SPARQL representation of the competency questions that have been introduced in [50], to perform the assessment of that ontology.

On the other hand, unfortunately, no SPARQL test suite is readily available in literature for the pizza ontology. A set of queries exists as the test suite for an alternative query language[7]. These could be used as a basis to assess the validity of the approach presented in this paper. The queries in that test suite were thus converted back to SPARQL. However, two more queries were added to the test suite, because the existing queries only search for very small parts of the ontology.

The complete experimental setup is available in the repository (see footnote 5).

To measure the coverage, the approach to measure the NCC of a set of SPARQL queries, as described in Sect. 4.1, was used. In both examples, this requires to slightly alter the structure of the SPARQL queries, as detailed in Sect. 4.1. Such a modification does not affect the content of the queries.

The NCC coverage of the set of SPARQL queries for the data protection ontology was measured as 62.50%. This means that the test suite (and, therefore, the competency questions from [50]) cover little more than half the named classes of the ontology. By measuring the coverage on the mutants, the results are highly variable: the minimum coverage is 31.03%, whereas the maximum one is 81.82%. The minimum coverage is reached on a single mutant of type ERE; the maximum coverage is reached on 17 mutants of type CAE and 9 mutants of type CAS. However, most of the mutants have the same coverage as the original SUT (62.50%).

On the other hand, the NCC coverage of the set of SPARQL queries for the pizza ontology was measured as 96.97%. This means that the test suite queries almost the whole set of named classes of the pizza ontology. With this SUT, The coverage on the mutants displays a very slight variation: the minimum coverage for the mutants is 95.96%, while the maximum is 97.96%. Specifically, all 95 mutants generated by the ERL operator (and only those) have the minimum coverage; whereas the maximum coverage is achieved by three of the mutants generated by the ERE operator.

The results of the validation is shown in Table 4, and a summary of killed mutants is shown in Fig. 1(a) and (b).

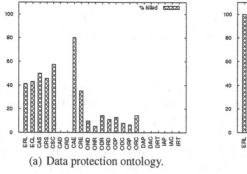

(a) Data protection ontology.

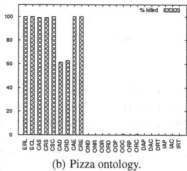

(b) Pizza ontology.

Fig. 1. Overview of killed mutants.

---

[7] https://code.google.com/p/twouse/wiki/SPARQLASExamples.

Table 4. Results of the mutation testing.

Operator	Data protection			Pizza		
	Killed	Total	Percent	Killed	Total	Percent
ERE	61	145	42.07%	108	112	96.43%
ERL	60	145	41.38%	95	95	100%
ECL	62	145	42.76%	95	95	100%
CAS	3542	7102	49.87%	8073	8151	99.04%
CRS	52	114	45.61%	253	255	99.22%
CSC	58	101	57.43%	83	83	100%
CAD	0	7084	0%	4536	7404	61.26%
CRD	0	18	0%	471	753	62.55%
CAE	5678	7076	80.24%	8133	8134	99.99%
CRE	13	37	35.14%	41	41	100%
OND	4	41	9.76%	0	6	0%
ONR	2	37	5.41%	0	7	0%
ODR	6	41	14.63%	0	6	0%
ORD	4	37	10.81%	0	7	0%
ODP	4	31	12.90%	0	6	0%
ODC	18	228	7.89%	1	250	0.40%
ORP	2	31	6.45%	0	7	0%
ORC	18	126	14.29%	1	253	0.40%
DAP	0	1	0%	0	0	0
DAC	0	3	0%	0	0	0
DRT	0	2	0%	0	0	0
IAP	0	12	0%	0	0	0
IAC	0	30	0%	0	0	0
IRT	0	12	0%	0	10	0%
Total	9,584	22,599	42.41%	21,890	25,675	85.26%

A brief analysis of the results elicits some interesting considerations. First, it is clear that the test suites mainly address classes, with little attention to the properties, especially in the pizza ontology. Thus, in both cases, additional tests, especially for the object properties, are required. Also, concerning the classes, the tests in the data protection ontology mostly cover some specific branches of the hierarchy, while almost no tests search through other branches. Finally, some considerations can be done on the ontologies themselves. For example, by examining the live mutants generated by the ERE operator on the pizza ontology, it emerges that some object properties are not used by any of the SPARQL queries. Depending on the purposes of the ontology, this might suggest that those properties are irrelevant and would call for a structural change in the ontology design. More significant insights could be offered by using richer test suites (possibly deriving the test cases from the coverage analysis), which are not currently available for the selected ontologies.

6   Conclusions and Future Work

The work presented in this paper extends and adapts some popular testing techniques from the software testing domain, namely mutation testing and coverage testing, to ontologies defined using the OWL language. The paper first gives a brief overview of the essentials of OWL ontologies. It then introduces a methodology and operators for mutation testing, and a possible approach to measure the coverage of an OWL ontology. Finally, it describes an implementation of the mutation and coverage testing techniques, and some basic experiments on previously-defined ontologies and SPARQL test suites.

The benefits of mutation testing are manifold: by analyzing the patterns of killed and alive mutants, testers can detect errors in the SUT and in the test suite. Equivalent mutants can help detect redundancies in the ontology, which may not be errors but still facilitate errors, for example when creating instances of the ontology.

On the other hand, combining mutation testing with coverage testing can assist in measuring the effectiveness of the test suite. In particular, measuring the coverage can help find the kinds of tests that need to be added to the test suite, and this in turn can lead to a higher percentage of killed mutants.

More in general, the extension of software engineering and testing approaches to ontologies and semantic knowledge bases can pave the way to the formalization of integrated design and testing patterns for semantics-based applications.

This work is at its initial stages, with many opportunities for future development. First off, the proposed methodology needs to be expanded to support a full test suite: a significant set of SPARQL queries, if the SUT is the ontology itself; or, if the SUT is an ontology-based software, testing it with its own test suite. The purpose would be to compare the outputs of the test suite when executed against the original ontology and against the mutants. In this phase, it is possible that the complexity of the mutation testing is excessive and causes performance problems, and it might be necessary to apply or develop algorithms designed to reduce the number of mutants.

Second, the mutation methodology can be improved, by extending it with additional mutation operators. With respect to the work presented in [56], additional mutation operators have been introduced, and these currently make up the bulk of the mutants generated. However, some features of the OWL language have not been exploited yet. For example, the mutation operators do not currently address annotations other than labels, or the value and cardinality constraints. Some of these OWL features can have a significant effect in the ontology definition, and mutants thus created might be useful in assessing the ontology.

Third, every mutation testing approach should be coupled with an algorithm to detect equivalent mutants, and the one proposed here makes no difference.

In particular, the newly-defined mutation operators (CAS, CAD and CAE) generate a very large number of mutants, possibly introducing performance issues. Identifying and removing equivalent mutants would then be of primary importance. In the specific domain of OWL ontologies, it is possible that the use of reasoners can provide an efficient means of detecting mutants.

Fourth, the mutation testing should take into account the peculiarities of ontology engineering. In particular, while the domain certainly imposes some constraints on the ontology developer, many decisions are based on discretionary choices, balancing different aspects such as human readability and efficiency of the ontology. Traditional mutation testing techniques might be extended to embrace these features, for example by separating those mutant operators that are likely to introduce errors in the domain (for example swapping a class with its parent) from those that simply change the ontology structure without making it inconsistent with the domain. If such a partition were possible, then mutation testing techniques could be used not only to detect errors in the design, but also to suggest different ontology architectures that the designer might overlook.

Finally, stretching along the line of the previous point, an extended mutation technique could be designed which alters the structure of the ontology. For example, there might be circumstances where using a hierarchical relationship (subclass axiom) might be an alternative to using an object property. An extended mutation technique that generates mutants based on a different structure of the ontology might offer a fast way to compare a wide number of ontology designs.

An even more significant amount of work would concern coverage testing. A very basic approach has been introduced in this work, which only takes into account OWL named classes, but measuring the coverage should involve much more than classes, e.g., addressing properties and individuals. Therefore, additional coverage criteria need to be defined.

Implementation-wise, OWL coverage testing also needs a lot of improvements. Specifically, due to the lack of instrumenting methodologies and tools for OWL ontologies, the coverage analysis currently requires to restructure the SPARQL queries so that it is possible to count the classes used. A more correct implementation would introduce instrumentation code that generates the coverage results. However, since SPARQL queries are not executable code but require a SPARQL engine to be run, the instrumentation should be performed on the latter. Since several SPARQL engines (including the one used in this work) have an open source implementation, such instrumentation is possible.

References

1. Quillian, M.R.: Word concepts: a theory and simulation of some basic semantic capabilities. Behav. Sci. **12**, 410–430 (1967)
2. World Wide Web Consortium (W3C): RDF 1.1 concepts and abstract syntax (2014)
3. World Wide Web Consortium (W3C): OWL 2 Web Ontology Language document overview, 2nd edn. (2012)

4. Antoniou, G., van Harmelen, F.: Web Ontology Language: OWL. In: Staab, S., Studer, R. (eds.) Handbook on Ontologies. International Handbooks on Information Systems, pp. 67–92. Springer, Heidelberg (2004)
5. Horrocks, I.: DAML+OIL: a description logic for the semantic web. Bull. Tech. Committee Data Eng. **25**, 4–9 (2002)
6. Horrocks, I.: What are ontologies good for? In: Küppers, B.O., Hahn, U., Artmann, S. (eds.) Evolution of Semantic Systems, pp. 175–188. Springer, Heidelberg (2013)
7. Rospocher, M., Serafini, L.: An ontological framework for decision support. In: Takeda, H., Qu, Y., Mizoguchi, R., Kitamura, Y. (eds.) JIST 2012. LNCS, vol. 7774, pp. 239–254. Springer, Heidelberg (2013). doi:10.1007/978-3-642-37996-3_16
8. Kershenbaum, A., Fokoue, A., Patel, C., Welty, C., Schonberg, E., Cimino, J., Ma, L., Srinivas, K., Schloss, R., Murdock, J.W.: A view of OWL from the field: use cases and experiences. In: Cuenca Grau, B., Hitzler, P., Shankey, C., Wallace, E. (eds.) Proceedings of the Second Workshop on OWL: Experiences and Directions (OWLED), vol. 216. CEUR Workshop Proceedings (2006)
9. Blomqvist, E., Seil Sepour, A., Presutti, V.: Ontology testing - methodology and tool. In: Teije, A., Völker, J., Handschuh, S., Stuckenschmidt, H., d'Acquin, M., Nikolov, A., Aussenac-Gilles, N., Hernandez, N. (eds.) EKAW 2012. LNCS, vol. 7603, pp. 216–226. Springer, Heidelberg (2012). doi:10.1007/978-3-642-33876-2_20
10. World Wide Web Consortium (W3C): OWL Web Ontology Language test cases (2004)
11. Wang, H., Horridge, M., Rector, A., Drummond, N., Seidenberg, J.: Debugging OWL-DL ontologies: a heuristic approach. In: Gil, Y., Motta, E., Benjamins, V.R., Musen, M.A. (eds.) ISWC 2005. LNCS, vol. 3729, pp. 745–757. Springer, Heidelberg (2005). doi:10.1007/11574620_53
12. García-Ramos, S., Otero, A., Fernández-López, M.: OntologyTest: a tool to evaluate ontologies through tests defined by the user. In: Omatu, S., Rocha, M.P., Bravo, J., Fernández, F., Corchado, E., Bustillo, A., Corchado, J.M. (eds.) IWANN 2009. LNCS, vol. 5518, pp. 91–98. Springer, Heidelberg (2009). doi:10.1007/978-3-642-02481-8_13
13. McGuinness, D.L., Fikes, R., Rice, J., Wilder, S.: An environment for merging and testing large ontologies. In: Proceedings of the Seventh International Conference on Principles of Knowledge Representation and Reasoning (KR 2000), pp. 483–493 (2000)
14. Gangemi, A., Catenacci, C., Ciaramita, M., Lehmann, J.: Modelling ontology evaluation and validation. In: Sure, Y., Domingue, J. (eds.) ESWC 2006. LNCS, vol. 4011, pp. 140–154. Springer, Heidelberg (2006). doi:10.1007/11762256_13
15. Burton-Jones, A., Storey, V.C., Sugumaran, V., Ahluwalia, P.: A semiotic metrics suite for assessing the quality of ontologies. Data Knowl. Eng. **55**, 84–102 (2005)
16. Ma, L., Yang, Y., Qiu, Z., Xie, G., Pan, Y., Liu, S.: Towards a complete OWL ontology benchmark. In: Sure, Y., Domingue, J. (eds.) ESWC 2006. LNCS, vol. 4011, pp. 125–139. Springer, Heidelberg (2006). doi:10.1007/11762256_12
17. Guarino, N.: An overview of ontoclean. In: Staab, S., Studer, R. (eds.) Handbook on Ontologies. International Handbooks on Information Systems, 2nd edn, pp. 201–220. Springer, Heidelberg (2009)
18. Poveda-Villalón, M., Suárez-Figueroa, M.C., Gómez-Pérez, A.: Validating ontologies with OOPS!. In: Teije, A., Völker, J., Handschuh, S., Stuckenschmidt, H., d'Acquin, M., Nikolov, A., Aussenac-Gilles, N., Hernandez, N. (eds.) EKAW 2012. LNCS, vol. 7603, pp. 267–281. Springer, Heidelberg (2012). doi:10.1007/978-3-642-33876-2_24

19. Poveda, M., Suárez-Figueroa, M.C., Gómez-Pérez, A.: Common pitfalls in ontology development. In: Meseguer, P., Mandow, L., Gasca, R.M. (eds.) CAEPIA 2009. LNCS, vol. 5988, pp. 91–100. Springer, Heidelberg (2010). doi:10.1007/978-3-642-14264-2_10

20. Vrandečić, D., Gangemi, A.: Unit tests for ontologies. In: Meersman, R., Tari, Z., Herrero, P. (eds.) OTM 2006. LNCS, vol. 4278, pp. 1012–1020. Springer, Heidelberg (2006). doi:10.1007/11915072_2

21. Granitzer, M., Scharl, A., Weichselbraun, A., Neidhart, T., Juffinger, A., Wohlgenannt, G.: Automated ontology learning and validation using hypothesis testing. In: Wegrzyn-Wolska, K.M., Szczepaniak, P.S. (eds.) Advances in Intelligent Web Mastering. Advances in Soft Computing, vol. 43, pp. 130–135. Springer, Heidelberg (2007)

22. Lee, S., Bai, X., Chen, Y.: Automatic mutation testing and simulation on OWL-S specified web services. In: Proceedings of the 41st Annual Simulation Symposium (ANSS), pp. 149–156. IEEE (2008)

23. World Wide Web Consortium (W3C): OWL-S: Semantic markup for web services (2004)

24. Wang, Y., Bai, X., Li, J., Huang, R.: Ontology-based test case generation for testing web services. In: Proceedings of the 8th International Symposium on Autonomous Decentralized Systems (ISADS), pp. 43–50 (2007)

25. DeMillo, R.A., Lipton, R.J., Sayward, F.G.: Hints on test data selection: help for the practicing programmer. Computer 11, 34–41 (1978)

26. Hamlet, R.G.: Testing programs with the aid of a compiler. IEEE Trans. Softw. Eng. SE-3, 279–290 (1977)

27. Lipton, R.: Fault diagnosis of computer programs. Technical report. Carnegie Mellon University (1971)

28. Ammann, P., Offutt, A.J.: 5. In: Syntax-Based Testing, pp. 170–212. Cambridge University Press, Cambridge (2008)

29. Howden, W.E.: Weak mutation testing and completeness of test sets. IEEE Trans. Softw. Eng. SE-8, 371–379 (1982)

30. Jia, Y., Harman, M.: An analysis and survey of the development of mutation testing. IEEE Trans. Software Eng. 37, 649–678 (2011)

31. Offutt, A.J.: A practical system for mutation testing: help for the common programmer. In: Proceedings of the International Test Conference (ITC). IEEE Computer Society, pp. 824–830 (1994)

32. Offutt, A.J., Untch, R.H.: Mutation 2000: Uniting the orthogonal. In: Wong, W.E. (ed.) Mutation Testing for the New Century. The Springer International Series on Advances in Database Systems, vol. 24, pp. 34–44. Springer, US (2001)

33. Bartolini, C., Bertolino, A., Marchetti, E., Parissis, I.: Data flow-based validation of web services compositions: perspectives and examples. In: Lemos, R., Giandomenico, F., Gacek, C., Muccini, H., Vieira, M. (eds.) WADS 2007. LNCS, vol. 5135, pp. 298–325. Springer, Heidelberg (2008). doi:10.1007/978-3-540-85571-2_13

34. Ma, Y.S., Offutt, A.J., Kwong, Y.R.: Mujava: an automated class mutation system. Softw. Test. Verification Reliab. 15, 97–133 (2005)

35. Offutt, A.J., Lee, A., Rothermel, G., Untch, R.H., Zapf, C.: An experimental determination of sufficient mutant operators. ACM Trans. Softw. Eng. Methodol. (TOSEM) 5, 99–118 (1996)

36. Offutt, A.J., Hayes, J.H.: A semantic model of program faults. SIGSOFT Softw. Eng. Notes 21, 195–200 (1996)

37. Mottu, J.-M., Baudry, B., Traon, Y.: Mutation analysis testing for model transformations. In: Rensink, A., Warmer, J. (eds.) ECMDA-FA 2006. LNCS, vol. 4066, pp. 376–390. Springer, Heidelberg (2006). doi:10.1007/11787044_28

38. Clark, J.A., Dan, H., Hierons, R.M.: Semantic mutation testing. In: Proceedings of the 3rd IEEE International Conference on Software Testing, Verification, and Validation Workshops (ICSTW), pp. 100–109. IEEE (2010)

39. Horridge, M., Drummond, N., Goodwin, J., Rector, A., Stevens, R., Wang, H.H.: The manchester OWL syntax. In: OWL: Experiences and Directions Workshop (OWLED) (2006)

40. Zhu, H., Hall, P.A.V., May, J.H.R.: Software unit test coverage and adequacy. ACM Comput. Surv. **29**, 366–427 (1997)

41. Yang, Q., Jenny Li, J., Weiss, D.M.: A survey of coverage-based testing tools. Comput. J. **52**, 589–597 (2009)

42. Ledgard, H.F., Marcotty, M.: A genealogy of control structures. Commun. ACM **18**, 629–639 (1975)

43. Huang, J.C.: An approach to program testing. ACM Comput. Surv. **7**, 113–128 (1975)

44. Chow, T.S.: Testing software design modeled by finite-state machines. IEEE Trans. Software Eng. **4**, 178–187 (1978)

45. Osterweil, L.J.: Data flow analysis as an aid in documentation, assertion, generation, validation, and error detection. Technical Report CU-CS-055-74, University of Colorado, Boulder, Colorado 80302 (1974)

46. Ammann, P., Offutt, A.J.: 2. In: Graph Coverage, pp. 27–103. Cambridge University Press, Cambridge (2008)

47. Tikir, M.M., Hollingsworth, J.K.: Efficient instrumentation for code coverage testing. In: Proceedings of the ACM SIGSOFT International Symposium on Software Testing and Analysis (ISSTA), pp. 86–96 (2002)

48. Ammann, P., Offutt, A.J.: 8. In: Building Testing Tools, pp. 268–279. Cambridge University Press, Cambridge (2008)

49. Bartolini, C., Muthuri, R.: Reconciling data protection rights and obligations: an ontology of the forthcoming EU regulation. In: Proceedings of the Workshop on Language and Semantic Technology for Legal Domain (LST4LD), Recent Advances in Natural Language Processing (RANLP) (2015)

50. Bartolini, C., Muthuri, R., Santos, C.: Using ontologies to model data protection requirements in workflows. In: Proceedings of the Ninth International Workshop on Juris-informatics (JURISIN), pp. 27–40 (2015). Extended version to be published in LNAI book

51. Reding, V.: The upcoming data protection reform for the European Union. International Data Privacy Law (2010)

52. Rodríguez-Doncel, V., Santos, C., Casanovas, P.: A model of air transport passenger incidents and rights. In: Proceedings of the 27th International Conference on Legal Knowledge and Information Systems (JURIX), pp. 55–60. IOS Press (2014)

53. Rodríguez-Doncel, V., Santos, C., Casanovas, P.: Ontology-driven legal support-system in the air transport passenger domain. In: Proceedings of the International Workshop on Semantic Web for the Law (SW4Law) (2014)

54. World Wide Web Consortium (W3C): RDF 1.1 Turtle (2014)

55. World Wide Web Consortium (W3C): Sparql query language for rdf (2008)

56. Bartolini, C.: Mutating OWLs: semantic mutation testing for ontologies. In: Proceedings of the workshop on domAin specific Model-based AppRoaches to vErificaTion and validaTiOn (AMARETTO), pp. 43–53 (2016)

Certification of Cash Registers Software

Isabella Biscoglio$^{(\boxtimes)}$, Giuseppe Lami, and Gianluca Trentanni

Institute of Information Science and Technologies "Alessandro Faedo"
of the National Research Council, Pisa, Italy
{isabella.biscoglio, giuseppe.lami,
gianluca.trentanni}@isti.cnr.it

Abstract. This paper presents the Italian scenario of cash register software certification. The basic concepts of certification are introduced together with involved actors, requirements and possible objects to be certified. Subsequently, the specific kind of fiscal device running fiscal software, that is the cash register, is outlined, and its certification process is described. The current technological adjustments of the cash register software according to the Italian legislation modifications are introduced and discussed.

Keywords: Certification · Requirements · Legislation · Cash register

1 Introduction

The certification of products, processes or services plays different roles according to the specific application domain. In the global market, the certification by independent and reliable bodies can be an economical and social benefit. Indeed, the assurance that a product, process or service is compliant with the requirements expressed by international standards or national legislation, can represent a real added value.

However, in specific domains the certification is mandatory before a product can be put into operation. E.g. in aviation, the new aircrafts must be certified before they are allowed to fly.

In the Italian fiscal domain, the certification of the fiscal software by a third party accredited body (an accredited University Lab or the National Research Council) is mandatory. Therefore, the fiscal software running into electronic devices suitable for storing, managing and tracing commercial transactions called *fiscal meters*, must be compliant with a set of requirements specified by the related national legislation [1] and must be certified before being put on the market. To this aim, by further laws and decrees [2–11], the Italian national legislation established modalities and terms for the release of fiscal meters, regulating both the record of the commercial transactions and the certification process. They shall follow to get the final approval by the Italian income revenue authority.

The software of a fiscal meter may implement also functionalities not directly related to the incomes record (the so-called fiscal functions); such software part is called "non-fiscal" software. The non-fiscal software usually carries out tasks related to goods management, accounting capabilities and so on. In this case it must not affect the

S. Hammoudi et al. (Eds): MODELSWARD 2016, CCIS 692, pp. 154–167, 2017.
DOI: 10.1007/978-3-319-66302-9_8

correct fiscal behavior of the remaining fiscal software and the non-fiscal software is not an object for the certification.

About the fiscal software, it is also opportune to specify that it runs on two types of fiscal meters: cash registers and automated ticketing systems. In this paper, only the first one will be considered.

Usually fiscal meters certification is carried out by accredited University Lab or the National Research Council, and it is based on inspection, evaluation and verification activities of both hardware and software components of the fiscal meter; it follows quite similar steps to be performed and differentiates mainly by the kind of the test cases applied for hardware or software components. The final approval for the market release of a cash register is up to Italian Income Revenue Authority (IRA), and it requires that both the certifications (the one related to hardware and the one related to software) end successfully. Nevertheless, for simplicity, this paper only addresses the steps required for the fiscal software certification (Fig. 1).

The aims of this paper are the followings:

1. to present, starting from general basic concepts of certification, the Italian fiscal software certification scenario, and the involved actors.
2. to describe the object of the certification: the *cash register*, its characteristics, and the requirements its software component shall comply with.
3. to illustrate the cash register certification process by means of a Business Process Model [12] and the fiscal software Testing Suite.
4. to highlight the challenges implied in the technological advancements according to the evolution of the Italian legislation.

In the following, the fiscal software certification scenario will be described. In Sect. 3 the cash register and its components will be presented. In Sect. 4 some fiscal requirements for cash register software will be listed and in Sect. 5 a Cash Registers Certification Process will be illustrated. Finally, some questions on technological evolution of the cash registers will be discussed and the conclusions will be provided.

2   Fiscal Software Certification Scenario

In this section, some general concepts about certification are introduced.

Starting from the general concept of certification, one more specific kind of software certification is considered along with involved actors, requirements to be met and objects to be certified.

2.1   Certification Basic Concepts

A generally accepted definition of certification can be taken from ISO [13]: "*a procedure by which a third party gives written assurance that a product, process or service conforms to specified requirements*".

Applied to the *software* area, the software certification is a procedure by which a third party gives written assurance that a *software* product, process or service conforms to specified *software* requirements.

The "assurance" can be given as a result of an activity, the "conformity assessment", defined in the same Guide but refined by the standard [14] as "an activity that provides demonstration that specified requirements relating to a product, process, system, person or body are fulfilled".

Nothing such as a "guarantee" is wanted. The "demonstration" should be perceived as "confidence" instead of "proof".

Besides the *conformity assessment* is a process which includes, but is not limited to, testing and analysis of the objects to be certified. Indeed, the certification process includes: (a) conformance assessment; (b) inspection and surveillance of the quality management system; (c) verification and surveillance of projects and production processes. In this context, independent testing laboratories or supplier/developer execute many tests, and subsequently the evidences of their activities (plans, procedures, reports) are used in the certification process.

In the software certification context, the certification purpose is to increment the confidence about the conformance of software products, processes or services towards some defined requirements.

Finally, the third-party certification should be meant as an independent assessment asserting that specified requirements pertaining to a product, person, process or management system have been met. In general, *the third-party certification* should provide more confidence than the *supplier certification* as there is no evidence that the supplier adopts a defined, controlled and verified process to produce and certify an object.

2.2 Actors, Requirements and Objects of the Certification

The actors involved in the certification process can be divided in two groups, *who want to give confidence on the object of certification* (certification and accreditation bodies, suppliers, sellers, standard makers…) and *who want to get confidence on the object of certification* (customers, users, end users, government…).

In the first group, there are different actors with corresponding different responsibilities. Among them, the most important subjects are the *certification body* and the *accreditation body*.

A *certification body* is an organism with internal rules, human/infrastructure resources and specific skills apt to perform certification procedures. In order to assess conformity in a repeatable and documented way, a certification body must follow a defined process, and it is important that all the certification bodies follow the same rules for the same object types. In some cases, the internal rules themselves might be required to be compliant to defined standards. In such a case, the certification bodies should be "accredited", that is declared capable of performing certification activities, upon periodical surveillance, by special organisms called *accreditation bodies*.

The accreditation increases the value of the product, process or service to be certified. The accreditation bodies are specialized per product category, and, also the accreditation bodies need the accreditation. As there are not many accreditation bodies, they can accredit each other by executing periodical conformity assessments with a "peer reviews" mechanism.

Among the actors that can give confidence on the object of certification, there are also the independent testing laboratories. These laboratories can be accredited according to opportune accreditation rules or standards by special accreditation bodies (usually different from those that accredit certification bodies).

In the second group, among who *want to get confidence on the object of certification*, there are customers, users, end users, government.... They are those who benefit from the certification as they experience the good and affordable added value of the certified products or processes or services. Among them, there are, for example, the customers or also the responsible manufacturers and service providers. For them, having their products assessed and certified as conformant to a commonly accepted international standard can allow to better distinguish themselves among less reputable suppliers.

Regarding the certification *requirements*, generally speaking, they are substantially standards or legislation. The standards can be grouped in requirements standards for products or requirements standards for processes, standards for enabling a certification body to assess conformance of products or processes to their requirements, and standards usable as internal rules by certification bodies for their certification activities.

Other standards can be added to this list: (a) standards for the accreditation of the software certification bodies; (b) standards for the accreditation of the software testing/evaluation laboratories; (c) standards for using test execution techniques and other evaluation processes. Besides, regarding the requirements standards for products, they are *functional standards* or *quality standards*.

The first indicate what a product is expected to do in defined working conditions. The latter cover specific product/process aspects that are relating to their performance, usability, and so on.

The standards should meet the criteria of suitability. Therefore, they should be easy to understand and to use, grounded on scientific bases, cost effective, able to capture user needs and to support evolving techniques.

About the *objects* of the certification, they are usually *processes*, *products*, *services* or *organizations*. In these cases, the certification concerns properties or attributes of these objects, and through verification of conformance to one or more defined requirement standard the conformity assessment is detailed.

The methods for assessing the conformance are depending on the application domain. Then they could include analyses, tests, extended surveillance over quality management systems, and so on. Changing the object of the certification, methods for assessing their conformance and standard change as a consequence. So various types of standards may be involved in a certification scheme.

In Fig. 1 the complete scenario is depicted.

2.3 Actors, Requirements and Objects of the Fiscal Software Certification

In the contest of the software certification, the request of more confidence that the software, during its exercise, be compliant to the requested requirements, is strong. In many case as in the case of the fiscal software, the software certification is mandatory before a product can be put into market.

In the Italian fiscal software certification scenario, the certification process is approved by the Minister of Finances, and on its behalf the certification against the

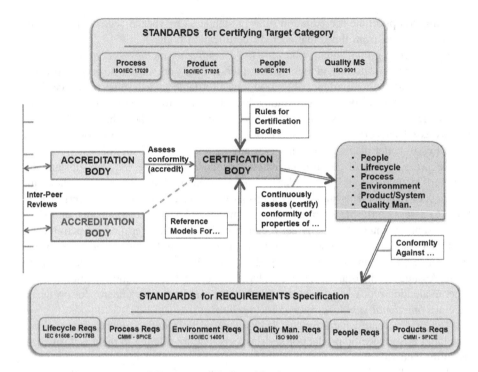

Fig. 1. Simplified certification scheme.

Italian fiscal legislation is provided. The Minister of Finances appoints the certification bodies and performs a sort of control on their certification activities.

In the case of the fiscal software certification, the Italian Fiscal Legislation is the reference as *requirements* collection. The conformity assessment that the legislation requests for the fiscal software is *functional* and, consequently, the requirements considered in the certification process express what a fiscal software is expected to do during its life.

The above cited suitability criteria are not always satisfied since in many cases the legislation (as it will be reported in the Sect. 6) is obsolete and not completely able to support evolving techniques. This is a challenge that the legislation should handle as soon as possible.

The *certification body* referred here is the System and Software Evaluation Centre (SSEC) of the National Research Council, and the *accreditation body* is the Minister of Finances. The SSEC has been working for a couple of decades in the 3rd party software products and processes assessment, improvement and certification.

In the case of the fiscal software, the object to be certified is the fiscal software of a cash register.

The graphic representation of the Certification and Accreditation scenario for the cash registers is depicted in Fig. 2.

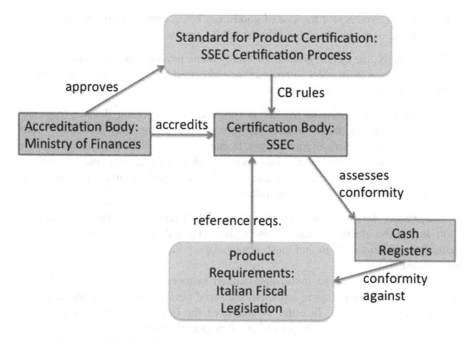

Fig. 2. SSEC certification and accreditation scenario.

3 Cash Registers

First of all, it is opportune to define what a cash register is.

The current Italian legislation specifies what is a cash register, why it was introduced, which are its components, what kind of documents it must issue, and the specific normative requirements that each issued document should satisfy.

What It Is: The cash register is a fiscal device designed to record and process numerical data entered by the keyboard or other suitable functional unit of information acquisition, equipped with the device to print on special supports the same data, and their total [3].

Why It was Introduced: in 1972 Italy has adjusted its tax policies to the other countries tax policies introducing the value added tax (V.A.T.) [15]. By V.A.T. introduction, a supplier of goods or services must charge to the customer the payment of a tribute, and in turn the supplier must pay that tribute to the Government. Subsequently to the V.A.T. introduction, the phenomenon of the tax evasion quickly increased. It was necessary to monitor the revenues of the commercial activities in order to check the regularity of their transactions in terms of data integrity and security. In this context, the fiscal receipt was considered the instrument to oppose the tax evasion since it allowed to keep trace of the payments and to monitor the revenues of the commercial activities. As result of this exigency, the law [1] established the duty for the cash register of issuing a fiscal receipt, at the time of the payment, for the sale of goods, not being subject to the emission of an invoice and occurring in shops or open public places.

Consequently, the cash register must satisfy some requirements of security and, in particular, of integrity in order to prevent "*unauthorized access to, or modification of, computer programs or data*" [16].

Its Components: the cash register is composed of indicating devices (typically *screens*), a printing device, a fiscal memory and the casing. Each component must satisfy specific normative requirements. In particular, the indicating devices must be two and must be placed on the two opposite sides of the cash register in order to allow to the purchaser an easy reading of the displayed amounts. The displayed characters must be at least seven millimeters high.

The *printing device* provides for the release of the fiscal receipt, daily fiscal closing report and of the electronic transactions register. Printed characters must be at least twenty-five millimeters high and must present appropriate requirements of clarity and easy readability.

The *fiscal memory* is an immovable affixed memory that contains fiscal data. It must record and store the fiscal logotype, the serial number, the progressive accumulation of the amount, etc. In order to guarantee the integrity of its data, the fiscal memory must allow, without the possibility of cancellation, only progressive increasing accumulations and the preservation of their contents over time.

Finally, the *casing* must foresee a unique fiscal seal by means of a single screw that ensures the inaccessibility of all hardware components involved in the fiscal functionalities of the cash register, except for the paper management. Also, onto the casing, must be applied in a well visible place on the front toward the buyer, a slab with reported data as mark of the manufacturer, machine serial number, data of the model approval document and the service centre.

What Kind of Documents it must Issue: The cash registers have to be able to print a fiscal receipt, a daily fiscal closing report, and an electronic transactions register. Each document must contain mandatory information specified for single indention, for instance: company name, owner name and surname, V.A.T. percentage and company address, accounting data, date and time of the fiscal receipt issue, the fiscal logotype, the total amount of the payments of the day, the cumulative total of the amounts of the daily payments, etc.

The Italian legislation provides a detailed refinement of this generic descriptions providing hardware and software requirements that better characterize the structure and functionalities of a valid cash register [3]. In particular, the legislation requires two separate certification processes: one for the hardware components and one for the software layer. The two processes are quite similar in the steps to be performed and differentiate mainly by the kind of the test cases to be applied. Only for aims of clarifying, the hardware components testing requires, for instance, water tightness or battery capacity, and evaluations of HW reliability, measured by Mean Time Between Failure (MTBF).

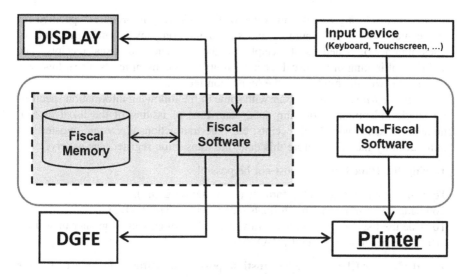

Fig. 3. Cash register scheme.

For the software components, black-box tests are performed, according to the software requirements required by legislation and below reported.

The certification of a cash register needs that both the processes terminate with successful results. For aim of simplicity this paper only details the steps required for the fiscal software certification.

4   Fiscal Requirements for Cash Registers Software

The cash register industrial life-cycle includes different situations like regular functioning, exhausted fiscal memory, disconnected devices, etc. From the ministerial decree [2] on, the Italian legislation has disciplined these different situations imposing precise technological constraints with a subtle level of detail.

The complete list of requirements that the cash register must satisfy can be extracted from the legislation, even though it is sometimes obscure and misunderstood. Anyway the legislation remains the reference point for fiscal software developers and certifiers.

In the following some extracted requirements will be introduced. These are organized according to the specific situations of the cash registers life-cycle.

During the Regular Fiscal Functioning (that is with a fiscal memory that records and storages accounting data), a cash register must issue:

- a *fiscal receipt* with some of the following information specified for single indention: company, company name, name and surname of owner, V.A.T. number and site of the company, accounting data, date, time of issuing of the fiscal receipt, fiscal logotype (compliant with the model that the legislation requires) etc.

- a *daily fiscal closing report* with some of the following information specified for single indention: V.A.T. number and site of the company, eventual amounts of sales, number of issued fiscal receipts, number of issued non-fiscal receipts, date and time of issuing of the fiscal receipt, number of the fiscal resets, fiscal logotype (compliant with the model that the legislation requires).
- an *electronic transactions register* with some of the following information specified for single indention: accounting data, date, time of issuing of the fiscal receipt, number of issued non-fiscal receipts, etc. The transactions *electronic* register was introduced by the [17]. Before this date, the transaction register was papery.

During the Data Input, it must not be possible:

- To change time in impossible formats (for instance: 26:44).
- To change date in impossible formats (for instance: 31/09/2012).
- To issue the fiscal receipt with a series of articles whose sum is greater than fixed max value per total of receipt (MAXSF).

Fiscal Memory Close to the Exhaustion (possible only from 2 to 5 closures to the exhaustion):

- In the daily fiscal closing report must appear the message "memory close to the point of exhaustion".
- In the last daily fiscal closing report must appear the message "memory exhausted".

With Exhausted Fiscal Memory:

- The command of issuing a fiscal receipt must not be executed.

After an Interruption of the Electricity:

- The fiscal receipt must be compliant to the legislation.
- Therefore, it must be report all information cited above.
- The last daily fiscal closing report must be compliant to the legislation.
- Therefore, it must report all information cited above.

If the Printing Device is Disconnected:

- Any issuing of fiscal documents by the cash register must be inhibited.
- Congruent warnings must be reported.

If the Indicating Device is Disconnected:

- Any issuing of fiscal documents by the cash register must be inhibited.
- Congruent warnings must be reported.

If the Fiscal Memory is Disconnected:

- Any issuing of fiscal documents by the cash register must be inhibited.
- Congruent warnings must be reported.

As mentioned above, these are only an extract of a broader collection of cash register software requirements that the legislation requests. They have been reported in order to underline the level of detail that the Italian legislation has identified in this matter.

The global collection constitutes a Requirements Repository that the SSEC keeps continuously updated and aligned to the continuous modifications in the legislation imposed by the designate authorities.

To each requirement collected in the requirements repository a set of specific test cases and responses is associated and executed during the test phase.

5 Cash Registers Certification Process

In this section, the fiscal software certification process is described. With the aim of making such a description clearer, a Business Process Model of the fiscal software certification process is provided as well.

The principal stakeholders involved in the fiscal software certification process are:

- The Cash Register Producer (from here in after called the "producer"). It develops the whole cash register including the fiscal software (the acquisition of fiscal software from a supplier, is allowed too). The producer is in charge of applying to the IRA to obtain the final approval. The cash register is expected to be completely developed and tested by the producer.
- The certification body. It is in charge of performing the certification of the cash register against the Italian fiscal legislation. Its activities consist of analysis of technical documentation, code inspection and fiscal software functional testing. The certification process described and discussed in this paper is related to the SSEC certification body.
- The Income Revenue Authority (IRA). It is in charge of releasing the final approval of the cash register. It can perform additional tests, mainly targeting special cases and exceptions.

In the following a representation of the Business Process Model of the cash registers certification is provided along with the description of the single tasks performed by the stakeholders involved in the cash register certification process.

5.1 The Certification Process Model

The fiscal software certification process can be divided into six steps:

- Cash Register Development. This step is performed by the Producer. The Producer, once the cash register development ends, shall provide the certification body with the fiscal software source code, and the technical documentation related to the cash register. Such a technical documentation shall include, at least, the system and software architectural design, the functional description of the fiscal software (e.g. state charts, control flow diagrams), the functional instructions for the user (e.g. the user manual of the cash register), and the maintenance procedures to be applied during the operational stage of the cash register.
- Documentation analysis and code inspection. This step is performed by the certification body possibly in co-operation with the producer. The information about the design, coding and functions implemented is gathered and analyzed by the

certification body with the aim of evaluating the structural and functional characteristics of the cash register, with particular focus on the fiscal part. Possible characteristics that may affect correctness and reliability of the cash register are pointed out.

- Test cases definition. The step is performed by the certification body. The knowledge acquired in step 2. Is used to define the set of test cases to be executed. Functions implemented and critical aspects of the technical solution adopted in the development of the cash register are taken into account to tailor, and possibly complete, a standard test suite prepared and maintained by the SSEC. Details on the test suite are provided in Sect. 5.2.
- Testing fiscal software. This step is performed by the certification body. Test cases are executed and results recorded. The test environment is the target cash register. The test cases aim at verifying the fiscal software requirements through the execution of cash register functionalities.
- Release of the certificate. In the case of all tests passed, documentation analysis passed and code inspection passed, the certification body releases a certificate of compliance of the cash register. The version of fiscal software used in testing is freezed and annexed to the certificate. In the case of test failure, the defect is identified, the producer is requested to fix the defects and a test is repeated according to a non regression testing strategy [18].
- Approval of the cash register. The IRA, taking into account the certificate of the certification body and, possibly, performing additional tests, issues a decree of approval of the cash register. Such a decree allows the cash register to be sold and used in the Italian market.

In Fig. 4 the process is represented by means of a business process representation [12].

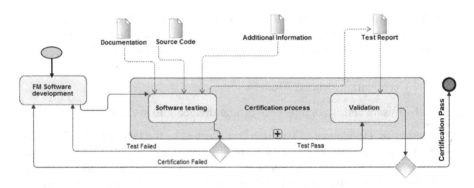

Fig. 4. Cash registers certification business process model.

5.2   The Fiscal Software Testing Suite

The test suite has been developed by the SSEC taking into account the required behavior of the cash register according to the law requirements and the possible abnormal conditions and malicious actions.

To increase the compliance in the completeness of the test suite, the traceability between fiscal law requirements and test cases is established. The test suite in divided into five parts.

Part 1. It addresses the set up phase and the behavior of the cash register in the pre-fiscal mode (i.e. the state of the cash register before the initialization of the fiscal me-mory). The transition from the pre-fiscal to the fiscal mode is also verified in Part 1.

Part 2. It addresses the nominal behavior of the cash register in fiscal mode. In this phase the correctness and security of the counters is verified, as well as the layout and contents of the fiscal documents produced.

Part 3. It addresses abnormal use of the cash register (i.e. possible anomalous and malicious use of the cash register).

Part 4. It addresses boundary conditions and recoverability i.e. the behavior of the cash register in case of exhausting resources (e.g. the fiscal memory exhaustion) or adverse events (e.g. power interruption).

Part 5. It addresses the behavior in the case of physical disconnections of cash register components (i.e. the DGFE or customer display).

6 Discussion

The paper reports an Italian experience of fiscal software certification inferring from the background knowledge collected over several decades of activity. In this long experience many exceptions with respect the normal process execution have been experienced. In the following, a not exhaustive list of some important challenges is discussed.

The first challenge concerns the legislation. Although it plays a central role in the certification process, often it is still too generic to cover all the possible exceptions and issues. Such a vagueness and incompleteness of the requirements determines misunderstandings, and may cause troubles in software development and errors in the final product. In order to reduce this risk, the SSEC tries to keep updated and aligned with the norms a proprietary Requirements Repository, that is the collection of cash register normative requirements, both from the hardware and software point of view, so to keep track of any possible non-compliance against the legislation. Besides, the SSEC collects and updates a set of practices provided by the designate authorities to avoid additional errors.

The second challenge concerns the documentation provided by the producers. The system and software architectural design, the functional description of the fiscal software, the functional instructions for the user (e.g. the user manual of the cash register), and the maintenance procedures to be applied are sometimes affected by incompleteness and ambiguity. As a consequence, the specification of software functionalities implemented, may not result complete and accurate enough to define appropriate software test cases. In these cases, the SSEC has to ask for important integrations to identify implemented software functionalities and set up a customized test plan.

The third challenge concerns the error handling discovered during the test plan execution. As in every testing activity, non-compliances or defects can be detected test sessions. In case of non-compliances, the cash register producers are requested to fix the source code. This task may have a rather high cost, in terms of time and effort, spent by both the certification body and the producer. Moreover the execution of regression testing aimed at verifying that the fixing did not determine side effects invalidating the already tested functionalities, is necessary. For these problems, the SSEC has adopted the *compartmentation of the source*, i.e. wherever possible, by the analysis of the available documentations as well as code inspection, source code is sliced into separate components so that only the test cases related to a specific part are selected and re-executed. However, this approach for test case selection and prioritization cannot be easily adopted because most of times the source code is implemented as firmware or middleware. Therefore, strengthening the actions in the previous directions (updating of the legislation and integration of the missing documentation) can further limit new problems during the testing session.

This list of challenges is partial but it can offer food for thought for the issues regarding the fiscal software certification.

7 Conclusions

In the paper the current scenario of cash register certification in Italy has been presented. After having considered the main concepts of the software certification, its actors and its requirements, the cash register, as object to be certified, has been introduced and some its software requirements have been presented. Subsequently, a Certification Process Model for the cash registers software and the Fiscal software Testing Suite have been shown. Finally a discussion about the most current challenges on this specific kind of software certification closes the paper. Although this is the current process required by the legislation before a cash register can be put into market, the same legislation is strengthening the transactions traceability as strategy to improve the effectiveness of the fight against tax evasion. From this point of view, the abolition of the fiscal receipt and the adoption of tools for the electronic invoice and the telematic transmission of the incomes are considered an effective solution. These changes require technological advancement and normative adjustments for the stakeholders involved in the certification process. The developers must adapt the fiscal software of their cash registers to the new normative issues, and the certification bodies must reorganize their certification process for the legislation compliance check. So new challenges are glimpsed in the cash registers software future [19].

References

1. L. 26 Gennaio 1983, n. 18. (Italian legislation, in Italian)
2. D.M. 03/23, Decreto Ministeriale 23 Marzo 1983 (1983). (Italian legislation, in Italian)
3. D.M. 03/23 all. A, Decreto Ministeriale 23 Marzo 1983, allegato A. (1983) (Italian legislation, in Italian)
4. D.M. 19/06, Decreto Ministeriale 19 Giugno 1984 (1984). (Italian legislation, in Italian)
5. D.M. 14/01, Decreto Ministeriale 14 Gennaio 1985 (1985). (Italian legislation, in Italian)

6. D.L. 326, Decreto Legge 4 Agosto 1987, n. 326 (1987). (Italian legislation, in Italian)
7. D.M. 4/04, Decreto Ministeriale 4 Aprile 1990 (1990). (Italian legislation, in Italian)
8. D.M. 30/03, Decreto Ministeriale 30 Marzo 1992 (1992). (Italian legislation, in Italian)
9. D.M. 04/03, Decreto Ministeriale 04 Marzo 2002 (2002). (Italian legislation, in Italian)
10. P.M. 28/07, Provvedimento Ministeriale 28 Luglio 2003 (2003). (Italian legislation, in Italian)
11. P.M. 16/05, Provvedimento Ministeriale 16 maggio 2005 (2005). (Italian legislation, in Italian)
12. vom Brocke, J., Rosemann, M.: Handbook on Business Process Management 1: Introduction, Methods and Information Systems. Springer, Germany (2014)
13. ISO/IEC Guide 2, Standardization and related activities – General vocabulary (1996)
14. ISO/IEC DIS 17000, Conformity assessment - Vocabulary and general principles (2004)
15. D.P.R. 633, Decreto del Presidente della Repubblica 26 Ottobre 1972, n. 633 (1972). (Italian legislation, in Italian)
16. ISO/IEC FDIS 25010, Systems and software engineering -(SQuaRE)- System and software quality models (2011)
17. P.M. 31/05, Provvedimento Ministeriale 31 Maggio 2002 (2002). (Italian legislation, in Italian)
18. Pezzè, M., Young, M.: Software Testing and Analysis: Process, Principles, and Techniques. Wiley (2008)
19. Prokin, M., Prokin, D.: GPRS terminals for reading fiscal registers. In: 2013 2nd Mediterranean Conference on Embedded Computing (MECO), pp. 259–262. IEEE (2013)

Methodologies, Processes and Platforms

Meta-Tool for Model-Driven Verification of Constraints Satisfaction

César Cuevas Cuesta[(✉)], Patricia López Martínez, and José M. Drake

Group of Software Engineering and Real-Time,
University of Cantabria, Santander, Spain
{cuevasce, lopezpa, drakej}@unican.es

Abstract. The work presented in this paper addresses the general problem of verifying if models structurally compliant to a given meta-model also satisfy the constraints specified on it, whether integrity or tool-specific ones. For accomplishing such constraints satisfaction verification, a completely model-driven strategy is proposed, whose core idea is to perform the checking by applying an M2M transformation to the model to verify, hence yielding a model which represents the verification result. This output model encapsulates every detected constraint violation, allowing their later manifestation, automatic fixing or any other kind of processing. Besides providing a meta-model for formalizing those diagnostic models gathering constraint violations, the presented methodology enables the systematic and straightforward development of verification tools, each one targeting a given couple of domain meta-model and constraints set. Therefore, it supports the actual objective of this work: A strategy for the development of a generic tool for the verification, suitable for any constraints set or meta-model. The functional foundation for designing such a generic tool is that it will be based on a generator (meta-tool) for the on-the-fly creation of the required specific tool (M2M checking transformation), thanks to the Higher Order Transformation (HOT) technique.

Keywords: MDSE · Meta-model · Constraints · Model transformation · HOT · Verification

1 Introduction

When a domain formalization does not only consist of a meta-model but also of a set of integrity constraints specified for it due to the existence of laxities within its formulation (which happens in most cases), model conformity encompasses the basic compliance to the meta-model structure as well as the satisfaction of every specified constraint. This work focuses on this second aspect, proposing a full-fledged model-driven strategy for verifying constraints satisfaction. This is a very important topic since, in addition to integrity constraints, it is quite common that model processing tools define additional specific constraints for proper actuation.

The core idea of the proposed strategy for constraints satisfaction verification is to perform it by applying an M2M transformation to the model to verify. Hence, the verification result is a new model, idea that is in complete agreement with the

S. Hammoudi et al. (Eds): MODELSWARD 2016, CCIS 692, pp. 171–193, 2017.
DOI: 10.1007/978-3-319-66302-9_9

MDSE principle [1, 2]. This output model does not only record which constraints have been violated but also encapsulates the data needed for describing those violations detected in the checked model. Since a meta-model is required in order to formalize the structure of such diagnostic models describing constraint violations, the methodology provides a preliminary and extensible one. Despite the extensibility feature, its initial design aims to achieve a high level of generality.

The approach is basically dependent on the couple domain meta-model + constraints at hand, since a different M2M checking transformation must be developed for each couple. Although at first glance it may contradict the benefits claimed by the MDSE, especially the productivity-related ones, indeed the presented methodology enables the systematic development of specific verification tools, being able in turn to support the actual objective of this work: To design a strategy for the development of a generic tool for constraints satisfaction verification, suitable for any constraints set or even for any meta-model. The functional foundation for designing such a generic tool is that it will be based on a generator for the on-the-fly creation of the required specific tool (M2M checking transformation).

Figure 1 shows an overview of the proposed strategy, which provides three assets that are applicable in any application domain:

- The **ConstraintViolationDescription (CVD)** meta-model. It is meant to formalize the structure of the models obtained as result of the verification.
- The **ConstraintCharacterization (CC)** meta-model. The domain expert shown in Fig. 1. is responsible for formulating the domain meta-model as well as the constraints. In our strategy, his responsibility goes one step forward and he must characterize every constraint, decorating their formulation with description data, in particular including the way in which their violations must be described, i.e. defining a mapping between them and a suitable CVD class. This CC meta-model is meant to support that collective characterization in model form.
- The **tool generator** that produces every specific verification tool. When the final user attempts to check a model, the automatically generated tool is used.

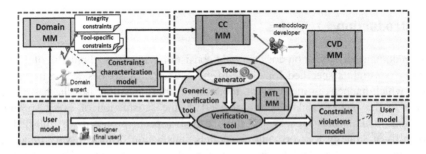

Fig. 1. Strategy overview.

This strategy is part of a more general work [3] about the design of generic MDSE tools (able to operate on models compliant to different meta-models) for alleviating the problems that meta-model evolution may induce in MDSE-based development environments. The background motivation is contributing to foster the adoption of MDSE as basis of domain-specific development environments by the domain experts who push forward the methodologies in their corresponding domains by designing new strategies, tools and environments. Although this wider context is largely out of the scope of this paper, it is worth to mention that the work here is a proof of concept of a technique for designing generic MDSE tools that receive instruction information for each meta-model to be supported. Such information actually instructs the tool in how to adapt itself for spanning its coverage to a new meta-model, thus being able to process models compliant to it. In this *instruction* technique, the information is formulated in model form and such models are formalized by means of an *instruction meta-model* specific for each tool. In the presented scenario, the CC meta-model plays that role.

The rest of the paper is organized as follows. Section 1 introduces and justifies the very frequent use of lax meta-models and specification of constraints while Sect. 2 describes the proposed approach for the systematic development of verification tools, ranging from the model-based representation of a verification result to the meta-model supporting these output models describing constraint violations. This section also explains the way in which an M2M strategy can support the approach. Section 3 exposes the final goal of the work: a strategy for the development of a generic tool for model verification. Section 4 addresses the implementation aspects using the ATLAS Transformation Language (ATL). Section 5 presents an application example on top of the MAST-2 meta-model. Finally, Sect. 6 is devoted to related work that can be found in the MDSE literature and Sect. 7 ends giving some conclusions and future work lines.

2 Lax Meta-Models and Constraints Definition

The formulation of meta-models describing every semantic detail of the corresponding target conceptual domain is an ideal situation where every instance model would correspond to a valid scenario within the domain. However, this is very difficult if not impossible to achieve, except for very simple cases. Hence, meta-models are usually formulated by only reflecting the big picture of the modelled domain, without covering every detail, which inevitably leads to the existence of laxities in them. Under this circumstance, there can be models that, although compliant to such lax-formulated meta-models, represent non-valid scenarios regarding the domain semantics.

As a trivial example, let's consider a meta-model containing a Person class which defines an integer age attribute. It is a clear laxity, because, although common sense dictates that only positive values should be assigned to that attribute in the instance models, nothing in the meta-model formulation establishes it and hence incoherent models could be formulated (people of age < 0) but still compliant to the meta-model.

In order to tackle this problem, integrity constraints should be specified for any lax meta-model, typically one constraint per laxity. When this specification is accomplished, the domain formalization is composed of the meta-model but also of the set of integrity constraints specified for it and, in addition to the basic structural compliance to the meta-model, model conformity also encompasses the satisfaction of every constraint. Hence, the existence of valid models representing invalid scenarios is avoided.

For enhancing the lax formulation of a domain meta-model by means of the specification of integrity constraints as well as for formulating tool-specific constraints, the standard language is OCL. Although OCL distinguishes several types of constraints (invariants, pre- and post-conditions, derivation rules, etc.), only invariants are considered in this work. Thus, in this paper *invariant* and *constraint* will be used indistinctly.

Since the problem of lax formulations is conveniently addressed by the use of integrity constraints, it is quite common to find meta-models formulated with an even greater degree of laxity than the one strictly due to the practical impossibility of a comprehensive description of the domain. There are several reasons for it, as for example:

- **Preserving as Simple as Possible the Meta-model Structure**, in order to ease future extensions and maintenance. If a meta-model is designed to cover the target domain semantics very deeply, a very complex internal structure would be required, featured by a large number of primitive types instead of the usual ones (int, real, boolean, char, string, etc.), as well as a very deep hierarchy of class inheritance, aiming at specializing at maximum the possible associations and their multiplicities.
- **Using a Single Meta-model** for supporting models that participate in different processes where different tools are applied on them. Because of their implementation maturity or their particular scope, it is very common that each tool enforces specific conditions or well-formedness rules on the models. In such context, it may be better to use a single and quite lax meta-model according to the core nature of the described system instead of defining a specialized meta-model for each tool. The tools can instead formalize their particular preconditions as sets of constraints analogous to the integrity ones but now called additional or tool-specific constraints.

As an example, Fig. 2 shows an overview of the MAST environment for analysis and design of real-time systems, in which the verification methods proposed in this work have been applied.

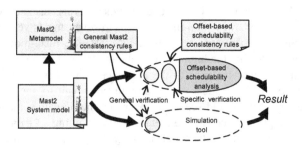

Fig. 2. The MAST-2 environment.

The environment is based on a meta-model, called MAST-2 [4], used to formalize models describing the timing behaviour of systems with real-time requirements to fulfil. The design of the meta-model tried to maintain a balance between faithfully describing the target domain without yielding an overwhelming internal structure.

Currently, the meta-model contains 143 classes and is lax-formulated. However, a set of OCL-formulated integrity constraints ensures that the models used to describe the timing behaviour of the targeted real-time systems correspond to valid scenarios. Section 5 will present a sample of those laxities/constraints.

In addition, the MAST environment is equipped with several real-time analysis and design tools that operate on the models compliant to the MAST-2 meta-model. Some of these tools, like the Simulator shown in Fig. 2, work on models that are simply required to be fully compliant to MAST-2 (including constraints satisfaction). Other tools, like the Offset-Based Schedulability Analysis Tool, can only work on models that satisfy certain additional constraints. Under a strategy of strict meta-modelling, the environment would have to manage tens of meta-models (very similar ones, but different), one for each available analysis tool, as well as the corresponding transformations between them. In contrast, using a lax meta-model only requires to specify an appropriate list of constraints for each environment tool.

3 M2M-Based Constraints Satisfaction Verification

3.1 Verification Result in Model Form

The result of verifying constraints satisfaction in a model can adopt several different forms. As depicted in Fig. 3, this work adopts the approach of representing it as another model whose elements correspond to constraint violations occurred in the verified model. This output model constitutes the base for a possible manifestation of those violations, allowing its management by tools in an MDSE environment. The provided information regarding the detected violations can be as rich as set in a hypothetical meta-model that the output model must conform to.

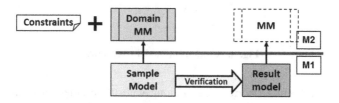

Fig. 3. Model representation of verification result.

The next subsection presents a meta-model for these models, output of the verification process. It defines the data required for describing, at higher or lower level of detail, the detected violations and it aims to cover the entire spectrum of constraints violations that may appear in MDSE models.

3.2 The CVD Meta-Model

The CVD (Constraint Violation Description) meta-model constitutes an initial proposal of meta-model for formalizing diagnostic models, i.e. those ones formulating the result of verifying if other models satisfy the constraints specified on their corresponding domain meta-model.

The meta-model presents a conventional structure, with a main container class (CVD_Model) and a class hierarchy oriented to model the data needed for the description of constraint violations, the more depth in the hierarchy, the more detail. This hierarchy has a root class (CVD) from which the rest of meta-model classes inherit. Figure 4 shows both the CVD_Model and CVD classes along with the top subclasses of the latter, which are briefly exposed below. Thus, a model compliant to CVD has a single CVD_Model instance, which contains through its descriptions association the rest of model elements, instances of CVD or of any of its subclasses.

- **CVD**: This class models violations generically, since it only has attributes for the constraint identifier along with an optional textual description and the severity assigned to the risen problem. It also references the model element where the violation is

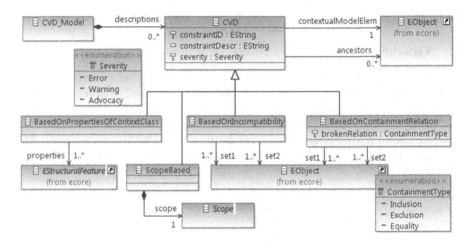

Fig. 4. CVD meta-model overview.

located (contextualModelElem) along with those other ones (ancestors) that constitute the path from it towards the model main container. Actually, this class is enough for formulating as a model the set of violations detected in another model, since the described information is suitable for any kind of constraint, regardless its nature, semantics or formulation.

- **BasedOnIncompatibility**: This class extends CVD by defining the set1 and set2 references, aimed at holding two sets of model elements that can be reached from the contextual model element through association chains. Hence, it is suitable for describing violations of constraints consisting in setting incompatibilities between subclasses of two classes (typically abstract) that are connected to the context class through association chains. The use of this class will be illustrated in Sect. 5.

- **BasedOnContainmentRelation**: This class extends CVD by defining the brokenRelation attribute, meant to specify a type of containment relationship (according to the ContainmentType enum), as well as the set1 and set2 references, aimed at holding two sets of *equally typed* model elements, which can be reached from the contextual model element through association chains. Hence, it is suitable for describing violations of constraints consisting in setting a containment relationship between the populations corresponding to the endpoints of two association chains starting from the context class. The use of this class will be illustrated in Sect. 5.

- **ScopeBased**: This class extends CVD by defining the scope containment reference, aimed at holding a scope definition, i.e. a population of model elements. Hence, it is suitable for describing violations of constraints whose satisfaction depends not only on the state of a model element but also on its siblings within the scope in which the first one is immersed.

- **BasedOnPropertiesOfContextClass**: This class extends CVD by defining the properties reference, aimed at holding properties of the context class. Thus, it is suitable for describing violations of constraints specified on properties of the context class.

In order to depict the class hierarchy more in depth, Fig. 5 shows the subclasses of BasedOnPropertiesOfContextClass, which are briefly exposed below. The CVD meta-model provides options for modelling violations of constraints consisting in reducing a property multiplicity, restricting the validity range for an attribute value or the valid types for a reference; or related to impose rules about the coexistence of optional properties or the order that the values of numeric attributes must hold.

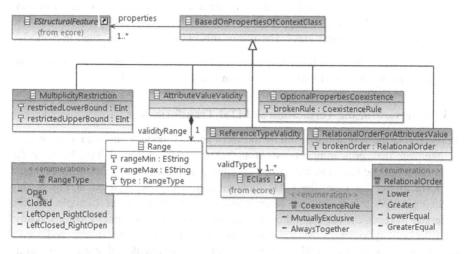

Fig. 5. BasedOnPropertiesOfContextClass subclasses.

- **MultiplicityRestriction**: This class extends BasedOnPropertiesOfContextClass by defining the integer restrictedLowerBound
  and restrictedUpperBound attributes, meant to specify the new multiplicity
  limits for the context class property pointed through the properties reference.
  Hence, it is suitable for describing violations of constraints reducing the multiplicity
  of a context class property.
- **AttributeValueValidity**: This class extends BasedOnPropertiesOf
  ContextClass by defining the validityRange containment reference, aimed
  at holding a Range instance describing a validity interval for the values of the
  context class attribute pointed through the properties reference. Hence, it is
  suitable for describing violations of constraints consisting in narrowing the range of
  values for a context class attribute. The use of this class will be illustrated in Sect. 5.
- **ReferenceTypeValidity**: This class extends BasedOnPropertiesOfContextClass by defining the validTypes reference, aimed at
  holding subclasses of the type of the context class reference pointed through the
  properties reference. Hence, it is suitable for describing violations of constraints consisting in selecting the valid subtypes for a context class reference.
- **OptionalPropertiesCoexistence**: This class extends BasedOnPropertiesOfContextClass by defining the brokenRule attribute, meant to
  specify a coexistence rule (according to the CoexistenceRule enum) that has
  not been respected. Hence, it is suitable for describing violations of constraints
  consisting in constraining the definition state of a set of optional properties of the
  context class.
- **RelationaOrderForAttributesValue**: This class extends BasedOn
  PropertiesOfContextClass by defining the brokenOrder attribute,
  meant to specify a relational order (according to the RelationalOrder enum)
  that has not been respected. Hence, it is suitable for describing violations of constraints consisting in enforcing a relational order for the values of a set of numeric
  attributes of the context class. The use of this class will be illustrated in Sect. 5.

Due to space reasons, the CVD meta-model is not presented in its entirety. Its
complete specification and Ecore formulation can be found in [5].

3.3   Overview of the Verification as M2M Transformation

Representing the verification result by means of another model leads in a natural way to
contemplate the verification process as an M2M transformation, defined between the
meta-model of the model to be verified and the meta-model that the result model must
conform to (in this case, the CVD meta-model). Thus, as depicted in Fig. 6, this
checking M2M transformation, when applied on a given model (Sample model),
generates as result the corresponding model describing the constraint violations, if any.

Like in any other M2M transformation, visibility over the source and target
meta-models (DomainMM and CVD, respectively) is required (dotted arrows). However,
in this M2M strategy, the source meta-model is constraints-naked, i.e. it is not required
neither including nor attaching the constraints to it. It is enough that the developer knows
them in order to incorporate their verification to the checking transformation.

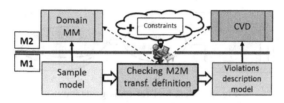

Fig. 6. Checking M2M transformation in action.

3.4 Extension of the Approach

So far, using an M2M-based strategy, a verification methodology has been designed. This solution solves the addressed conformity verification problem but without sidestepping the fact that the strategy implies the development of a different verification tool (implementation of a different checking transformation) for every pair domain meta-model + set of constraints. Figure 7 (left side) shows this drawback.

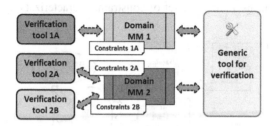

Fig. 7. Specific verification tools vs. generic tool.

Therefore, once that methodology for the systematic (but manual) development of specific tools for model verification has been set, it seems logic to envision a step forward, a generic tool that could be applied for the verification of models regardless their meta-models and corresponding constraints, as shown in Fig. 7 (right side). Thus, the design of a strategy that enables the development of such a generic tool for verification has been accomplished. It is based on code generation, as explained in the next section.

4 Generic Tool for Verification

4.1 Foundation: Meta-Tool for Automating Tools Generation

Trying to abstract the infinite number of domain meta-models that the Domain-Specific Language (DSL) approach promotes, does not seem a suitable option for creating a generic tool for verification. Hence, our solution has been the development of a meta-tool for the on-the-fly construction of the specific tool corresponding to each case. Such a strategy (Fig. 8) leads to the area of code generation, in this case the code of a checking M2M transformation.

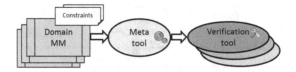

Fig. 8. Meta-tool for tools generation.

To perform this task, the meta-tool receives as input the constraints along with the mapping between each constraint and a CVD class, i.e. the way selected to model the violation of each constraint. More specifically, it is not only required information about what type of violation description is assigned to a constraint, but also information relative to which domain meta-model elements (typically attributes, associations or association chains) are assigned to the properties of the CVD instance. This whole information related to a constraint (its own data – name, OCL expression and context class – as well as mapping data) constitutes the *constraint characterization*.

Thus, as shown in Fig. 9, our meta-tool for the generation of *ad hoc* tools accepts as input the models encapsulating the set of constraint characterizations.

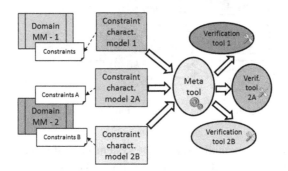

Fig. 9. Input models for the meta-tool.

In order to formalize the structure of these characterization models, a meta-model has been designed. It is called the ConstraintsCharacterization (CC) meta-model and its role in the developed scenario is shown in Fig. 10.

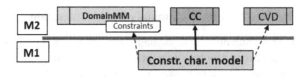

Fig. 10. CC meta-model role.

The CC meta-model is exposed in the next subsection. Later, in Subsect. 4.3, the design and operational mode of the created meta-tool is analysed. Since its purpose is the on-the-fly generation of every specific tool for verification, the field of generation of M2M transformations is naturally reached.

The elegance of the model-driven paradigm allows the reutilization of the same transformation-based infrastructure. This technique is known as Higher Order Transformation (HOT) [6], i.e. a transformation that operates on transformations – in this work, a transformation that generates a transformation –. To achieve this objective, the concept of M2M transformation needs to be extended with that of transformation model, so that an M2M transformation is represented by a model compliant to the meta-model of the used model transformation language (MTL).

4.2   The CC Meta-Model

The CC meta-model formalizes the models through which the constraints specified on a domain meta-model are characterized, in order to feed the meta-tool. This meta-model presents a structure closely aligned to the one of the CVD meta-model, even maintaining name parity between counterpart classes wherever possible. As CVD, it has a main container class (CC_Model) and a hierarchy root class (CC) from which the rest of the meta-model classes inherit. A model compliant to CC has a single CC_Model instance, which contains through its constraintCharacterizations association the rest of model elements, instances of CC or of any of its subclasses. This main container instance also references the domain meta-model (an EPackage instance in Ecore).

Figure 11 shows the meta-model main container and root classes along with the top-subclasses of the latter. Briefly said, each of them is appropriate to characterize constraints whose violations will be described by the corresponding CVD

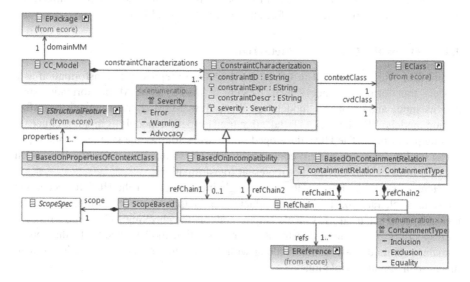

Fig. 11. CC meta-model overview.

counterpart class. The mapping could also be established to a superclass of the counterpart one, although this option will lead to a loss of description information available in the characterization. However, what is prohibited is to establish a mapping to a subclass of the CVD counterpart. In this case, a problem about inexistent required information would arise when trying to encode the generation of a violation description instance during the automatic creation of the checking M2M transformation.

In order to depict the class hierarchy more in depth, Fig. 12 shows the subclasses of BasedOnPropertiesOfContextClass. The meta-model offers options for characterizing constraints whose violations will be described by instances of the CVD counterpart classes, hence showing the alignment between both meta-models.

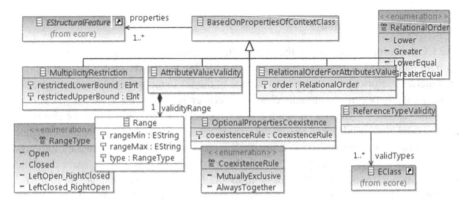

Fig. 12. BasedOnPropertiesOfContextClass subclasses.

Due to space reasons, the CC meta-model is not presented in its entirety. Its complete specification and Ecore formulation can be found in [5].

4.3   HOT as the Core of the Meta-Tool

In an M2M working context in which it is possible to represent a transformation as a model – transformation model–, a HOT can be defined as an M2M transformation such that its input and/or output models are themselves M2M transformations (transformation models) [7]. Hence, HOTs take 0..n transformation models as input, produce 0..n as output or both. The HOT developed in this work follows the synthesis pattern [6]. It can be defined as the pattern corresponding to HOTs that generate a transformation (model) from models that do not represent transformations.

Here, as shown in Fig. 13, there is a single input model for the HOT to accept, the constraints characterization one, producing as output a model compliant to the meta-model of the used MTL. This output model is the checking M2M transformation corresponding to the input constraints characterization model, specific to the couple domain meta-model + constraints along with the mapping decisions regarding how to model their possible violations.

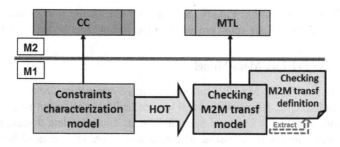

Fig. 13. HOT generates checking M2M transformation.

The final step is the serialization (extraction) of the produced model in order to obtain the checking M2M transformation encoded in the MTL textual concrete syntax.

4.4 ATL Implementation

The widespread ATL is the MTL chosen in this work for implementing M2M transformations: the HOT and consequently every generated M2M checking transformation. ATL is the *de facto* standard for M2M purposes, belonging to the AMMA platform [8], a complete modelling infrastructure very well integrated with Eclipse/EMF. ATL is very suitable for developing HOTs because, although not all M2M transformation frameworks provide a meta-model formalizing the abstract syntax of the transformation language, AMMA/ATL indeed does. Another interesting feature is that the serialization of an ATL model to its textual representation is also very well supported through the AMMA technical projectors.

The ATL code for the HOT at the heart of the presented methodology as well as the ATL code of a sample M2M checking transformation (the one corresponding to the MAST-2 meta-model and its integrity constraints) can be found at [5]. For the generated M2M checking transformations, an implementation style based on helpers and on called rules has been selected. One of the main advantages of this choice is that the resultant ATL code has a very regular structure, following a uniform pattern easy to automate. This structure is also properly documented at [5].

5   Use Case Example

In order to illustrate the presented methodology, let's consider an example based on the MAST-2 meta-model. The following Subsect. 5.1 reflects the lax nature of its formulation by exposing a selection of four laxities along with the corresponding integrity constraints. Subsection 5.2 addresses the CC model characterizing the MAST-2 integrity constraints, model from which the M2M checking transformation specific for them is generated. In particular, it is shown the model portion corresponding to the four constraints selected in Sect. 5.1. Subsection 5.3 introduces a very tiny MAST-2 model which violates every considered constraint and Subsect. 5.4 focuses on the use of

Eclipse OCL for verification. Finally, Subsect. 5.5 shows the CVD model produced when applying the checking transformation to the sample incoherent model.

5.1   The MAST-2 Lax Meta-Model

As exposed in Sect. 2, the MAST-2 meta-model has a non-trivial size (143 classes) and it is lax-formulated, i.e. it presents several tens of laxities of different nature. Hence, a set of integrity constraints has been specified for it. The complete documentation for these laxities/constraints is accessible at [9]. Below, there is a reduced but representative sample of such laxities, along with the corresponding preventing constraints.

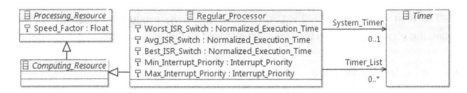

Fig. 14. The Regular_Processor class.

As shown in Fig. 14, the Regular_Processor class defines two integer-like attributes for describing the managed interrupt priorities, namely Max_Interrupt_Priority and Min_Interrupt_Priority. A laxity is located here because any compliant model could present the incoherency of a minimum value greater than the maximum (an analogous discussion arises when considering the three ISR_Switch attributes). Thus, an integrity constraint (*i_2_2_a*) has been specified. Its OCL formulation is trivial:

```
context Regular_Processor inv i_2_2_a:
    Max_Interrupt_Priority >= Min_Interrupt_Priority
```

Figure 14 also shows that the Regular_Processor class inherits the Speed_Factor attribute from the Processing_Resource abstract superclass. This attribute represents the processing capacity of the processor regarding a reference processor and, obviously, it cannot take a non-positive value. So another laxity is located here because, since the attribute is typed as float, any compliant model could have the incoherency of presenting a non-positive value for it. Thus, an integrity constraint (*i_1_1_a*) has been specified. Its OCL formulation is also trivial:

```
context Processing_Resource inv i_1_1_a:
    Speed_Factor > 0.0
```

Finally, Fig. 14 also shows that the Regular_Processor class defines two references of Timer type, namely Timer_List and System_Timer. The first one represents the set of timing objects associated to a processor, if any, while the second one specifies the main one among them. Hence, a laxity is located here because any MAST-2 model could present the incoherency of having processors specifying a system timer among those ones in the model not included in the timers list. Thus, an integrity constraint (*i_4_1_a*) has been specified. Its OCL formulation is also pretty straightforward:

```
context Regular_Processor inv i_4_1_a:
  if not System_Timer.oclIsUndefined() then
    Timer_List -> includes(System_Timer)
  else
    true
  endif
```

Next, Fig. 15 shows that both the Scheduler and Schedulable_Resource classes have their Policy and Scheduling_Parameters references defined in terms of the abstract classes Scheduling_Policy and Scheduling_Parameters, allowing the assignment of objects of respectively any concrete type of policy or parameters. However, a laxity emerges regarding the association between a scheduler and a schedulable resource because the corresponding policy and scheduling parameters objects may be incompatible (the compatibilities are shown by dotted red lines in Fig. 15) in a compliant model.

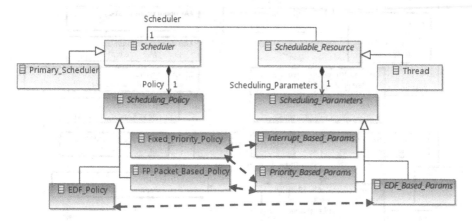

Fig. 15. Compatibility between policy and parameters. (Color figure online)

Consequently, a constraint (*i_4_4_a*) has been defined, setting the appropriate correspondences. Its OCL code appears below:

```
context Schedulable_Resource inv i_4_4_a:
  self.Scheduling_Parameters.oclIsKindOf(Priority_Based_Params)
  and
  self.Scheduler.Policy.oclIsTypeOf(Fixed_Priority_Policy)or
  self.Scheduling_Parameters.oclIsKindOf(Priority_Based_Params)
  and
  self.Scheduler.Policy.oclIsTypeOf(FP_Packet_Based_Policy)or
  self.Scheduling_Parameters.oclIsKinOf(Interrupt_Based_Params)
  and
  self.Scheduler.Policy.oclIsTypeOf(Fixed_Priority_Policy)or
  self.Scheduling_Parameters.oclIsKindOf(EDF_Based_Params)
  and
  self.Scheduler.Policy.oclIsTypeOf(EDF_Policy)
```

5.2   CC Model

For generating the checking M2M transformation applicable to MAST-2 models, it is necessary to feed the meta-tool with a CC model that encapsulates the characterization of the MAST-2 integrity constraints. Figure 16 shows that model portion corresponding to the four sample constraints considered above.

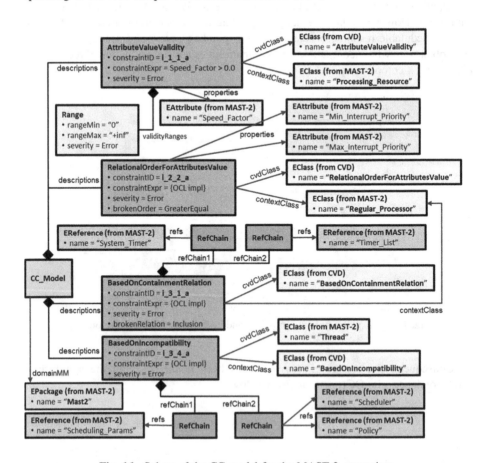

Fig. 16. Subset of the CC model for the MAST-2 constraints.

- The *i_2_2_a* constraint is characterized through an instance of `CC::RelationalOrderForAttributesValue`, referencing its context class as well as the CVD class selected for describing any possible violation and formulating the severity to be associated. It also defines the specific information required by the concrete characterization class, which in this case applies for the attributes involved in the constraint and the relational order to be respected.

Analogously:

- The *i_1_1_a* constraint is characterized through an instance of `CC::AttributeValueValidity`.
- The *i_4_1_a* constraint is characterized through an instance of `CC::BasedOnContainmentRelation`.
- The *i_4_4_a* constraint is characterized through an instance of `CC::BasedOnIncompatibility`, which in addition to the severity, and context and CVD classes, specifies association chains indicating how to reach the potentially incompatible model elements from the contextual one.

It is worth remarking that, although the CC model could seem a bit complex, it needs to be formulated only once, just like the domain meta-model itself, to generate the corresponding M2M checking transformation, which will be later used multiple times with any instance model.

5.3   MAST-2 Sample Model

A MAST-2 sample model for illustration purposes is partially shown in Fig. 17. It represents a system consisting of a mono-processor platform with fixed-priority scheduling policy. The platform is modelled by the processor *Proc1* with its hosted scheduler (*Proc1_Sched*) along with its scheduling policy object. The platform sub-model also encompasses the timers associated to the processor. A schedulable resource (*Thread1*), which is part of the reactive section of the model (not depicted), along with its scheduling parameters object, and scheduled by the only existing scheduler,

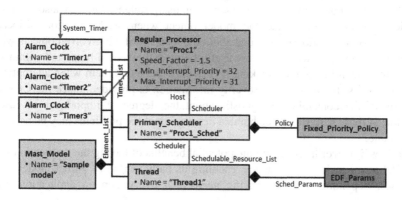

Fig. 17. A sample incoherent MAST-2 model (partially shown).

completes this partial model visualization. As can be seen at a glance, the model violates the four constraints presented above.

5.4   Validation with Eclipse OCL

The presented methodology has been implemented by means of the Eclipse/EMF [10] modelling platform and its ATL component. Atop EMF resides another component, Eclipse OCL, an implementation of the OMG OCL 2.3 specification for definition of constraints in OCL and verification of models using conventional EMF tooling. Therefore, it seems logical to briefly elaborate on its application, outlining some shortcomings it may present and for which our approach can provide better capabilities. This discussion is presented here, in the context of this use case example.

The default functionality provided by Eclipse OCL is completely trustworthy for the detection of constraint violations, presenting in an error dialog box the corresponding diagnostic report. However, it presents limitations. For instance, Fig. 18 shows the standard diagnostic report corresponding to the previous MAST-2 sample model.

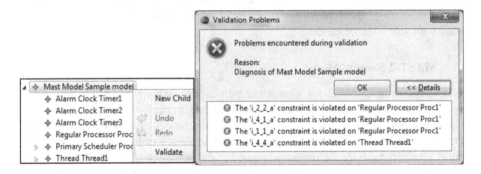

Fig. 18. Eclipse OCL verification report.

As it can be observed, the report only details the name of the violated invariants (which could roughly indicate the essence of the problems but can also be totally cryptic, as happens here) and the model object where each violation is located. Moreover, no information is provided about the location of the involved objects within the model, although it would be very useful because they could be nested within very deep containment hierarchies, making it very difficult to find them when attempting to solve the errors. In addition, no severity information is provided, since the OCL formulation of the constraints is agnostic about the degree of importance in case of violation. A more verbose and elaborated description of the problems may be necessary or desirable.

Besides, it is worth remarking the potential benefits of having the verification result in model form, such as for instance, enabling its participation in further model-driven processes, depending on the specific needs that every domain application might present.

5.5   CVD Model

When applying the checking M2M transformation for MAST-2 (obtained from the CC model partially presented in Subsect. 5.2) to the MAST-2 sample model in Subsect. 5.3, the CVD model shown in Fig. 19 is produced as result. As it can be observed, each constraint violation has produced a corresponding description object:

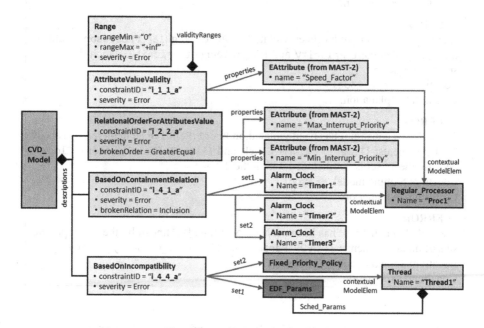

Fig. 19. Resultant CVD model.

- For the interrupt priorities incoherency, i.e. the violation of the $i\_2\_2\_a$ constraint, an instance of CVD::RelationalOrderForAttributesValue is generated. As expected, it formulates the ID of the violated constraint, the severity assigned to the risen problem and the contextual model element where the violation is located, as well as the properties involved in the constraint (the attributes Max_Interrupt_Priority and Min_Interrupt_Priority) and the relational order that has been broken (max $\geq$ min).

  Analogously:

- For the speed factor incoherency, i.e. the violation of the $i\_1\_1\_a$ constraint, an instance of CVD::AttributeValueValidity is generated.
- For the timers incoherency, i.e. the violation of the $i\_4\_1\_a$ constraint, an instance of CVD::BasedOnContainmentRelation generated.
- For the violation of the $i\_4\_4\_a$ constraint, an instance of CVD::BasedOn Incompatibility is generated. It points out the two incompatible model

Table 1. Possible diagnostic report.

− ERROR: The *i_1_1_a* constraint has been violated on `Proc1:Regular_Processor` by attribute `Speed_Factor`. Its value -1.5 is not within the valid range (0, +inf). Location: `Sample model >> Proc1` Constraint explanation: …
− ERROR: The *i_2_2_a* constraint has been violated on `Proc1:Regular_Processor` by attributes `Max_Interrupt_Priority` and `Min_Interrupt_Priority`, which do not respect the order >=. Location: `Sample model >> Proc1` Constraint explanation: …
− ERROR: The *i_4_1_a* constraint has been violated on `Proc1:Regular_Processor` by sets of model elements: {`Timer1`} : `Alarm_Clock` and {`Timer2, Timer3`} : `Alarm_Clock` because the 1st set is not included within the 2nd one. Location: Sample model >> Proc1 Constraint explanation: …
− ERROR: The *i_4_4_a* constraint has been violated on `Thread1:Thread` by the incompatible sets of model elements: {} : `EDF_Params` and {} : `Fixed_Priority_Policy` Location: `Sample model >> Thread1` Constraint explanation: …

elements, in this case the `EDF_Params` and `Fixed_Priority_Policy` instances.

In contrast to the Eclipse OCL report of Fig. 18, Table 1 shows a possible comprehensive report that could be presented to the modeller from the information encapsulated in the prior CVD model.

6   Related Work

Addressing constraints satisfaction verification through an M2M transformation approach is not new. To the best of our knowledge, it has already been outlined in [11] and applied in later works, like [12, 13].

In Bézivin's seminal work [11], applying an M2M transformation on the model to verify yields as result a so called diagnostic model, compliant to a proposed meta-model, called *Problems*. It is an extremely simple meta-model, with a single class that defines three attributes, namely `severity`, `location` and `description`. Moreover, the authors simply outline a pattern for implementing manually the transformation corresponding to each case. Our work extends that core idea developing a much more ambitious strategy built on top of a more complete target meta-model (CVD).

In Diguet's work [12], in the context of a MARTE [14] to AADL [15] process, the author proposes a diagnosis meta-model called VERIF and uses ATL for implementing an M2M transformation for checking syntactic correctness constraints on input MARTE models as a preliminary step before the main transformation. However, although more elaborated than the *Problems* meta-model, the VERIF one is still quite simple and, again, the work is only focused on a specific transformation for a specific case, although it can be taken as a template. Our proposal goes beyond these works by aiming at providing a generic solution independent of the domain formalization.

This genericity is also claimed in [13], which addresses the detection of modelling problems through QVTr transformations from input models (conforming to any MOF-based meta-model) to result models (conforming to the *pResults* meta-model) where problem occurrences are reported in a structured and concise manner.

A relatively close work, although following a different approach is [16]. The authors propose a method for efficient checking of OCL constraints by means of SQL. The core idea consists in reducing the problem to check the emptiness of SQL queries. Given an OCL constraint, it is possible to build an SQL query that returns all instances that violate it. Hence, the OCL constraint is satisfied if and only if its corresponding SQL query returns the empty set. Such queries are incrementally computed by a relational DBMS.

An inspiring work for the design of the CVD meta-model is [17], where an exhaustive constraints taxonomy is proposed in order to achieve well-formedness and good quality of conceptual models. Our CVD meta-model is slightly different oriented. It does not aim at revealing types of constraints but at providing suitable modelling of the data needed for describing constraint violations, envisioning their later manifestation or automatic treatment.

It should be remarked that the problem we address, i.e. the verification of invariants satisfaction, does not deal with the validation of the domain formalization (meta-model + constraints) itself. In this sense, when considering a set of invariants specified on a domain meta-model, we suppose that set to be perfectly valid, satisfying the typical correctness properties: syntactic correctness, no meta-model over-restriction or under-restriction, consistency, independence, satisfiability, no subsumption, no redundancy, etc. See [18] for a clear distinction between verification of instance models vs. validation of domain formalization design. In fact, there exists an important amount of published research on the topic of validation, like [19–21]. However, this dimension is out of the scope of our work.

7   Conclusions and Future Work

A strategy for verifying constraints satisfaction along with a meta-tool implementing it has been presented. The approach is based on the representation of the verification result as a diagnostic model generated by means of a so called M2M *checking transformation*. Although every couple of domain meta-model and constraints set requires a specific verification tool (checking transformation), the proposed strategy allows their systematic and straightforward development. Therefore, a HOT-based generic tool for verification, regardless the domain meta-model or particular set of constraints, has been implemented, allowing the generation of every required checking transformation. The meta-models needed to support this model-driven approach have been presented.

This strategy is part of a more general work [3] about the design of generic MDSE tools to foster the adoption of MDSE as basis of domain-specific development environments. The presented proposal, although domain independent, has been applied in our research group as part of the development of a complete model-driven strategy and infrastructure for the design of real-time systems. The asset at the core of this effort is the MAST-2 meta-model. Due to its laxity, a set of integrity constraints has been specified for it and in addition, the different analysis and design tools of the overall MAST environment require specific conditions (tool-specific constraints) for the models to be processed. The presented verification mechanism alleviates the implementation of future design and analysis tools since they will not be required to implement a preliminary verification step. Moreover, the representation of the verification result as a model allows an agile processing, in order, for instance, to give some guidance to the user about how to solve the inconsistencies.

Since the approach has been only applied within our in-house real-time field, we are looking forward to apply it in different domains in order to get valuable feedback about the level of genericity of the CVD and CC meta-models and their potential extension.

From a purely functional viewpoint, we are currently assessing the applicability of the OCL meta-model provided by the EclipseOCL component in order to inject textual OCL specifications into model form and directly link them from our CC models.

Acknowledgements. This work has been partially funded by the Spanish Government and FEDER funds, with references TIN2011-28567-C03-02 (HI-PARTES) & TIN2014-56158-C4-2-P (M2C2).

References

1. Bézivin, J.: On the unification power of models. Softw. Syst. Modell. **4**, 171–188 (2005)
2. Schmidt, D.C.: Guest editor's introduction: model-driven engineering. Computer **39**, 25–31 (2006)
3. Cuevas, C.: Metaherramientas MDE para el diseño de entornos de desarrollo de sistemas distribuidos de tiempo real. Ph.D. Thesis (2016)
4. Cuevas, C., Drake, J.M., López Martínez, P., Gutiérrez García, J.J., González Harbour, M., Medina, J.L., Palencia, J.C.: MAST 2 Metamodel (2012)
5. http://www.istr.unican.es/members/cesarcuevas/phd/3.2-constraintsVerification.html
6. Tisi, M., Jouault, F., Fraternali, P., Ceri, S., Bézivin, J.: On the use of higher-order model transformations. In: Model Driven Architecture-Foundations and Applications, pp. 18–33 (2009)
7. Bézivin, J., Büttner, F., Gogolla, M., Jouault, F., Kurtev, I., Lindow, A.: Model transformations? Transformation models!. In: Model Driven Engineering Languages and Systems, pp. 440–453 (2006)
8. Bézivin, J., Jouault, F., Touzet, D.: An introduction to the ATLAS Model Management Architecture. Research report, LINA, (05-01) (2005)
9. http://www.istr.unican.es/members/cesarcuevas/phd/artifactsMAST2.html

10. Steinberg, D., Budinsky, F., Paternostro, M., Merks, E.: EMF: Eclipse Modeling Framework, 2nd revised edition (rev) edn. Addison-Wesley Longman, Amsterdam, (2009)
11. Bézivin, J., Jouault, F.: Using ATL for checking models. Electron. Notes Theoret. Comput. Sci. **152**, 69–81 (2006)
12. Diguet, J.L.: Checking syntactic constraints on models using ATL model transformations. In: Model Transformation with ATL, p. 140 (2009)
13. Elaasar, M., Briand, L., Labiche, Y.: Domain-specific model verification with QVT. In: France, Robert B., Kuester, Jochen M., Bordbar, B., Paige, Richard F. (eds.) ECMFA 2011. LNCS, vol. 6698, pp. 282–298. Springer, Heidelberg (2011). doi:10.1007/978-3-642-21470-7_20
14. formal/2011-06-02: UML Profile for MARTE: Modelling and Analysis of Real-time Embedded Systems, v1.1 (2011)
15. Feiler, P.H., Gluch, D.P., Hudak, J.J.: The architecture analysis & design language (AADL): an introduction (2006)
16. Oriol, X., Teniente, E.: Incremental checking of OCL constraints through SQL queries. In: CEUR Workshop Proceedings, pp. 23–32 (2014)
17. Miliauskaite, E., Nemuraite, L.: Taxonomy of integrity constraints in conceptual models. In: IADIS Virtual Multi Conference on Computer Science and Information Systems (2005)
18. Delmas, R., Pires, A.F., Polacsek, T.: A verification and validation process for model driven engineering. In: Progress in Flight Dynamics, Guidance, Navigation, Control, Fault Detection, and Avionics, pp. 455–468 (2013)
19. Anastasakis, K., Bordbar, B., Georg, G., Ray, I.: UML2Alloy: a challenging model transformation. In: Engels, G., Opdyke, B., Schmidt, Douglas C., Weil, F. (eds.) MODELS 2007. LNCS, vol. 4735, pp. 436–450. Springer, Heidelberg (2007). doi:10.1007/978-3-540-75209-7_30
20. Cabot, J., Clarisó, R., Riera, D.: UMLtoCSP: a tool for the formal verification of UML/OCL models using constraint programming. In: Proceedings of the Twenty-Second IEEE/ACM International Conference on Automated Software Engineering, pp. 547–548 (2007)
21. Pérez, C.A.G., Buettner, F., Clarisó, R., Cabot, J.: EMFtoCSP: a tool for the lightweight verification of EMF models. In: Formal Methods in Software Engineering: Rigorous and Agile Approaches (FormSERA) (2012)

A Model-Driven Adaptive Approach for IoT Security

Bruno A. Mozzaquatro[1]([✉]), Carlos Agostinho[2], Raquel Melo[2],
and Ricardo Jardim-Goncalves[1]

[1] Universidade Nova de Lisboa (UNL), DEE/FCT, 2829-516 Caparica, Portugal
b.mozzaquatro@campus.fct.unl.pt, {ram,rg}@uninova.pt
[2] Centre of Technology and Systems, UNINOVA, 2829-516 Caparica, Portugal
ca@uninova.pt

Abstract. Internet of Things (IoT) and sensor networks are improving the cooperation between organizations, becoming more efficient and productive for the industrial systems. However, high iteration between human, machines, and heterogeneous IoT technologies increases the security threats. The IoT security is an essential requirement to fully adoption of applications, which requires correct management of information and confidentiality. The system and devices' variability requires dynamically adaptive systems to provide services depending on the context of the environment. In this paper, we propose a model driven adaptive approach to offer security services for an ontology-based security framework. Model-Driven Engineering (MDE) approach allows creating secure capabilities more efficient with the generation of security services based on security requirements in the knowledge base (IoTSec ontology). An industrial scenario of C2NET project was analyzed to identify the transformation of a system design of security solution in a platform specific model.

Keywords: Model-driven engineering · Adaptive approach · Security management · Internet of things · Ontology

1 Introduction

Smart devices integrated with different Future Internet technologies allow several industrial applications with sensing, identification, localization, networking and processing capabilities. The information technology (IT) standards have beneficiated the industrial manufacturing by the evolution of industrial systems [1]. The adoption of the Internet creates new business opportunities as well as exploiting collaborative work based on IT infrastructure in system environments. These aspects have potential to develop industrial systems like environmental monitoring, healthcare service, inventory and production management, food supply chain, transportation, workplace and home support, security and surveillance [2].

Nevertheless, heterogeneous environments with smart devices interconnected with the Internet also increases the security threats. The main problem of IoT

© Springer International Publishing AG 2017
S. Hammoudi et al. (Eds): MODELSWARD 2016, CCIS 692, pp. 194–215, 2017.
DOI: 10.1007/978-3-319-66302-9_10

security is the high interaction between humans, machines and IoT technologies with constraints in terms of connectivity, computational power, and energy [3]. Furthermore, IoT network is a dynamically changing environment and security issues require making-decision systems to change security mechanisms at runtime [4]. Therefore, it is necessary to learn and adapt for adjusting on-demand security attributes and anticipate new threats in an information system [5]. In contrast, severals security models, trust management, identity management and security mechanisms are used to ensure the privacy and security, keeping security goals, such as availability, confidentiality, integrity, authentication, non-repudiation, and authenticity [6–8].

Information security is an important requirement to fully adoption of IoT applications and must be considered by information system designers and by administrators of organizations that depends on the correct management of information security and confidentiality [7]. However, IoT is still in a conceptual phase. The field is very dynamic and security challenges are less structured, somewhat disorganized causing confusion amongst concepts and terms to software developers. Ontology characterizes an interesting domain with classes and relationships among them and implements a data model to share a common base knowledge in the particular domain [9].

Model-Driven Engineering (MDE) has relevant aspects that contribute to design adaptive systems considering contextual information and to adopt suitable secure solutions at runtime [10]. In this context, the integration of MDE approach with an ontology-based system to generate services from security requirements could improve the real-time detection of vulnerabilities, prediction, and assessment of security risk management and intrusion detection [11–13]. MDE consists of the principles of the generation of models in software development [14]. However, this approach provides a way to generate models high-level of abstraction to transform into code from system design models. The models are commonly used to represent of real-world contexts. Therefore, several distinct representations of the same context are possible. In Software Engineering, models could be represented in differents Domain Specific Languages (DSL) or software factories.

In this work we propose an ontology-based framework with an integrated model-driven adaptive approach for IoT security, to identify common security issues and become able to dynamically adapt security mechanisms and services to possible threats. This approach explores the generation of security services at runtime from security requirements models through an analysis in the IoT-Sec ontology. The main contribution is an adaptive approach to transforming dynamic changes on the context of the environment, generating security services on demand to protect IT infrastructures.

The rest of paper is organized as follow: Sect. 2 presents the background of security ontologies and adaptive security model. The related works are presented in Sect. 2.3. Section 3 presents details of the C2NET project, which the supply network optimization of manufacturing and logistic assets based on collaborative demand, production and delivery plans. Section 4 describes the framework proposed for ontology-based security framework. An adaptive form with the use of MDE approach to generate security services from security requirements models is presented in Sect. 4.2. Section 5 describes a case study with examples coming from C2NET project. Finally, Sect. 6 presents the conclusion about this work.

2 Background

This section describes main subjects involved in this work that contributes to improve the security aspects in the context of Internet of Things. In Sect. 2.1 existing security ontologies (i.e. IoTSec ontology) are discussed and an adaptive security model to adopt mechanisms in a suitable solution. Also, related works are presented to demonstrate the positioning of the paper.

2.1 Security Ontologies

Security issues are important for all contexts with personal data exchanges and sensitive information, but for IoT has differentiating characteristics and a big concern with the high iteration between humans, machines, and IoT technologies. It is justified by the heterogeneity of different smart devices connected to the Internet. Therefore, ensuring security and privacy of applications and services is critical to improving trust and use on the Internet.

In this context, the first step to mitigate these issues is to understand the relation between the security aspects of security management and identify situations of misunderstood concepts around information security and IoT. For that, ontology is an essential tool largely utilized for structuring an area of interest. According to the state of the art, several existing security ontologies have been proposed in the literature, but only a few are available (Fig. 1): security overview ontology [15–18] and security ontology applied to specific domain [9,11,19,20].

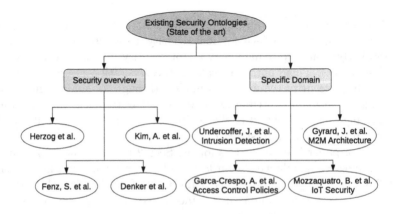

Fig. 1. Existing security ontologies.

Some ontologies address only one part of security domain (e.g. computer attacks) and others explore the overview of information security. [9] proposes a reference ontology for security in the IoT (IoTSec) with harmonization of ontologies based on ontology development methodology.

IoTSec Ontology. IoTSec ontology is a reference ontology for IoT security [9]. IoTSec ontology was proposed to explore aspects of relationships among basic components of the risk analysis of ISO/IEC 13335-1:2004 and National Institute of Standards and Technology (NIST) Special Publication 800-12 [21] such as Assets, Threats, SecurityMechanism, Vulnerability and Risk. Figure 2 presents an arrangement of top-level classes to modeling information security based in works [15–19].

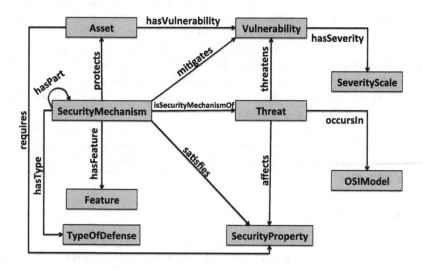

Fig. 2. Reference ontology for security in IoT [9].

IoTSec ontology was designed based on information security issues that can be represented using a structured knowledge. It explores relationships among classic components of risk analysis to provide an overview of the domain of security in IoT. IoTSec ontology was developed using the OWL (Web Ontology Language) ontology language.

These components allow identifying relations between relevant situations in an IoT network with risk analysis of potential threats. For example, the vulnerability class describes the potential weakness of M2M technologies associated with Asset class (hasVulnerability property). In this ontology, many technologies are considered assets such as Wi-Fi, Web, GSM (2G), UTMS (3G), LTE (4G), Ethernet, Bluetooth, Sensor, etc. Assets require security properties to be considered secure such as availability, confidentiality, integrity, etc. Vulnerabilities are flaws in software or hardware and when they are discovered, vendors publish a patch to fix it. For instance, vulnerability notes database (VND)[1] is one example that provides information about software vulnerabilities including summaries, technical details, remediation information, and lists of affected vendors.

Meanwhile, security mechanisms are used to avoid that threats exploit vulnerabilities found. These mechanisms are categorized according to the type of defense to protect the assets. A security mechanism is composed of several types of defense i.e., detective, preventive, corrective, recovery, response, etc.

Threat class describes information about attacks and others ways to exploit the applications' weakness and, sometimes, they explore one or more vulnerabilities. For instance, Wormhole attack replays messages from a system with the vulnerability of unprotected communication channel of a sensor network of an organization. This threat occurs in the network layer of OSI Model (occursIn property). In this situation, SecurityMechanism class contains tools to protect using cryptography algorithms, but need to consider their strengths and weaknesses such as energy consumption, flexibility, high cost, etc.

Organizations may prevent exploitation of its vulnerabilities using security tools or algorithms to protect (mitigates property) the systems' weakness. Mitigates property represents the relationship between SecurityMechanism and Vulnerability class. Vulnerabilities are qualified regarding its severity level (SeverityScale class) to an organization. Sometimes, organizations need to monitor the vulnerability with severity scale high, when systems have behavior unpredictable, and they can have become exposed to new threats. Each threat affects one or more security properties and the security mechanisms could satisfy these security properties.

2.2 Adaptive Security

Adaptive security is an approach to adjust attributes based on the behavior at runtime to respond to new and unusual threats in critical services [5,22,23]. This approach is found in the literature with concepts of self-adaptive software [24,25] and autonomic computing [26]. It is a solution that learns and adapts to the changing environment at runtime in face of changing threats, and anticipates threats before they are manifested.

This approach is a continuous process to learn, adapt, prevent, identity and respond to unusual and malicious behavior in runtime. For that, the adaptive security model proposed by [22] is composed of four components as depicted in Fig. 3: monitor, analyzer, adapter, and adaptive knowledge database. The monitor collects attributes; the analyzer determines the adaptation requirements; and the adapter decides the adaptation plan for execution.

The continuous cycle of security monitoring is needed for the use of suitable mechanisms depending on the information about the context and status of IoT devices. It is appropriated for IoT scenario because high interactions among heterogeneous devices and environment with critical risks to our lives. Monitoring

---

[1] http://nvd.nist.gov/.

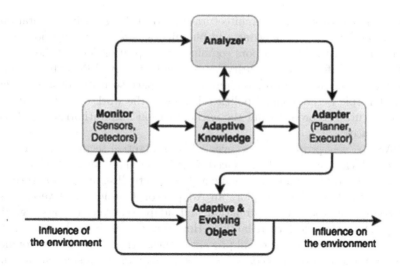

Fig. 3. Adaptive and evolving security model [22].

information context at runtime allows to choose or adapt a suitable security service to ensure one or more security properties.

According to [5] there is a little work on adaptive security mechanisms to secure IoT. Each work proposed explores static platforms, and specific aspects improve IoT security as well as security policies, encryption, secure communication, and intrusion detection. There is a need for IoT security to adapt and adjust attributes when there is a change in the context. Nevertheless, the reliability and performance of the adaptive security approaches are directly related with security mechanisms used to identify the threats in the system.

Within the scope of Model-Driven Engineering (MDE), adaptive security could be addressed to provide customization as a service in a runtime architecture. MDE is an approach composed of several theories and methodological frameworks for industrialized software development using models inside of software development cycle [27]. These models are described based on standard specification languages and code is generated automatically or semi-automatically from others abstract models. One relevant aspect of MDD to the adaptive security is the automation, which non-code artifacts are produced totally or partially from models [27] such as: documentation, test artifacts, build and deployment scripts, and other models.

2.3   Related Works

Ontologies have been explored in several aspects to improve information security, identifying vulnerabilities of systems, assessment of the threat against targets using differents approaches, such as intrusion detection [11], correlation of context-aware alert analysis [12], identification of complex network attacks [13].

The work [4] proposes an architectural approach for security adaptation in smart spaces utilized for analyzing and planning access control decision at runtime and design-time. The authors combine an adaptation loop of the adaptive security model, Information Security Measuring Ontology (ISMO) to offer input knowledge for the adaptation loop and a smart space security-control model to enforce dynamic access control policies. However, the work only illustrates the adaptive security approach from the authentication and authorization of users of smart spaces.

EDAS [28] was proposed as an event driven adaptive security model to IoT to protect devices against threat faced at runtime. The authors use an Open Source Security Information Management (OSSIM) to filter and normalize events collected from *things*. They explore an Adaptation Ontology to leverage risks' information from the event correlation and adapt security settings regarding usability, QoS, and security reliability. However, the authors do not consider potential vulnerabilities that could prevent eventual threats in the environment. In this case, the approach needs an occurrence to verify the suitable action to mitigate it.

The work [29] proposes an MDS@run.time approach to intercept services and identify security requirements are fitting the execution context. For that, the authors consider security policies as models interpreted at runtime. Nevertheless, the policy orchestration is integrated into cloud environment and different policies are attached to each execution context. The MDS@run.time was evaluated in the framework OW2 FraSCAti middleware with relevant results compared with other approaches to managing security in collaborative processes.

In this context, this work explores a knowledge base supported by a reference ontology for security in the IoT through a framework for IoT security. It is composed of the basic components of risk management and the relation between threat, vulnerability, asset, security mechanism, and security property. It provides a knowledge base for making decision with the suggestion of potential solutions or identify weakness of resources, ensuring the secure environment IoT-enabled industrial systems. Usually, these security recommendations need adoption of security mechanisms to have an impact on the environment. For that, the model-driven adaptive approach explores the generation of security services identified through the queries on the ontology as essential in the environment. It transforms platform specific models or code artifacts from security requirements models.

3   C2NET Platform

C2NET[2] (Cloud Collaborative Manufacturing Networks) is a research and development project, funded by the European Commission H2020 programme. The goal of the project is the design of cloud-enabled tools for supporting the small-medium enterprises (SME) supply network optimization of manufacturing and logistics assets based on collaborative demand, production, and delivery plans.

---

[2] http://c2net-project.eu/.

The project consists of a scalable real-time architecture, platform and software to optimize the manufacturing and logistics process by the collaborative computation through efficient delivery plans.

The main problem of traditional supply chains has centralized decision-making approaches, which make difficult for companies to react to current highly dynamic markets. C2NET platform is proposed to contribute in several aspects of industrial manufacturing, exploring data collection of IoT devices on the companies' shop floor, combining this information with contextual information of the business environment to improve decision making. However, these devices are vulnerable to several threats, and it needs to be addressed using a set of security mechanisms. Moreover, some of these devices use different IoT technologies. The C2NET platform ensures IoT interoperability by defining two components of the entire C2NET system: Data Collection Client (DCC) and Data Collection Framework (DCF). See [30] for more information on the C2NET DCC/DCF architecture.

3.1 C2NET Data Collection Client

The C2NET Data Collection Client (DCC) is a component that provides services for collecting and sending all the required data from the legacy systems of the company (e.g. its planning, logistics and operations) and data arriving from IoT devices on the shop floor (e.g. machine availability, performance, etc.). This component can connect the different data sources (both legacy systems and IoT devices), and will store the data gathered, submitting it to C2NET DCF when needed (both on a periodical basis or under demand). Consequently, the C2NET DCC will adopt an ESB pattern.

3.2 C2NET Data Collection Framework

The C2NET Data Collection Framework (DCF) is a domain module that offers functionality for managing data from different heterogeneous sources and providing necessary information for other modules of the C2NET system. This module enables uniform accessibility of structured information for data consumers. It also resolves challenges concerning integration and interoperability across data producers and consumers caused by differences in industrial processes, data models, methods, technologies, and devices. It takes into consideration the homogenous integration of legacy systems and IoT devices.

3.3 Security Requirements

Being a real-time architecture, C2NET has several security aspects need to be considered to ensure the security properties of its application. Hence, some requirements will be described according to their relevance for the C2NET platform:

– Access Control consists of two essential aspects of the security to identify users and their permissions on the platform: authorization and authentication.

- Encryption is a security requirement responsible for providing the protection of the information. It consists in the modification of the original content to make incomprehensible for active/passive attackers, even though they have access to the information. This requirement can also provide the integrity because the attackers can not modify the original content.
- Digital Signature consists on a set of rules and parameters to identify the sender and verify the integrity of the stored data as well as transmitted data. It detects unauthorized manipulations during the transmission and shows the evidence to the receiver of the signature is generated by the claimed sender.

4 Ontology-Based Security Framework for Adaptive Security

The authors propose an ontology-based security framework, designed to use an adaptive security model with an integrated model-driven approach. The security model is suitable for the dynamic environment of IoT, monitoring the behavior of the environment, learning and adapting security services to malicious behavior. In this context, the support of an adaptive knowledge base enables to anticipate threats before they are manifested in the IoT network. An approach of Model-Driven Engineering (MDE) to transform security requirements found on the ontology into security services is presented in Sect. 4.2.

Several industries are using IoT devices to different applications to provides new opportunities based on sensing, ubiquitous identification, and communication capabilities [2]. IoT devices transmit sensitive information of companies, if not addressed properly, can be vulnerable to internal and external attacks.

The ontology-based security framework proposed in this paper explores the adaptive security model to making decisions based on knowledge base for information security issues. For that, this security framework is integrated with the platform of C2NET project, enriching it in regards to the security of IoT devices. In this context, the architecture of ontology-based security framework is depicted in Fig. 4. The architecture aims to improve security issues of industrial manufacturing integrated with the C2NET platform.

The C2NET platform uses IoT devices to collect data from the industrial environment using a C2NET Data Collection middleware. Security mechanisms (i.e. based on rules, security protocols) are applied in data communication to protect sensitive information between IoT devices and middleware. Nevertheless, several vulnerabilities of devices and software appear every day, which is making the assets vulnerable to attacks. Hence, continuous assessment and suitable adaptations need to be enforced to ensure the security properties such as availability, confidentiality, and integrity.

The security framework is proposed with two approaches to improving security issues of C2NET platform: design and execution. Follow specific characteristics of each approach:

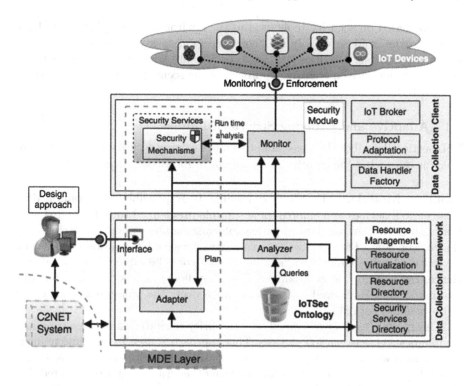

Fig. 4. An architecture of ontology-based security framework with MDE approach proposed with the C2NET platform.

- Design: install an IoT device/sensor in the network, based on the IoTSec ontology [9] to identify potential security solutions to protect itself and configure the suitable security mechanisms of the DCC.
- Execution: the monitor module detects an anomaly behavior or vulnerability if it can not resolve immediately in real time, then the analyzer module consults to the ontology (actualized continuously), and the adapter module generates new services with suitable security mechanisms for the middleware to enforce those; the device needs to be stored momentaneously.

The design approach of the security framework explores the previous knowledge to adopt new technologies or products considering security issues. On the other hand, run time approach monitors IoT devices based on security metrics and attributes to identify malicious behaviors in the smart environment. Consequently, configurations and/or rules need to be adapted according to the knowledge base, when security tools trigger alerts. For that, IoT ontology (IoTSec) contributes to identifying relations between threat, asset, vulnerability, security mechanism and security property. The adapter infers new information on the knowledge base to deploy new approaches for specifics situations or malicious behaviors. The runtime approach uses an analyzer module to identify anomaly behavior based on security tools used in the environment (e.g. IDS, IPS, Firewalls, Proxies, and so on). In this context, security attributes are monitored to detect malicious activities and, then, actions are triggered to adjust settings using the model-driven adaptive approach of the security framework (described in Sect. 4.2).

4.1 Adaptive and Evolving Security Modules

This section describes the three adaptive and evolving security modules responsible for improving the security management of industrial systems.

Monitor Module. The Monitor module is responsible for monitor data between IoT devices and enforce some suitable pre-defined rules to the IoT network. These devices are used to gather information about security attributes of the environment. The monitor only considers device's information collected by devices to identify potential vulnerabilities that could be explored by the threats. Hence, raw data of the environment (e.g. shop floor) also is collected, but this information only is filtered by the platform to verify the proper operation based in the semantic of data.

This module uses a pre-defined set of security rules to ensure the secure data communication between IoT devices. This approach is used in run time to make the decision without delay. In this case, this set is fed with previous knowledge of ontology according to device's information of security attributes collected. For that, monitor module realizes a fast analysis of parameters upward of threshold defined to verify anomalies. For instance, any unusual behavior identified by security tools like intrusion detection system or firewall are forwarded to DCF component of C2NET platform to realize the deepest analysis of ontology-based security framework.

Analyzer Module. The Analyzer module of the security framework is responsible for consulting activities mapped in the knowledge base but in the case of new occurrences (e.g. zero-day threats) reported by security tools, resulting in unusual behavior for the security framework. So, it needs to be adapted to avoid critical damage to the organizations.

Also, this module consists of the composition of queries semi-structured to retrieve information about security solutions or security issues about the context presented. Some IoT networks reveal severe problems according to the heterogeneity of devices used to data collection, enabling potential threats for the organization. So, through the use of queries to the knowledge base, future security issues can be avoided. For example, based on the specific device used in the network, is possible to relate their vulnerabilities and potential security mechanisms used to mitigate them specific security property. A semi-structure query can be composed as follow:

$$\ll SecMechanism \gg \Longleftarrow \ll AssetK \gg \wedge \ll VulnerabilityY \gg \wedge \\ \wedge \ll ThreatX \gg \wedge \ll SecPropertyZ \gg \tag{1}$$

More information about the correlation between main security concepts of ontology can be found in [9].

The DCF component of the C2NET platform manages the virtual instances of IoT devices to control their behavior in the physical world. The Resource Virtualization is responsible for minimizing the distance between physical devices and their virtualized devices in the IoT network. This information is important to analyzer module make decisions for adaptation for potential security solutions between IoT devices.

Adapter Module. The Adapter module provides methods for selecting and configure security mechanisms according to the security policies received by the Analyzer module. It is responsible for the policy resolution, adoption of multiple security mechanisms and relation of the security properties. This module has an interface with Analyzer module to gather results of the queries on the knowledge base according to the context identified. This module starts the adaptation process that will be finalized using the MDE approach described in Sect. 4.2.

The correlation of potential security solutions and security property identified on the IoTSec ontology allows categorizing the results to select the security components to generate artifacts from specific models. Hence, the security policies can be composed of several security mechanisms to be implemented using security tools (Fig. 5). Each model used in this module is composed of one or more security mechanisms to achieve the security requirements.

However, each adaptation of specific security and business services is necessary to generate or deploy services at run time. Depending upon the security analysis on the IoTSec ontology, new security services can be applied. Some

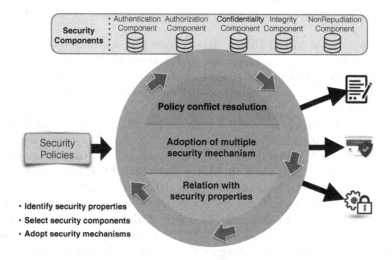

Fig. 5. Continuous adaptation process to select and generate security solutions.

services can be deployed at run time [31]: authentication, authorization, confidentiality, integrity, non-repudiation, and so on.

4.2 MDE Layer

The Model-Driven Engineering (MDE) layer consists of applying the principles of models to the transformation for generation of software artifacts from systems design models [14]. The main idea of this layer is to generate artifacts and codes from requirements obtained on the knowledge base (IoTSec ontology) according to the security needs of the IoT network in industrial systems.

A Model-Driven Adaptive Approach. The model-driven adaptive approach is an integration of the MDE with an ontology-based security framework to generate security services. MDE approach considers models as the core and its manipulation at high-level of abstraction to transform into code. The models are commonly used to represent of real-world contexts. Therefore, several distinct representations of the same context are possible. In Software Engineering, models could be represented in differents Domain Specific Languages (DSL) or software factories.

Several changes are necessary to make a secure environment with dynamic and heterogeneous devices. However, an adaptive way for the framework to generate, in a semi-automatic process, security services with adjustments in the same service requiring a development of functionalities for some distinct technologies like C, Java, Python or devices as tiny devices or legacy systems. The MDE approach has the potential to address this context. It has the ability to synthesize artifacts and source codes from security models through transformation mapping and rules and helps ensure the consistency between application implements and analysis information associated with security requirements by models.

MDE follows the Model-Driven Architecture (MDA), from Object Management Group (OMG), as the reference architecture to the development, integration, and interoperability of object-oriented software artifacts [32]. Figure 6 presents the MDA architecture instantiated with examples applied in the context of IoT security.

Also following MDA, the adaptor module has three levels of abstraction to transform models in the software development process. (i) Computation Independent Model (CIM) level defines the functionalities that the system needs to do (i.e. requirements); (ii) Platform Independent Model (PIM) presents how the system achieves its requirements and technical details; and (iii) Platform Specific Model (PSM) defines specific aspects of each platform or technology [33]. In the context of security, it is following the approach of Model-Driven Security (MDS) [34], a specialization of the MDE has already successfully resulted in industrial systems [35], process-oriented systems [36], complex distributed systems [37], multi-cloud systems [38], and using runtime models [29]. This concept allows designers create system models according to security requirements to generate system architectures from the models.

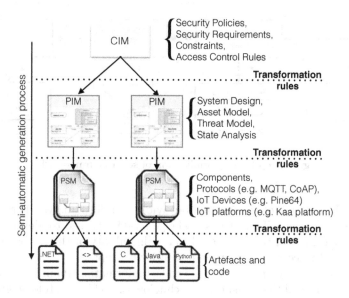

Fig. 6. The model transformation process of MDA architecture.

5 Ontology-Based Adaptive IoT Security Scenario

In this section, the application of the ontology-based security framework and model-driven adaptive security into a validation scenario of metalworking industry to improve the security issues between IoT devices and C2NET platform.

The IoTSec ontology was designed to allow decision-making following main classes of security: assets (K and X), vulnerabilities (Y), threats (Z), security mechanisms (G), and security properties. For instance, a sensor K (K requires some security properties J) based on technology X has vulnerabilities Y that can threaten by attack Z, but if the company use a security mechanism G, he could neutralize potential threats. Also, organizations need to define restrictions that can be represented by security policies, and it means the security properties addressed for security framework. Figure 7 presents a step-by-step of the data flow of the security framework.

It demonstrates the application and the generation of security services according to the contextual information collected in the environment. Also, the integration of the IoTSec ontology with the framework. Here, this ontology has an essential role to make support for decision making about the security issues in the IoT security.

- 1° step: After the data collection of the monitoring of security attributes, a primer analysis of security rules is realized to mitigates potential threats or vulnerabilities found.
- 2° step: A brief set of security rules is used to apply in mechanisms to protect devices and data transmissions. It is used with a run time approach, which requires a fast decision-making based on the knowledge already queried.

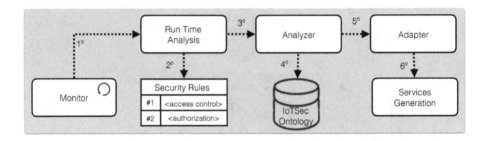

Fig. 7. Step-by-step application of security framework.

- 3° step: In the case of the unusual behavior, so a deep analysis is required to find other solutions. Thus, the knowledge base is checked to identify suitable security mechanism that is related to a vulnerability or threat. Some queries can be used to correlate with main security concepts.
- 4° step: SPARQL queries are used to collect information about unusual behaviors or vulnerabilities in specific technologies. IoTSec ontology gives support to decision-making using contextual information (security attributes) collected by IoT devices.
- 5° step: Security solutions are suggested by the ontology to mitigate threats or avoid exploitation of vulnerabilities. For that, security services need to be selected for solve the problems found.
- 6° step: Based on the security requirements, a set of mechanisms and tools are used to create new security services.

An overview of the scenario is described to understand the applicability of security framework and what information are essential to monitoring for security level assessment. According to the restrictions and contextual information, security framework checks the knowledge base using SPARQL Protocol and RDF Query Language (SPARQL)[3] queries and relates with others queries to identify suitable security mechanisms or potential threats, for example. Hence, in this work the scenario presented is vulnerable only to digital threats, such as disclosure information, replay attack, spoofing and others attacks to smart devices.

5.1 Non-conformity Scheduling Scenario

Non-conformity scheduling is a validation scenario composed of several IoT devices/sensors to feed the C2NET platform with realtime detection of non-conformity products during the production process. It reduces the quantity of waste and non-conformity products that may arise during the production process.

This scenario is the most critical in case of security issues because the C2NET platform collects information about the shop-floor production.

---

[3] http://www.w3.org/TR/rdf-sparql-query/.

Then, any violation in data communication between IoT devices and C2NET platform could compromise the production or to result critical problems to the company. Figure 8 depicted a scenario of data collection using an IoT devices in a sensor network about the shop-floor production to identify occurrences of non-conformities.

Fig. 8. Communication aspects of a metalworking industry scenario [39].

This industrial scenario is composed of four steps to detect occurrences of non-conformities in the production. The Step 1 of the scenario, C2NET platform collects information about the shop-floor production. This information can be gathered directly via sensor network, through the connection to legacy systems or quality control workers can manually insert it. Considering to the platform only verify the semantic of information. If non-conformities are detected in the quality control by direct matching between what was expected in the production and what is being produced, C2NET informs the Production Manager (Step 2). At the same time, Step 3, C2NET can make suggestions to the Production Manager about the actions to be performed related with the non-conformity detected, such as: stop production, make an intervention on the machine, or continue production. In Step 4, C2NET informs the Company Manager about the non-conformities detected, and the actions took by the Production Manager. Through earlier detection the Production Manager can act faster and reduce the waste of raw materials, thus reducing costs.

To ensure all steps of this process of production, the main security properties as well as integrity, confidentiality, and non-repudiation need to be ensured. The integrity and confidentiality properties are two important aspects to avoid access to the information transmitted. For that, security framework contributes to choosing suitable security tools with the relation between vulnerabilities, threats and security mechanisms. Algorithm 1.1 shows an SPARQL query and how this information is obtained of IoTSec ontology, considering the variables ?threat (threat), ?secmec (security mechanism) and ?secprop (security property).

Algorithm 1.1. SPARQL query on the IoTSec ontology.

```
SELECT DISTINCT ?threat ?secmec ?secprop
WHERE {
    ?threat rdfs:label ?label .
    ?threat iotsec:hasSecurityMechan ?secmec .
    ?secmec iotsec:satisfies ?secprop
}
```

In the case of confidentiality, if an attacker has got access to the information transmitted, he can not understand this information because it must be encrypted. Moreover, the authentication property is related only to the access control of the information by the C2NET platform.

5.2   Evaluation of a Model-Driven Adaptive Approach

The validation of our proposal is used a metalworking industry scenario to the adaptive generation of security services with the use of an ontology-based security framework. Considering to the scenario present in Sect. 5.1, the flexibility offered by a security framework is often very limited:

- Sensors and actuators do not need to be physically coupled, but they need to be prepared to have any future reconfiguration or adaptation of the use of different security tools (e.g. change a cryptographic algorithm).
- The architecture has a sensor network collecting information about the shop-floor production with a central gateway server (i.e. data collection client). The sensors need to communicate with a gateway to monitoring with security tools (e.g. firewalls, IDS, IPS, Proxies) to execute event-driven security policies that orchestrate the network. A security policy can change one or more security mechanisms to attend a specific security requirements identified by the IoTSec ontology.

The objective of security framework is to ensure the security management between requirements and support dynamic adaptation of a running system with the orchestration of security capabilities on heterogeneous devices independently of each platform. Suppose that this scenario is totally unprotected, so the monitoring with security tools will generate alerts of intrusion attempts, fraud and information theft. Each alert will be queried on the IoTSec ontology to get suggestions of the security approach to mitigate these problems.

To supply the security properties of confidentiality, non-repudiation, and integrity, the security framework identified through the IoTSec ontology the use of Digital Signature to the message authentication, ensuring the authenticity of digital messages. Based on model-driven adaptive, Fig. 9 presents the class diagram of the PIM to be deployed in a security service (Digital Signature).

The digital signature model employs asymmetric cryptography to provide authenticity of digital messages that are sent through a non-secure communication channel. This model of security solution gives the receiver to believe

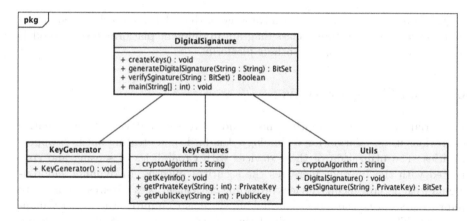

Fig. 9. PIM of a security service model of the Digital Signature.

the message was sent by the claimed sender. For instance, the model presented uses specific algorithms (e.g. RSA, DSA, ECDSA, ElGamal) to create private and public keys for the digital signature. Usually, these algorithms are modified according to the context and device used in the environment.

The transformation process allows to generate code only changing a parameter in the system design and each method in the class diagram is implemented by the Java language. Algorithm 1.2 presents the main classes generated by the model-driven adaptive approach.

Algorithm 1.2. Java code of the class diagram of the Digital Signature.

```
public class DigitalSignature {
  /*
  *   Generate Digital Signature
  */
  public static byte[] generateDigitalSignature(String
      message, String keyPath) {
    PrivateKey privKey = KeyFeatures.getPrivateKey(keyPath);
    return signBytes = Utils.getSignature(message, privKey);
  }

  public static void main(String[] args){
    KeyGenerator();
    String msg = args[0];
    String keyPath = args[1]; // path to privatekey.key
    byte[] signedMsg = generateDigitalSignature(msg,
        keyPath);
  }
}
```

Our approach proposed takes advantage of the MDE approach to generation of a security solution from a class diagram in different platform specific models as C, Python, Java or also for others platforms.

6   Final Considerations

Industrial systems are adopting more and more smart devices to automatize operations using information technology standards and creating business opportunities. The utilization of these devices with capabilities of sensing and connected with the Internet increases the security concerns. In dynamic environments with heterogeneous devices providing critical services requires attention to improving security using decision-making systems to improve the security management. The real-time approach of the security management allows realizing fast changes through of policies or configurations to attend security requirements. By another hand, to attend some security requirements, the availability of the critical business services is affected when they need modifications in mechanisms or tools. For that, the runtime approach involves security services provisioning, the proposal in this paper, to generate new secure solutions to reach a security requirement, even though the critical services of industrial systems need to stop, but by a short time if it is compare with security software development of new services.

The authors proposed a model-driven adaptive approach to provides security services for the IoT security. This proposal uses an ontology-based security framework to suggest security solutions at runtime and codes are generated from security requirements according to the context environment. Nevertheless, IoTSec ontology provides the relation between main concepts of risk management using semantic web technologies. This knowledge base provides suggestions of security solutions based on the contextual information identified by the security framework.

This paper shows the main contribution of a model-driven engineering applied in an industrial scenario to generate security services according to the security recommendation of the ontology-based framework. The generation of security services at runtime provides making decision and enforcement of new solutions with less time of development and reconfiguration of resources because transformation models are faster transition to create new source codes or configuration scripts of a security mechanism. Considering to the industrial scenario, it has huge business impact ensuring the availability of providing critical services. In future works, security service provisioning must be better analyzed to identify which are the mechanisms and tools appropriate for model-driven adaptive approach.

Acknowledgements. The research leading to this work has received funding from CAPES Proc. No.: BEX 0966/15-0 and European Commission's Horizon 2020 Programme (H2020/2014-2020) under grant agreement: C2NET No.: 636909.

References

1. Bi, Z., Xu, L.D., Wang, C.: Internet of things for enterprise systems of modern manufacturing. IEEE Trans. Industr. Inf. **10**, 1537–1546 (2014)
2. Xu, L.D., He, W., Li, S.: Internet of things in industries: a survey. IEEE Trans. Industr. Inf. **10**, 2233–2243 (2014)
3. Sicari, S., Rizzardi, A., Grieco, L., Coen-Porisini, A.: Security, privacy and trust in internet of things: the road ahead. Comput. Netw. **76**, 146–164 (2014)
4. Evesti, A., Ovaska, E.: Comparison of adaptive information security approaches. ISRN Artificial Intelligence (2013)
5. Habib, K., Leister, W.: Adaptive security for the internet of things reference model. Norsk informasjonssikkerhetskonferanse (NISK) 13–25 (2013)
6. Roman, R., Zhou, J., Lopez, J.: On the features and challenges of security and privacy in distributed internet of things. Comput. Netw. **57**, 2266–2279 (2013)
7. Yan, Z., Zhang, P., Vasilakos, A.V.: A survey on trust management for internet of things. J. Netw. Comput. Appl. **42**, 120–134 (2014)
8. Granjal, J., Monteiro, E., Silva, J.S.: Security in the integration of low-power wireless sensor networks with the internet: a survey. Ad Hoc Netw. **24**, 264–287 (2014)
9. Mozzaquatro, B.A., Jardim-goncalves, R., Agostinho, C.: Towards a reference ontology for security in the internet of things. In: IEEE International Workshop on Measurement and Networking, pp. 1–6 (2015)
10. Soylu, A., De Causmaecker, P.: Merging model driven and ontology driven system development approaches pervasive computing perspective. In: 2009 24th International Symposium on Computer and Information Sciences, ISCIS 2009, pp. 730–735. IEEE (2009)
11. Undercoffer, J., Joshi, A., Pinkston, J.: Modeling computer attacks: an ontology for intrusion detection. In: Vigna, G., Kruegel, C., Jonsson, E. (eds.) RAID 2003. LNCS, vol. 2820, pp. 113–135. Springer, Heidelberg (2003). doi:10.1007/978-3-540-45248-5_7
12. Xu, H., Xiao, D., Wu, Z.: Application of security ontology to context-aware alert analysis. In: 2009 Eighth IEEE/ACIS International Conference on Computer and Information Science, ICIS 2009, pp. 171–176 (2009)
13. Frye, L., Cheng, L., Heflin, J.: An ontology-based system to identify complex network attacks. In: 2012 IEEE International Conference on Communications (ICC), pp. 6683–6688 (2012)
14. Bézivin, J.: Model driven engineering: an emerging technical space. In: Lämmel, R., Saraiva, J., Visser, J. (eds.) GTTSE 2005. LNCS, vol. 4143, pp. 36–64. Springer, Heidelberg (2006). doi:10.1007/11877028_2
15. Herzog, A., Shahmehri, N., Duma, C.: An ontology of information security. J. Inform. Secur. **1**, 1–23 (2007)
16. Fenz, S., Ekelhart, A.: Formalizing information security knowledge. In: Proceedings of the 4th International Symposium on Information, Computer, and Communications Security, ASIACCS 2009, pp. 183–194. ACM, New York (2009)
17. Kim, A., Luo, J., Kang, M.: Security ontology for annotating resources. In: Meersman, R., Tari, Z. (eds.) OTM 2005. LNCS, vol. 3761, pp. 1483–1499. Springer, Heidelberg (2005). doi:10.1007/11575801_34
18. Denker, G., Kagal, L., Finin, T., Paolucci, M., Sycara, K.: Security for DAML web services: annotation and matchmaking. In: Fensel, D., Sycara, K., Mylopoulos, J. (eds.) ISWC 2003. LNCS, vol. 2870, pp. 335–350. Springer, Heidelberg (2003). doi:10.1007/978-3-540-39718-2_22

19. Gyrard, A., Bonnet, C., Boudaoud, K.: An ontology-based approach for helping to secure the ETSI machine-to-machine architecture. In: 2014 IEEE International Conference on Internet of Things (iThings), and Green Computing and Communications (GreenCom), and Cyber, Physical and Social Computing(CPSCom), pp. 109–116. IEEE (2014)

20. García-Crespo, Á., Gómez-Berbís, J.M., Colomo-Palacios, R., Alor-Hernández, G.: Securontology: a semantic web access control framework. Comput. Stand. Interfaces **33**, 42–49 (2011)

21. Stoneburner, G., Goguen, A.Y., Feringa, A.: Spp. 800–30. Risk management guide for information technology systems (2002)

22. Abie, H.: Adaptive security and trust management for autonomic message-oriented middleware. In: 2009 IEEE 6th International Conference on Mobile Adhoc and Sensor Systems, pp. 810–817 (2009)

23. Shnitko, A.: Adaptive security in complex information systems. In: Proceedings of 2003 the 7th Korea-Russia International Symposium on Science and Technology, KORUS 2003, pp. 206–210 (2003)

24. Laddaga, R., Robertson, P.: Self adaptive software: a position paper. In: SELF-STAR: International Workshop on Self-* Properties in Complex Information Systems, vol. 31, p. 19 (2004)

25. Agostinho, C., Jardim-Goncalves, R.: Sustaining interoperability of networked liquid-sensing enterprises: a complex systems perspective. Ann. Rev. Control **39**, 128–143 (2015)

26. Dobson, S., Zambonelli, F., Denazis, S., Fernández, A., Gaïti, D., Gelenbe, E., Massacci, F., Nixon, P., Saffre, F., Schmidt, N.: A survey of autonomic communications. ACM Trans. Autonom. Adapt. Syst. **1**, 223–259 (2006)

27. Picek, R., Strahonja, V.: Model driven development-future or failure of software development. IIS **7**, 407–413 (2007)

28. Aman, W., Snekkenes, E.: Event driven adaptive security in internet of things. In: UBICOMM 2014: The Eighth International Conference on Mobile Ubiquitous Computing, Systems, Services and Technologies, pp. 7–15 (2014)

29. Ouedraogo, W.F., Biennier, F., Merle, P.: Optimizing service protection with model driven security@ run. time. In: 2015 IEEE Symposium on Service-Oriented System Engineering (SOSE), pp. 50–58. IEEE (2015)

30. Ghimire, S., Melo, R., Ferreira, J., Agostinho, C., Goncalves, R.: Continuous data collection framework for manufacturing industries. In: Ciuciu, I., Panetto, H., Debruyne, C., Aubry, A., Bollen, P., Valencia-García, R., Mishra, A., Fensel, A., Ferri, F. (eds.) OTM 2015. LNCS, vol. 9416, pp. 29–40. Springer, Cham (2015). doi:10.1007/978-3-319-26138-6_5

31. Hafner, M., Memon, M., Breu, R.: Seaas-a reference architecture for security services in SOA. J. Univ. Comput. Sci. (J.UCS) **15**, 2916–2936 (2009)

32. Bézivin, J., Gerbé, O.: Towards a precise definition of the OMG/MDA framework. In: 2001 Proceedings of the 16th Annual International Conference on Automated Software Engineering, (ASE 2001), pp. 273–280. IEEE (2001)

33. Kleppe, A.G., Warmer, J., Bast, W.: MDA Explained: The Model Driven Architecture: Practice and Promise. Addison-Wesley Longman Publishing Co. Inc., Boston (2003)

34. Lúcio, L., Zhang, Q., Nguyen, P.H., Amrani, M., Klein, J., Vangheluwe, H., Traon, Y.L.: Advances in model-driven security. Adv. Comput. **93**, 103–152 (2014)

35. Clavel, M., Silva, V., Braga, C., Egea, M.: Model-driven security in practice: an industrial experience. In: Schieferdecker, I., Hartman, A. (eds.) ECMDA-FA 2008. LNCS, vol. 5095, pp. 326–337. Springer, Heidelberg (2008). doi:10.1007/978-3-540-69100-6_22
36. Basin, D., Doser, J., Lodderstedt, T.: Model driven security for process-oriented systems. In: Proceedings of the Eighth ACM symposium on Access control models and technologies, pp. 100–109. ACM (2003)
37. Lang, U., Schreiner, R.: Model driven security management: making security management manageable in complex distributed systems. In: Workshop on Modeling Security (MODSEC08)-International Conference on Model Driven Engineering Languages and Systems (MODELS) (2009)
38. Ouedraogo, W.F., Biennier, F., Ghodous, P.: Model driven security in a multi-cloud context. Int. J. Electron. Bus. Manage. **11**, 178 (2013)
39. C2NET, P.: Deliverable D1.3: C2NET platform validation scenarios. Version R0.1 (2015)

Identifying Performance Objectives to Guide Service Oriented Architecture Layers

Tehreem Masood$^{(\boxtimes)}$, Chantal Bonner Cherifi, and Néjib Moalla

Decision and Information Sciences for Production Systems (DISP),
Université Lumière Lyon 2, Lyon, France
{tehreem.masood, chantal.bonnercherifi,
nejib.moalla}@univ-lyon2.fr

Abstract. Service oriented architecture is emerging as a powerful paradigm for organizations that need to integrate their applications within and across organizational boundaries. Organizations need to take decisions more quickly and need to change those decisions dynamicaly. Delivering an adequate level of performance is a critical and significant challenge that requires monitoring along the different layers of service oriented architecture. Current monitoring systems are designed to support specific layers but do not fulfil the requirements of all the layers of service oriented architecture. Ontologies on the semantic web standardize and formalize the concepts and store domain knowledge for effective decision making. In this paper, we propose performance monitoring framework for various layers of service oriented architecture. It integrates various ontologies to monitor the performance at the service oriented layers in order to ensure their sustainability. We design a Service Performance Ontology that captures all the information about the service domain. Along with that we design ontologies for ensuring performance at service level, binding level, composition level and server level. We conduct a performance evaluation over real web services using suitable estimators for response time, delay, loss and more.

Keywords: Web services · Service Oriented Architecture (SOA) · Performance · Decision making · Ontology

1 Introduction

Web Services is a software system designed to support interoperable machine to machine interaction over a network [1]. It uses open standards like XML [2], SOAP [3], WSDL [4]. Web-service based applications are applications built by using web services provided by third-parties. The SOA Reference Architecture (SOA RA) has nine layers that emerge in the process of designing an SOA solution or defining an enterprise architecture standard [5]. SOA RA is shown in Fig. 1.

The component services access the Data abstraction layer to fetch and retrieve data. Messaging through SOAP provides the ability to perform the necessary message transformation to connect the service requestor to the service provider and to publish and subscribe messages and events asynchronously [6]. In this way services are published in the service layer. On the top level layer, BP applications provide process

© Springer International Publishing AG 2017
S. Hammoudi et al. (Eds): MODELSWARD 2016, CCIS 692, pp. 216–226, 2017.
DOI: 10.1007/978-3-319-66302-9_11

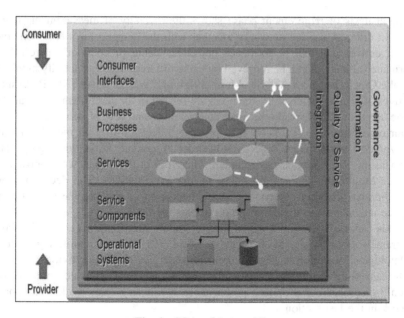

Fig. 1. SOA ref Layers [5].

orchestration mechanism to execute enterprise business processes. BP application use Business Process Modeling Notation (BPMN) [7] to design their business processes. Governance rules are the set of policies like service will be available for one year etc. Security is used to provide some integrity to the system like authentication with the help of user name and password. Quality of service layer is used to provide the agreed quality as defined in service level agreements.

Ontologies play an important role in both semantic web applications and knowledge engineering systems [8]. Numerous tasks such as information storage, processing, retrieval, decision making etc. are done on the basis of ontologies.

Web service performance metrics are classified as client-side and server-side. Load generators are used together with profiling tools to measure and optimize the performance of web service based applications. Examples are JMeter [9], soapUI [10], Eclipse TPTP [11] and JProbe [12].

Software performance engineering is a systematic approach to construct software systems that meet performance objectives (PO's). As part of software performance engineering, we focus on establishing PO's. PO's can be monitored at service or process execution time. PO's that we have specified are related to availability, reliability, response time, throughput, resource utilization and bandwidth of SOA layers. It helps to determine that how the SOA layers performs under a particular workload. It demonstrates that the system meets performance criteria.

Companies need to know the performance of web services for a number of reasons. Some of the reasons are: Clients need to know and demand efficient PO's. Multiple service providers offering same or similar service take advantage. Also, It is required to know the resource demands of the system at different workloads.

The analysis of requirement phase shows the diversity of measurements that are applied in different service networks together with the demand for a common framework. It derives a list of performance objectives being of common interest. These performance objectives can be retrieved by using different business activity monitoring tools like Oracle Business Activity Monitoring [13], WSO2 server [14]. Performance objectives of primary interest for the users are related to the performance degradations that include availability, response time, delay, failure and loss of service.

Our objective in this research is to propose a decision-making model combining service/process performance objectives in order to generate validation arguments for the expansion of the service environment. Therefore in this paper, we propose a Performance Monitoring Framework based on the Service SOA. The decision support covers the unavailability of services, recommendation of services based on key performance indicators and the composition of existing ones.

In this paper, we introduce a performance monitoring framework for SOA layers. The framework consists of two major steps (i) Service monitoring ontology (ii) Ontologies for performance measurement of service oriented activities.

The remaining of the paper is organized as follows: Sect. 2 includes related work. Section 3 discusses our proposed performance monitoring framework. We conclude our work in the last section.

2 Requirements

Performance monitoring framework that is addressed in this paper should be able to fulfill the requirements of different user perspectives.

2.1 Service Network or Business Activity Users

In this case the framework shall provide a view of the service network which allows to easily track the failing service by analyzing the network of services. Service network involves service tasks and business processes. Service task issues a single business action for the most part. Its interactions involve the execution of a single business function or an inquiry against a single core business entity. Business Process is a sequence of tasks triggered by business events. It issues a series of business actions that could involve the invocation of one or more granular business services. This perspective is related to those users who are managing the network of services or business activities to identify and replace the faulty service. This perspective is important to address business activities are the core part of a value chain in the enterprise.

2.2 Performance Emergency Response Team (PERT)

It is important to gather the information from various sources to get clear view of performance degradations. It can be done by setting up performance objectives for monitoring along SOA layers. Performance objectives to analyze performance degradations are availability, response time, delay, loss and many others. There are different tools available to monitor these performance objectives. It is extremely important to manage the performance problems by providing some alternate solutions. Framework shall provide a mechanism to recommend alternate solutions under these circumstances.

3 Related Work

This section is divided into four parts. The first part is related to the end user requirement in performance monitoring. The second part deals with Performance based monitoring projects related to SOA paradigm are evaluated. The third part deals with the decision making models to support SOA. The fourth part evaluates the Ontology based QoS Analysis Techniques.

3.1 Performance Based Monitoring Projects

INTERMON [15] project is inter-domain QoS monitoring. This project is based on abstractions for traffic, topology. It centralizes the collection of pre-defined measurements. It cannot be guaranteed that an entity has a complete control of other networks.

JRA1 [16] project is inter-domain QoS monitoring. This architecture uses authentication and authorization rules, schedule new types of measurements. It provides metrics concatenation and aggregation. The constraint is requesting data for day-to-day operation of the networks. Other constraints are to allow distributed policies among the different networks, for exchange of monitoring data and access to on-demand test tools.

The MonALISA project [17] also provide a framework for distributed monitoring. It consists of distributed servers which handle the metric monitoring for each configured host at their site and for WAN links to other MonALISA sites. This system relies on JINI for its discovery service.

The PlanetLab [18] is a huge distributed platform over 568 nodes, located in 271 different sites. It enables people being members of the group to access the platform to run networking experiments. PlanetLab infrastructure service is centralized and relies on a single database. Similar to INTERMON it can therefore not be applied as is to a multi-domain environment.

The perfSONAR framework [19] is a service-oriented monitoring architecture to monitor the performance in multi-domain networks. It is mainly used in large-scale environments and less suited for service monitoring where fine quality is important (such as for video quality monitoring). The focus of perfSonar is on troubleshooting across network boundaries.

Top-Hat [20] federate different measurement infrastructures to provide researchers with valuable information during the discovery and selection of resources for their experiments. It interconnects measurement systems to monitor performance in multi-domain networks. It provides experiment support. This tool is used to ping a large amount of hosts with the least possible resources.

3.2   Decision in SOA

Decision as a Service [21] separates the decisions logic from the application logic. The decision process is completely put into one service. It is a method used to describe decision logic in scenarios with many input parameters. It allows to use separate services for every step of the process locally.

SOA+d [22] creates an approach bridge for the gap between SOA and decision automation. They focus on intelligent design choice model of Simon to suggest this meta-model. They integrate elements into two dimensions: conceptual and methodological. New concepts like concept of decision, intelligence, design and the choice service. Meta model purpose is to define, organize and reuse knowledge about concepts involved in the business processes and their decisional aspect as well as their design and implementation based on services and the relationship between them.

3.3   Ontology Based QoS Analysis Techniques

MonONTO [23] provides ontology to propose recommendation for the advanced internet applications users. They have considered information concerning the application type, traffic generated and user profile along with network performance metrics. Their expert system monitors the performance of advanced internet applications. Their ontology serves as a support to a decision reference tool by providing high-level information to the user about the agreement of the network facing the service level demands. They have used a fixed list of network parameters. Therefore, it does not deal with the heterogeneity and extensibility issues. Implementations of web services have not been done by them. Additionally, it does not deal with QoS mapping.

Another technique named as Semantic Web Service Discovery Based on Agents and Ontologies [24] considers the fuzzy constraints. Their framework is modelled by adding semantics of QoS attributes with web service profiles. It describes the design and implementation of a web service matchmaking agent. Agent uses an OWL-S based ontology and an OWL reasoner to compare ontology based service descriptions. They have used fuzzy constraints increases the efficiency of the web service discovery approach by providing the customers the web services which are not actually satisfying the input QoS constraints, but are close to the QoS constraints specification.

4   Performance Monitoring Framework

This section presents our Performance Monitoring Framework as shown in Fig. 2. The first step of our framework is the requirement to use service or business process. This analysis is typically performed on user requirement or business goals in a certain time period to create a specification of requirements.

Next step is the identification, defining and collection of performance objectives. Performance requirements of SOA layers are monitored in terms of PO's. These PO's have target values that are required to achieve in a certain time period. We identify PO's at the service layer, orchestration layer, resource layer and binding level. We design performance based ontologies for service oriented architecture layers.

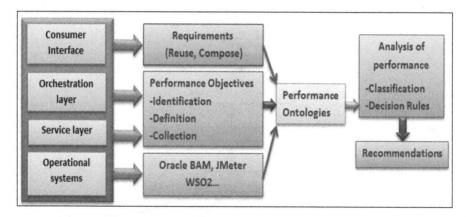

Fig. 2. Performance Monitoring Framework.

We classify these performance objectives and define decision rules based on these ontological concepts to make recommendations like yes and no to reuse existing service.

Major steps for the creation of performance profile are:

- Specifying ontological concepts
- Management of common concepts
- Quality assurance on the performance profile

In the following sub sections we explain service performance ontology and ontologies at the service layer, orchestration layer, resource layer and binding level.

4.1   Service Performance Ontology

In this step we design Service Performance ontology (SPOnt) as a base infrastructure. It aggregates the main concepts and relationships between them. QoS requirements, service domain concepts, key performance indicators and performance levels are the major concepts. SPOnt is shown in Fig. 3.

Service
This concept has various data type properties to capture different attributes in SPOnt. It also has various object properties that links Service concept to other concepts. The details are as follows:

Performance Level
This concept conceptualizes the level where a service network can be monitored. It has various sub concepts, each for capturing the performance levels such as Domain Level, Node level, Server Level, Service Level, Operation Level, and Messaging Level.

QoS Level
Quality of service model is classified as metrics into time based, size based and combined (both time based and size based) metrics. Key performance indicator (KPI)

222   T. Masood et al.

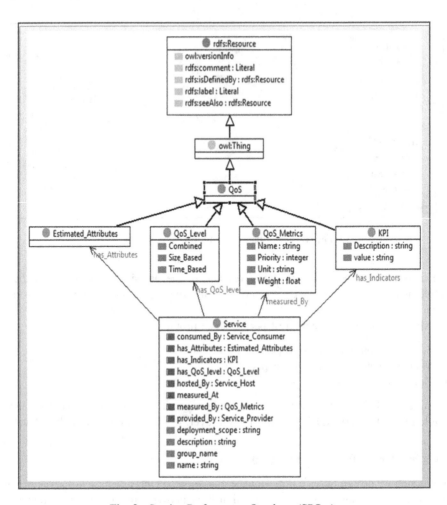

Fig. 3. Service Performance Ontology (SPOnt).

assessment model has classified the indicators as response time, delay, error, loss, SLA, number of operations per second and average data blocks per time unit.

Time based

Time based classification includes all those indicators that can be measured in time units like availability, delay, response time. Availability is defined as the total down time per service. Delay is defined as downtime divided by uptime. Response time is also called latency. It is the time perceived by a client to obtain a reply for a request for a web service. It includes the transmission delays on the communication link. It is measured in time units.

Size based

Size based classification includes all those indicators that can be measured in size units. For example reliability. Reliability can be analyzed as loss or error of service. It is measured as number of successful invocations divided by total number of invocations.

Combined

Combined based classification includes all those indicators that can be measured by both time and size units like bandwidth and throughput. Bandwidth is defined as the tasks per time unit and average data blocks per time unit. Throughput is defined as the number of operations per second.

4.2   Performance Objectives for SOA Layers

In this step, we explain the ontological concepts of the performance at service layer, orchestration layer, resource layer and binding level. Ontologies for all these layers are shown below step by step. Figure 4 shows the ontology of performance at service layer. PO's at service layer are explained below.

Response Time: captures the response time of a service/operation. It has three sub concepts to record Maximum, Minimum and Average response time.

Request Count: shows the number of invocation of a service.

Response Count: shows the number of replies for an invocation of a service.

Fault Count: shows the number of invocations the service has not replied.

Deploy Time: shows when the service is deployed at the server

Up Time: shows the time period the service is available since its deployment

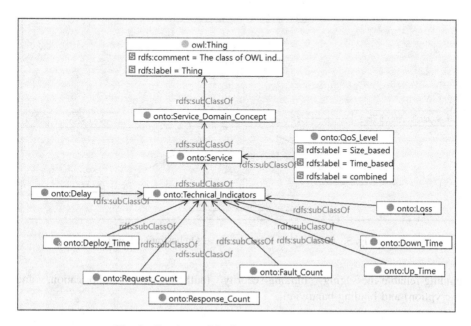

Fig. 4. Ontology of Performance at Service Layer.

Down Time: shows the time period of un-availability of a service since its deployment
Delay: shows the average response time of a service.
Loss: shows that the service is un-available (i.e., it cannot be invoked).

Figure 5 shows the ontology of performance at orchestration layer. PO's at orchestration layer are explained below.

Process-Response-Time: captures the response time of a business process. It has three sub concepts to record Maximum, Minimum and Average response time.
Process-Up-Time: shows the time period the business process is available since its deployment
Process-Down-Time: shows the time period of un-availability of a business process.
Process-Delay: shows the average response time of a business process.
Process-Loss: shows that the business process is un-available (i.e., it cannot be invoked).
Process-Duration: shows the time duration of business process since it is deployed, executed and remained in process.

Some other PO's at service layer are also used in order to estimate their value at composition level like availability and service response time.

Figure 6 shows the ontology of performance at binding level. Binding level means at the messaging level. PO's at transport messaging level are binding-throughput,

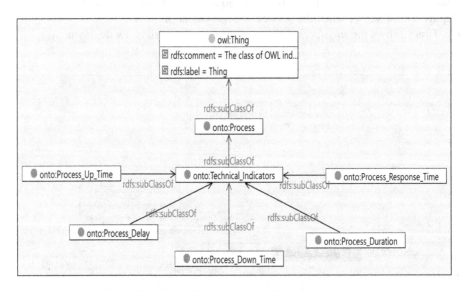

Fig. 5. Ontology of Performance at Orchestration Layer.

binding-reliable-messaging, binding-security (authentication, authorization, and encryption) and binding-bandwidth.

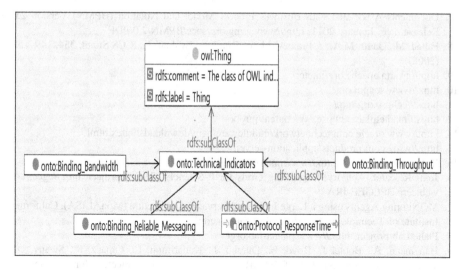

Fig. 6. Ontology of Performance at Integration Layer.

5 Conclusion

In this paper, we propose a framework to identify the performance objectives along the service oriented architecture layers. The proposed research work accelerates the analysis of existing service networks in order to validate service reuse capabilities. First of all we design our service performance ontology SPOnt to show the relationships of all the concepts. Then we identify the performance objectives at the service layer, orchestration layer, resource layer and binding level. Then we use performance objectives of these aforementioned layers to provide decision making capabilities. We will enhance our work to cover the recommendation based on the decision rules for service reuse and service composition problem. We will implement our work by using real time case study.

References

1. Gottschalk, K., Graham, S., Kreger, H., Snell, J.: Introduction to web services architecture. IBM Syst. J. **41**(2), 170–177 (2002)
2. Extensible Markup Language (XML) 1.1 (2nd edn.) (2006). World Wide Web Consortium. http://www.w3.org/TR/xml11/
3. Simple Object Access Protocol (SOAP) 1.2, Part 0, Primer (2007). World Wide Web Consortium. http://www.w3.org/TR/soap12-part0/
4. Web Services Description Language (WSDL) 2.0, part 1: Core Language (2007). World Wide Web Consortium. http://www.w3c.org/TR/wsdl20/
5. https://www.opengroup.org/soa/source-book/soa_refarch/layers.htm
6. Tari, Z., Phan, A.K.A., Jayasinghe, M., Abhaya, V.G.: Benchmarking soap binding. In: On the Performance of Web Services, pp. 35–58. Springer (2011)

226   T. Masood et al.

7. Documents Associated with Business Process Model and Notation (BPMN) Version 2.0 Release date. January 2011. http://www.omg.org/spec/BPMN/2.0/PDF
8. Fahad, M., Qadir, M.A.: A Framework for Ontology Evaluation. ICCS Suppl. **354**, 149–158 (2008)
9. http://jakarta.apache.org/jmeter/
10. http://www.soapui.org/
11. https://eclipse.org/tptp/
12. https://marketplace.eclipse.org/content/jprobe
13. http://www.oracle.com/technetwork/middleware/bam/downloads/index.html
14. http://wso2.com/products/application-server/
15. INTERMON project. http://www.intermon.org/
16. Joint Research Activity 4, Enabling Grids for E-SciencE (EGEE) project. http://egeejra4.web.cern.ch/EGEE-JRA4/
17. MONitoring Agents using a Large Integrated Services Architecture (MonALISA). California Institute of Technology. http://monalisa.caltech.edu/
18. PlanetLab project. http://www.planet-lab.org/
19. Hanemann, A., Boote, J., Boyd, E., Durand, J., Kudarimoti, L., Łapacz, R., Swany, D., Trocha, S., & Zurawski, J. PerfSONAR: a service oriented architecture for multidomain network monitoring. In: Proceedings of 3rd International Conference Service Oriented Computing (ICSOC 2005). Amsterdam, The Netherlands. doi:10.1007/11596141_19
20. Bourgeau, T., Augé, J., Friedman, T.: TopHat: supporting experiments through measurement infrastructure federation. In: Proceedings of the 6th International ICST Conference on Testbeds and Research Infrastructures for the Development of Networks and Communities (TridentCom 2010)
21. Zarghami, A., Sapkota, B., Eslami, M. Z., van Sinderen, M.: Decision as a service: separating decision-making from application process logic. In: EDOC, pp. 103–112. IEEE (2012)
22. Boumahdi, F., Chalal, R., Guendouz, A., Gasmia, K.: SOA+d: a new way to design the decision in SOA-based on the new standard Decision Model and Notation (DMN). SOCA **10** (1), 35–53 (2016). http://link.springer.com/search?query=Boumahdi&search-within=Journal&facet-journal-id=11761
23. Moraes, P., Sampaio, L., Monteiro, J., Portnoi, M.: Mononto: A domain ontology for network monitoring and recommendation for advanced internet applications users. In: Network Operations and Management Symposium Workshops. IEEE (2008)
24. Benaboud, R., Maamri, R., Sahnoun, Z.: Semantic Web Service Discovery Basedon Agents and Ontologies. Int. J. Innov. Manage. Technol. **3**(4), 467–472 (2012)

Applications and Software Development

Empirical Investigation of Scrumban in Global Software Development

Ahmad Banijamali$^{(\boxtimes)}$, Research Dawadi, Muhammad Ovais Ahmad,
Jouni Similä, Markku Oivo, and Kari Liukkunen

M3S Research Unit, Faculty of Information Technology and Electrical Engineering,
University of Oulu, PO box 4500, 90014 Oulu, Finland
{ahmad.banijamali,muhammad.ahmad,jouni.simila,markku.oivo,
kari.liukkunen}@oulu.fi, research.dawadi@student.oulu.fi

Abstract. Scrumban combines two Agile approaches (Scrum and
Kanban) to create a management framework for improving software engineering practices. Scrumban is expected to override both Scrum and
Kanban, as it inherits the best features of both. However, there is little
understanding of the possible impact of Scrumban on software development in prior studies. This study first makes a comparison among Scrum,
Kanban, and Scrumban and then investigates the impact of Scrumban
on six major challenges of global software development. This study was
conducted in a distributed project at two Software Factories in two universities in Finland and Italy. The results show that Scrumban could
positively affect issues such as evenness of different sites, communication,
and cultural issues as well as leveraging resources among sites. However,
there are still few challenges that require alternative methodologies and
tools other than Scrumban to be overcome.

Keywords: Agile · Distributed software development · Kanban ·
Scrum · Scrumban · Software factory

1 Introduction

The success of software development projects depends heavily on the use of appropriate software development methodology. According to a report by Standish
Group, 42% of project cases which have used an Agile approach were successful, which is considerably more than what has been achieved using traditional
project management methods [1]. Agile methods are iterative, incremental, and
enhance collaboration between self-organizing cross-functional teams [2]. Scrum is
the most frequently used Agile method in software development [3]. Scrum reaches
its objective through time-boxed iterations based on continuous feedback and task
prioritization [4].

Kanban, on the other hand, has not been widely adopted in software development [5]. In 2004, Kanban entered into the Agile realm when David Anderson introduced it in practice while assisting a software development team at Microsoft [6].

© Springer International Publishing AG 2017
S. Hammoudi et al. (Eds): MODELSWARD 2016, CCIS 692, pp. 229–248, 2017.
DOI: 10.1007/978-3-319-66302-9_12

Kanban proposes to defer the project commitments, set constraints on the amount of work in progress (WIP), and limit the project promises that cause project failure [7]. The high expectations for Kanban are the result of its adaptability regarding changes in requirements, its ability to visualize project processes, and its role in increasing communication and cooperation among team members [8].

A study by Ladas [9] combined Scrum and Kanban to introduce a methodology which represents the best elements of those methodologies. According to that study, Scrumban is more appropriate for teams that are already using Scrum. Scrumban applies Scrum as a prescriptive method of team-work to complete the work, while it encourages process improvements through Kanban to allow projects to continuously optimize the processes and number of tasks [10].

There are limitations with respect to Scrum which can be mitigated by using Kanban alongside it. For example, Scrum does not consider the organization as a whole during its implementation [11] and has limitations such as lack of work visibility and changing task priorities [12]. Scrumban thus inhibits companies from embracing change and establishing better relationships between business and information technology departments [13]. Scrum and Kanban can be combined for high throughput and visibility into the development process.

Geographically distributed teams with poorly planned coordination often end up with unmatched deadlines, cost overruns, and even cancelled projects [14]. Distributed software development settings (DSD) often have additional challenges such as different locations, times, cultures, and languages among team members which can add more complexities to software development [15]. The idea of utilizing manpower from different locations is tempting, but it creates excessive coordination tasks in projects makes it difficult to ensure that everyone has a clear idea of the project goals and is committed to achieving them.

A study conducted by Šmite et al. [16] compares the characteristics of Agile and DSD and declares that communication in Agile projects is informal, face-to-face, and synchronous, while DSD projects require formal, computer-mediated, and often asynchronous communication. Moreover, Agile projects apply change-driven and self-managed coordination and light-weight control. However, DSD settings need plan-driven and standardized coordination among sites, which is achieved through several command and control methods. Despite their opposing characteristics, the combination of Agile and distributed development is of high interest to companies [17].

Geographically distributed development, in itself, is a vague term because there can be different types of distributed teams based on the time difference between the involved team members [18]. Two configurations of distributed teams that can be taken into consideration are North-South and East-West. North-South distributed teams do not have a considerable difference in time-zones, while the East-West configuration involves a significant time-zone difference [18]. Our investigated software factories (described in Sect. 3.1) were distributed from the North to South of Europe; hence, the East-West setting is beyond the scope of this research.

According to Šmite et al. [16], there is limited research and understanding about the application of Agile methodologies in DSD. In addition, Scrumban is a new development approach in the software engineering domain, and existing literature provides little information on Scrumban's impact on DSD projects. Increasing interest in globally distributed software development practices has motivated us to investigate the following research question: "How does Scrumban methodology affect global software development?" As coordination among developers is a critical issue within those environments, we have mainly investigated Scrumban from this perspective.

This paper is structured as follows: Sect. 2 presents an overview of previous studies on Scrum, Kanban, and Scrumban in the context of software engineering and similarities and differences among them. Further, it discusses global software development. Section 3 provides a brief introduction to the Software Factory settings and then elaborates on the T-Bix project case which has been used for this research. Next, it shows the project coordination model and the applied research approach. Section 4 presents findings of this study, the limitations, and direction for future studies. Section 5 concludes the paper and highlights the main contributions of our work.

2   Related Works

This section discusses Scrum, Kanban, and Scrumban with respect to their similarities and differences. It also describes software development practices in a global context.

2.1   Scrum

The first implementation of Scrum in the field of software development was at Easel Corporation in the USA in 1993 [19]. Scrum advocates small teams that work independently and create more efficiency at work [20]. Scrum is an incremental Agile software development methodology that operates through a series of iterations that require continuous planning, defined roles, and project artefacts [21,22]. Scrum is the most frequently applied Agile software development method [3] for achieving small but continuous deliverables. It facilitates regular feedback after each iterative development process, called a "sprint" [23]. According to Rising and Janoff [20], Scrum is beneficial, particularly for projects in which all the requirements are not clear in advance.

Implementation of Scrum allows self-organization which can result in a high-performance team even if the team comprises average developers [19]. The most important roles in Scrum include: (1) product owner, who serves as an interface among developers and other stakeholders, (2) Scrum master, who is the person responsible for leading scrum meetings, identifying tasks to be completed within the sprints, and measuring progress [20], and (3) development team. Since companies from Western countries often tend to outsource their software development to Eastern countries [19], applying Scrum in such situations can induce independency of teams as well as increase communication and productivity.

2.2   Kanban

Kanban is a relatively new concept in the field of software engineering that was originally applied in Lean manufacturing [6]. While Scrum focuses on one iteration at a time, Kanban supports a continuous workflow [5]. Kanban provides the flexibility of managing the workflow within teams. It limits WIP in each activity to a maximum number of tasks or items at any given time. Moreover, it does not suggest strictly defined roles and sprints [24]. It provides a clear visualization of the phases in the project lifecycle.

Kanban reduces lead time and improves quality and productivity [25]. Kanban helps team members to identify constraints of a process and focus on a single item or task at a time [26]. In traditional software development methods, several works are assigned to a team member, which is defined as a push method [26]. In that case, the work to be completed is sent to the team member regardless of the status of other work. On the other hand, Kanban suggests assigning a developer to one particular job. When the work is completed, the developer can pull another task from the Kanban board and work on it. According to Polk [27], provision of a Kanban board changed the thinking of team members by making them realize that they are not just developing code but developing a complete product. With Kanban, team members, stakeholders, and customers can get a real-time view of project progress [26]. Implementation of Kanban also lowers the risk of communication and coordination breakdown [28].

2.3   Scrumban

By combining Lean and Agile methodologies, project members can receive rapid and iterative feedback while they have the ability to implement the necessary changes and respond to the feedback. The combination of Agile and Lean in co-located projects enhances coordination among team members, increases team morale, and produces better outcomes [13]. Lean increases the scale of the development process and makes it efficient, while Agile principles help to make the process flexible [11].

Table 1 summarizes the key points of using Scrum and Kanban in the same project by showing several examples from the literature. In Sect. 4.1, we will use these points for our analysis in the context of distributed software development.

Scrum and Kanban are similar in the sense that both improve transparency, aim to release software as soon as possible, work on the principle of breaking work into pieces, and continuously optimize the project plan [29]. It is argued that if Kanban is used alongside Scrum, they can complement each other [30]. Scrumban incorporates the iterative planning of Scrum but is more responsive and adaptive to changes in user requirements. Project members who have had good experience with Scrum can benefit from Scrumban, as it improves their knowledge and capabilities [30]. By combining Scrum and Kanban, researchers hope to create more flexibility in projects as well as maintaining the iterative pace that Scrum has provided [30].

Table 1. Scrum and Kanban methodological elements.

ID	Study place	Key points	Reference
P01	Vietnamese office of a Swedish software development company	Scrum: Iterative and incremental Regular feedback Strict roles and rules Kanban: Visualization Limiting WIP Scrumban: Self-organizing Collaborative teamwork	Nikitina et al. [24]
P02	Faculty of Computer and Information Science, University of Ljubljana	Scrum: Incremental and iterative Planned project Regular feedback Kanban: Maximize workflow Visualization Limiting WIP	Mahnic [5]
P03	Arrk Group: a multinational software development company	Scrumban: Limiting WIP Optimal resource utilization Collaborative teamwork Quick decisions Customer satisfaction	Joshi and Maher [31]
P04	GoGo: offers services such as Internet, entertainment, messaging, voice in the aviation market	Scrumban: Visualization of workflows Transparency Increased team participation	Brinker [32]

One factor that Scrumban inherits from Kanban is the visualization of workflows [10]. Scrum completes tasks through sprints that are planned in advance, but Scrumban allows more flexibility and planning only for the following sprint. This helps projects to limit WIP. When the limit of tasks in a particular workflow is reached, team members help each other to complete the tasks in that workflow rather than starting a new one. This increases the coordination among team members and also reduces the possibility of a bottleneck [10].

Scrumban, unlike Scrum, has no strict rules and roles and encourages self-organized teams. As a result, team members manage their tasks by themselves and make quicker decisions. According to Khan [10], Scrumban reduces the relevant tasks of planning for the whole iteration (the same as Scrum), as meetings are set only when required and tasks are changed depending on the output of the ongoing sprint.

A real case example of a company's transition from Scrum to Scrumban [4] reports that implementation of Scrumban provided a systematic improvement in the performance of developers. Additional features of Scrumban over Scrum such as WIP limit and pull-based task management are received well by the team members. Table 2 has summarized findings from Yilmaz and O'Connor [4], Reddy [7], and Ahmad et al. [33] to highlight the similarities and differences between Scrum, Kanban, and Scrumban.

Table 2. Similarities and differences among Scrum, Kanban and Scrumban [4,7,33].

Kanban	Scrum	Scrumban
No predefined roles for members	Predefined roles of Scrum master and team members	Predefined roles of Scrum master and team members may vary within project time
Continuous delivery	Time-boxed sprints	Task board-based iterations
WIP limits amount of work	Sprint limits amount of work	WIP limits amount of work
Changes can be made at any time	No changes allowed mid-sprint	Changes allowed mid-sprint
Earlier planning and documentation necessary	Planning done after each sprint	Planning on demand, also within sprints
Kanban board is persistent	Scrum board is reset after each sprint	Scrumban board is persistent
Size of task is not limited	Size of task limited to a sprint	Size of task is not limited
Pull-based work management	Sprint backlog-based work management	Pull-based work management

The implementation of Scrumban, however, presents several challenges. The flexibility regarding production changes can cause new challenges in, for example, assigning resources and developing project time-tables. Because Lean methodology calls for considering the whole organization through implementation [34], the combination of Kanban and Scrumban increases the complexities of planning for activities across the whole organization. Moreover, it is not always possible to include business personnel or management executives developing project backlogs or contributing regular feedback [11].

2.4 Distributed Software Development

Finding resources globally creates the possibility of mobility in resources and of accessing new knowledge of skilled people around the world [17]. Global software development is applied through multi-geo, multicultural, and multi-temporal environments to benefit from access to new markets, lower costs, increased operational efficiency, improved quality, and less time to markets [35].

DSD could have different configurational characteristics, which refers to the structural properties of the global environment, different ways of distributing developers, and differences in time and physical distance. A study by Ramasubbu et al. [36] examined how configurational dimensions can affect productivity, quality, and profit outcomes of distributed projects. This study explains aspects of dispersions including spatial dispersion to measure the physical distance, temporal dispersion to measure the time-zone difference, and configurational dispersion to measure structural properties such as number of distributed sites and homogeneity of distributed people and skills across different sites.

Šmite et al. [17], Jiménez et al. [37], and Nakamura et al. [38] declare that realizing the DSD benefits come with associated challenges in terms of communication gaps between multiple sites, group awareness, software configuration management, knowledge management, flexible coordination, collaboration, project management, process support, tools support, quality management, and risk management.

Coordination is a pressing issue in global software development. People at the research and development center of Yahoo in Norway mentioned that the time-zone difference was a major cause of problems when dealing with dislocated teams [18]. According to Noll et al. [39], the main barriers to coordination in distributed projects are geographic, temporal, cultural, and linguistic differences. That study proposed that project teams should enhance site visits, use synchronous communication technology, and apply knowledge-sharing infrastructure to transform implicit knowledge to explicit knowledge [39]. Other scholars such as Mak and Kruchten [40], Redmiles et al. [41], and Sidhu and Volberda [42] have argued that coordination issues come from (1) lack of flexibility and integration, (2) poor role support, (3) decreasing informal communication and workplace transparency, and (4) limitations imposed on formal communication. However, the levels of impact of these issues are different in different dispersion configurations; for example, a study conducted by Ramasubbu et al. [36] suggests that establishing a project in an East-West geographical setting requires radically more consideration of time-zone classifications than North-South settings.

There are several instances of the application of Scrum in distributed development projects [1,16,18,43]. The American software consulting company Agile Factori implemented a successful software development project using Agile methodologies. The project was provided by Big Oil, an American company consisting of four teams, two of which were located in America and the other two in Brazil and Argentina. All four teams had a real-time video screen with audio that showed activities at the other sites. In addition, one screen at each site showed a dashboard of in-process software components. This allowed other sites visualization, increased awareness, and better coordination among teams [18].

SirsiDynix (U.S) has successfully implemented distributed Scrum since 2005 [19,43]. Using distributed Scrum, SirsiDynix collaborated with the Russian company Exigen in 2005 for a large project [43] employing more than 50 members in total and producing over one million lines of code. The output of this distributed team was estimated to be equivalent to the work of a 350 co-located-person team working in a waterfall model [43].

An international Agile software development company, Xebia, located in France, India, and the Netherlands, also implemented Scrum successfully between 2006 and 2008 [43]. Distributed Scrum was used alongside XP programming in multiple projects by Xebia, and the results showed that the distributed teams were as effective as co-located teams. These instances show that globally distributed teams can be as productive as co-located teams when Scrum is applied effectively [19,44].

3   Research Process

3.1   Software Factory

Software Factories (SF) include structured sets of related software assets to provide developers with a development setting consisting of domain-specific tools that help to transform abstract models into implementations [26,45,46]. Through the SF settings, reusable development practices such as patterns, models, guidelines, and transformations are accessible from the viewpoint of a specific aspect in the development context. This enables domain-specific validation and guidance delivery [47].

The SFs increase productivity from the business perspective, improve quality and consistency of architectures and designs, reduce development lifecycle, and consolidate operational efforts [47]. Also, SFs established in the context of universities are perfect avenues for exploiting technological research for innovation. A study by Taibi et al. [48] declares that such an SF environment benefits both business by receiving innovative, new ideas and academia by presenting new skills, frameworks, and models. Therefore, academic Software Factories can be additionally considered as a new concept of collaboration among universities and companies [48].

3.2   T-Bix Project Case

A joint five-month software development project called T-Bix was initiated between the University of Oulu, Finland and the University of Bolzano, Italy in their respective Software Factories. The aim of the project was to develop a single common platform for the time-banking system to be operational in South Tyrol in Italy. The platform allows users to register their own profiles, search for jobs and products, post jobs and products, send requests for jobs and products, and communicate their feedback. The target group was young, unemployed people as well as senior citizens hit by the socio-economic crisis.

Because T-Bix project teams were located in Europe (North-South dispersion configuration), they did not experience drastic temporal differences; however, the long physical distance and diverse cultures, languages, and social behaviors remained as challenges in the project. The Finnish team consisted of one PhD candidate and four master's degree students who were working locally in Oulu. The team from Italy had a Software Factory coordinator with a PhD degree and four master's degree students. A member of the Italian team was working remotely from Lithuania. There was one student on each team with industrial experience; however, the rest of the teams did not have prior experience in industry. Each team comprised one project manager and three developers. The Finnish team used Scrumban, while the other team used Scrum as the development methodology in Italy. Teams frequently used available tools and assets in SFs, including Rise Editor, Myeclipse, Dreamweaver, JIRA, and GitHub. There was an Italian entrepreneur (customer of the T-Bix project) who was in direct contact with both teams. The customer communicated his needs through meetings and emails; teams attempted to interpret the customer's requirements into user stories and backlogs.

The front-end of the application was developed with direct contact with the customer in Italy. The back-end, including the database development and integration of the front-end and back-end, was developed in Finland. The codes were shared on GitHub, where some feedback and comments were also shared.

An identical Kanban board was created in JIRA by the Oulu team and shared with the team members in Bolzano. The Kanban board was updated regularly, providing visibility of the board and tasks across both teams.

In addition to JIRA boards, the Software Factory in Oulu was equipped with physical Kanban boards that were utilized throughout the project lifetime. The boards were divided into four sections: backlog (features), to do, in progress (WIP), and done, and was populated with user stories planned in each sprint. Once each sprint was completed, the team in Finland updated the boards with new tasks and shifting completed jobs to the "done" section. Figure 1 shows a snapshot of the board.

Teams used collaboration tools such as Skype and Google Hangout to communicate and verify the requirements, monitor the project progress, present the sprint deliverables, discuss the challenges, and set new milestones. After each sprint, teams presented their respective outcomes and progress and received feedback from both the customer and other team members.

Finding the best time for meetings is a major concern in global software development [18]. Members from the T-Bix project met on a planned time-table which considered the temporal difference between Italy, Finland, and Lithuania. To accommodate other sites and the customer, the meetings were often held in the afternoon. This ability to hold meetings during the daytime without much time shifting is an advantage provided by North-South collaboration.

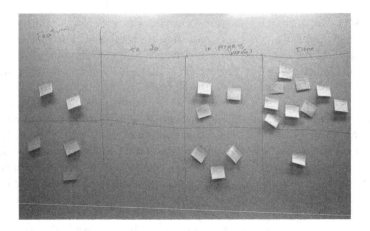

Fig. 1. A physical Kanban board in Oulu software factory.

3.3 Project Coordination Model

The project was proposed by the customer to the University of Bolzano with the aim of decreasing the rate of unemployment in South Tyrol. Subsequently, the University of Bolzano had the idea of making the project a distributed Software Factory project between the two universities.

The customer was in contact with the teams with respect to the elicitation of requirements, acceptance testing, and the validation of artefacts. The user interface of the website was designed and validated through regular meetings with the customer. The codes and designs were continuously uploaded in GitHub, in which both teams updated their latest work. The next sprint was planned according to the feedback and suggestions made by the customer and both teams. The following model (Fig. 2) shows how the project was carried out among the teams.

3.4 Research Approach

This study exploits empirical software engineering methods. The authors have applied semi-structured interviews to collect the data. The participants of this study are members of the Oulu Software Factory who were interviewed after completion of the project. The authors provided a set of open-ended questions covering the scope and objectives of this paper. Four rounds of interviews were conducted, which lasted from 45 min to 2 h. All interviews were recorded and transcribed, enabling authors to analyze them based on the needs of this study.

A semi-structured interview format was preferred, as it provides a clear set of instructions for the interviewer, who usually follows a paper-based interview guide during the interview. The availability of questions beforehand makes the interviews easier for the interviewer and the openness of this type of interview provides the interviewees with the freedom to express their views using their own terms.

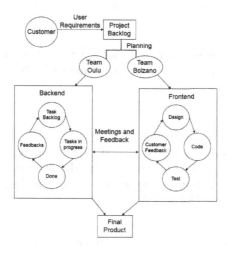

Fig. 2. Project coordination model.

Table 3. Interviewees' backgrounds.

Interviewee	Role in the project	Empirical experience	Expertise
D1	Project manager	10 years	Project management, UI Design, JIRA&GitHub
D2	Programmer	—	PostgreSQL, JIRA&GitHub
D3	Programmer	—	PostgreSQL, Java, JIRA&GitHub
D4	UI Designer	—	UI Design, Java, JIRA&GitHub

In addition, the comparable qualitative data obtained from semi-structured interviews is regarded as reliable for analysis [49]. Table 3 summarizes the roles, empirical experiences, and expertise of the interviewees.

We have defined a set of the coding categories based on the top challenges of the DSD projects. Those challenges have been extracted from prior studies in the DSD domain. The categories were discussed and confirmed by two authors of this paper. All challenges are defined in detail in the next section. Afterward, authors read through the transcripts and underlined each fragment of relevant information and specified which fragment fell into which DSD challenges categories. We have provided some examples of the specified fragments in the next section. Finally, the reliability of the results was tested separately by two authors of this paper, and they each found the same results.

4   Results

This section summarizes key findings regarding Scrumban's impact on the T-Bix project as well as the limitations and opportunities for future research.

4.1   Findings

Table 4 explains how the impact of Scrumban has been realized in the coordination between North-South distributed sites. For this purpose, we have investigated the top issues in DSD projects as already introduced by other scholars, including Carmel and Espinosa [18], Barcus and Montibeller [50], Espinosa et al. [51], and Nidiffer and Dolan [52].

Table 4. Impact of Scrumban on coordination in DSD environments.

Scrumban aspects		Issues in distributed software development					
	Strategic	Project and process management	Communication	Cultural	Technical	Security
Iterative and incremental development	Highly improved toward latest sprints	Highly improved toward latest sprints	More sprints, smoother	More iterations, fewer challenges	Slightly improved	No evidence
Predictable and well-planned project	No meaningful impact on leveraging resources at the other site	More iterations, more improvement	Effective communication for the planned tasks	No evidence	Slightly improved toward latest sprints	No evidence
Transparency	Positively impacted leveraging resources at both sites	Positively impacted task management within sites	No evidence	Slightly reduced challenges	No evidence	No evidence
Regular feedback	Slightly improved	Positively impacted task management within sites	Demands of both formal and informal feedback	Improved toward latest sprints	No evidence	No evidence
Limiting WIP	Positively impacted resource management	Decreased challenges slightly	No evidence	No evidence	No evidence	No evidence
Self-organizing	Slightly improved	Positively impacted task management within sites	Improved informal communication	No evidence	No evidence	No evidence

Strategic issues within DSD settings are concerned with the difficulty in leveraging available resources. Issues in which stakeholders can anticipate and manage risks should be identified carefully [52]. Because T-Bix was an evolutionary project done through iterative sprints, teams were able to find new ways to leverage available resources and skills. Within the initial meetings, two teams discussed the experience and expertise of their members, clarifying how the project resources were divided between the two sites and how the project duties should be assigned.

However, the team members mentioned their increasing responsibility during the later sprints of the project. The project manager [D1] explained that they were asked to accomplish some additional work on coding. Adapting to these workflow changes made it difficult to complete the project. A developer [D4] explained that after much discussion, the two teams decided to assign additional tasks to the Oulu team, as they had more technical skills:

"After much discussion, we had to accept more work, as Bolzano was not able to complete it. We should provide more deliverables at the end of the project. We had no choice because we wanted the project done."

The teams applied JIRA to establish the project structure and define the roles of the two sites. Project tasks were assigned to the teams' members according to their roles and skills. Furthermore, JIRA created visibility in the WIP for each role compared to other developers. The project manager [D1] confirmed this:

"Using JIRA, I could monitor the progress of different completed tasks with respect to the roles. It provided me an opportunity to recognize the tasks that required extra coordination."

Project and process management in DSD involves discussing problematic situations in synchronizing work between distributed sites [50]. Integrated quality, shared workspaces for storing files, and engineering tools are potential enablers of this issue. Complexity also arises from the fact that there should be sufficient communication between two teams before they can prioritize project tasks and decide which one is to be carried out by which team, as in the case of the T-Bix project discussed. The teams had agreed upon a preliminary division of work, but additional tasks were later added to the project by the customer. The members mentioned that the added tasks caused several challenges in managing their ongoing tasks. To control the scope of the project, the involved teams should manage changes in a planned way. Any changes in the project scope may affect the priority and division of work among the sites. The project manager [D1] declared the following primary decision criterion for allocating tasks between sites:

"Consistency between the requested feature and available skills and knowledge at the sites was our decision criterion for allocating tasks to sites."

Using Kanban boards in JIRA improved the visualization and transparency of the completed, ongoing, and planned tasks. One developer [D3] mentioned the following:

"The Kanban board in JIRA was quite helpful because we could not frequently update the pictures of the physical Kanban board for the other team. We applied JIRA's Kanban board to share the tasks we had completed and planned to do."

Using JIRA and GitHub, project members received feedback on their jobs, for example, for the codes that were uploaded in GitHub. One of the developers [D2] stated the following:

"For example, when the scripts in the database had problems, one of the programmers in Bolzano was using GitHub to send feedback regarding the issues and asking for solutions."

Another developer [D4] also believed the following:

"JIRA is a tool developed for task management purposes, but you cannot upload all project deliverables into it. It is not a shared platform, so we needed to use other tools, in which we could share other data."

Communication issues are related to the lack of effective communication mechanisms. It is very important to convey information such as the current state of the project as well as project challenges, schedule, and cost. In the case of distributed projects, communication plays an important role in collaboratively planning the project stages. Along with formal communication, informal communication between team members and with stakeholders can ease the working environment and facilitate coordination among them [29]. Applying Scrumban in DSD projects demands both formal and informal styles of communication. Informal communication facilitates project implementation; however, formal communication creates a disciplined environment, which is necessary for coordination in DSD sites.

Communication was regarded as an important tool for ensuring that the T-Bix teams were placed at the same level of understanding regarding the project. A developer [D4] highlighted the following:

"The Bolzano team had their own understanding of the project and we had ours. We had discussions to resolve the discrepancies and create balance between the two teams. Scrumban provoked us to have regular meetings with team members as well as the customer. This increased the level of communication in the project." However, the project manager [D1] mentioned that different time-zones created little discomfort for arranging meetings.

Scrumban leads to a great deal of communication. One developer [D4] argued the following:

"At first, we had many problems in our communication because the project members complained that the other site hindered the project progress and was not completing its tasks well."

However, new communication channels as well as more effective planning in the project led to a higher level of communication between teams. It was claimed that:

"We had many challenges in our discussions, but since people have had more communication and became increasingly more acquainted with the way the other team works, communication became smoother."[D1]

Cultural issues involve the conflicting behavioral processes and technologies among various team members [52]. Different socio-cultural backgrounds make communication more complicated due to lack of understanding of other social behaviors, cultures, and languages. The T-Bix project shows that people have different expectations regarding working in multinational teams; for example, one developer [D2] explained the following:

"It was quite good for distributed software development to include multiple cultures. It was interesting to work with people with different backgrounds."

However, other people found multi-cultural settings more difficult than co-located projects.

Due to the nature of Software Factory projects, team members were completely new to each other and they were assigned to this project with no prior knowledge of the other team members. At the beginning of the project, they had several challenges in communicating with each other and establishing good organization for their project; however, the evolution of the teams and the feedback on the requirements and skills alleviated cultural barriers after people had met for several sprints.

Technical issues in DSD environments are related to incompatible data formats and exchanges. Creating standards and web services could be seen as potential ways to resolve this issue. The T-Bix case shows that during different sprints, teams progressively realized the technical abilities and needs of other sites. The iterative nature of Scrumban helped them to meet those needs and prepare to meet the internal project standards and agreements.

Security, on the other hand, involves ensuring electronic transmission confidentiality and privacy [52]. It can be improved through emerging standards for secure messaging. The T-Bix project did not provide meaningful evidence of Scrumban's impact on improving security issues in DSD settings. However, this study was conducted with respect to coordination issues, and other project issues are beyond its scope.

4.2 Limitations

The research was conducted in a Software Factory where we collected member experiences from a business case with a real customer outside the university. According to Fagerholm et al. [53], student selection process can serve as a limitation in Software Factory projects because universities apply different prerequisites and standards for their selection process. In our case, the two universities followed different selection methods, resulting in differences in the level of knowledge and skills between the two teams.

The authors believe that the limited number of the interviewees is the most critical limitation of this paper. The semi-structured interview design for the university environment led to both the benefits and the limitations of this research. Prior studies argue for the clear benefits of using students as empirical research subjects [54,55]; although academic projects rarely can be defined on a large scale. To that end, it is necessary to carry out further studies within a larger context in an industrial setting to verify our findings.

This research was done within three European countries. Therefore, the DSD configuration is North-South, with little difference in time-zones. We assume that management of teams with a higher level of time variation, for example East-West configuration, might have more issues. Greater differences in time-zones, for instance from India to the U.S., will cause more coordination challenges for joint meetings and on-time responses to emails, as well as more drastic changes in culture and languages.

4.3   Future Research

There are a limited number of studies and industrial practices on the applicability, challenges and benefits of Scrumban in software engineering. The Software Factory setting is an attractive concept for testing new ideas and methodologies related to software development. However, there are challenges related to maintaining software artefacts after the completion of Software Factory projects [56]. The authors believe that the results of the T-Bix project can be maintained in future academic research, for example, by involving other Software Factories from different time-zones. It is important to continue studying the impact of Scrumban on East-West distributed teams with a greater variation in time-zones. In addition, companies with distributed sites suffer from similar challenges; therefore, they would be the best candidates to apply Scrumban and provide feedback for designing future Software Factory projects.

An interesting future study would be investigating how the results of this study would work in a large industrial environment where there are multiple sites involved at a variety of locations. We believe that those environments could nicely validate the capability of Scrumban to improve coordination in DSD projects.

This study primarily emphasized coordination aspects within distributed sites. Other issues require further investigation with respect to proper methodologies, workflows, and tools. Also, we did not consider impact parameters such as age, education, and years of experience on the use of Scrumban, which could apparently be a very good research topic.

5   Conclusions

Current software companies tend to establish their production units in different locations in order to optimize skilled workforces to produce products at higher quality and lower cost. In that regard, companies need adequate methodologies, techniques, and tools to improve efficiency and decrease challenges in DSD. Software Factory settings can reuse existing assets, architectures, knowledge, and components to develop software artefacts by imitating industrial processes.

The current study has used Software Factories to investigate how coordination among distributed sites is effected by the combination of Scrum and Kanban. Our research shows that the full extent of Scrumban capability is still unknown because it has not been researched a great deal. Therefore, the results of this research can be used as the initial steps for developing and validating an efficient methodology for software engineering practices, particularly in distributed sites.

There are different issues which should be considered before companies decide to locate their branches in various remote sites. This study argues that Scrumban could alleviate some of those challenges, but further solutions are needed to make

DSD more reasonable than co-located developments. Furthermore, companies must restructure their organizations to include proper roles and processes to improve transparency, change management, communication, coordination, and resources in DSD.

Future scholarly studies could investigate perspectives other than coordination for the usability of Scrumban. Moreover, they could propose new domain-specific tools and approaches for DSD projects which impose different constraints, for example, East-West distributed projects. However, companies, as the real users of Scrumban methodology, should be aware of its challenges as well as its benefits in planning project deliverables and coordination among teams.

Acknowledgements. This research was supported by the DIGILE Need for Speed program, and partially funded by Tekes (the Finnish Funding Agency for Technology and Innovation). We would like to thank DIGILE and Tekes for their support and the University of Bolzano for its excellent collaboration.

References

1. Schwaber, K., Sutherland, J.: Software in 30 Days: How Agile Managers Beat the Odds, Delight Their Customers, and Leave Competitors in the Dust. John Wiley & Sons Press, Hoboken (2012)
2. Alam, S.S., Chandra, S.: Agile software development: novel approaches for software engineering. Int. J. Eng. Sci. (IJES) **3**(1), 36–40 (2014)
3. Rodriguez, P., Markkula, J., Oivo, M., Turula, K.: Survey on agile and lean usage in finnish software industry. In: Proceedings of the ACM-IEEE International Symposium on Empirical Software Engineering and Measurement, pp. 139–148. ACM Press (2012)
4. Yilmaz, M., O'Connor, R.: A Scrumban integrated gamification approach to guide software process improvement: a Turkish case study. Tehnicki Vjesnik **23**(1), 237–245 (2016)
5. Mahnic, V.: Improving software development through combination of scrum and Kanban. Recent Advances in Computer Engineering, Communications and Information Technology, Spain (2014)
6. Ahmad, M.O., Markkula, J., Oivo, M.: Kanban in software development: A systematic literature review. In 39th EUROMICRO Conference on Software Engineering and Advanced Applications (SEAA), pp. 9–16. IEEE Press (2013)
7. Reddy, A.: The Scrumban [R]Evolution: Getting the Most Out of Agile, Scrum, and Lean Kanban. Addison-Wesley Professional, Boston (2015)
8. Kniberg, H., Skarin, M.: Kanban and Scrummaking the most of both. The InfoQ Enterprise Software Development (2010)
9. Ladas, C.: Scrumban. Lean Software Engineering-Essays on the Continuous Delivery of High Quality Information Systems (2008)
10. Khan, Z.: Scrumban-adaptive agile development process: using scrumban to improve software development process. Master's Thesis, Finland (2014)
11. Rodriguez, P., Partanen, J., Kuvaja, P., Oivo, M.: Combining lean thinking and agile methods for software development: a case study of a finnish provider of wireless embedded systems detailed. In: 47th Hawaii International Conference on System Sciences (HICSS 2014), pp. 4770–4779. IEEE Press (2014)

12. Tripathi, N., Rodríguez, P., Ahmad, M.O., Oivo, M.: Scaling Kanban for software development in a multisite organization: challenges and potential solutions. In: Lassenius, C., Dingsøyr, T., Paasivaara, M. (eds.) XP 2015. LNBIP, vol. 212, pp. 178–190. Springer (2015). doi:10.1007/978-3-319-18612-2_15
13. Auerbach, B., McCarthy, R.: Does agile+ lean= effective: an investigative study. J. Comput. Sci. Inf. Technol. 2(2), 73–86 (2014)
14. Smith, J.L., Bohner, S., McCrickard, D.S.: Toward introducing notification technology into distributed project teams. In: 12th IEEE International Conference and Workshops on the Engineering of Computer Based Systems (ECBS 2005), pp. 349–356. IEEE Press (2005)
15. Gupta, M., Fernandez, J.: How globally distributed software teams can improve their collaboration effectiveness? In: 6th IEEE International Conference on Global Software Engineering (ICGSE), pp. 185–189. IEEE Press (2011)
16. Šmite, D., Moe, N.B., Ågerfalk, P.J.: Fundamentals of agile distributed software development. In: Šmite, D., Moe, N., Ågerfalk, P. (eds.) Agility Across Time and Space. LNCS, pp. 3–7. Springer (2010). doi:10.1007/978-3-642-12442-6_1
17. Šmite, D., Moe, N.B., Agerfalk, P.J.: Agility Across Time and Space: Implementing Agile Methods in Global Software Projects. Springer Science & Business Media, Heidelberg (2010)
18. Carmel, E., Espinosa, J.A.: I'm Working While They're Sleeping: Time Zone Separation Challenges and Solutions. Nedder Stream Press, Washington, DC (2011)
19. Sutherland, J., Viktorov, A., Blount, J., Puntikov, N.: Distributed scrum: agile project management with outsourced development teams. In: 40th Annual Hawaii International Conference on System Sciences (HICSS 2007). IEEE Press (2007)
20. Rising, L., Janoff, N.S.: The scrum software development process for small teams. IEEE Softw. 17(4), 26–32 (2000)
21. Schwaber, K.: Agile Project Management with Scrum. Microsoft Press, Redmond (2004)
22. Schwaber, K., Beedle, M.: Agile Software Development with Scrum. Pearson International Edition, New York (2002)
23. Nikitina, N., Kajko-Mattsson, M.: Guiding the adoption of software development methods. In: Proceedings of the 2014 International Conference on Software and System Process, pp. 109–118. ACM Press (2014)
24. Nikitina, N., Kajko-Mattsson, M., Strale, M.: From scrum to scrumban: a case study of a process transition. In: Proceedings of the International Conference on Software and System Process, pp. 140–149. IEEE Press (2012)
25. Sjøberg, D.I., Johnsen, A., Solberg, J.: Quantifying the effect of using kanban versus scrum: a case study. IEEE Softw. 29(5), 47–53 (2012)
26. Ahmad, M.O., Liukkunen, K., Markkula, J.: Student perceptions and attitudes towards the software factory as a learning environment. In: Global Engineering Education Conference (EDUCON), pp. 422–428. IEEE Press (2014)
27. Polk, R.: Agile and Kanban in coordination. In: AGILE Conference, pp. 263–268 (2011)
28. Ikonen, M., Pirinen, E., Fagerholm, F., Kettunen, P., Abrahamsson, P.: On the impact of Kanban on software project work: an empirical case study investigation. In: 16th IEEE International Conference on Engineering of Complex Computer Systems (ICECCS), pp. 305–314. IEEE Press (2011)
29. Barash, I.: Use of agile with XP and Kanban methodologies in the same project. PM World J. 2(2), 1–11 (2013)
30. Ladas, C.: Scrumban-Essays on Kanban Systems for Lean Software Development. Modus Cooperandi Press, Seattle (2009)

31. Our Journey into Scrumban. http://www.arrkgroup.com/thoughtleadership/our-journey-into-scrumban/
32. Using Scrumban (Scrum Kanban) for Agile Marketing - Chief Marketing Technologist. http://chiefmartec.com/2014/12/using-scrumbanlean-agile-marketing/
33. Ahmad, M.O., Kuvaja, P., Oivo, M., Markkula, J.: Transition of software maintenance teams from scrum to Kanban. In: 49th Hawaii International Conference on System Sciences (HICSS 2016), pp. 5427–5436. IEEE Press (2016)
34. Karvonen, T., Rodriguez, P., Kuvaja, P., Mikkonen, K., Oivo, M.: Adapting the lean enterprise self-assessment tool for the software development domain. In: 38th EUROMICRO Conference on Software Engineering and Advanced Applications (SEAA), pp. 266–273. IEEE Press (2012)
35. Sutanto, J., Kankanhalli, A., Tan, B.C.: Deriving it-mediated task coordination portfolios for global virtual teams. IEEE Trans. Prof. Commun. **54**(2), 133–151 (2011)
36. Ramasubbu, N., Cataldo, M., Balan, R.K., Herbsleb, J.D.: Configuring global software teams: a multi-company analysis of project productivity, quality, and profits. In: Proceedings of the 33rd International Conference on Software Engineering, pp. 261–270. ACM Press (2011)
37. Jiménez, M., Piattini, M., Vizcaino, A.: Challenges and improvements in distributed software development: a systematic review. Adv. Soft. Eng. **2009**, 3 (2009)
38. Nakamura, K., Fujii, Y., Kiyokane, Y., Nakamura, M., Hinenoya, K., Peck, Y.H., Choon-Lian, S.: Distributed and concurrent development environment via sharing design information. In: The Twenty-First Annual International Computer Software and Applications Conference, 1997, COMPSAC 1997, Proceedings, pp. 274–279. IEEE Press (1997)
39. Noll, J., Beecham, S., Richardson, I.: Global software development and collaboration: barriers and solutions. ACM Inroads **1**(3), 66–78 (2010)
40. Mak, D.K., Kruchten, P.B.: Task coordination in an agile distributed software development environment. In: Canadian Conference on Electrical and Computer Engineering, CCECE 2006, pp. 606–611. IEEE Press (2006)
41. Redmiles, D., Van Der Hoek, A., Al-Ani, B., Hildenbrand, T., Quirk, S., Sarma, A., Filho, R., de Souza, C., Trainer, E.: Continuous coordination: a new paradigm to support globally distributed software development projects. Wirtschafts Informatik **49**(1), 28–38 (2007)
42. Sidhu, J.S., Volberda, H.W.: Coordination of globally distributed teams: a co-evolution perspective on offshoring. Int. Bus. Rev. **20**(3), 278–290 (2011)
43. Sutherland, J., Schoonheim, G., Rijk, M.: Fully distributed scrum: Replicating local productivity and quality with offshore teams. In: 42nd Hawaii International Conference on System Sciences (HICSS 2009), pp. 1–8. IEEE Press (2009)
44. Paasivaara, M.: Coaching global software development projects. In: 6th IEEE International Conference on Global Software Engineering (ICGSE), pp. 84–93. IEEE Press (2011)
45. Abrahamsson, P., Kettunen, P., Fagerholm, F.: The set-up of a software engineering research infrastructure of the 2010s. In: Proceedings of the 11th International Conference on Product Focused Software, pp. 112–114. ACM Press (2010)
46. France, R., Rumpe, B.: Model-driven development of complex software: a research roadmap. In: 2007 Future of Software Engineering, pp. 37–54. IEEE Computer Society (2007)

47. Greenfield, J., Short, K.: Software factories: assembling applications with patterns, models, frameworks, and tools. In: 3rd International Conference on Object-Oriented Programming, Systems, Languages and Applications (OOPSLA). ACM Press (2004)
48. Taibi, D., Lenarduzzi, V., Ahmad, M.O., Liukkunen, K., Lunesu, I., Matta, M., Fagerholm, F., Münch, J., Pietinen, S., Tukiainen, M., Fernández-Sánchez, C., Garbajosa, J., Systä, K.: "Free" innovation environments: lessons learned from the software factory initiatives. In: 10th International Conference on Software Engineering Advances (ICSEA 2015), pp. 25–30 (2015)
49. Cohen, D., Crabtree, B.: Qualitative Research Guidelines Project. Robert Wood Johnson Foundation, Princeton (2006)
50. Barcus, A., Montibeller, G.: Supporting the allocation of software development work in distributed teams with multi-criteria decision analysis. Omega 36(3), 464–475 (2008)
51. Espinosa, J.A., Slaughter, S.A., Kraut, R.E., Herbsleb, J.D.: Team knowledge and coordination in geographically distributed software development. J. Manag. Inf. Syst. 24(1), 135–169 (2007)
52. Nidiffer, K.E., Dolan, D.: Evolving distributed project management. IEEE Softw. 22(5), 63–72 (2005). IEEE Press
53. Fagerholm, F., Oza, N., Munch, J.: A platform for teaching applied distributed software development: the ongoing journey of the Helsinki software factory. In: 3rd International Workshop on Collaborative Teaching of Globally Distributed Software Development (CTGDSD), pp. 1–5. IEEE Press (2013)
54. Höst, M., Regnell, B., Wohlin, C.: Using students as subjects a comparative study of students and professionals in lead-time impact assessment. Empirical Softw. Eng. 5(3), 201–214 (2000)
55. Madeyski, L.: Test-Driven Development: An Empirical Evaluation of Agile Practice. Springer Science & Business Media, Heidelberg (2009)
56. Chao, J., Randles, M.: Agile software factory for student service learning. In: 22nd Conference on Software Engineering Education and Training (CSEET), pp. 34–40. IEEE Press (2009)

Verifying Atomicity Preservation and Deadlock Freedom of a Generic Shared Variable Mechanism Used in Model-To-Code Transformations

Dan Zhang[1], Dragan Bošnački[1(✉)], Mark van den Brand[1], Cornelis Huizing[1],
Bart Jacobs[2], Ruurd Kuiper[1], and Anton Wijs[1]

[1] Eindhoven University of Technology, Eindhoven, Netherlands
`D.Bosnacki@tue.nl`
[2] KU Leuven, Leuven, Belgium

Abstract. A challenging aspect of model-to-code transformations is to ensure that the semantic behavior of the input model is preserved in the output code. When constructing concurrent systems, this is mainly difficult due to the non-deterministic potential interaction between threads. In this paper, we consider this issue for a framework that implements a transformation chain from models expressed in the state machine based domain specific language SLCO to Java. In particular, we provide a fine-grained generic mechanism to preserve atomicity of SLCO statements in the Java implementation. We give its generic specification based on separation logic and verify it using the verification tool VeriFast. The solution can be regarded as a reusable module to safely implement atomic operations in concurrent systems. Moreover, we also prove with VeriFast that our mechanism does not introduce deadlocks. The specification formally ensures that the locks are not reentrant which simplifies the formal treatment of the Java locks.

Keywords: Model transformation · Code generation · Concurrency · Atomicity · Formal verification · Separation logic · Deadlock freedom

1 Introduction

Model transformation is a powerful concept in model-driven software engineering [15]. Starting with an initial model written in a domain specific language (DSL), other artifacts such as additional models, source code and test scripts can be produced via a chain of transformations. The initial model is typically written at a conveniently high level of abstraction, allowing the user to reason about complex system behavior in an intuitive way. The model transformations are

D. Zhang, D. Bošnački, R. Kuiper and A. Wijs—This work was done with financial support from the China Scholarship Council (CSC) and ARTEMIS Joint Undertaking project EMC2 (grant agreement 621429).

© Springer International Publishing AG 2017
S. Hammoudi et al. (Eds): MODELSWARD 2016, CCIS 692, pp. 249–273, 2017.
DOI: 10.1007/978-3-319-66302-9_13

supposed to preserve the correctness of the initial model, thereby realising a framework where the generated artifacts are correct by construction. A question that naturally arises for model-to-code transformations is how to guarantee that functional properties of the input models are preserved in the generated code [21]. In particular, this requires semantic conformance between the model and the generated code. For models in the area of safety-critical concurrent systems, the main complication to guarantee this equivalence involves the potential of threads to non-deterministically interact with each other.

Specifically, when variables are shared among multiple threads, the absence of race conditions is crucial to guarantee that no undesired updates of those variables can be performed. This relates to the notion of *atomicity* of the instructions executed by the threads. For instance, if two threads both increment the value of a variable x by one, then only when each of those increments can be performed atomically is it ensured that the final value of x equals the initial value plus two. Achieving atomicity of program instructions can be done using various techniques, such as locks, semaphores, mutexes, or CPU instructions such as *compare-and-swap*.

Also in modeling languages, atomicity is an important concept, to simplify the reasoning about program instructions by abstracting away the atomicity implementation details. Hence, an important requirement for model-to-code transformations is that the atomicity of the statements in the modeling language is preserved in the code. A conceptual solution would be to map each statement to an atomic block in the implementation language. Strictly speaking, a block of instructions is atomic if during its execution no instruction of another thread is allowed to be executed. However, such a definition is too strong for practical purposes, since it excludes the possibility for threads to run truly concurrently in cases when they access different variables, and therefore do not interfere with each other. For this reason, it is usually replaced with weaker notions that still ensure non-interference. One such version, sometimes called *serializability* [2], allows instruction blocks to be executed concurrently as long as their individual results are not affected by the other blocks.

In this paper, we demonstrate how one can establish that a model-to-code transformation transforms atomic statements in modeling languages to blocks of program instructions that are serializable. To illustrate this, we focus on a DSL called Simple Language of Communicating Objects (SLCO) [7], on the one hand, and the Java programming language on the other hand. It should be stressed, though, that our approach is suitable for any combination of a modern imperative programming language with concurrency and a modeling language that is, like SLCO, based on state machines that can be placed in parallel composition, and can change state by firing transitions with atomic statements (for instance, UML state machines).

SLCO was originally introduced to model complex embedded concurrent systems by means of state machines in combination with variables. A technique to verify SLCO-to-SLCO transformations has been proposed in [20, 26–28]. In this paper we focus on the correctness of a fully automated model-to-code transformation in which each SLCO state machine is transformed to an individual Java thread. In order to define the transformation in a modular way, and thereby improving its maintainability, we divide it into two parts, one part transforming SLCO concepts into *generic code*, and the other part transforming the aspects that are specific for the particular input SLCO model into *specific code*. The specific code may refer to the generic code to use the model-independent concepts. An example of a generic SLCO concept is the communication channel, while a particular state machine is an example of a concept specific for a given SLCO model. This way of working provides a clear maintenance advantage, as the implementations of generic concepts can be updated without affecting the overall transformation machinery. Another benefit is that the generic code needs to be verified only once. Each class of the generic code can be specified and verified in isolation, allowing for modular verification.

In the past, we have outlined the approach described above in [29], in which we have also identified the main challenges. As a first step towards having completely verified generic code, we focused on the SLCO communication channel, and formally verified, using the VeriFast tool [12], that its semantics is captured by the Java construct to which we transform it [4].

Contributions. First, we discuss how we have implemented, specified, and verified a protection mechanism to access shared variables in such a way that the code blocks implementing atomic DSL statements are guaranteed to be serializable. This generic mechanism is used in our framework to automatically transform SLCO models into multi-threaded Java code, but the solution is general enough to be used in other model-to-code transformations as well.

The mechanism employs a fine-grained ordered-locking approach. A coarse-grained approach tends to negatively impact the performance of multi-threaded software, while a lock-free approach, in particular using atomic instructions such as *compare-and-swap*, is necessarily restricted to work only for statements that involve a single shared variable.

Second, we show the feasibility to verify the atomicity of generic statements by focusing on the SLCO assignment statement. We formally prove its implementation against a specification of non-interference using the VeriFast tool [12]. Being based on separation logic [22], VeriFast is suitable to deal with aliasing and concurrency in Java, as well as with race conditions using the concept of ownership of shared resources between multi-threaded programs.

Third, we introduce a wrapper class pattern to perform modular verification. With the wrapper class, it is possible to encapsulate data structures that are used in the code, but are not subjected to verification (for instance, because they have already been verified at an earlier stage possibly using a different tool).

This paper is an extended version of previous work [30]. In addition to the three contributions mentioned above, we also discuss how we can automatically prove that our mechanism to ensure the atomicity of statements does not introduce, what we call, *lock-deadlocks*. A lock-deadlock occurs when each thread in a set S is blocked trying to acquire a lock which is held by another thread in S. Since the methods involved in the mechanism are the only ones which manipulate locks, the mechanism being free of lock-deadlocks implies that our model-to-code transformation always produces programs that are lock-deadlock free. In our previous work in [30] this was informally ensured by the assumption that the locks are always acquired in a certain fixed order. Using the implementation in VeriFast [13] of several modular verification techniques [13,17], we are able to formally specify this requirement in the contracts of the relevant methods and to verify in a modular fashion that deadlocks are not introduced.

As an added value, we prove that in our generated programs there is no need for reentrant locks. This allows us to simplify the formal specification of the locks used in our mechanism. In [30], our verification already relied on this observation, but the current specification formally ensures adherence to it.

The remainder of the paper is structured as follows. In Sect. 2 we briefly explain SLCO, the model transformation from SLCO to Java, and the essentials of separation logic and VeriFast. Section 3 describes the implementation of atomicity of SLCO statements in Java, as well as the implementation of the generic wrapper class. In Sect. 4, we demonstrate how to specify and verify the Java implementation with regard to the atomicity property. Section 5 contains the specification and verification of the deadlock and reentrance avoidance. Related work is discussed in Sect. 6, and Sect. 7 contains our conclusions and a discussion about future work.

2 Preliminaries

2.1 SLCO

In SLCO, systems consisting of concurrent, communication components can be described using an intuitive graphical syntax. Objects, as instances of classes, can communicate via channels, over which they send and receive signals. Objects are connected to channels via their ports. Each object consists of a number of finite state machines and shared variables. The state machines in an object can use private, local variables, and communicate with each other via the shared variables in the object. Each transition of a state machine may have an associated SLCO *statement*.[1] SLCO offers five types of atomic statements: SendSignal, ReceiveSignal, (Boolean) Expression, Assignment, and Delay.

State machines, like the ones in Fig. 1, are used to specify object behavior. Each transition has a source and target state, and the statement associated with a transition is executed when the transition is fired. Parallel execution of transitions is formalized in the form of interleaving semantics. A transition is enabled if the statement is enabled or there is no statement associated with the transition. For communication between objects, there are statements for sending and receiving signals. The statement **send** *T(s)* **to** *InOut*, for instance, sends a signal named T with a single argument s via port *InOut*. Its counterpart

---

[1] There is an extended version of SLCO allowing multiple statements per transition. In this paper, we consider the basic language, since extended SLCO models can be translated to basic SLCO models [7].

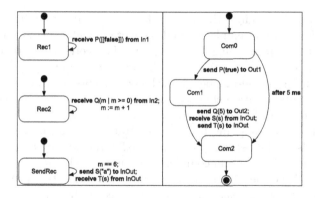

Fig. 1. Behaviour diagram of an SLCO model.

receive $T(s)$ **from** *InOut* receives a signal named T from port *InOut* and stores the value of the argument in variable s. Statements such as **receive** $Q(m \mid m >= 0)$ **from** *In2* offer a form of conditional signal reception. In this example, only those signals are accepted whose argument is at least equal to 0. Boolean expressions, such as $m=6$, denote statements that block until the expression holds. Assignment statements, such as $m := m + 1$, are always enabled, and are used to assign values to variables. Finally, time is incorporated in SLCO by means of delay statements. For example, the statement **after** 5 **ms** blocks until 5 ms have passed since the moment the source state was entered.

As already mentioned, variables can be shared by multiple state machines. In Fig. 1, the three state machines in the left rectangle are part of the same object, and m is shared by them: assigning a value to m in the second state machine may affect the truth-value of the expression in the third. Statements of types Expression, Assignment, ReceiveSignal and SendSignal can all refer to variables shared by multiple state machines.

2.2   Model Transformation

Recently, we developed an automated model-to-code transformation from SLCO models to multi-threaded Java programs.[2] The transformation consists of multiple steps. Here we focus on the last step that transforms SLCO models to Java code. The preceding steps are transformations from SLCO models to more refined SLCO models using Xtend.[3] These steps are used to deal with potential semantic and platform differences.

After this problem has been resolved, the last step from SLCO to Java is applied, which is implemented in the Epsilon Generation Language (EGL) [16] based on Eclipse. The output is defined by means of templates that are used

---

[2] The files can be obtained from http://www.mdsetechnology.org/attachments/ article/3/LockingUnlockingSpec.zip.

[3] http://www.eclipse.org/xtend.

by the generator to produce the Java code. The generator applies transformation rules, defined in the template, to all the meta model objects which results in generation of the corresponding Java code. This Java code is constructed by combining specific code implementing the behavior of the input model with generic code implementing model-independent SLCO concepts. Examples of such concepts are the communication channel, the various types of statements, and a list datatype to store the shared variables owned by an object. The transformation achieves a one-to-one mapping between the state machines in an SLCO model and the threads in the derived program. Finally, the specific code is combined with the generic code to obtain complete, executable code that should behave as the SLCO model specifies. In order to guarantee that important properties of the input model are preserved, the transformation needs to be verified. In this paper, we focus on verifying that the atomic nature of SLCO statements is preserved when they are transformed to blocks of Java instructions. The main complication when verifying this lies in the fact that the statements may access shared variables, and hence can potentially interfere with each other when executed concurrently. We use separation logic to specify the code blocks.

2.3   Separation Logic

Separation logic [18,22] is an extension of Hoare logic [19] that supports reasoning about shared memory which can be referenced from more than one location. Therefore, separation logic is used to describe the heap – a mapping from object IDs and object fields to values, where a value is an object or a constant. The basic heap expressions are **emp**, the empty heap, satisfied by states having a heap with no entries, and $E \mapsto F$ (read as "E points to F"), a singleton heap, satisfied by a state with a heap consisting of only one entry on address E with content F. For instance, $o.f \mapsto v$ means that field f of object o has value v. To represent complex heaps (e.g., dynamic data structures) the logical operator '$*$', called *separation conjunction* is used. Expression $P*Q$ asserts that the heap contains disjoint parts such that P holds in one part and Q holds in the other. So, unlike its counterpart $o.f \mapsto v \wedge o.f \mapsto v$, the expression $o.f \mapsto v * o.f \mapsto v$ evaluates to **false** because the two heap components are not disjoint. In a concurrent setting, this is used to detect data races, i.e., a simultaneous access to the same memory objects by two different threads.

In addition to the standard rules of the Hoare framework, separation logic has the *frame rule*. It allows to extend the specification of a program segment C with assertion R. The axiom requires that no free variable in R is modified by C:

$$\frac{\{P\}\ C\ \{Q\}}{\{P * R\}\ C\ \{Q * R\}} \qquad \text{(frame)}$$

Separation logic uses the principle of a minimal memory footprint, meaning that a separation assertion describes a unique heap. For example, the assertion $o.f \mapsto a * o.g \mapsto b$ describes a heap consisting of exactly two entries. This property together with the requirement that the heaps of two separate threads are disjoint, makes it possible to give a natural ownership interpretation of a shared resource. If a separation logic assertion P holds at some program location on a thread, we say that the thread owns the part of the heap described by P at that location.

The portions of the heap associated with each thread are always mutually disjoint. When a thread acquires a shared object, it claims the ownership of the state associated with the variable; when releasing the variable, it must return the ownership of the corresponding piece of state. At all stages, our use of separation logic ensures that each piece of the heap is accessed by at most one thread. It thus becomes possible to reason about concurrent programs in which ownership of a shared variable can be perceived to transfer dynamically between threads. We achieve this dynamic transfer by associating invariants to locks of shared objects. The invariant representing the environment of the thread expresses the ownership of the shared variable.

By acquiring a lock, the verified program component also acquires the lock invariant representing the heap that corresponds to the shared variables. The invariant carries a full permission to change the actual shared variables. By releasing the lock, the component releases, together with the invariant, also the acquired ownerships. This is expressed by the following rules for the *lock* and *unlock* operations

$$\{\textbf{emp}\} \ \texttt{v.lock()} \ \{I_v(l)\} \tag{L}$$

$$\{I_v(l)\} \ \texttt{v.unlock()} \ \{\textbf{emp}\} \tag{UL}$$

where $I_v(l)$ is the invariant associated with lock l of variable v.

To specify read-only sharing of variables, fractional ownerships (permissions) are used. A fractional permission with fraction ϕ is denoted by $[\phi]o.f \mapsto v$, where $0 < \phi \leq 1$. When $\phi = 1$, the fraction is omitted and we obtain the usual $o.f \mapsto v$. This case expresses *full ownership*, allowing both read and write access.

2.4 VeriFast

The VeriFast tool is a program verifier for sequential and concurrent C and Java programs. Programs are annotated with assertions written as separation logic formulae. The verifier can check for `NULLPointerException` or `ArrayIndexOutOfBoundsException`. For concurrent programs, it checks that the program does not contain data races (memory safety). When the verification succeeds and it reports no error, the assertions and method contracts (preconditions and postconditions) are respected in every program execution. In the verification, VeriFast executes method bodies symbolically. The symbolic execution of a triple $\{P\} \ C \ \{Q\}$ starts in the symbolic state corresponding to the precondition P. If the triple is correct, each finite execution should eventually reach a symbolic state implying Q.

3 Implementing SLCO Atomicity

In this section, we give the formal definition of atomicity of SLCO statements as well as a semantically comparable form of non-interference called serializability [2] for the Java blocks implementing those statements. Furthermore, to facilitate the transformation of SLCO statements to Java code, specifically to handle accessing shared variables, we introduce the generic data structure `SharedVariableList`.

In our model-to-code transformation, each SLCO statement s in a state machine M is transformed into a block of Java instructions $\sigma = s_0; s_1; \ldots; s_n$ to be executed by a thread t_M. Strictly speaking, preserving atomicity of s in σ means that no instruction s' of some thread $t \neq t_M$ is allowed to be executed between the beginning and end of the execution of σ.

However, implementing atomicity in this strict sense is undesirable when constructing multi-threaded software, since it disallows true parallelism. That is why we replace this strong atomicity requirement with serializability. Serializability guarantees that for any concurrent execution of (atomic) Java blocks there exists a sequential execution of those blocks that is indistinguishable from the concurrent execution, in terms of the final effect on the global system state. More explicitly, let σ and σ' be two different instruction blocks to be executed by different threads t_M, t'_M. Let q_0 be a global state in the Java model in which both σ and σ' can start a concurrent execution and let q_1 be a state in which the system ends up after the execution of both σ and σ'. Then, q_1 also is obtained after sequential execution of the sequence $\sigma\sigma'$ or $\sigma'\sigma$ (or both). Hence, we may reason about their execution as if σ was first completely executed before σ' was started, or vice versa. (Note that this also covers the case when σ may prevent the execution of σ' or vice versa.) The extension of the concept of serializability to an arbitrary number of instruction blocks σ_i is straightforward.

The state of a system is determined by the values of its variables. In SLCO, statements may access variables shared by multiple state machines (see Sect. 2) (with respect to atomicity, accessing a channel is similar to accessing a shared variable). Therefore, in the corresponding Java code, multiple threads may access the same shared variables. In order to realize serializability in such a setting, it must be ensured that an instruction s' of some thread t cannot affect the variables accessed by the instructions in a block σ of thread $t_M \neq t$ running concurrently.

The way in which shared variables are protected has a significant impact on the overall performance of concurrent programs. For example, using one single global lock to protect a list frequently accessed by several threads is likely to scale much worse than when each element in that list is individually lockable.

SLCO statements may require access to just a subset of the shared variables of an object. Therefore, each element in the list of shared variables is assigned its own lock for read and write access. This gives a better performance than using a single lock for the complete list. In this way we achieve serializability, as shown in Sect. 4.2.

Individual locking may introduce deadlocks. We use the technique of ordered locking [11] to prevent them. The ordered locking mechanism guarantees that when multiple threads compete over a set of variables, one thread is always able to acquire access to all of them. Of course, other threads requiring access to different shared variables are able to access these concurrently.

Note that the locks can be released in an arbitrary order. Obviously there is no deadlock during the releasing since at least one method - namely, unlockV is active. After the locks are released we again have the situation in which multiple threads compete for the locks in fixed order.

Our synchronization mechanism for shared variables is shown in Listing 1.1. The SharedVariableList, as a wrapper class, is introduced to abstract away how the list of shared variables is implemented. It can be used to encapsulate Java data structures. The methods lockV and unlockV are used to acquire and release each lock of the shared variables in the list.

Listing 1.1. Class Statement.

```
1  public abstract class Statement {
2    protected SharedVariableList variablesList;
3    ...
4    public void lockV() {
5      for (int i = 0; i < variablesList.size(); i++) {
6        variablesList.get(i).lock.lock();
7      }
8    }
9    public void unlockV() {
10     for (int i = 0; i < variablesList.size(); i++) {
11       variablesList.get(i).lock.unlock();
12     }
13   }
14 }
```

The class Assignment as a subclass of class Statement (Listing 1.2) contains a method called lockAndAssign that can be used to safely assign a new value to a shared variable. The abstract method assign is implemented in the subclass which is related to a concrete SLCO assignment. When a thread attempts to execute the method assign, it will be delayed until all locks in the variablesList of variables to be accessed by the assign method are not being used anymore by other threads.

Listing 1.2. Class Assignment.

```
1  public abstract class Assignment extends Statement {
2    ...
3    public abstract void assign();
4    public void lockAndAssign() {
5      lockV();
6      assign();
7      unlockV();
8    }
9  }
```

As already mentioned, to store shared variables, we use a wrapper class SharedVariableList. Listing 1.3 shows its declaration. The concept of wrapper classes is quite common in object-oriented programming and is a pattern in object-oriented development. The wrapper class is used to hide information of concrete Java data structures, which allows modular verification. Parts of the code that use SharedVariableList can be verified without involving the data structure; in fact, it may not even have been implemented yet. This helps to scale verification to larger programs, since the wrapper class needs to be analyzed only once, instead of once per call. Finally, modifying the implementation of the data structure encapsulated by the wrapper class never breaks correctness of its callers. This allows for simultaneous development and verification of code.

Listing 1.3. Declaration of class `SharedVariableList`.

```
1 final class SharedVariableList{
2     public SharedVariableList();
3     public int size();
4     public SharedVariable get(int index);
5     boolean add(SharedVariable e);
6 }
```

4   Specifying and Verifying SLCO Atomicity

In the previous section, we explained how the atomicity of SLCO statements can be implemented using serializability. We can use separation logic in VeriFast to verify the serializability, i.e., the fact that there is non-interference between different threads.

The interpretation of correctness depends crucially on rules L and UL for the *lock* and *unlock* operations from Sect. 2.3. In our case in rules L and UL invariant $I_v(l)$ is of the form $v \mapsto \_$, i.e., expresses ownership of the variable v. By rule L, $I_v(l)$ is guaranteed to hold after `lock`, i.e., in the beginning of the protected code block. This means that the corresponding thread acquires the ownership of v. Similarly, at the end of the block, after `unlock`, the ownership of v is released and the invariant $I_v(l)$ is no longer guaranteed to hold. Let V be the list of shared variables associated with the statement implemented in the block. By executing `lock` for each variable in V, using a combination of the L and UL rules and the frame rule from Sect. 2.3, an assertion I_V is established which is the conjunction of the invariants $I_v(l)$, for all $v \in V$. I_V can be seen as an invariant of the list V which expresses ownership of all variables in V by the thread. The concrete setting of our model transformation ensures that no shared variable in V is acquired or released within the protected code block. This is achieved by simply not using `lock` and `unlock` within the protected block, since these are the only statements with which one can acquire or release ownership. Together with the fact that invariant I_V holds at the beginning and at the end of the block, this implies non-interference since all variables are held exclusively by the thread during the execution of the block.

VeriFast supports modular verification in the sense that each method is verified separately. In this, each method relies on its environment to comply with the invariant. This is checked during the verification when several threads are combined. In the following sections, we specify and verify the atomicity of Java constructs corresponding with SLCO statements using separation logic via VeriFast.

In VeriFast, for each verified Java source file (.java) there is a corresponding specification file (.javaspec). The .java file contains implementations, specifications, annotations, and predicates, while the .javaspec file contains only declarations of predicates and specifications of methods with a semicolon instead of a method body. A .javaspec file can be used to verify client programs even without having the corresponding .java file that contains the definitions and the implementations mentioned in the .javaspec file. Thus, the client programs are users of the .javaspec files. For example, we only need to provide a pure (i.e., containing no implementations) specification file SharedVariableList.javaspec to VeriFast in order to verify the Statement class.

4.1   Class SharedVariableList Specification

Class SharedVariableList is specified in separation logic in a way that is in fact independent of the Java programming language. In Listing 1.4, the class SharedVariableList provides methods for modifying and querying its instances, such as size, add and get.

Listing 1.4. Specification of class SharedVariableList.

```
 1 final class SharedVariableList{
 2    /*@ predicate List(list<SharedVariable> elements); @*/
 3    public SharedVariableList();
 4    //@ requires true;
 5    //@ ensures List(nil);
 6    public int size();
 7    //@ requires [?f]List(?es);
 8    //@ ensures [f]List(es) &*& result == length(es);
 9    public SharedVariable get(int index);
10    //@ requires [?f]List(?es) &*& 0 <= index &*& index < length(es);
11    //@ ensures [f]List(es) &*& result == nth(index, es);
12    boolean add(SharedVariable e);
13    //@ requires List(?es);
14    //@ ensures List(append(es, cons(e, nil))) &*& result;
15 }
```

The VeriFast specific text, e.g., specifications and declarations of auxiliary variables introduced only for verification purposes, is located inside special comments delimited by @.

We express the state of the sharedVariableList instances using a mathematical list predefined in VeriFast as follows: The empty list is denoted by nil and a nonempty list starting by an element h and a tail t is denoted by cons(h,t). In particular, predicate List is an abstract predicate that provides an abstract representation of the contents of the list of shared variables. More concretely, parameter elements is a mathematical list containing the actual program variables that are stored in the list. The actual implementation can be, for instance, a dynamic list or an array. Using the abstract predicate we can hide such implementation details during the verification. Note that List remains undefined in this specification stage. Its definition can be provided later together with the implementation of SharedVariableList.

The pre- and postconditions form the *contracts* of the methods and are denoted by the keywords requires and ensures, respectively, like in lines 4–5 in Listing 1.4. This contract of the constructor guarantees that an object is created corresponding to an empty list, regardless of the precondition.

The specification of `size` in lines 7 and 8 states that the method returns the length of the list. Component assertions of pre- and postconditions are separated by the spatial conjunction denoted by `&*&`. Both `[?f]` and `[f]` are fractional ownerships. The question mark `?` in front of a variable means that the matched value is bound to the variable and all later occurrences of that variable in the contract refer to this matched value. In our case the value of the fractional permission `f` in the precondition in line 7 must be the same as the one in the postcondition in line 8. Hence, the precondition in line 7 `[?f]List(?es)` expresses both that a fractional ownership with fraction `f` is required for the shared variable list corresponding with the mathematical list `es`, and records `f` and `es`. The postcondition specifies that the method returns the ownership of `es` to the caller with the same fraction `f` and the result that is returned by `size` is the length of `es`. `result` is a reserved variable name representing the return value of the method.

The precondition of `get` (line 10) requires that a valid element `index` is provided as an input parameter. The postcondition expresses that the element at position `index` in list `es` is returned using the mathematical function `nth`.

Unlike for other methods, the precondition of `add` (line 13) requires full ownership of the list `es`. As a result, the caller who owns `es` is allowed to insert an element into the list. Finally the method `add` returns the ownership of a new list that combines the list `es` with the newly inserted element `e` using the function `append`.

4.2   Class Statement Specification

The specification of class `Statement` is shown in Listing 1.5. The predicate constructor `lock_inv` in line 2 is essential for the preservation of serializability. It defines the lock invariant $I_v(l)$ associated with the lock of a variable v passed as a parameter. The assertion `v.value |->_` asserts the full ownership of $v.value$. The underscore '_' denotes an arbitrary value.

The recursive predicates `locks` and `invariants` in lines 3–4 and 5–6, respectively, are used to specify data structures without static bound on their size. The body of each predicate is a conditional assertion. If `vs` is `null` (the base case of the induction) then the value of predicate `locks` is `true` (line 4); otherwise, the inductive step asserts that the lock of the first element of the list `vs`, `head(vs)` is partially owned. This is given by `return [_]head(vs).lock |-> ?lock`, where `[_]` denotes an unspecified fraction. Besides that, invariant `lock_inv(head(vs))` is associated with the lock of the first element, via the predicate `ReentrantLock`. Predicate `ReentrantLock` is defined by VeriFast as a specification of the `ReentrantLock` class. In a similar fashion, the recursive predicate `invariants` states that a conjunction of invariants corresponding to the (locks of the) variables in list `vs` is recursively built. As mentioned above, for each variable the corresponding invariant is given by the specification `lock_inv(head(vs))`.

Predicate `Statement_lock()` is actually defined in Listing 1.6 and denotes that the `Statement` object is in a valid state corresponding to an abstract value given by the mathematical object list of shared variable objects `vs`. The body of method `lockV` needs to establish the above mentioned invariant I_V of each variable in list `vs`, which is expressed by the postcondition `invariants(vs)`. The postcondition `invariants(vs)` is also one part of the precondition in the method `unlockV`. By calling the method `unlockV`, invariant I_v of each variable in list `vs` is not guaranteed to hold anymore. After that, other threads can acquire the ownership of those variables through the method `lockV`.

Listing 1.5. Abstract Specifications of Class `Statement`.

```
1  /*@
2  predicate_ctor lock_inv(SharedVariable v)(;) = v.value |-> _;
3  predicate locks(list<SharedVariable> vs;) =
4      vs == nil ? true : [_]head(vs).lock |-> ?lock &*& [_]lock.
             ReentrantLock(lock_inv(head(vs))) &*& locks(tail(vs));
5  predicate invariants(list<SharedVariable> vs;) =
6      vs == nil ? true : lock_inv(head(vs))() &*& invariants(tail(vs));
7  @*/
8  class Statement {
9      //@ predicate Statement_lock(list<SharedVariable> vs);
10     void lockV();
11     //@ requires [_]Statement_lock(?vs);
12     //@ ensures invariants(vs);
13     void unlockV();
14     //@ requires [_]Statement_lock(?vs) &*& invariants(vs);
15     //@ ensures true;
16 }
```

4.3 Class Statement Verification

Above we gave the formal specification of the class `Statement` in an abstract, mathematically precise and implementation-independent way. The specification of `SharedVariableList` is a critical factor to verify the implementation of class `Statement`. Additional predicates and annotations are also needed to verify the implementation of class `Statement`, as shown in Listing 1.6.

Listing 1.6. Verification annotations for class `Statement`.

```
1  /*@
2  predicate_ctor lock_inv(SharedVariable v)(;) = ...
3  predicate locks(list<SharedVariable> vs;) = ...
4  predicate invariants(list<SharedVariable> vs;) = ...
5  @*/
6  class Statement {
7      SharedVariableList variablesList;
8      //@ predicate Statement_lock(list<SharedVariable> vs) = this.
             variablesList |-> ?a &*& a.List(vs) &*& locks(vs);
9      void lockV()
10     //@ requires [_]Statement_lock(?vs);
11     //@ ensures invariants(vs);
12     {
13         for (int i = 0; i < variablesList.size(); i++)
14         //@ requires [_]variablesList |-> ?b &*& [_]b.List(vs) &*& [_]locks(
                drop(i,vs)) &*& i >= 0 &*& i <= length(vs);
15         //@ ensures invariants(drop(old_i, vs));
16         {
17             //@ drop_n_plus_one(i,vs);
18             variablesList.get(i).lock.lock();
19         }
20     }
21     void unlockV()
```

```
22    //@ requires [_]Statement_lock(?vs) &*& invariants(vs);
23    //@ ensures true;
24    {
25      for (int  i = 0; i < variablesList.size(); i++)
26      //@ requires [_]variablesList |-> ?b &*& [_]b.List(vs) &*& [_]locks(
            drop(i,vs)) &*& invariants(drop(i,vs)) &*& i >= 0 &*& i <= length
            (vs);
27      //@ ensures true;
28      {
29        //@ drop_n_plus_one(i,vs);
30        variablesList.get(i).lock.unlock();
31      }
32    }
33 }
```

The part in lines 1–5 in Listing 1.6 is identical to lines 1–7 in the specification Listing 1.5. Line 8 in Listing 1.6 contains the definition of predicate `Statement_lock` which in Listing 1.5 was only specified. The part `this.variablesList |-> ?a` states that field `variableList` is defined. The last two conjuncts `a.List(vs) &*& locks(vs)` relate `variableList` with the mathematical variable `vs` of type `list` and moreover the variables in `vs` are connected to their corresponding locks. The contract of method `lockV` in lines 10–11 is the same as the one in Listing 1.5.

In line 13 we use a `for` loop to obtain the lock of each element in the `SharedVariableList`. Besides loop invariants, VeriFast supports also loop verification by specifying a loop contract consisting of a precondition and a postcondition [24]. Then the loop is verified as if it were written using a local recursive function. The contract specifies the permissions used only by a specific recursive call (i.e., corresponding to a specific value of the loop counter i). The precondition in line 14 matches `variablesList` with variable b (`[_]variablesList |-> ?b`), relates b to vs (`[_]b.List(vs)`), associates the variables from the i-th to the `vs.length-1`-th in list vs (`[_]locks(drop(i,vs))`) to their locks, and finally limits the range of the counter i(`i >= 0 &*& i <= length(vs)`). The segment vs from i to `vs.length-1` is obtained using the built-in function on lists `drop`. In a similar way in the postcondition in line 15, the list tail starting with `old_i` is obtained as an argument of the predicate `invariants`. Variable `old_i` refers to the value of the variable i at the start of the virtual function call (loop body). After the top virtual recursive call backtracks, i.e., after the loop termination, `old_i` equals 0. This implies the validity of the conjunction of all lock invariants and consequently the ownership of all variables in `vs`.

Lemma functions are used to help VeriFast transform one assertion to another. The contract of a lemma function corresponds to a theorem, its body to the proof, and a call to an application of the theorem. Lemma function `drop_n_plus_one(i,vs)` in line 17 tells the verifier that `drop(n,vs)` is equivalent to the concatenation of the element `nth(vs)` with the list `drop(n+1,vs)`.

The detailed annotation of `unlockV` (lines 21–32) uses the same concepts as the annotation of `lockV`, therefore we do not discuss the former explicitly. It expresses that in each iteration the loop invariant shrinks instead of growing with the addition of a new conjunct, i.e., invariant associated to a lock.

The specification and annotation in the current section is sufficient to prove that predicate `invariants`, which corresponds to I_V, holds at the beginning and at the end of the block implementing the statements. In Listing 1.2 this means that `invariants` holds immediately after `lockV` in line 5 and immediately before the `unlockV` in line 7. The validity of `invariants` ensures ownership of the variables in `sharedVariables`. As discussed above, by construction of our transformation (i.e., by not using `lock` and `unlock` within the protected block of the statement translation) we ensure that the block does not release this ownership. For example, in Listing 1.2 methods `assign` in line 6, as well as the implementations of all other types of SLCO statements, satisfies this property. VeriFast is able to verify that all relevant variables are held by the thread executing the method corresponding to the implementation of the SLCO statement. This implies serializability of the programs as can be seen from the following arguments.

Consider two instruction blocks σ and σ' which both implement an SLCO statement. Hence, they both contain a lock protected code block. We show that they are serializable. Let V and V' be the set of variables accessed by σ and σ', respectively. Consider first the case when $V \cap V' \neq \emptyset$. Suppose that σ first acquires the ownership of all variables in V. Then σ' must wait until those variables are released. If there is some prefix σ'' of σ' which has been executed before σ acquired the variables in V, then σ' could have modified only variables which are not in V. So, this prefix could have been executed after σ terminated and therefore the sequence $\sigma\sigma'$ will produce the same variable changes, i.e., the same state as the concurrent execution of σ and σ'.

A similar argument can be used for the case $V \cap V' = \emptyset$. In this case the individual statements in σ and σ' are independent of one another and can be permuted in an arbitrary order. The set of possible sequences includes both $\sigma\sigma'$ and $\sigma'\sigma$ and they confluently lead to the same end state.

5   Specifying and Verifying Lock-Deadlock Freedom

In this section, we show how in addition to specifying and verifying atomicity preservation, we can also verify that programs generated by our model-to-code transformation are guaranteed to be free of lock-deadlocks. We first discuss the theory behind the approach and after that we present the concrete specification and verification in VeriFast.

5.1   Lock-Deadlock Freedom for Generated Code

Code generation from models should preserve deadlock freedom: if the model is deadlock free, the generated code should be deadlock free. This places demands on the generic code and on the translation.

Here, we consider an important category of deadlocks: *lock-deadlock* - a set of threads is lock-deadlocked if all threads in the set are blocked because they try to acquire locks that are already acquired by some thread in the set [13,17].

In the spirit of model-driven development we treat lock-deadlock freedom as a property to be ensured by the code generation rather than having to establish this for each specific instance of generated code.

A well-established way to obtain lock-deadlock freedom is putting an ordering on acquiring locks. To achieve lock ordering at the level of code generation we put requirements on the order of acquiring locks by means of the specification of the lock, the lock API. This specification is such that any code (generated or obtained otherwise) that satisfies the precondition of the lock method of this API is lock-deadlock free. (Note that here the approach is SLCO independent and not Java specific.) We show how these requirements are met by the generic code and the way it is used in the translation from SLCO to Java.

Conditions for Lock-Deadlock Freedom. Let the locks be ordered by an anti-reflexive partial order $<$. In the API specification of the lock, the auxiliary variable $lockset(T)$ represents the locks acquired by thread T, which is maintained by the methods lock() and unlock(). The following assumption is a cornerstone of the lock-deadlock avoidance approach:

Assumption 1 (Lock Acquire Precondition). The precondition of method lock of lock lck which is to be acquired implies that $lck < l$ for any l in $lockset(T)$, where T is the current thread.

Theorem 1 (Lock-deadlock Freedom). *Code adhering to the precondition of method* lock *as in Assumption 1 is lock-deadlock free.*

Proof. Suppose, by contradiction, that we have a lock-deadlock. Then there is a set S of threads that are all waiting for each other. I.e., every thread in S is waiting for a lock that has already been acquired by a thread in S. Call this set of acquired locks L. We now construct a cycle in the order, which gives the contradiction.

Suppose lock l_1 in L is tried, by a call to lock(), by thread T_1, which has lockset LS_1. LS_1 is the set of locks acquired by T_1. By the definition of S, there has to be a lock L_2 in LS_1 that is in L. Then the precondition of lock() requires that $l_1 < l_2$. Since l_2 is in L, there is a thread T_2 waiting for l_2. By repeating this argument we get an infinite chain $l_1 < l_2 < \ldots$. Since all locks l_i are in L and L is finite, there has to be a repetition in the chain: $l_i < \cdots < l_i$ So we have a cycle in $<$, which is in contradiction with the fact that $<$ is an anti-reflexive partial order. □

Lock-Deadlock Freedom for Java Code Generated from SLCO Models. We show that code as generated from SLCO specifications adheres to the precondition of method lock as in Assumption 1 and hence is, by Theorem 1, lock-deadlock free.

Lemma 1. *If the precondition of* lockV *of class* Statement *in Listing 1.8 is satisfied, the generic code adheres to the precondition of method* lock *as in Assumption 1.*

Proof (sketch). The only place where lock is called in the generic code is in the method lockV. There lock methods are called in the designated order (since the precondition implies the correct ordering of variables/locks) and hence the locks will be acquired in the same correct descending order. The only possible problem is the first lock to be acquired, if it is greater than some of the locks in *lockset(T)*. Therefore, the precondition of lockV additionally requires that all locks that are acquired by lockV are below all locks in lockV. (Actually, in our translator we enforce a stronger condition that *lockset(T)* is empty when lockV is called.) □

The proof sketch above has been carried on formally below using VeriFast (Subsect. 5.2).

Lemma 2. *The generated code adheres to the specification of class* Statement.

Proof. Inspecting the translator shows that the methods of instance s of class Statement are called only in the template method lockAndAssign as shown in Listing 1.2. We give a pseudo-formal annotation, where V is the set of locks that correspond to the variables of s.

$$\{lockset(T) == \emptyset\}$$
$$\text{lockV();}$$
$$\{lockset(T) == V\}$$
$$\text{assign();}$$
$$\{lockset(T) == V\}$$
$$\text{unlockV();}$$
$$\{lockset(T) == \emptyset\}$$

Method assign is implemented in the translation according to the specific assignment statement in the SLCO model. Inspecting the translator shows that it will not call lock, hence keeping the lockset invariant. To satisfy the above annotation it is needed that the precondition of assign is implied by the postcondition of lockV, and that the postcondition of assign implies the precondition of unlockV, which can be shown straightforwardly by inspecting the code of the translator. □

Lemmas 1 and 2 and Theorem 1 imply lock-deadlock freedom immediately.

5.2 Formal Specification and Verification of Lock-Deadlock Freedom in VeriFast

To implement the theoretical considerations from the previous section we use the feature of VeriFast that ensures lock-deadlock freedom based on ordered lock acquisition [13]. To this end we first need to adapt VeriFast's lock specification for C to Java.

Class ReentrantLock Specification. To simplify the specification we rely on the fact that the locks in our mechanism are never reacquired, i.e., a thread already holding a lock never attempts to acquire it again. Later, we prove that the VeriFast specification is free of deadlocks, which formally guarantees absence of lock reentrance. The specification of the class `ReentrantLock` is given in Listing 1.7.

Listing 1.7. Abstract Specifications of Class **Statement** to Avoid Deadlock.

```
1  //@ predicate lockset(int threadId, list<ReentrantLock> lockIds);
2  public class ReentrantLock {
3    //@ predicate ReentrantLock(predicate() inv);
4    //@ predicate ReentrantLocked(predicate() inv, int threadId, real frac)
         ;
5    public ReentrantLock()
6    //@ requires create_lock_ghost_args(?inv, ?ls, ?us) &*& inv() &*&
         lock_all_below_all(ls, us) == true;
7    //@ ensures [_]ReentrantLock(inv) &*& lock_above_all(this, ls) == true
         &*& lock_below_all(this, us) == true;
8
9    public void lock();
10   //@ requires [?f]ReentrantLock(?inv) &*& lockset(currentThread, ?locks)
         &*& lock_below_top(this, locks) == true;
11   //@ ensures ReentrantLocked(inv, currentThread, f) &*& inv() &*&
         lockset(currentThread, cons(this, locks));
12
13   public void unlock();
14   //@ requires ReentrantLocked(?inv, currentThread, ?f) &*& inv() &*&
         lockset(currentThread, ?locks);
15   //@ ensures [f]ReentrantLock(inv) &*& lockset(currentThread, remove(
         this, locks));
16 }
```

The abstract predicate `lockset` in line 1 is defined by the client that uses the specification. It states that the `ReentrantLock` list `lockIds` contains the locks held by thread `threadId`. The abstract predicate `ReentrantLock` associates the invariant `inv` with the lock. Predicate `ReentrantLocked` denotes that the lock is associated with invariant `inv` and it is held (owned) by `threadId` with fraction `f`.

The contract of the constructor `ReentrantLock` associates the created lock with its invariant `inv` and places the lock in the partial ordering above the locks in set `ls` and below the locks in set `us`. Ghost variables `inv`, `ls`, and `us` are created in the precondition. A precondition for the lock creation is that `inv` holds and also that the lower and upper limit of the lock are consistent, i.e., that the locks in `ls` are all below all locks in `us`.

The precondition of method `lock` expresses the decreasing order of lock acquisition, i.e., the requirement that the lock needs to be below all locks currently held by the thread. Note that if the lock is reacquired, it is already held by the current thread, i.e., included in `locks`, therefore an error will be signaled by VeriFast. Hence, the specification also implies absence of reentrance. Predicate `ReentrantLock` in the precondition expresses the fact that the lock is available with fraction `f`. The postcondition states that the lock is owned (locked) with fraction f, that the associated invariant holds at this point and that the lock is added to the lockset held by the current thread.

The specification of unlock is a mirror image of the contract of lock in the sense that basically the postcondition of postcondition of the former is a precondition of the latter and vice versa.

Class Statement Specification. The updated specification of class Statement is shown in Listing 1.8. Predicates lock_inv in line 2 and invariants in lines 5–6 are the same as in Listing 1.5. The recursive predicate locks in lines 3–4 has an output parameter called ll that is a ReentrantLock list associated with the SharedVariable list vs. The body of locks is a conditional assertion. If vs is null then ll is null (line 4) too; otherwise, the inductive step asserts that the lock of the first element of the list vs, head(vs) is added at the head of ll denoted by ll == cons(lock, ll0). Besides that, lock_above_all is a fixpoint function defined by VeriFast to ensure the level of lock is above the level of each element in list ll0 which is the tail of ll. In a similar fashion, the recursive predicate locked in lines 7–8 states that invariant lock_inv(head(vs)) is associated with the lock of the first element, via the predicate ReentrantLocked. Predicate ReentrantLocked also states that thread t is the current thread holding the lock of the first element. The semicolon (;) in the parameter list of predicate locked is used to declare locked as precise, which enables VeriFast's logic for automatically opening and closing this predicate.

The lemma function extend_upper_bound_at_top in lines 9–14 states that if the lock list ys is an upper bound of list xs, i.e., the level of each lock in list xs is below the level of each lock in list ys, and the level of lock x is above the level of locks in list xs, then we can add x at the top of ys and the new list cons(x,ys) will remain an upper bound of xs. The lemma_auto function is another type of lemma which can be implicitly called by VeriFast. locks_inv() in lines 15–20 instructs VeriFast to always replace the chunk [?f]locks(?vs, ?ls) with [f]locks(vs, ls) &*& vs != nil || ls == nil. (The lemma is proved by opening the predicate locks explicitly.)

Predicate Statement_lock() in line 23 is similar to the one defined in Listing 1.5 but has two parameters in its parameter list. The list of ReentrantLock objects ll is used to extract the list of locks associated with shared variable objects vs.

The precondition of lockV, given in line 25, plays a crucial role in Lemma 1. The predicate lockset states that the list levelList is a list of locks acquired so far by the current thread. Predicate lock_all_below_all requires that levels of the locks to be acquired in list ll are below levels of the locks in levelList, i.e., the locks acquired so far by the current thread.

The postcondition of method lockV implies the correctness of the annotation in Lemma 2. It asserts that all variables in vs are locked by the current thread and that consequently each element in list ll is added to the list levelList. VeriFast requires that the order of lock acquisition in list levelList is descending. However, the order of locks in list ll is ascending, which is defined during the

SLCO-to-Java transformation. Therefore, the order of elements in list ll should be reversed before appending the list ll to the list levelList. This is expressed by the predicate lockset(currentThread,append(reverse(ll),levelList)) in line 26. Actually our transformation ensures that the list of acquired locks levelList is always empty at the precondition in line 25. So, the requirement that all locks in ll are below all locks in levelList is trivially satisfied.

The postcondition lockset(currentThread,?levelList) and invariants (vs) of the method lockV are also part of the precondition in the method unlockV. By calling the method unlockV, invariant I_v of each variable in list vs is not guaranteed to hold anymore and all locks in ll are also removed from the list levelList as expressed by remove_all(ll,levelList).

Listing 1.8. Abstract Specifications of Class **Statement** to Avoid Deadlock.

```
1  /*@
2  predicate_ctor lock_inv(SharedVariable v)(;) = v.value |-> _;
3  predicate locks(list<SharedVariable> vs; list<ReentrantLock> ll) =
4      vs == nil ? ll == nil : [_]head(vs).lock |-> ?lock &*& [_]lock.
           ReentrantLock(lock_inv(head(vs))) &*& locks(tail(vs), ?ll0) &*&
           ll == cons(lock,ll0) &*& lock_above_all(lock,ll0) == true;
5  predicate invariants(list<SharedVariable> vs;) =
6      vs == nil ? true : lock_inv(head(vs))() &*& invariants(tail(vs));
7  predicate locked(list<SharedVariable> vs, int t;) =
8      vs == nil ? true : [_]head(vs).lock |-> ?lock &*& lock.
           ReentrantLocked(lock_inv(head(vs)), t, _) &*& locked(tail(vs),t);
9  lemma void extend_upper_bound_at_top(ReentrantLock x, list<ReentrantLock>
        xs, list<ReentrantLock> ys)
10 requires lock_all_below_all(xs, ys) == true &*& lock_above_all(x,xs)==
        true;
11 ensures lock_all_below_all(xs, cons(x, ys)) == true;
12 {
13     switch (xs) { case nil: case cons(h, t): extend_upper_bound_at_top(x,
           t, ys); }
14 }
15 lemma_auto void locks_inv()
16 requires [?f]locks(?vs, ?ls);
17 ensures [f]locks(vs, ls) &*& vs != nil || ls == nil;
18 {
19     open locks(vs, ls);
20 }
21 @*/
22 class Statement {
23     //@ predicate Statement_lock(list<SharedVariable> vs, list<
           ReentrantLock> ll);
24     void lockV();
25     //@ requires [_]Statement_lock(?vs,?ll) &*& lockset(currentThread,?
           levelList) &*& lock_all_below_all(ll,levelsList) == true;
26     //@ ensures invariants(vs) &*& lockset(currentThread,append(reverse(ll)
           ,levelList)) &*& locked(vs,currentThread);
27
28     void unlockV();
29     //@ requires [_]Statement_lock(?vs,?ll) &*& invariants(vs) &*& lockset(
           currentThread,?levelList) &*& locked(vs,currentThread);
30     //@ ensures lockset(currentThread, remove_all(ll,levelList));
31 }
```

Class Statement Verification. Above we provide the formal specification of the class `Statement` to avoid lock-deadlock in an abstract and modular way. Here, we verify the implementation of this class, as shown in Listing 1.9.

The definition of predicates in lines 2–7 in Listing 1.9 can be found in Listing 1.8 in lines 2–20. Line 11 in Listing 1.9 shows the definition of predicate `Statement_lock` in line 23 in Listing 1.8. It states that the field `variableList` of class `Statement` is defined (`this.variablesList |-> ?a`) and it is related with the mathematical variable `vs` of type `list` (`a.List(vs)`). Moreover, the variables in `vs` are connected to their corresponding locks which are stored in the list `ll` (`locks(vs, ll)`). The precondition and postcondition of method `lockV` in lines 13–14 are the same as the one in lines 15–26 in Listing 1.8.

Similar to the contract of the `for` loop for proving atomicity in Listing 1.6, we introduce the level of locks associated with `variablesList` into the contract of the `for` loop in Listing 1.9 to prove lock-deadlock freedom. In the precondition, the conjunct `[_]locks(drop(i,vs),?lll)` associates the variables in `vs` from index `i` to `vs.length-1` with their locks and stores them in the list `lll`. In a similar way in the postcondition in line 18, the list tail starting with `old_i` is obtained as an argument of the predicates `invariants` and `locked`. The predicate `invariants` in the postcondition ensures the ownership of all variables in `vs`. The predicate `locked` in the postcondition implies the validity of the postcondition of each `lock.lock()` of all locks associated with `vs`. After the execution of the `for` loop, `levelList1` is updated by appending the lock list `lll` to it. To ensure that the locks in list `levelList1` are placed in descending order, the order of list `lll` is reversed before appending it to the list `levelList1` via `reverse(lll)`.

The `switch` statement in line 21 helps VeriFast to access the list `levelList1` even if it is `null`. The lemma function `extend_upper_bound_at_top` in line 23 works as described in the specification above.

Another lemma function provided by VeriFast `append_assoc()` states the associative property of the `append` operator, which can append one list to another.

Instead of using `true` as the postcondition of method `unlockV` for proving the atomicity property, here we use the predicate `lockset(currentThread, remove_all(lll,levelList1))`. It expresses that the locks of the variables in the list `lll` are removed from the list `levelList1` after the execution of method `unlockV`. In each iteration of the `for` loop, the element that is equal to the head of list `lll` is removed from `levelList1`. The lemma function `remove_all_head(lll, levelList1)` tells VeriFast that `remove_all(lll, levelList1)` is equivalent to `remove_all(tail(lll), remove(head(lll), levelList1))`. The fixpoint function `remove(head(lll), levelList1)` removes the element that is equal to the head of `lll` from `levelList1` and `remove_all(lll, levelList1)` removes all elements that occur in list `lll` from `levelList1`.

Listing 1.9. Verification annotations for class **Statement** to Avoid Deadlock.

```
1  /*@
2  predicate_ctor lock_inv(SharedVariable v)(;) = ...
3  predicate locks(list<SharedVariable> vs;) = ...
4  predicate invariants(list<SharedVariable> vs;) = ...
5  predicate locked(list<SharedVariable> vs, int t;) = ...
6  lemma void extend_upper_bound_at_top(ReentrantLock x, list<ReentrantLock>
        xs, list<ReentrantLock> ys)...
7  lemma_auto void locks_inv()...
8  @*/
9  class Statement {
10   SharedVariableList variablesList;
11   //@ predicate Statement_lock(list<SharedVariable> vs,list<ReentrantLock
        > ll) = this.variablesList |-> ?a &*& a != null &*& a.List(vs) &*&
        locks(vs,ll);
12   void lockV()
13   //@ requires [_]Statement_lock(?vs,?ll) &*& lockset(currentThread,?
        levelsList) &*& lock_all_below_all(ll,levelsList) == true;
14   //@ ensures invariants(vs) &*& lockset(currentThread,append(reverse(ll)
        ,levelsList)) &*& locked(vs,currentThread);
15   {
16     for (int i = 0; i < variablesList.size(); i++)
17     //@ requires [_]variablesList |-> ?b &*& [_]b.List(vs) &*& [_]locks(
          drop(i,vs),?lll) &*& i >= 0 &*& i <= length(vs)&*& lockset(
          currentThread,?levelsList1) &*& lock_all_below_all(lll,
          levelsList1) == true;
18     //@ ensures invariants(drop(old_i, vs)) &*& lockset(currentThread,
          append(reverse(lll),levelsList1)) &*& locked(drop(old_i, vs),
          currentThread);
19     {
20       //@ drop_n_plus_one(i,vs);
21       //@ switch (levelsList1) { case nil: case cons(h,t): }
22       //@open(locks(_,_));
23       //@extend_upper_bound_at_top(head(lll), tail(lll), levelsList1);
24       //@append_assoc(reverse(tail(lll)), {head(lll)}, levelsList1);
25       variablesList.get(i).lock.lock();
26     }
27   }
28
29   void unlockV()
30   //@ requires [_]Statement_lock(?vs,?ll) &*& invariants(vs) &*& lockset(
        currentThread,?levelList) &*& locked(vs,currentThread);
31   //@ ensures lockset(currentThread, remove_all(ll,levelList));
32   {
33     for (int  i = 0; i < variablesList.size(); i++)
34     //@requires [_]variablesList |-> ?b &*& [_]b.List(vs) &*& [_]locks(
          drop(i,vs),?lll) &*& invariants(drop(i,vs)) &*& i >= 0 &*& i <=
          length(vs) &*& lockset(currentThread,?levelList1) &*& locked(drop
          (i,vs),currentThread);
35     //@ ensures lockset(currentThread,remove_all(lll,levelList1));
36     {
37       //@ drop_n_plus_one(i,vs);
38       //@ open(locked(_,_));
39       //@ open(locks(_,_));
40       //@ remove_all_head(lll, levelList1);
41       variablesList.get(i).lock.unlock();
42     }
43   }
44 }
```

6 Related Work

The detection of race condition violations in concurrent code using the lock mechanism has been addressed by a number of type-based [9], static [1,8] and dynamic analysis [6] tools. However, as shown in [10], a code block free of race conditions may still contain errors caused by simultaneous access to shared objects. Therefore, stronger concepts of non-interference are needed. In [10], a relaxed definition of atomicity was used and an atomic type system was implemented to check it. The tool DoubleChecker [2] checks for serializability of concurrent programs based on run-time information about the dependences between threads. The above mentioned works check the correctness of programs a posteriori, i.e., after they have been fully implemented. In contrast, our approach statically verifies generic code to be used in the construction of complete programs.

There exists a substantial amount of work that deals with model-to-code transformations. For an overview, see [21]. Here we focus on relevant work that deals with model-to-code transformations and uses verification based on deductive methods, like theorem proving.

In [3], a formal verification using the Isabelle/HOL theorem prover is presented of a concrete algorithm that generates Java code from UML Statecharts. It is shown that the source UML model and the generated Java code are bisimilar. This is a one stage model transformation. In [23], a Java code generation framework is presented. The framework is based on the transformation language QVT. The theorem prover KIV is used to prove security properties and syntactic correctness. In both these works, one of the major concerns is the scalability when the transformations are applied on complex models. By splitting the transformation into producing generic and specific code, and verifying the generic concepts in isolation, we aim to have a more scalable approach.

Finally, software model checking techniques, e.g., [5,14], offer a supporting approach to verify code resulting from model-to-code transformations. These techniques could in particular be useful to verify the generic code. Tools like Java PathFinder [25] are natural candidates for this task. It remains to be investigated how feasible it is to apply these techniques in a modular approach like ours.

7 Conclusions

We have presented an approach for the verification of atomicity preservation in model-to-code transformations based on separation logic using the tool VeriFast. We applied this approach in the transformation from the domain specific language SLCO to Java.

To improve performance, we replaced the strong atomicity requirement of SLCO with the semantically relaxed notion of serializability. This was implemented by a fine-grained deadlock-free ordered locking mechanism allowing true parallelism. We stated the serializability in terms of ownership of shared variables expressed by means of lock invariants. Using VeriFast we verified non-interference in the Java code.

A nice aspect of our approach is that we can also formally prove that our mechanism does not introduce so-called lock-deadlocks caused by mutual blocking of threads waiting to acquire locks. We can do this in an automatic and modular fashion using VeriFast. The same specification for showing absence of lock-deadlocks allows us to prove that the locks are not reentrant. This simplifies the specification and formal reasoning.

Future Work. Besides shared variables, SLCO also allows the use of channels for communication. As a next step, we want to verify that programs generated by our transformation using both locks and message-passing are free of deadlocks. Another plan for future work is to address the verification of model-specific code. This would allow us to conclude that our transformation is guaranteed to produce correct code.

References

1. Abadi, M., Flanagan, C., Freund, S.N.: Types for safe locking: static race detection for java. ACM Trans. Program. Lang. Syst. **28**(2), 207–255 (2006)
2. Biswas, S., Huang, J., Sengupta, A., Bond, M.D.: DoubleChecker: efficient sound and precise atomicity checking. In: ACM SIGPLAN Notices, vol. 49, pp. 28–39. ACM (2014)
3. Blech, J., Glesner, S., Leitner, J.: Formal verification of java code generation from UML models. In: Fujaba Days, pp. 49–56 (2005)
4. Bošnački, D., Brand, M., Gabriels, J., Jacobs, B., Kuiper, R., Roede, S., Wijs, A., Zhang, D.: Towards modular verification of threaded concurrent executable code generated from DSL models. In: Braga, C., Ölveczky, P.C. (eds.) FACS 2015. LNCS, vol. 9539, pp. 141–160. Springer, Cham (2016). doi:10.1007/978-3-319-28934-2_8
5. Chaki, S., Clarke, E., Groce, A., Jha, S., Veith, H.: Modular verification of software components in C. In: ICSE, pp. 385–395. IEEE (2003)
6. Choi, J.D., Lee, K., Loginov, A., O'Callahan, R., Sarkar, V., Sridharan, M.: Efficient and precise datarace detection for multithreaded object-oriented programs. In: ACM SIGPLAN Notices, vol. 37, pp. 258–269. ACM (2002)
7. Engelen, L.: From Napkin sketches to reliable software. Ph.D. thesis, Eindhoven University of Technology (2012)
8. Engler, D., Ashcraft, K.: RacerX: effective, static detection of race conditions and deadlocks. In: ACM SIGOPS Operating Systems Review, vol. 37, pp. 237–252. ACM (2003)
9. Farzan, A., Madhusudan, P.: Causal atomicity. In: Ball, T., Jones, R.B. (eds.) CAV 2006. LNCS, vol. 4144, pp. 315–328. Springer, Heidelberg (2006). doi:10.1007/11817963_30
10. Flanagan, C., Qadeer, S.: A type and effect system for atomicity. In: ACM SIGPLAN Notices, vol. 38, pp. 338–349. ACM (2003)
11. Havender, J.W.: Avoiding deadlock in multitasking systems. IBM Syst. J. **7**(2), 74–84 (1968)
12. Jacobs, B., Smans, J., Philippaerts, P., Vogels, F., Penninckx, W., Piessens, F.: VeriFast: a powerful, sound, predictable, fast verifier for C and java. In: Bobaru, M., Havelund, K., Holzmann, G.J., Joshi, R. (eds.) NFM 2011. LNCS, vol. 6617, pp. 41–55. Springer, Heidelberg (2011). doi:10.1007/978-3-642-20398-5_4
13. Jacobs, B., Bosnacki, D., Kuiper, R.: Modular termination verification: extended version. Technical report, Department of Computer Science, KU Leuven (2015)

14. Jhala, R., Majumdar, R.: Software model checking. ACM Comput. Surv. **41**(4), 1–54 (2009)
15. Kleppe, A., Warmer, J., Bast, W.: MDA Explained: the Model Driven Architecture: Practice and Promise. Addison-Wesley Professional, Boston (2005)
16. Kolovos, D., Rose, L., Garca-Dominguez, A., Paige, R.: The Epsilon Book. Eclipse (2011)
17. Leino, K.R.M., Müller, P., Smans, J.: Deadlock-free channels and locks. In: Gordon, A.D. (ed.) ESOP 2010. LNCS, vol. 6012, pp. 407–426. Springer, Heidelberg (2010). doi:10.1007/978-3-642-11957-6_22
18. O'Hearn, P., Reynolds, J., Yang, H.: Local reasoning about programs that alter data structures. In: Fribourg, L. (ed.) CSL 2001. LNCS, vol. 2142, pp. 1–19. Springer, Heidelberg (2001). doi:10.1007/3-540-44802-0_1
19. Owicki, S., Gries, D.: Verifying properties of parallel programs: an axiomatic approach. Commun. ACM **19**(5), 279–285 (1976)
20. Putter, S., Wijs, A.: Verifying a verifier: on the formal correctness of an LTS transformation verification technique. In: Stevens, P., Wąsowski, A. (eds.) FASE 2016. LNCS, vol. 9633, pp. 383–400. Springer, Heidelberg (2016). doi:10.1007/978-3-662-49665-7_23
21. Rahim, L., Whittle, J.: A survey of approaches for verifying model transformations. Softw. Syst. Model. **14**(2), 1003–1028 (2015)
22. Reynolds, J.C.: Separation logic: a logic for shared mutable data structures. In: 17th Annual IEEE Symposium on Logic in Computer Science, pp. 55–74. IEEE (2002)
23. Stenzel, K., Moebius, N., Reif, W.: Formal verification of QVT transformations for code generation. In: Whittle, J., Clark, T., Kühne, T. (eds.) MODELS 2011. LNCS, vol. 6981, pp. 533–547. Springer, Heidelberg (2011). doi:10.1007/978-3-642-24485-8_39
24. Tuerk, T.: A formalisation of smallfoot in HOL. In: Berghofer, S., Nipkow, T., Urban, C., Wenzel, M. (eds.) TPHOLs 2009. LNCS, vol. 5674, pp. 469–484. Springer, Heidelberg (2009). doi:10.1007/978-3-642-03359-9_32
25. Visser, W., Havelund, K., Brat, G., Park, S., Lerda, F.: Model checking programs. Autom. Softw. Eng. **10**(2), 203–232 (2003)
26. Wijs, A.: Define, verify, refine: correct composition and transformation of concurrent system semantics. In: Fiadeiro, J.L., Liu, Z., Xue, J. (eds.) FACS 2013. LNCS, vol. 8348, pp. 348–368. Springer, Cham (2014). doi:10.1007/978-3-319-07602-7_21
27. Wijs, A., Engelen, L.: Efficient property preservation checking of model refinements. In: Piterman, N., Smolka, S.A. (eds.) TACAS 2013. LNCS, vol. 7795, pp. 565–579. Springer, Heidelberg (2013). doi:10.1007/978-3-642-36742-7_41
28. Wijs, A., Engelen, L.: REFINER: towards formal verification of model transformations. In: Badger, J.M., Rozier, K.Y. (eds.) NFM 2014. LNCS, vol. 8430, pp. 258–263. Springer, Cham (2014). doi:10.1007/978-3-319-06200-6_21
29. Zhang, D., Bošnački, D., van den Brand, M., Engelen, L., Huizing, C., Kuiper, R., Wijs, A.: Towards verified java code generation from concurrent state machines. In: AMT. CEUR Workshop Proceedings, vol. 1277, pp. 64–69. CEUR-WS.org (2014)
30. Zhang, D., Bošnački, D., van den Brand, M., Huizing, C., Jacobs, B., Kuiper, R., Wijs, A.: Verification of atomicity preservation in model-to-code transformations. In: Fourth International Conference on Model-Driven Engineering and Software Development (MODELSWARD 2016), pp. 578–588. SCITEPRESS (2016)

Process Oriented Training with ADOxx: A Model-Based Realisation in Learn PAd

Robert Woitsch$^{(\boxtimes)}$, Nesat Efendioglu, and Damiano Falcioni

BOC Asset Management, Operngasse 20b, 1040 Vienna, Austria
{robert.woitsch,nesat.efendioglu,
damiano.falcioni}@boc-eu.com

Abstract. Process Oriented Training can be applied in two different approaches: (a) processes describing the methodology of training and learning as well as (b) processes describing the organizational context that need to be learned. This paper introduces the results of the EU project Learn PAd that developed prototypes of modelling tools enabling the latter - the usage of business processes to describe the organizational context. Flexibility of business processes have been introduced with case management and knowledge artefacts had been integrated to provide a homogeneous modelling environment. The requirements of such a modelling environment had been collected and implemented with the meta-modelling platform ADOxx®. The meta-model approach has been used to implement the modelling language as well as the mechanisms and the algorithms. The architecture of the modeling tool is introduced and a use case feedback is provided.

Keywords: Meta modelling · Modelling method development · Process-Oriented learning

1 Introduction

This paper revisits the contents of [29] and extends it with findings of [6]. This paper elaborates application scenarios for process-oriented training and learning, derives relevant requirements for modelling languages and introduces how the Learn PAd modelling method can be implemented with ADOxx® [2].

In [29] process oriented learning is introduced, which(1) compares the business process with a curriculum, (2) exploit the so-called knowledge products within a business process to define the required knowledge and (3) the knowledge sources to identify the available knowledge. The end users are using the business processes and the corresponding description for learning, whereas the responsible trainers manage the training by appropriately configuring the business process models.

The EU project Learn PAd [19] applied this process-oriented training approach at two governmental use cases, first at a University and second in a municipality.

The technological infrastructure is introduced and some guidelines for the change towards process-oriented learning are highlighted.

This paper focus on the realisation of process oriented learning and training with ADOxx®, by discussing application scenarios, modelling method requirements,

© Springer International Publishing AG 2017
S. Hammoudi et al. (Eds): MODELSWARD 2016, CCIS 692, pp. 274–292, 2017.
DOI: 10.1007/978-3-319-66302-9_14

development tools, modelling features and their implementation and technical deployment of realized prototype. Use case expertise is reflecting based on [6]. Public results are introduced in form of proof of concept evaluation from the adoxx.org community [2].

In Sect. 2 we present the identified scenarios on process oriented training. Section 3 introduces the meta-modelling approach as a realisation technique. In Sect. 4 implemented Learn PAd modelling method is introduced. Possible deployment architecture is discussed in Sect. 5. Afterwards use case scenarios are briefly elaborated in Sect. 6. Finally, outlook and conclusion is reflected in the last section.

2 Application Scenarios

In this section we shortly revisit the five application scenarios identified [30].

2.1 Individual Training

Individual training will support novices. The assessment of trainings enables much better insights into training demands.

The education of new employees is time consuming, as new employee typically lacks the organizational context. Hence, many questions or knowledge gaps are the result of fundamentally missing baseline knowledge of the organization.

Individual training is supported by the definition of different learning goals for different skill profiles, so that a learner can continuously improve their own skills through executing the business process.

Learn PAd merges the training and working environments, so that changes to business processes affect both the working environment for the daily tasks and the corresponding training environment.

2.2 Organizational Evolution

This process-oriented approach can also be applied to the development of the whole workforce within an organization.

In order to organizationally evolve the business process, learning goals need to define which part of the business process is to be changed, and – by involving skill profiles of team members – analyse how certain skill profiles are to be educated.

In addition to changes in the sequence of a particular process, knowledge of existing business processes can also change. Here the situation is different to individual training as users are very familiar with the process and usually claim that they know exactly what to do. The challenge is therefore to increase sensibility to minor, but important, changes.

2.3   Business Process Support and Reflection

The use of business processes and their explanatory documents as learning objects forces the public administration to critically reflect the current way of working and enables the detection of error prone parts.

Learning goals are defined in order to support the performance and reflect on the current business processes, which part needs to be improved.

An honest reflection on business process performance is usually very difficult as employees ideally need to critically reflect on their daily business within a so-called "failure-culture" in the organization – a culture that appreciates the identification of failures instead of pseudo-blaming some responsible actors.

Performance analysis needs a guiding structure. Business processes are an ideal candidate for such a structure as they enable a step-by-step analysis of daily operations that must result in an efficient sequence of activities that achieve organizational goals.

2.4   Process Optimization and Improvement

Process optimization and improvements are closely linked to performance support and reflection, which rely on the existing competencies of team members.

In order to support continuous improvement and optimization of a business process, learning goals can be used to identify the organizational learning objectives and identify the corresponding measures.

In this scenario, the team members use the learning platform as a communication and collaboration portal. The intention is to use business process based collaborative learning not only for the initial identification of improvements, but also to use those improved processes when performing the aforementioned organizational learning scenario.

2.5   Citizens Transparency

This use case is not a traditional training scenario but is an add-on use case with the aim of addressing the citizen that interacts with the Public Administration.

Learning goals are defined in order to increase transparency for citizens, addressing the misunderstandings reduction, incorrect submitted documents or increase appreciation.

Under such special conditions, the collaborative process-oriented training platform can be provided to citizens who interact with the administration.

Of course, the process will not be represented in detail, but on a higher abstraction to only point out the relevant decisions for the citizens, as well as only including high-level information.

3   Realization Approach

3.1   Modelling Method Requirements

The five application scenarios on process-oriented training have been analysed using an open requirement harvesting approach [7]. Modelling method relevant requirements have been filtered, grouped and detailed to end up with the following high level list:

- Modelling Language requirements: (a) access rights on models, (b) filtered model view to simplify the usage of the modelling tool, (c) questionnaire modelling, (d) textual annotation of models to semantically lift the models (e) bar display to have a better overview on used and created knowledge, (f) people-like view to simplify the graphical representation for non-modelling experts and (g) realizing a meta model that integrates the different relevant standards like BPMN, DMN, CMMN and others.
- Mechanisms and Algorithms: (a) track changes to see enable collaborative modelling, (b) process simulation to check consistency, (c) role based process skeleton to identify role-specific tasks, (d) model validation check, (e) critical path analysis, (f) model exchange with collaboration platform, (g) verification component and (h) evaluation component using a dashboard.

In the following the realisation approach of aforementioned requirements is introduced.

3.2   Conceptual Modelling as an Instrument

Conceptual models belong to the family of linguistic models that use an available set of pre-defined descriptions to create a model, and enrich the pure textual models (such as mathematical formula) with diagrammatic notations [9].

Hence, targeting aforementioned process-oriented training scenarios with conceptual models, means that pre-defined diagrammatic concepts are available that have a specific meaning enabling to reconstruct relevant parts of the reality with these

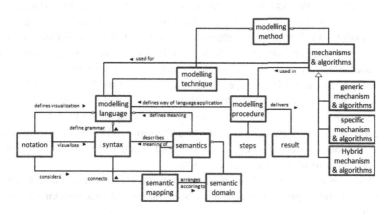

Fig. 1. Modeling method framework based on [11].

concepts in order to either (1) specify, (2) support execution, (3) represent knowledge or (4) evaluate the different dimensions of process-oriented training. The generic framework introduced in Fig. 1 enables the specification of conceptual models.

The framework identifies three building blocks: (1) the modelling language that is most prominently associated with conceptual models, as available concepts to be used for such models are pre-defined according their semantic, their syntax and their graphical notation, (2) the modelling procedure defines the stepwise usage of the modelling language and hence is not always available, this means there are modelling languages that have not a pre-defined way of usage but leave the modeller freedom in the sequence of modelling, (3) mechanisms and algorithms enable the computer-based processing of models and hence provide an IT support for the aforementioned modelling scenarios – specification, execution support, knowledge representation and evaluation.

3.3   Meta Models as Realization Approach

Meta modelling is introduced as a realization approach to develop domain-specific modelling tools and hence enable IT-supported concept modelling [11]. Based on [12, 15, 24] Fig. 2 introduces the different layers.

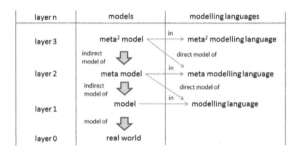

Fig. 2. Meta model layers.

Relevant parts of the real world – in our case the process oriented training – are seen as layer 0. Relevant concepts are provided in form of a modelling language and the corresponding mechanisms and algorithms to enable the creation of a model on layer 1. The modelling language is understood as the meta model, as it is a model of the concepts available for the model. This meta model is for example defined in a meta model language like ALL [2]. The specification of the meta model can again be defined by a model – the so called meta model or as a synonym meta^{2}model.

ADOxx$^®$ provides a meta^{2}model to simplify the development of modelling tools by using the provided meta^{2}model elements. Furthermore ADOxx$^®$ provides also an abstract meta model, which defines the context and functional behaviour of concepts, which can be used to inherit the own concepts.

The challenge is now to find the most appropriate abstract meta model classes to realise the modelling approach that covers aforementioned process-oriented training requirements.

3.4   Realization Technology with ADOxx®

This section introduces the development platform adoxx.org [2]. It is therefore seen as a short overview on how to implement an individual modelling solution for process-oriented training. Due to space restriction a brief overview is provided with the intension to raise the interest for detailed reading in the tutorial sections of adoxx.org.

The modelling tool is realized by configuring the meta modelling platform with a so-called application library. The model type is a package of modelling classes, enabling the separation of concerns within the meta model. Modelling classes are concepts of the meta model that are instantiated by the user while modelling. Each class is defined by its attributes, which are instantiated with attribute values during modelling. The user interface and interaction with the model concepts, are defined in the so-called notebooks class attribute "AttrRep". In the class attribute Graphical representation (GraphRep), the graphical notation –with other words, the concrete syntax- of the class is defined. The semantic of a model class is defined by the inheritance from the pre-defined meta model.

3.4.1   Relevant Technology for Modelling Languages

The context, semantic as well as the functional behaviour of modelling classes are realised by inheriting the most appropriate pre-defined meta model class, and adapting the missing structural, semantical or functional elements. In the following the two ADOxx abstract meta models are discussed. First, the dynamic meta model realizes a directed graph and hence provides start, activity, decision, parallelism, merging, and graph-end. Additional to these elements with operational graph-based semantic, there are two classes with container semantic the aggregation and the swim lane that automatically groups elements that are inside. Beside these two groups of classes there are some additional objects.

The static meta model realizes an organizational structure with persons and resources. Similar to the above mentioned containers there are aggregations and swim lanes. A new meta model is developed, when inheriting from the pre-defined classes. In case graph-based algorithms are used, the concepts are inherited from the dynamic meta model. In case a tree-based algorithm is used the classes are inherited from the static meta model. In case no corresponding class is found an own class hierarchy must be implemented.

3.4.2   Relevant Technology for Mechanisms and Algorithms

In order to upgrade a simple model editor to a full fletched modelling tool, the previously defined modelling language is enriched with corresponding mechanisms and algorithms. Generic functionality is provided for (a) modelling, (b) query, (c) transformation and (d) simulation. Some features need no configuration like querying a model or running a path analysis, whereas some functionality needs domain specific configurations like the transformation of a model into another format.

Basic components and their configurations can be extended by a script language called AdoScript that provide more than 400 APIs in form of message ports for: (i) acquisition, (ii) modelling, (iii) analysis, (iv) simulation, (v) evaluation, (vi) import/export, (vii) documentation and (viii) query. Ports for user interfaces are

(i) AdoScript language, (ii) Core user interface and the (iii) Explorer, whereas APIs for manipulating the models are (i) the Core – the actual model representation, (ii) the data base and (iii) the user management. Finally the application API of the modelling tool is provided in form of (i) drawing and (ii) application. This set of APIs provides the functionality that can be implemented either within the modelling tool, or via APIs that are accessed from third party components.

In third party components interact, there are three concepts available: (1) file based communication that triggers the export in a specific format (e.g. XML), (2) batch mode, where an AdoScript is invoked from outside the application or (3) via a Web/REST-Service that enables the invocation of all AdoScript APIs. In this way also SOAP messages can be exchanged and the modelling tool can be integrated into a collaborative learning platform.

4   The Learn PAd Modelling Method

The Learn PAd modelling method applies business process management for process oriented learning, hence the core concepts focuses on business process management. As Learn PAd uses the business processes for learning aspects, the idea is to use also the model-based approach for learning related modelling and identify applicable relations between the business processes that represent the object under observation as well as the learning models that describe the Learn PAd approach.

Business processes and learning models are both representatives of concept models hence have a tight relationship with semantics. Therefore, the integration of so-called modelling utilities such as ontologies or more human oriented knowledge acquisition tools, seems appropriate.

This results in a hybrid modelling approach; combining (a) business process related, (b) learning management related and (c) so-called modelling utilities together.

Figure 3 depicts current high level conceptual architecture on the Learn PAd modelling method, indicating the conceptual environment of the Learn Pad modelling method.

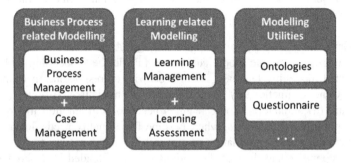

Fig. 3. High level building block of learn PAd modelling method.

Business Process Related Modelling: The major aspect in business process-oriented learning is the appropriate representation of a business process within the public administration. Beside the typical standard approach in using BPMN 2.0 for covering the business process management, Learn PAd additionally requires to specify relevant knowledge and skill profiles. In particular the business goals, strategies and business motivations, the organizational structure, the document and knowledge models are seen as the context of the business process model in Learn PAd.

In order to enable collaboration mechanisms for models on the Wiki platform, the corresponding concepts for such collaborative concepts need additionally to be reflected in the business process modelling language.

As Learn PAd deals with differently structure business process, ranging from well structure processes – that are typically covered in BPMN-like notations – but also weakly structured processes – that may be covered in Case Management Model Notation CMMN – there is the necessity to cover hybrid modelling within Learn PAd.

This conceptual concern is the basis of the Learn PAd modelling method.

Learning Related Modelling: deals with the specification of learning goals, definition of the learning content and the teaching path in presenting the content in the ideal way for each individual learner. Typical aspects are learning goal, curricula, skill profiles, teaching content and the packaging towards a learning management platform. Current state of research is to continuously asses the learning progress and hence combines the teaching path with assessment models that specify the goals that need to be achieved and also the assessment method.

Depending on the level of detail, the learning management will be performed using the ECAAD (Evidence Centred Design Methodology) [20, 21] method. Conceptual linkage is foreseen, so that Learn PAd business processes are seen as content packages of the ECAAD method, as well as different business processes models correspond to different phases of the learning process in ECAAD.

Modelling Utilities are modelling concepts that may or may not be used and hence can be flexibly added to the meta model. Current identified aspects are ontologies for semantically lifted log mining or questionnaires models for a model-driven development of tests.

Although those modelling utilities are not mandatory, the Learn PAd modelling method foresees as possible interaction, such as using the so-called "semantic lifting" approach to integrate ontologies, or to investigate a "graph rewriting" to export and transform relevant parts of the business process to questionnaire models.

Understanding the Learn PAd modelling method within its conceptual environment, it is now possible to distinguish between concepts that must be included into the Learn PAd modelling method (e.g. such as BPMN, CMMN, Roles and knowledge), concepts that are may be included as nice to have (e.g. such as business motivation, Key Performance Indicators, or skill profiles) and concepts that are not appropriate to be put into the Learn PAd modelling method (e.g. learning goals, learning assessment indicators, questionnaires).

Figure 4 introduces the conceptual Learn PAd Meta Model that introduces the high level concepts (a) process in both forms – procedural and case based processes, (b) organisation that are responsible in performing the processes, (c) the competency and required knowledge map appropriate organisations to processes, as well we as finally

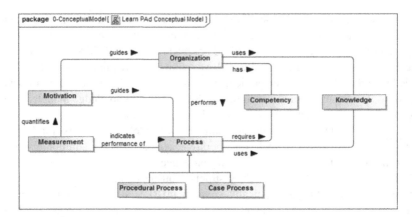

Fig. 4. The learn PAd meta model.

(d) the motivation and goals that guide the performance of processes and well as the corresponding measurement.

The next section introduces some selected parts of the method conceptualization in more detail.

4.1   Modelling Language

The modelling language has been developed following the meta model based approach and is described in detail in D3.2 [18].

The core domain is the business process model (using BPMN [22]) and the flexible case management (using CMMN [23]), which is linked to the business processes. Both are performed by workers, who are described in the organizational (structure) model. In order to perform skill-management, there is also a competence models, which details the traditional work place description of the organizational model.

Document and knowledge models provide the organizational knowledge in order to perform and execute the business processes and the cases.

In order to enable continues improvement, the business motivation model describes goals, intensions and rules, whereas the KPI (Key Performance Indicator) model, collects and aggregates measures and construct measurable indicators to assess the evolution of the learning organization.

Some other model types like the process map or the knowledge system model are introduced. Those model types do not carry own domain information but mainly act as a navigation support to navigate between the different aforementioned models.

A sub-set of BPMN 2.0 has been realized in Learn PAd focusing on those aspects which are relevant for human – learning – interaction, and leave out – technical – aspects, which are not relevant.

Although all concepts are specified in the BPMN 2.0 standard, its realization including abstract classes as well as references to other model types (– so called model type weaving.

More information on the BPMN realization is provided on the Learn PAd development space at ADOxx.org [1], as well as in [18].

The use of flexible case management, hence the description and collection of different cases introduces not only a flexibility into the business processes but also enables collaboration in form of discussions, recommendations and lessons learned in exceptional cases.

Due to the absence of appropriate standards that describe the organizational structure, Learn PAd used the meta model from the first and most successful community business process management tool ADONIS® Community Edition.

Organizational units describe the different departments, sections or the enterprises, hence define organizational boundaries. The roles describe the ideal representation of competences, whereas the performer describes the current workplace holder and hence describes the actual competences.

The Document and Knowledge Model type specification, that is interesting for learning and/or knowledge management models, traditionally, is a document pool, that lists all documents that are needed – either as input, as a resulting output, as a guidance or as a support document – when executing a business process. This traditional view is highly important in quality management scenarios or in keeping the business process documentation clear and simple.

In the context of learning, we enriched this model type with elements from the PROMOTE® modelling language [26]. A language that was first implemented in 2000 in a research project [25] and now founds its way into teaching and industrial projects.

Knowledge resources are described in three forms: (a) the document as an atomic knowledge carrier with a unique identifier, (b) the knowledge source that is – often a very large – container of documents, which collects, manages and encapsulates the big amount of documents like databases, document management systems or file directories, as well as (c) the knowledge resource, which represents not only complicated but also complex knowledge carries such as humans, or communities.

The difference between knowledge source and knowledge resource is that a knowledge source provided predictable results, hence a formal correct query into a database or file repository, will result in a predicable list of documents. Knowledge resource in contract, represent the complex knowledge resources and hence do not provide predictable results. The assessment of the opinion of an "expert community", the forming of a "committee" or the "impressions of an exhibition" may be valuable knowledge resources but in contract to a document by far not predictable. Hence those artefacts can be described in the knowledge resource.

When realizing a knowledge management or learning environment, the pure knowledge carrier like documents, sources or resources are often not relevant, but the so-called knowledge products. The knowledge product is a successful artefact that enables the consumption of knowledge in the similar way, like the consumption of any other non-physical good [27, 28].

It is based on implicit and explicit knowledge, hence can be distinguished in (a) information products that realize the internalization, (b) the service, that realizes the socialization and finally (c) the application that realizes the combination of external knowledge. For completeness reasons it is stated that (d) the externalization is not considered as it is a knowledge production and not a knowledge consumption.

Hence, typically a business process consumes knowledge products that are prepared for the use. Information products are mainly provided as documents, services as "responsible" colleagues and applications as "IT-resources" to be used.

As we consider the knowledge product as the essential carrier of knowledge and hence the essential artefact for learning, which is important to be observed, supported and measured, the consortium decided to include the knowledge product into the document and knowledge model type although this seems not obvious from a business process management point of view.

In that form, knowledge products can be integrated into the business processes and into cases, their responsibilities can be defined in the organizational structure and their quality and evolution can be measured with key performance indicators.

The full specification of the modelling can be downloaded in form of D3.2 [18] from the Learn PAd webpage. Additional material and specification on aforementioned modelling language implementation can be downloaded from the Learn PAd development space of ADOxx.org [1].

4.2 Mechanisms and Algorithms

Mechanisms and algorithms implement the model value by processing the models and by introducing features for modelling. Here, some relevant features are introduced.

4.2.1 People Oriented View

Business process models belong to the family of concept models, hence they consist of a graphical representation of concepts, which are often unintuitive to agents from public administration or to citizens. In order to ease the interpretation of business processes, so-called people oriented view has been introduced that enables the switch form a business process in the traditional graphical notation to a new graphical notation, where icons graphically describe the nature of the activity. Hence, instead of "blue boxes", an iconic representation of the action is provided, as shown in Fig. 5.

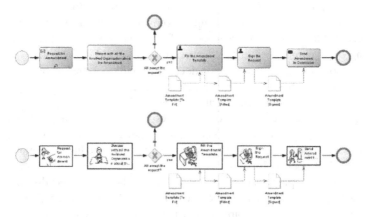

Fig. 5. Standard and people-like View of a business process.

This is achieved, by a so-called semantic lifting of each concept, hence the relation of a model object with an ontological description. A list of explanatory graphical icons is also annotated to the same ontological description. Hence, when switching into the people-like view, the images that are annotated with the model object are included in the new graphical description.

Current set of graphical description is based on the artefact types in the BPMN 2.0 specification. As the approach is open, other graphics can be included.

A detailed instruction of this feature is described in the Learn PAd development space in ADOxx.org.

4.2.2   Semantic Lifting of Business Processes

Semantic lifting is a form of a loose coupled model weaving, where concepts of a business process – e.g. tasks – are semantically lifted. This semantic lift is implemented by annotating the BPMN objects with an ontological concept [10].

There are different forms of semantic lifting, hence three cases that explain the different nature of semantic lifting are explained.

First, the direct lifting within the model is a simple copy/paste of the ontology URI into a generic or specially adapted attribute of the business process object. In this form, no changes in the modelling languages are necessary, but the usability is low and error prone is high.

The import ontological concept into the modelling tool and the selection of the semantic concepts within one modelling tool – e.g. via the former introduced pointer concept the so-called INTERREF – has the benefit that all concepts are safely managed in one repository and in one tool. As concept modelling and semantic have differences in the tool handling, it is likely that the ontology is maintained in the separate tool, which raises redundancies, requires replications and raises challenges in maintaining objects in the concept model repository. Therefore, this approach is not applicable if the ontology changes, but is required to stay stable.

The third approach is the invocation of an ontology management system out of the modelling environment. Hence, each model object of a business process, can access an interface of an ontology management system and can select one of the concepts, which are then stored in form of the URI in a special annotation attribute.

Finally, it has to be mentioned that there are many combinations of the introduced approaches, where the second and third approaches are combined to realize also complex scenarios and use the second approach as a pre-selection of stable part and the third approach for the identification of the concrete concept.

A discussion on the different implementations in more detail as well as the necessary development tools can be downloaded from the Learn PAd development space form ADOxx.org.

4.2.3   Business Processes in Collaboration Portals

The graphical representations of business processes is used to simplify the introduction of the business process tasks and link the corresponding description and attached document to the graphical representation. Although this form of process documentation is widely known and applied, the use within collaboration portals raises new challenges.

The simple export of graphical representations and model information is typically performed via Web-enabled APIs. In the ADOxx® case in form of Web-Services that deliver the (a) table of content, (b) model image, (c) model information and (d) model image map to enable click-able interaction in the Browser.

While user interface technology improves – e.g. Ext JS – the interaction possibilities improve. Former file based interaction, or static Web-API approaches are now exchanged by the attempt to continuously interact with a WIKI portal or realize Widgets that run within different Web-user interfaces.

Traditional Web-Service interaction and creation of WIKI pages can be downloaded from the Learn Pad development space from the ADOxx.org community. The mentioned Widget interaction is currently under development.

4.2.4   Business Process Verification

Business process design is an error prone process. The domain expert acting as modeler of the BP can easily introduce logical errors especially on complex and high collaborative business processes, which can results in failures at the execution time.

Verifying some quality properties over a Business Process in a formal and rigorous way is the safer way to avoid such kind of situations [5, 8].

The Learn PAd platform integrates a Formal Verification component in order to provide such kind of functionality. This component interact with the Learn PAd Modeling environment prototype through the Learn PAd platform in order to verify some properties like soundness or critical path existence, and visualize the results on the model.

The Fig. 6 is an example of the resulting of such interaction. In this case, deadlock presence is checked on a Business Process model and the found trace that lead to deadlock is shown on the model. Deadlock verification is only one of the supported properties that can be verified. For a complete list, please refer to the Deliverable 4.1 of the Learn PAd project.

The full support of this interaction scenario is under development. More details are available on the Learn Pad development space from the ADOxx.org community.

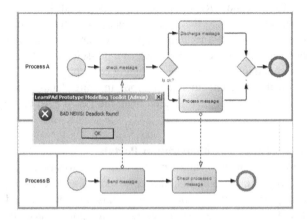

Fig. 6. Deadlock trace highlight on business process.

5   Process Oriented Learning Deployment

Process oriented Training and Learning has in principle two main categories with different technical realization:

- Process Oriented Training and Learning, where the process describes the training and learning method.
- Process Oriented Training and Learning, where the process describes the organizational content.

The technical realization in the first case can be realized by a process oriented training and learning methodology like ECAAD, (Evidence Centred Design Methodology) [20, 21] whereas the training and learning environment are Learn Management Systems like Moodle or Blackboard [3].

The technical realization of the second case can be realized by using business process modelling method like the extended BPMN 2.0 as developed in Learn PAd but then faces the challenge to be integrated into an existing legacy application.

Learn PAd dealt with the latter case and hence had to challenge the installation of this organizational learning-add on into existing legacy infrastructure.

5.1   High Level Reference Architecture

Learn PAd indicates functional capabilities for process oriented training and learning in organization, based on the knowledge management high level reference architecture.

Figure 7 indicates the major building blocks from the reference architecture: (1) Knowledge, Learning and Business Process Context that considers the complex and heterogeneous operative legacy systems of the end users organization, (2) Collaborative Business Process and Knowledge Based Learning that enables a process-oriented learning from knowledge workers, (3) Business Process and Knowledge Based Learning Modelling enables the definition of learning processes that are then realized in

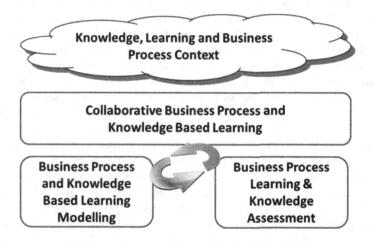

Fig. 7. Tools and applications for process-oriented learning.

the aforementioned execution environment, and finally (4) Business Process Learning and Knowledge Assessment introduces monitoring and dashboard functionality to identify improvements opportunities.

In the following the four building blocks are described:

- "Knowledge, Learning and Business Process Context": is a collection of relevant legacy applications that are necessary to execute the business process. In order to enable the seamless implementation of process oriented learning within an organization, the available IT infrastructure has to be considered as it is, and the process oriented learning framework has three choices to interact with the existing applications.

First integration is a loose link from the learning system to the legacy applications. This is most likely the first choice, ideally if the legacy application is a Web-application. Hence, this will be a Hyperlink to the Web-interface of the legacy application

Second integration is via an implemented API. This will be used if valuable learning or feedback information is required from the concrete legacy application. In the case where a social enterprise tool, enterprise wikis or similar are already in place, it may be worth implementing an interface. (e.g. KPI container).

Third integration are learning system components that are added to the IT infrastructure, hence the integration is given by the use of the learning system.

Pragmatically, a Wiki environment that describes how to access the legacy systems and providing the necessary links is the most appropriate way to start with a process oriented learning system.

- "Collaborative Business Process and Knowledge Based Learning": is a collaborative platform that is specially configured to support business processes. Traditional business process descriptions that are exported in collaborative Web-platforms are enriched with learning functionalities, such as stepping through a process, starting simulations, commenting on documents and knowledge as well as assessing learning progress.

Business processes can be trained by the user either in a manual or automatic way. The manual way is performed by stepping through a business process, reading the documents and discussing with colleagues whether the decision that would have been taken is the correct one. Automatic training of a business process is understood as simulation, whereby the process is triggered and the trainees have to commit their decisions into the system. Collaborative Business Process and Knowledge Based Learning workspace provides all functional capabilities for a user-friendly entry point into the process documentation, the manual stepper and the automatic simulation. Business processes are presented graphically, the corresponding documents, the required skill level and the capability to provide feedback and comments in form of an intuitive Wiki are provided in the form of a collaborative environment. Process Simulation for Learning is used by the knowledge worker in order to learn how the process has to be executed. Depending on different skill levels the process is simulated in a form that the knowledge worker performs each step with the correlated content. Hence the process is not executed directly but simulated with the aim to derive findings from recorded clicks and links. Focus is the end users interaction with the platform and with the process so that the user learns to perform the process in practice.

- "Business Process and Knowledge Based Learning Modelling": is used by trainers to design business process models for public administration. Typical conceptual and semantic modelling will be applied to define relevant conceptual artefacts that are processed for management and improvement. Modelling covers typical capabilities like (1) graphical visualization of models, (2) query and analysis features of models, (3) simulations of graphs as well as (4) transformation into different input and output formats. Depending on the platform and usage scenario the aforementioned generic modelling feature are differently grouped or detailed. Collaboration and Feedback transforms the previously made "Wiki-like" collaboration functionality into the modelling tool. Hence track changes, ratings or comments may be considered in this group.
- "Business Process Learning & Knowledge Assessment": is used by experts and trainers to analyses the use of the business processes and assess which part of the process is well supported and trained and which needs adjustments. A dashboard displays key performance indicators that enable the assessment of the maturity, skills and training levels of the process and its end users. It is seen as a cockpit for the trainer that represents KPIs for learning and knowledge maturity in a Scorecard like presentation.

The aforementioned grouping of high-level functional building blocks describes the major components, which can be added into an existing working infrastructure and the organization's site.

5.2   Modelling Tool Deployment

This section introduces the business process and knowledge based learning modelling tool, which can be downloaded in form of the first prototypes at the development space of ADOxx.org, or can be tested in the online version at advisor.boc-group.eu.

There are two prototypes: (a) the standalone rich client installation, which can be downloaded from the development space at ADOxx.org, as well as (b) the Web-based training and learning modeller on advisor provide modelling features, shown in Fig. 8.

The deployment of the full fletched rich client is in form of a local installation of the prototype. Export can be performed using the transformation features in order to generate special formats for learning simulation engines or collaborative portals. A server side installation may be required, in case the collaboration portal interacts with the modelling tool not via file exchange using the transformation features, but via the Web API. For such more complicated scenarios, additional effort is required to evolve the current prototype to an operational execution environment.

The deployment of the Web-based training and learning prototype in Learn PAd is a hosted deployment in form of a Web-application to flexibly instantiate modelling tools for different organizations. Cloud technology is available, in case such a service should be offered as SaaS.

In general, both modelling tools provide the basic concept modelling features, which can be extended on both prototypes.

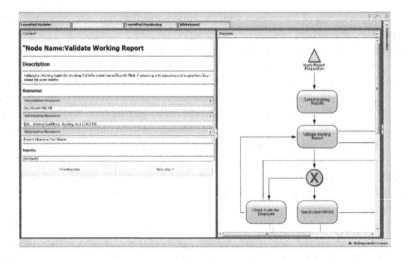

Fig. 8. Learn PAd prototype: modelling tool.

Modelling features are distinguished in: (a) model repository and access management, (b) Visualization, model management and graphical design, (c) Query, analysis and semantic inference of models as well as (d) Transformation from the model repository in requested output formats for documentation, execution or interchange.

Beside those generic functional capabilities, the feature details described in Sect. 3 are implemented in the standalone modelling prototype.

5.3   Use Case Realisation

The use case is the University of Camerino with strong background in BP modelling and software engineering. The team consists of on Learn PAd modeller and five so-called tellers who describe the organisational context and the processes.

The management of national and international research projects with the faculty was the use case scenario that starts when receiving an invitation to a project, and ends with archiving the finished project.

The processes deal with knowledge about research project form, the faculty council report, the consortium agreement and the grant agreement.

There are two sub-divisions that have been modelled according persons and their roles, hence each role described the required competence profile for executing the corresponding tasks within the business process.

This classification of skills had been distinguished in (i) analytical skills referring to selection and gathering of information, (ii) diagnostic skills referring to comprehension-evaluation of working activities and (iii) Implementation skills referring to accomplishment of tasks and transformation into results with appropriate quality.

For the successful evaluation, the European Quality Framework (EQF) has been used to formulate Key Performance Indicators that define the progress in individual and organisational learning.

After realising Learn PAd at the use case, the initial qualitative feedback is positive, hence further use cases are currently identified to be worked out during the final phase of the project and afterwards.

6 Conclusions

Process Oriented Training and Learning supports two approaches, one where process models are used to describe the teaching and one, where process model are used to describe the organizational context and content.

In Learn PAd the latter approach is applied for civil servants in five application scenarios: (a) individual training, (b) organizational evolution, (c) support and reflection, (d) process optimization and improvements as well as (e) citizens transparency.

The Modelling Method with its core languages has been introduced and some special features has been proposed, like the people oriented view, the semantic lifting and the business process verification. In the end the deployed architecture has been presented focusing on the high level architecture.

Acknowledgements. We thank the Learn PAd consortium for the fruitful research cooperation within the project. Especially we thank Prof. Dr. Knut Hinkelmann and his team from Fachhochschule Nordwestschweiz, which cooperated in the specification and development of this prototype also outside the research project in a separate cooperation on ADOxx.org.

References

1. ADOxx.org Development Space (2015). www.adoxx.org/live/web/learnpad-developer-space/space
2. ADOxx.org. 22 June (2015). www.adoxx.org
3. Blackboard (2015). blackboard.com
4. CompSysTech. CompSysTech. (2011). www.compsystech.org
5. Corradini, F., Polini, A., Polzonetti, A., Re, B.: Business processes verification for e-Government service delivery. Inf. Syst. Manage. **27** (2010)
6. De Angelis, G., Pierantonio, A., Polini, A., Re, B., Thönssen, B., Woitsch, R.: Modelling for learning in public administration - the learn PAd approach. In: Karagiannis, D., Mayr, C.H., Mylopoulos, J. (eds.) Domain-Specific Conceptual Modelling, pp. 575–594. Springer, Heidelberg (2016)
7. De Angelis, B., Ferrari, A., Gnesi, S., Polini, A.: Software Requirements Elicitation in the Context of a Collaboration Research Project: Technical Report, http://puma.isti.cnr.it/dfdownloadnew.php?ident=/LPAd/2014-TR-001&langver=en&scelta=NewMetadata, Accessed 28 May 2016
8. Falcioni, F., Polini, A., Polzonetti, A., Re, B.: Direct verification of BPMN processes through an optimized unfolding technique. In: QSIC 2012 (2012)
9. Fill, H.G., Karagiannis, D.: On the conceptualistion of modelling methods using the adoxx meta modelling platform, In: Enterpise Modelling and Information Systems Architectures, vol. 8(1). SIG EMISA 2013, March 2013

10. Hrgovcic, V., Karagiannis, D., Woitsch, R.: Conceptual modeling of the organisational aspects for distributed applications: the semantic lifting approach. In: IEE CAISE 2013 (2013)
11. Karagiannis, D.: Agile modelling method engineering. In: Proceedings of the 19th Panhellenic Conference on Informatics. ACM, New York (2015)
12. Karagiannis, D., Kühn, H.: Metamodelling platforms. In: Bauknecht, K., Tjoa, A.M., Quirchmayr, G. (eds.) EC-Web 2002. LNCS, vol. 2455, p. 182. Springer, Heidelberg (2002). doi:10.1007/3-540-45705-4_19
13. Karagiannis, D., Woitsch, R.: Model-driven design applied for e-learning and experiences from european projects. In: International Conference on Computer Systems and Technologies, CompSysTech 2011 (2011)
14. Mak, K., Robert, W.: Der Einsatz des prozessorientierten Wissensmanagementwerkzeuges PROMOTE® in der Zentraldokumentation der Landesverteidigungsakademie. Schriftenreihe der Landesverteidigungsakademie (2005)
15. Kühn, H.: Methodenintegration im Business Engineering. PhD Thesis. University of Vienna (2004) (in German)
16. Learn PAd D1.1 Requirements Report (2015). www.learnpad.eu
17. Learn PAd D1.2 Requirement Assessment Report (2015). www.learnpad.eu
18. Learn PAd D3.2. Learn PAd Meta Model (2015). www.learnpad.eu
19. Learn PAd EU Project, 22 June (2015). www.learnpad.eu
20. Misley, R.J., Steinberg, L.S., Almond, R.G.: Evidence-Centered Assessment Design (2015). www.education.umd.edu/EDMS/mislevy/papers/ECD_overview.html
21. NEXT TELL. Evidence Centered Design Methodology (2015). www.nexttell.eu
22. OMG BPMN (2015). http://www.omg.org/spec/BPMN/2.0/
23. OMG CMMN (2015). http://www.omg.org/spec/CMMN/1.0/
24. Strahringer, S.: Metamodellierung als Instrument des Methodenvergleichs: eine Evaluierung am Beispiel objektorientierter Analysemethoden. Shaker, Aachen (1996)
25. Telesko, R., Karagiannis, D., Woitsch, R.: Knowledge management, concepts and tools: the PROMOTE project. Forum Wissensmanagement, Systeme – Anwendungen – Technologien (2001)
26. Woitsch, R.: Process-Oriented Knowledge Management: A Service-Based Approach. Dissertation (2004)
27. Woitsch, R., Mak, K., Göllner, J.: Grundlagen zum Wissensmanagement, Teil 1: Ein WM-Rahmenwerk aus der Sicht praktischer Anwendungen. Schriftenreihe der Landesverteidigungsakademie (2010)
28. Woitsch, R., Hrgovcic, V.: Knowledge product modelling for industry: the PROMOTE approach. In: INCOM 2012 (2012)
29. Woitsch, R., Efendioglu, N.: Business process oriented learning: a collaborative approach of organisational learning. In: Proceedings of the 15th International Conference on Knowledge Technologies and Data-driven Business. I-KNOW 2015, pp. 491–494. ACM (2015)
30. Woitsch, R.: Business Oriented White Paper in Learn PAd, 22 June (2015)

Model-Based Architecture for Learning in Complex Organization

Francesco Basciani[(✉)] and Gianni Rosa[(✉)]

Dipartimento di Ingegneria e Scienze dell'Informazione e Matematica,
Università degli Studi dell'Aquila, L'Aquila, Italy
{francesco.basciani,gianni.rosa}@univaq.it

Abstract. To improve their service quality modern organization employees have to understand and put in action latest procedures and rules while coping with quickly changing contexts and decreasing resources. To this end a model-based architecture with interrelated enriched models is required in order to fosters an informative learning approach in the learning-by-doing paradigm. Such architecture enables organization employees to learn by accessing and studying enriched business process models and related material in a process-driven learning approach. Zachman Framework is used to organize all the models through the definition of the relations among them.

Keywords: Model driven engineering · Enterprise architecture · Zachman framework · Learning · Organizations

1 Introduction

In the complex organization domain it is increasingly demanded greater effort in terms of quality and efficiency in the services provided by employees in doing their jobs. To ensure this efficiency and this quality is necessary that employees with expertise in a given task (process) can share their experience. To facilitate both the knowledge elicitation and the learning process, a wide variety of models, tools and techniques have to be provided and integrated. In this respect several technical spaces are identifiable. This represents a major challenge because while the informative content of the various models is comparable, the way they are represented is based on different formats and standards. Furthermore, all these artifacts at the same time may confuse organizations, because it is not very obvious which one to choose or which purpose is served and bridging the different notation presents intrinsic difficulties whenever the artifacts are not belonging to the same technical space regardless of their content. Moreover, all the process and its sub-processes have to be developed and managed independently from other domains processes. Integrated models are needed, which put the various approaches into perspective. Such integration is meant to improve the speed of working, improve quality of documentation, products and processes, reduce costs, enhance responsiveness to customer needs and handle the overall system inherent complexity.

© Springer International Publishing AG 2017
S. Hammoudi et al. (Eds): MODELSWARD 2016, CCIS 692, pp. 293–311, 2017.
DOI: 10.1007/978-3-319-66302-9_15

In this paper we propose a model-based architecture conceived to provide a learning experience in which learner acquires knowledge while serving real requests, supporting an informative learning approach besides the learning-by-doing paradigm. For being effective, the architecture must provide the requirements for a modeling notation which describe the learners level, the acquired competencies and knowledge to perform a procedure described by means of a business process. This approach permits the learner to access and study these enriched models and operate within a simulated environment reproducing real requests through the promulgation of a process and monitoring activities in order to provide feedbacks for the evaluation of learners, business processes, and associated learning contents. To fulfill the need of share knowledge, manage and improve the processes in enterprise, the Learning Architecture LA provide a machine-processable model that exploit the correlation among the activities and/or concerns in order to provide enriched informations to the organization. The Zachman Framework [29] is used to describe all the interrelations, that provides a logic structure for classifying and organizing the knowledge about business activity of an organization in different dimensions, and each dimension can be perceived in different perspectives with respect to the Enterprise Architecture.

Structure of the Paper. The paper is organized as follows. Next section illustrates a motivating example related to a complex organization. In Sect. 3 we present an analysis of the required informations in order to design a LA; in Sect. 4, we outline how are integrate all the artifacts involved in learning in complex organizations using the Zachman Framework. Related work is discussed in Sect. 5 and finally, in Sect. 6 we draw some conclusions and future work.

2   Motivating Example

In this section, we present an example where an organization submits a project to the European Union (EU). To do that, the organization have to be aware of the environment complexity in which it is working because the ability to deal with this complexity is critical for the success of the project proposal. They must be able to handle in different ways a process as well as use different tools, models, reporting documentation and so on. Moreover, to successfully participate in a project proposal and to support administrative reporting activities, for a complex organization is required to involve a unit of administrative personal. For this reason, and also due to the typical employees high mobility, the availability of an electronic learning platform is therefore highly desired.

In order to better understand the complexity of managing public administrative procedures, a real world scenario is presented. Such scenario reference the administrative offices of an Italian public research body and is related to his participation to an European Project Budget Reporting (EPBR) [7]. We will start from the University organization structure description to the detail of the Business Process under analysis.

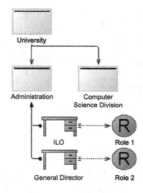

Fig. 1. Organization model: university organization (partial).

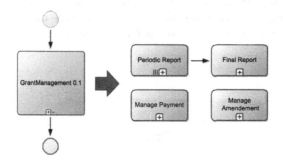

Fig. 2. Grant management different level of detail.

Figure 1 denotes a fragment of the University organization in which there is an administration and different schools (e.g. the Computer Science Division). In turn, an administration may have several employees, each one with its own role.

This scenario engages different partners in the definition of models and documentation for a Business Process and will permit to assess applicability of the proposed solution within real working contexts. For the sake of clarity, we are going to explain only a portion of the entire process and, after a first analysis of the domain, the Grant Management BP has been selected as reference point (see Fig. 2). It includes some sub-process, such as: Periodic Report, Final Report, Manage Payment and eventually Manage Amendment.

Without going into the details of each of the sub-processes involved in the scenario (this is not the purpose of our work) we consider the *Periodic Report* as motivating example. It is the data object representing the periodic report written by each partner participating to the project. In this process are involved different participants such as the officer, the coordinator (one pool), the grant beneficiary (multiple in parallel) and optionally the third part. Figure 3 describes how the coordinator organizes the process of periodic reports with respect to all the involved stakeholders.

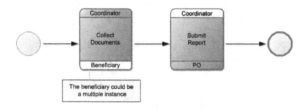

Fig. 3. Periodic report - choreography diagram.

Moreover, each Public Officer (PO) according to her experience, might have her own view of the process for the production of her private periodic report (Fig. 4 shows an example of a private process done by an EU public officer). In this way, different versions of the same process could be created, so we may have different diagrams for the same process. All these diagrams should have documentation so we need other models for this purpose.

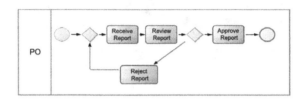

Fig. 4. Periodic report - private process of EU Officer.

In its turn, a documentation have to describe, textually and graphically, the state of the data-object. In particular, Fig. 5 shows as the Periodic Report is composed by a set of data-objects.

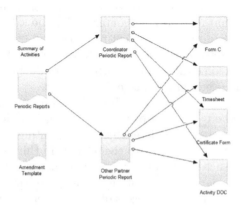

Fig. 5. Document model: periodic report.

Focusing on the role of Coordinator, they can be determined specific data-object: Amendment Template, Summary of Activities and Periodic Reports. Finally, Fig. 6 shows the private process of the Coordinator in relation to these documents.

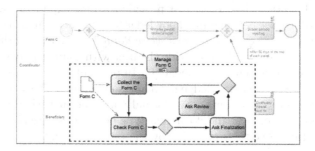

Fig. 6. Periodic report - private process of coordinator relationship with documents.

This scenario shows the use of a wide variety of models and diagrams (i.e. organization model, choreography diagram, collaboration diagram, Document Model, etc.) at different levels of detail both in term of modelling and learning (i.e. according to the learner skill you should focus on different abstraction level regarding how to deal with reporting).

The disadvantage in using all these models is represented by the increase of the whole process complexity and the problem of proper integration of all these artifacts. In the next section, we will show how the complexity emerged in this scenario is handled and the integration is done.

3   Learning Architecture

As illustrated in [17], in complex organisations there are many information resources that represents the complete set of activities consumed to perform missions, goals, and objectives. The knowledge must be systematically formalized, organized and consistently categorized in order to support effectiveness in learning. The architecture proposed in this paper supports:

- *informative learning* by which the learner can access and study the enriched BP model and related material with additional descriptive contents and,
- *procedural learning*, by which the learner operate within a simulated environment reproducing real requests through the enactment of a process and monitoring activities (*learn by doing* approach). Such environment allows us to capture useful feedback for the evaluation of: *(i)* learners, *(ii)* business processes, and *(iii)* associated learning contents. To this end, open-source communities principles and cooperation spirit will be fostered: contents are produced by the community, and meritocracy is naturally promoted, with leaders emerging because of their skill and expertise.

The above strategies, are *off-line* because the learner acquire such knowledge before serving real requests. However the typical complexity of processes defeats the human capacity to acquire a full knowledge on any aspect just through informative and procedural approaches. It is necessary that learner can retrieve and process useful and context-dependent information while she is working on real cases. The architecture therefore, must provide learning experience with *on-line* strategies in which learner acquires knowledge while serving real requests, supporting *"training on the job"* or *"learn while doing"* approach. To this end, it is of crucial relevance to be able to provide the user with contextually selected task and user-specific background knowledge [6]. In particular, the learner should be able to access the required knowledge in an optimal manner. This can be achieved by coupling the process (formal or informal) description with the descriptive units about the kind of data and document type being considered by the process. Ideally, the notion of context provided by the process permits users to know:

- what to do,
- who does what, and
- what to do after the task.

In this context arise the necessity to analyze the business process from a knowledge-management perspective and this is largely recognized (for instance, see [16]). In such a way the users engaged in their daily work routines have not to spend much time and effort in knowledge, information retrieval and management activities additional to their operative ones. Starting from the aforementioned premises, the LA exploits models in order to have informative specifications *(i)* for the learners and *(ii)* at the same time informations able to simulate and monitor the processes in organizations. The architecture proposed in this paper is composed by two main components as illustrated in Fig. 7:

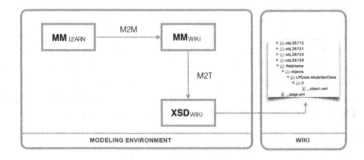

Fig. 7. The learning architecture.

- the Modeling Environment *ME* adopts state-of-the-art techniques and tools provided by the Eclipse Modeling Framework (EMF)[1]. The component provide metamodels, transformation and tools able to create a WIKI structure

---

[1] https://eclipse.org/modeling/emf/.

representing the processes starting from the diagrammatic modeling stage. The generation of e-learning artifacts out of specified business processes will be performed by LA means of horizontal (Model-to-model) and vertical (Model-to-code) model transformations as discussed in Sect. 4. Each of them represents an overall process phase that, starting from a representation of the modeled business process, create the XWiki structure from which will be created the wiki pages. The availability of complex meta-models for representing the business process structure, its data, and its business rules, permits to exploit its use also to assess the quality of the provided documentation with natural language processing techniques;

- the integration of a WIKI platform as a space for collaborative learning. The wiki-based content can be edited directly by the *experts* in order to enrich the learning material and to provide support to colleagues. Sharing and cooperation will be strongly fostered by the platform, introducing mechanisms inspired by the open source and open model communities. The WIKI is able to automatically reflect the structure of the specified BP.

The ME must be able to represent and transform by means of metamodels and model knowledge used in complex organization including factual, conceptual, procedural and meta-cognitive artifacts. Following we briefly illustrate the metamodeling architecture MM_{LEARN} involved in organizations that represent knowledge needed for learning as discussed in [24].

The models, as shown in Fig. 8, are obtained with an in-depth analysis of *(a)* three business processes in the domain of the Italian *Public Administration*

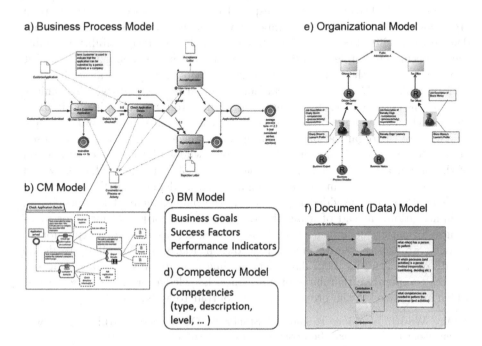

Fig. 8. Models involved in learning.

(the family reunion, the grant citizenship, and the bouncer registration); and
(b) a number of relevant modeling notations [6]. The business modelling language, defined to provide a process notation that could be easily understood by
all business stakeholders is BPMN 2.0 [1] as represented in Fig. 8(a). BPMN is a
standard for modeling processes described as a predefined sequences of activities
with decisions (gateways) to direct the sequence along alternative paths or for
iterations, flow of activities. Unfortunately, its semantic, as discussed in [6], is
limited, and it is not useful for some organizational aspects as for instance when
the activities in a process

- can occur in any order and/or in any frequency,
- are not predefined, repeatable and knowledge intensive,
- depend on evolving circumstances and ad-hoc decisions by knowledge workers
  regarding a particular situation.

The standard notation CMMN [2] as depicted in Fig. 8(b), allows us to deal
with the aforementioned limits. As discussed in [27], the importance to introduce intentional modeling in enterprise architecture entails potential benefits
and pitfalls. In learning context, it is of crucial relevance to model intentionality
providing a scheme for developing, communicating and managing business plans
in an organized manner. The BMM [3] focuses on that. It has been proposed
as a standard under the Object Management Group (OMG) and provides elements and relationships of intentional modeling as depicted in Fig. 8(c). Central
elements include *Means, Ends, Influencer, Potential Impact* and *Assessments*
that are specialized into more detailed elements as discussed in [24]. The modelling notation in learning must be able to describe the learners level, acquired
competency and learning progress respect to a business process or procedure in
organizations. In Fig. 8(d), the Competency model unlike the other models is not
defined in specific standard leaving to the modeller the responsibility to define
such aspects. The implementation we take into account is defined in [5] and it
is partly based on the framework the European Committee for standardisation,
CEN WS-LT LTSO (Learning Technology Standards Observatory)[2]. To achieve
their means and ends, organizations are structured (often hierarchically) in units
where each one has a set of job functions or tasks assigned to a group of people
belonging to the organization. Therefore, an organization structure is composed
of units, each encompassing the relevant people who work to achieve the mission
of the organization [22]. The need to keep track of "who does what, how and
when" is demanded to in Organizational model as depicted in Fig. 8(e) whose
implementations is provided in [5]. About the management of knowledge and
documentation, instead of using the BPMN 2.0 data object element for modeling information/documents used in a process, e.g. as input or output for an
activity, we use a separate model, as shown in Fig. 8(f). This allows to define
a data object (and its meta data), and adding more details, e.g. providing references to operative templates or guidelines, knowledge products or resources,
which are utilized in the processes (input, output to activities etc.).

---

[2] 2EN WS-LT Learning Technology Standards Observatory. URL: http://www.
cen-ltso.net/Main.aspx. Main contact: University of Vigo 36213 SPAIN.

4   Learning Using the Zachman Framework

The huge amount of informations and resources gathered from models in Sect. 3 is not independent because several technical spaces are identifiable. This represents a challenge because while the informative content of the various models is comparable, the way they are represented is based on different formats and standards. Bridging the different notation presents intrinsic difficulties whenever the artifacts are not belonging to the same technical space regardless of their content.

To fulfill the need of learning in enterprise, the *Learning Architecture* provides a machine-processable model that exploits the correlation among the activities and/or concerns in order to provide enriched informations to the organization. In the following we use the Zachman [29] framework to describe:

- the interrelations of above mentioned models,
- the logic structure for classifying and organizing the knowledge about business activity of an organization in different dimensions and perspectives with respect to the Enterprise Architecture.

Specifically, the Zachman Framework is a framework for enterprise architecture, which provides a formal and highly structured way of defining an enterprise. In essence, the framework is a two dimensional matrix consisting of 6 rows and 6 columns which defines 6 levels relevant to any enterprise, as well as 6 aspects. The structuring provided by the Zachman Framework provides that attention is placed on all the relevant scales, as well as on all relevant aspects, of any situation under consideration. Any Zachman Framework should be calibrated so that all relevant scales occur within its boundaries. Each row represents a total view of the enterprise from a particular perspective. These rows starting from the top include: Planner's View (Scope), Owner's View (Enterprise or Business Model), Designer's View (Information Systems Model), Builder's View (Technology Model), Subcontractor's View (Detail Representation), and Actual System View (The Functioning Enterprise). The columns describe various abstractions that define each perspective. These abstractions are based on six questions that one usually asks when s/he wants to understand an entity. The columns include: The Data Description (What?), The Function Description (How?), The Network Description (Where?), The People Description (Who?), The Time Description (When?), The Motivation Description (Why?). Further information and cell definitions of Zachman Framework can be found in [28]. The Zachman Framework can form the backdrop for a decision making process, ensuring that no mistaken collapse of attention occurs.

In this respect in Fig. 9 we outline how the models can be structured by Zachman's matrix [29]. The vertical dimension (the rows) in Fig. 9, describes the perspectives in terms of the participants involved in the organization's Information Systems [18] that use the models or descriptions contained in the cells. The top row represents the most generic perspective of an organization, while lower rows are successively more concrete, i.e.:

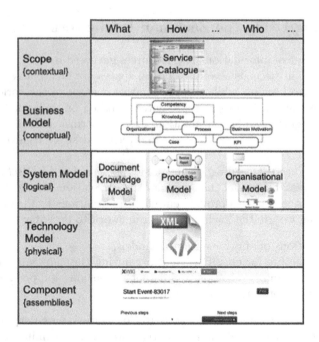

Fig. 9. The learning architecture structured by Zachman's matrix.

- *Scope* (Planner's Perspective), the planner defines the catalogue of services and the boundary of an organization which describe concrete information about a specific organisation, the context of learning, and business scope. The specification is written in natural languages and structured by means of a table that gather the aforementioned information;
- *Business Model* (Owner's Perspective), the owner is interested in modelling, at high abstraction level, the services defined in the *Scope*. The relevant data involved in a learning architecture, consists of a number of component meta-models illustrated in Fig. 10. The following have been defined by adapting current industrial standards:
    - business motivation (BMM) [3];
    - business process management and notation (BPMN) [1];
    - case management and notation (CMMN) [2].
  The remaining have been defined from scratch and are described in [24]:
    - competency metamodel (CM);
    - document and knowledge metamodel (DKM);
    - key performance indicator metamodel (KPI);
    - organization metamodel (OM).
  The relations are implicit and, hence, a process defined in a service catalogue (Scope Concepts level), may occur in the process description on the Business Concepts level but that relation is not formalized and therefore hard to trace;
- *System Model* (Designer's Perspective) the designer works with the specifications defined above, instantiating all elements involved in business organization to ensure that it will, in fact, fulfill the owner's expectations.

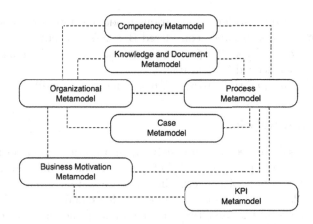

Fig. 10. The conceptual model.

The problem about tracing the relation between a process model on the System Logic Layer and the process description (at conceptual level), holds true;

- *Technology Model* (Builder's Perspective) the builder manages the process of define the language and functionalities able to satisfies the requirement of the learning platform. To this respect, the model set defined in *System Model* must be transformed in a standard exchange format, eg. XMI (see Sect. 4.2), in order to be machine readable;
- *Component* (Learning platform's Perspective) the learning architecture takes the instance models provided by the *Technology Model* and enables process-driven learning, fostering the cooperation and knowledge sharing among the learners.

While the horizontal dimension in the Zachman Framework describe the participants involved in the learning architecture, the columns provide a focus on each dimension [15]: What, How, Where, Who, When, Why and each of them is a descriptive of a single model. The architecture exploit a subset of them as following:

- Data (What?): in this column, "Document and Knowledge" concepts are defined. In particular, about the perspectives *Business Model, System Model*, and *Component*, the enterprise's informations about knowledge and resources used for business activity;
- Function (How?): the process of the organization are defined in several abstraction level. Starting from a service catalogue, the models are refined and enriched with structured information. In such way, learner can retrieve and process useful and context-dependent information while she is working on real cases;
- People (Who?): describes who is involved in activities, assigning them to business or IT perspective and classifying them w.r.t. to several aspects.

The matrix structure of the LA, allow us to perform an in depth analysis on some intrinsic characteristics:

- *horizontal relations*: bridging the various modeling notations (and their representation formats) between considered Business Objects;
- *vertical relations*: factorizing part of the transformation chaining in order to produce artifact needed for learning;
- enhance relevant quality factors, e.g. maintenance, extendibility, etc.

4.1 Horizontal Relations

As already discussed in Sect. 3 there are many information resources in an enterprise that serve several purposes and that usually reside in different information systems. The separation of concerns in software system modeling avoids the construction of large and monolithic models which could be difficult to handle, maintain and reuse. At the same time, having different models (each one describing a certain concern) requires their integration into a final model representing the entire domain [25]. The integration in LA is made through horizontal relations in Zachman Framework and, for the sake of clarity, only relations between models on the *System Model* layer will be discussed in this paper (see the related row in Fig. 9). To make these relations explicit and machine processable we provided the specification in terms of weaving models for defining correspondences between modeling elements belonging to different metamodels[3].

The concept of weaving is not new. Typical applications of model weaving are database metadata integration and evolution as in [21] which proposes Rondo, a generic metamodel management approach which uses algebraic operators such as Match and Merge to manage mappings and models. In [14] a UML extension is introduced to express mappings between models using diagrams, and illustrates how the extension can be used in metamodeling. The extension is inspired by mathematical relations and is based upon ideas presented in [4] which proposes an approach for defining transformation relationships between different components of a language definition rendered as a metamodel. The definition of model weaving that will be considered in this paper is that provided by Didonet Del Fabro et al. in [12]. They leverage the need of a generic way to establish model element correspondences by proposing a solution aimed at reaching a trade-off between genericity, expressiveness and efficiency of mappings which are considered models that conform to a weaving metamodel. The weaving metamodel is not fixed since it might be extended by means of a proposed composition operation to reach dedicated weaving metamodels. A weaving model *WM* represent the mapping between the *LeftMM* and *RightMM* metamodels. Like other models, this should conform to a specific weaving metamodel *WMM*.

In the context of *horizontal relations* we use the weaving models for specifying some form of semantics of given modeling elements. For instance, in BPMN the semantics of *Lane* is not precisely given, therefore we provide a weaving model which can associate a *Lane* to an *OrganizationalUnit* deferring the semantics of

---

[3] Implemented metamodel resources can be found in the repository: https://github.com/LearnPAd/learnpad/tree/master/lp-model-transformer/src/main/resources/metamodels.

the former to the latter (see diagram in Fig. 13). This technique is a simplification of the semantic anchoring [10] which adopts model transformations for anchoring the meaning of a concept from a metamodel into a concept to another metamodel (for which typically the semantics is already given). In other cases, the weaving is more relational and serves the scope to link different entities, like a competence profile which points to a document describing a job description.

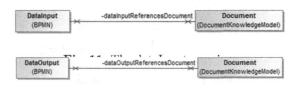

Fig. 12. The dataOutput weaving.

Fig. 13. The swimlane-lane weaving.

In the following, each weaving is given by means of a weaving metaclass denoting the correspondences between two or more metaclasses in different meta-models. The weaving models are given according to the component metamodels defined in [24], and the definition of each model can encompass one or more association:

- Business Process Modelling Notation (BPMN 2.0)[4]: several kinds of weaving are defined; the link with Document Knowledge Model permit to have the resources used as input (Fig. 11) and/or output (Fig. 12) in a process or activity.

  The lack of a specific semantic in the BPMN specification for the *Lane* concept required the definition of the Lane-weaving (Fig. 13). Such interconnection links a *Lane* in BPMN, with respectively *(i) OrganizationalUnit*, *(ii)* the *Perfomer*, and *(iii)* the *Role* in the Organisational Model. Finally, the Activity-weaving interconnects information linked to a given activity in accordance with the Fig. 14. In particular, given an *Activity*, it denotes: *(i)* the competencies needed for realizing it; *(ii)* the criteria used for evaluating its performance; *(iii)* the organizational unit, which has been assigned the responsibility; *(iv)* who is performing it; *(v)* the performer position and *(vi)* her role.

---

[4] http://www.omg.org/spec/BPMN/2.0/.

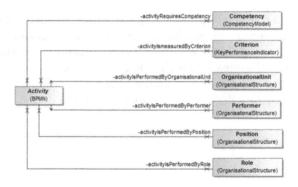

Fig. 14. The activity weaving.

- Case Management and Notation (CMMN)[5]: the ProcessTask-weaving denotes the reference to an *Activity* (regular task) to be invoked by the process task (Fig. 15).
- Organization Model: the Position-weaving links the *Position* described or reported in a resource in a Document and Knowledge Model, e.g., a job description (Fig. 16).

The above relations are just only a subset of all possible ones, according to motivating scenario in Sect. 2. A more in depth analysis, and other kind of relationship tailored for learning in complex organizations, like the Public Administrations, are discussed in [5].

Fig. 15. The process task weaving.

Fig. 16. The process task weaving

4.2 Vertical Relations

The LA exploits models in order to have informative specifications for the learners and, at the same time, informations able to simulate and monitor the processes in organizations. As said, models in the Zachman matrix are organized using different abstraction levels, therefore, the learning contents that describe multiple aspects of processes in organizations, should rely on adequate means that automatically relate and trace over the multiple views. The generation of learning artifacts out of specified business processes will be performed

---

[5] http://www.omg.org/spec/CMMN/.

by means of vertical model transformations chain as depicted in Fig. 17[6]. In order to enhance the automation in finding model transformation chains, we use the proposed process of deriving model transformation chaining depicted in [8]. Moreover, there is the need of techniques introducing automation in the management of artifacts that have to be kept consistent to each other.

In this respect the modeling facilities offered by the Eclipse Modeling Environment (EMF) can be used in order to support the management of the artifacts involved in the vertical relations. Specifically, EMF is part of the Eclipse project[7], whose goal is to provide a highly integrated tool platform. With EMF it is possible to explicitly define the domain model and this helps to provide clear visibility of it. Indeed, EMF has a distinction between the metamodel and the actual model: the metamodel describes the model structure (*System* and *Technology Metamodel* in Fig. 17(a)) while an actual model is a concrete instance of this metamodel (*System* and *Technology Model* in Fig. 17(a)). Another benefit is that EMF allows to persists the data model; the default implementation uses a data format called XML Metadata Interchange (XMI) that is a standard for exchanging meta-data information via Extensible Markup Language (XML). The EMF integration in the platform offer the advantage to perform different kind of transformations. For example, both the model-to-model and the model-to-code transformations, or a combination of them. This leads to modularity improvement, indeed, instead of making a single big transformation it can be divided into smaller once increasing, also, the overall process maintenance.

Therefore, in the Zachman vertical dimension, model transformations play a central role since they represent the glue between the several levels of abstraction and enable the generation of: *(i)* different artifacts for learning purposes using ATL[8] in *Model2Model* (see Fig. 17(a)) transformation languages and *(ii)* the generation of implementation code [9] by means of Acceleo[9] in *Model2Code* transformation (see Fig. 17(b)).

5 Related Work

Many efforts have been done in order to support the integration of models, tools and techniques used to describe various aspects of a complex organization.

[20] tackle the issue of integration of all the concepts and modelling techniques used by architects to describe their architectural domains, presenting an enterprise modelling approach. In this approach several abstract layers are integrated combining several existing languages. Unlike the work presented in

---

[6] Implemented ATL and Acceleo transformations resources can be respectively found in the repository: https://github.com/LearnPAd/learnpad/blob/master/lp-model-transformer/src/main/resources/transformation/ado2xwiki.atl   and https://github.com/LearnPAd/learnpad/blob/master/lp-model-transformer/src/main/java/eu/learnpad/transformations/model2text/main/generate.emtl.

[7] https://eclipse.org/.

[8] https://eclipse.org/atl/.

[9] https://eclipse.org/acceleo/.

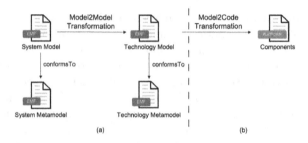

Fig. 17. The vertical Zachman transformation chain.

this paper, they propose a workbench for enterprise architecture that supports the integration of models in existing modelling languages and the integration of existing modelling tools. We choose to perform a similar integration using the Zachman Framework mainly because we are aware that the communication is important.

Indeed, thanks to the Framework's perspective, which allows us to answer the *what, how, where, who, when,* and *why* questions, we are able to create different descriptive representations (i.e., models), which translate from higher to lower perspective. This guidance is both clear and complete and as result these perspectives, in relation with these questions, determine a communication matrix. Furthermore, the Zachman Framework permits us to understand where completeness lies, and how to asses when we've achieved it. Indeed, *"Zachman's framework suggests that an architecture can be considered a complete architecture only when every cell in that architecture is complete. A cell is complete when it contains sufficient artifacts to fully define the system for one specific player looking at one specific descriptive focus"* [26].

Although we do not use the tools which they have defined, we still followed the method defined in [23]. In the article, in fact, they propose a method to achieve an Enterprise Architecture Framework based on the Zachman Framework Business. Furthermore, the authors identify a new concept related to this framework defined as "anchor cell" that defines the semantic relationships existing between cells on any of the framework's perspectives. In our work, we developed this "anchor cells" that represents vertical relationships with model transformations that transform a model in a perspectives in another model in another perspective. Moreover we have horizontal relationships through the rows (dimensions) using the weaving model [12].

6   Conclusion

In this paper, we presented a model-based architecture that fosters an *informative* learning approach based on simulation and monitoring besides the learning-by-doing paradigm. This enables complex organization employees also a *procedural* learning by accessing and studying organized business process models and related material. However, the enriched business models might not convey enough information to support on the one side the enactment of the represented complex organization process, and on the other side the training of the civil servant who is assigned to the tasks. Thus, it is of great relevance to be able to trace and relate all the models and the informative artifacts that structure and represent information with the specific tasks to which they refer. This is done by means of advanced model-driven techniques able to keep aligned different views (i.e., models specified at the same level of abstraction) and to manage multiscale models (i.e., models in which parts of the system are specified at different level of detail) by means of bidirectional transformations [11] and uncertainty management [13]. However, these approaches testify the benefits and advantages of applying theory and results from MDE on learning [19].

The inherit complexity arising using these models both in horizontal and vertical dimension is managed through the Zachman Framework adoption that helps in the in the models organization through the definition of the relations among them.

Acknowledgements. We thank our colleague Barbara Re from University of Camerino who provided us model fragments in the scenario discussed in Sect. 2. We also thank professor Alfonso Pierantonio for the precious comments that greatly improved the manuscript.

This research was supported by the EU through the Model-Based Social Learning for Public Administrations (Learn Pad) FP7 project (619583) For further informations visit the website: http://www.learnpad.eu. It is possible to find the repository hosting the platform implementation, concerning the part described in this article, here: https://github.com/LearnPAd/learnpad/tree/master/lp-model-transformer.

References

1. Business Process Model OMG. Notation (BPMN) 2.0. Object Management Group: Needham, MA, 2494:34 (2011)
2. OMG. Case Management Model and Notation (CMMN), V 1.0. Technical report, Object Management Group OMG (2013)
3. OMG. Business Motivation Model (BMM). Technical report, Object Management Group OMG (2014)
4. Akehurst, D., Kent, S.: A relational approach to defining transformations in a metamodel. In: Jézéquel, J.-M., Hussmann, H., Cook, S. (eds.) UML 2002. LNCS, vol. 2460, pp. 243–258. Springer, Heidelberg (2002). doi:10.1007/3-540-45800-X_20
5. Pierantonio, A., Rosa, G.: Design and initial implementation of metamodels for describing business processes in public administrations. Deliverable D3.2 - EU FP7 Project Learn PAd
6. Pierantonio, A., Rosa, G.: Domain Analysis of business processes in public administrations. Deliverable D3.1 - EU FP7 Project Learn PAd
7. Re, B., Sergiacomi, A.: Demonstrators BP and Knowledge models. Deliverable D8.1 - EU FP7 Project Learn PAd

8. Basciani, F., Ruscio, D., Iovino, L., Pierantonio, A.: Automated chaining of model transformations with incompatible metamodels. In: Dingel, J., Schulte, W., Ramos, I., Abrahão, S., Insfran, E. (eds.) MODELS 2014. LNCS, vol. 8767, pp. 602–618. Springer, Cham (2014). doi:10.1007/978-3-319-11653-2_37

9. Bézivin, J.: On the unification power of models. Softw. Syst. Model. 4(2), 171–188 (2005)

10. Chen, K., Sztipanovits, J., Abdelwalhed, S., Jackson, E.: Semantic anchoring with model transformations. In: Hartman, A., Kreische, D. (eds.) ECMDA-FA 2005. LNCS, vol. 3748, pp. 115–129. Springer, Heidelberg (2005). doi:10.1007/11581741_10

11. Czarnecki, K., Foster, J.N., Hu, Z., Lämmel, R., Schürr, A., Terwilliger, J.F.: Bidirectional transformations: a cross-discipline perspective. In: Paige, R.F. (ed.) ICMT 2009. LNCS, vol. 5563, pp. 260–283. Springer, Heidelberg (2009). doi:10.1007/978-3-642-02408-5_19

12. Del Fabro, M.D., Bézivin, J., Jouault, F., Valduriez, P., et al.: Applying generic model management to data mapping. In: Proceedings of the Journées Bases de Données Avancées (BDA 2005) (2005)

13. Eramo, R., Pierantonio, A., Rosa, G.: Managing uncertainty in bidirectional model transformations. In: Proceedings of the 2015 ACM SIGPLAN International Conference on Software Language Engineering, SLE 2015, pp. 49–58, New York, NY, USA. ACM (2015)

14. Hausmann, J.H., Kent, S.: Visualizing model mappings in UML. In: Proceedings of the 2003 ACM Symposium on Software Visualization, pp. 169–178. ACM Press (2003)

15. Hay, D.C.: The Zachman Framework: An Introduction. The Data Administration Newsletter, Issue 1. Essential Strategies Inc. (1997)

16. Heisig, P.: Process modelling for knowledge management

17. Hinkelmann, K., Merelli, E., Thönssen, B.: The role of content and context in enterprise repositories. In: Proceedings of 2nd International Workshop on Advanced Enterprise Architecture and Repositories - AER 2010 (2010)

18. Inmon, W.H., Zachman, J.A., Geiger, J.G.: Data Stores, Data Warehousing and the Zachman Framework: Managing Enterprise Knowledge. McGraw-Hill Inc., New York (1997)

19. Laforcade, P., Choquet, C.: Next step for educational modeling languages: the model driven engineering and reengineering approach. In: Null, pp. 745–747. IEEE (2006)

20. Marc, M., Lankhorst, M.M.: Enterprise architecture modelling-the issue of integration. Adv. Eng. Inf. 18(4), 205–216 (2004)

21. Melnik, S., Rahm, E., Bernstein, P.A.: Rondo: a programming platform for generic model management. In: Proceedings of International Conference on Management of Data, pp. 193–204. ACM Press (2003)

22. Oh, S., Sandhu, R.: A model for role administration using organization structure. In: Proceedings of the Seventh ACM Symposium on Access Control Models and Technologies, pp. 155–162. ACM (2002)

23. Pereira, C.M., Sousa, P.: A method to define an enterprise architecture using the Zachman framework. In: Proceedings of the 2004 ACM Symposium on Applied Computing, pp. 1366–1371. ACM (2004)

24. Pierantonio, A., Rosa, G., Silingas, D., Thönssen, B., Woitsch, R.: Metamodeling architectures for business processess in organizations. Projects Showcase@ STAF 2015, p. 27 (2015)

25. Reiter, T., Kapsammer, E., Retschitzegger, W., Schwinger, W.: Model integration through mega operations. In: Accepted for Publication at the Workshop on Model-driven Web Engineering (MDWE 2005) (2005)
26. Tupper, C.: Data Architecture: from Zen to Reality. Elsevier, Amsterdam (2011)
27. Yu, E., Strohmaier, M., Deng, X.: Exploring intentional modeling and analysis for enterprise architecture. In: 10th IEEE International Enterprise Distributed Object Computing Conference Workshops, EDOCW 2006, pp. 32–32. IEEE (2006)
28. Zachman, J.A.: The framework for enterprise architecture-cell definitions. ZIFA report (2003)
29. Zachman, J.A.: The Zachman Framework For Enterprise Architecture. A Primer For Enterprise Engineering And Manufacturing (2012)

An Assessment Environment for Model-Based Learning Management

Antonello Calabrò[1], Sarah Zribi[2], Francesca Lonetti[1], Eda Marchetti[1(✉)],
Tom Jorquera[2], and Jean-Pierre Lorré[2]

[1] Istituto di Scienza e Tecnologie dell'Informazione "A. Faedo", CNR, Pisa, Italy
eda.marchetti@isti.cnr.it
[2] Linagora, 75 Route de Revel, 31400 Toulouse, France

Abstract. Assessing the acquired competencies during a learning activity as well as the possibility of simulating difficult situations or scenarios are important challenges in learning management. The current uses of (semi) formal models representing the knowledge domain open the possibility of advanced techniques of simulation and monitoring. In this paper, we propose an assessment environment for model-based learning management that integrates simulation and monitoring facilities. In particular, we describe its architecture and main functionalities and its application inside an ongoing EU project. The proposed framework allows for user-friendly learning simulation with a strong support for collaboration and social interactions. Moreover, it monitors the learners' behavior during simulation execution and it is able to compute the learning scores useful for the learner knowledge assessment.

Keywords: Model-based learning · Simulation · Monitoring · Business process

1 Introduction

Recently a lot of attention has been devoted to the monitoring of the acquired competencies during a learning activity as well as to the possibility to learning by using simulation of difficult situations or scenarios. Independently by the context, usually simulation attempts to mimic real-life or hypothetical behavior to see how processes, systems or hardware devices can be improved and to predict their performance under different circumstances. Commonly, monitoring focuses on data collection and supervision of activities during the real-life execution of a process, systems or hardware components to ensure they are on-course and on-schedule in meeting the objectives and performance targets. Currently, inside the learning engineering area the use of Business Process Modeling Notation (BPMN) [1] makes easier the simulation and monitoring activities due to the possibility of exploiting concise definitions and taxonomies, and developing executable frameworks for overall management of the process itself. Indeed best practice of Business Process modeling lets the use of methods, techniques, and

S. Hammoudi et al. (Eds): MODELSWARD 2016, CCIS 692, pp. 312–332, 2017.
DOI: 10.1007/978-3-319-66302-9_16

tools to support the design, enactment and analysis of the business process and to provide an excellent basis for simulation and monitoring purposes. Examples can be found even in different environments such for instance the clinical one, for assessing and managing the patient treatment, and the financial sector for verifying and checking the bank processes. In all these application contexts, a key role is played by the data collected during the business process execution or simulation, which lets the possibility of reasoning about and/or improving the overall performance of the business process itself.

In the specific area of learning management, simulation and monitoring enhances student's learning and improves their knowledge; they are also very important for assessment of the teaching performance. Indeed different conceptual and mathematical models have been proposed for model-based learning and several type of simulations, including discrete event and continuous process simulations have been considered [2]. However, the main challenges of existing learning simulation and monitoring proposals are about collaborative simulation, gamification and the derived learning benefits. In particular, gamification is becoming one of the main challenges in the simulation activity, that can be incorporated with the aim of using game-based mechanisms and game thinking to engage, motivate action, promote learning and solve problems [3]. Moreover, rewarding strategies are encouraged in order to stimulate intrinsic motivations within the members of a community.

In this paper, we address model-based learning management through the evaluation of some performance indicators useful for learning assessment. We present a Simulation and Monitoring framework able to support collaboration and social interactions, as well as process visualization, monitoring and learning assessment. The proposed approach can be compared to a collaborative game where a team of players composed of one coach and any number of learners work together in order to achieve a common goal. The main objective is consequently to provide an easy to use and user-friendly environment for the learners in order to let them take part of the process when their turn comes, assuming different roles according to the content they have to learn. The principal contribution of this paper is the architecture of a framework for simulation and monitoring of model-based learning able to provide feedback for evaluating the learner competency and the collaborative learning activities. The proposed simulation and monitoring framework has been applied to a case study developed inside the Learn PAd project in the context of Marche Region public administration and important feedback and hints have been collected for the improvement of the framework itself over the Learn PAd project duration.

In the rest of the paper we first briefly introduce some background concepts and related work (Sect. 2), then is Sect. 3 we present the main components of the simulation and monitoring framework architecture whereas in Sect. 4 we describe its main functionalities. Finally, Sect. 5 shows the application of the proposed framework to a case study and conclusion concludes the paper.

2   Background and Related Work

The proposal of a simulation and monitoring framework for model-based learning originated in the context of the Model-Based Social Learning for Public Administrations (Learn PAd) European project [4] addressing the challenges set out in the "ICT-2013.8.2 Technology-enhanced learning" work programme. Learn PAd project envisions an innovative holistic e-learning platform for Public Administrations (PAs) that enables process-driven learning and fosters cooperation and knowledge sharing. The main Learn PAd objectives include: (i) a new concept of model-based e-learning (both process and knowledge); (ii) an open and collaborative e-learning content management; (iii) an automatic, learner-specific and collaborative content quality assessment; and finally (iv) an automatic model-driven simulation-based learning and assessment. The developed Learn PAd platform will support an informative learning approach based on enriched BP models, as well as a procedural learning approach based on simulation and monitoring that will allow users to learn by doing.

Recently other EU funded projects of 6th and 7th framework programmes have been financed in the area of Technology Enhanced Learning. Among the relevant ones there are: (i) MATURE [5] which interlinks individual learning processes in a knowledge maturing process. In particular, the focus has been in the maturing process and in building tools and services to reduce maturing barriers, to embed learning more seamlessly in work processes and knowledge management systems; (ii) Mirror [6] which delivered a set of real-time, interoperable learning applications, based on a conceptual model of holistic continuous learning by reflection. The project incorporates in particular (collaborative) knowledge construction and creative problem solving and innovation; (iii) Target [7] which is based on a gaming activity so to deal with complex situations and results in experiences that are gradually honed into knowledge; (iv) Prolix [8] which aligned learning with business processes in order to enable organizations to faster improve the competencies of their employees according to continuous changes of work requirements. The solution to develop includes also workflows for competence building, simulations, and games for process-oriented learning and information exchange.

Considering the industrial and research learning context, BP simulation approaches are very popular since learners prefer simulation exercises to either lectures or discussions [9]. Simulations have been used to teach procedural skills and for training of software applications and industrial control operations as well as for learning domain specific concepts and knowledge, such as business management strategies [10]. Nowadays, more attention is given to business process oriented analysis and simulation [11]. Studies have shown that the global purpose of these existing business process simulation platforms is to evaluate BPs and redesign them, whereas in the last years simulation/gaming is establishing as a discipline [12]. However, these platforms present several shortcomings regarding their applicability to a collaborative learning approach. Namely, no existing platform regroups all of the main functionalities of a learning simulation solution such as facilities for providing a controlled and flexible simulated environment (for example allowing to switch between possible outcomes of a task, in order to explore the different paths of a process), good visualization and monitoring of a process execution flow (in order both to assist and evaluate the learners) [12]. The main challenges of a learning simulation are about collaborative simulation and the derived learning benefits. To answer all of these concerns a new learning simulation and monitoring framework is designed in this paper, providing a flexible simulation framework with a strong support for collaboration and social interactions, as well as process visualization, monitoring and learners assessment.

Concerning monitoring, existing works [13] combine modeling and monitoring facilities of business process. PROMO [13] allows to model, monitor and analyze business process. It provides an editor for the definition of interesting KPIs (Key Performance Indicator) to be monitored as well as facilities for specifying aggregation and monitoring rules. Our proposal is different since it addresses a flexible, adaptable and dynamic monitoring infrastructure that is independent from any specific business process modeling notation and execution engine. Other approaches [14] focus on monitoring business constraints at runtime by means of temporal logic and colored automata. They allow continuous compliance with respect to predefined business process constraint model and recovery after the first violation. Differently from these approaches, the proposed solution does not allow to take counter measures for recovering from violation of defined performance constraints. Moreover, in our solution these constraints are not specified in the business process but they are dynamically defined as monitoring proprieties that can be applied to different business process notations. In the context of learning, monitoring solutions can be used for providing feedback on training sessions and allow KPI evaluation. Some learning systems such as that in [15] propose customized learning paths that learners can follow according to their knowledge, learning requirements or learning disability. Changing and management of learning pathways as well as adaptation of learning material are made according to the monitored data. However, contemporary Learning Content Management Systems (LCMS) provide rather basic feedback and monitoring facilities about the learning process, such as simple statistics on technology usage or low-level data on students activities (e.g., page view). Some tools have been developed for providing feedback on the learning tasks by the analysis of the user tracking data and monitoring of the simulation activity. The authors of [16], for instance, propose LOCO-Analyst, an educational tool aimed at providing educators with feedback on the relevant aspects of the learning process taking place in a web-based learning environment such as the usage and the comprehensibility of the learning content or contextualized social interactions among students (i.e., social networking). The main goal of these tools is to support educators for creating courses, viewing the feedback on those courses, and modifying the courses accordingly. Differently from these solutions, other proposals [17,18] focus on model-based learning and monitoring of business process execution. Specifically, [17] presents a flexible and adaptable monitoring infrastructure for business process execution and a critical comparison of the proposed framework with closest related works whereas [18] presents an integrated framework that allows modeling, execution and analysis of business process based on a flexible and adaptable monitoring infrastructure. The main advantage of this last solution is that it is independent from any specific business process modeling notation and execution engine and allows for the definition and evaluation of user-specific KPI measures. The monitoring framework presented in this paper has been inspired by the monitoring architecture presented in [17,18]. It includes new components specifically devoted to the computation of the evaluation scores useful for the learning assessment.

3   Simulation and Monitoring Framework Architecture

Extending the preliminary version of [19] in this section, we describe the high level architecture of the proposed Simulation and Monitoring framework, its main components, their purpose, the interfaces they expose, and how they interact with each others. In particular, as depicted in Fig. 1 each component is exposed as a service and provides an API as a unique point of access. Inside the Learn PAd infrastructure, the proposed simulation framework interacts with the Learn PAd components by means of the *Learn PAd Core Platform* and specifically through the *Bridge* and the *Core Facade* interfaces. Moreover, in the Learn PAd vision two levels of learners have been considered: the civil servant who is the standard learner, and the civil servant coordinator who is a generalization of the civil servant who is in charge to activate and manage a simulation session.

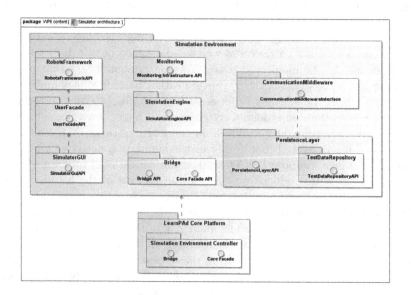

Fig. 1. Simulation Framework Architecture.

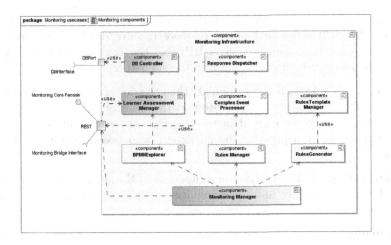

Fig. 2. Monitoring Framework Architecture.

The simulation framework components are:

SimulationGUI: it is in charge of the interactions between learners and simulator's components. It provides different facilities that are: (i) `Chat areas` that represents a space for learners to chat either one by one, one with the group of civil servants or with experts connected to the current simulation; (ii) `Notification area` which provides notifications to the learner; (iii) `User input/output panel`: this area contains forms for learners interactions; (iv) `Context area`: provides the documents related to the simulation, additional information or links to material that may be useful during the simulation activity; (v) `Simulation teams members`: learners involved in the simulation have a special placeholder so to distinguish them from the coordinator; (vi) `Contextual search`: allows to search among different kinds of information depending on the current displayed layout (users, processes, simulations, etc.); (vii) `Simulation lifecycle menu`: it allows the learner to choose among different views that are: *Business process view* allows to obtain a graphical representation of the current BP; *Play*: allows to run a simulation as an instance of a given BP; *Save*: allow to save the current simulation and restart it from the point in which it has been saved; *Pause* allow to pause the running of the current simulation; *Stop*: allow to stop the current simulation and exit; *Coordinator*: provides the name of the coordinator of the current session and allows him/her to modify it. Only the civil servant coordinator has the possibility to designate another civil servant to be the new coordinator of the simulation session; *Stats&Logs*: using an analytic dashboard, it allows the learner to display statistics and logs about all activities carried out during the simulation.

PersistenceLayer: it stores the status of the simulation at each step (i.e. BP executed task) in order to give to the civil servant the ability to stop it and restart when needed. Its main sub-components are: (i) the `Logger` that is in charge of storing time-stamped event data coming from the simulation engine; (ii) the `BPStateStorage` that allows to store/retrieve/delete/update the state of a given simulation associated to a BP; (iii) the `TestDataRepository` that collects the historical data that relate to the simulations executions.

RobotFramework: it allows to simulate the behavior of civil servants by means of robots. The Robots are implemented on the basis of the availability of historical data, i.e. the data saved in the *TestDataRepository* during a previous simulation session and provided by an expert who takes the role of the civil servant.

SimulationEngine: this is the core component of the simulation framework. It enacts business processes and links activities with corresponding civil servants or robots.

Monitoring: it collects the events occurred during the simulation and infers rules related to the business process execution.

Communication Middleware: it provides event-based communication facilities between the simulation components according to the publish/subscribe paradigm.

UserFacade: it is in charge of encapsulating real or simulated civil servants (i.e. robots) in order to make the learner interaction transparent to the other components of the architecture.

In the following more details about the simulation engine and monitor components are provided. More details about the simulation and monitoring design are in [20].

3.1 Simulation Engine

Simulation engine takes in charge the simulation of a given business process instance. It takes the form of an orchestration engine that invokes treatments associated to each activity of the current process. Such workflow may involve multiple civil servants taking different roles that may be present or not. For those that are not available, robots are used in order to mimic their behavior. A simulation manager is provided in order to manage BP lifecycle according to the current context (create, stop, resume, kill, etc.). Business processes are made of two kinds of activities: (i) Human activities involve civil servants who should provide information in order to complete the task. The concept of human activity is used to specify work which has to be accomplished by people; (ii) Mocked activities involve robots to compute the treatment associated to the activity. When the simulation engine invokes a human activity the corresponding civil servant is asked to provide input through a form. Those forms are managed by a form engine that delegates task to a robot if necessary. All the state information necessary to restart a specific simulation are stored "on the fly". The civil servant may decide to freeze a running simulation, to store it, to backtrack to a previous stored state and to logout. He/she will be able to resume it later.

Business Process orchestrator takes in charge the step by step execution of a given BP instance. Such BP instance is made of a BPMN description enriched with necessary run-time information such as end-points of software applications mocks, user id, etc. The BP engine is connected with the Forms Engine in order to take in charge users and robots input/output. Different solutions for the business process execution engine are: Activiti [21], Camunda [22] and jBPM [23]. In this paper, we rely on Activiti [21]. In order to collect inputs from learners during a simulation session, a form engine has been defined so to design and run the proper corresponding forms. Forms Engine allows dynamic forms creation and complex forms processing for web applications. The processing of a form involves the verification of the input data, calculation of the input based on the information from other input fields as well as dynamic activation or hiding of the data fields depending on the user input. Inside our solution the javascript Form editor, called FormaaS, has been adopted. It allows to design and run javascript forms and to quickly define forms and executable code.

3.2 Monitoring

The simulation framework is equipped with a monitoring facility that allows to provide feedback on the business process execution and learning activities. Figure 2 shows the architecture of the proposed monitoring infrastructure. The design of this monitoring infrastructure has been inspired by [17].

For aim of readability, we list below the monitoring components presented in [17] and refer to [17] for the complete description of their functionalities:

- Complex Event Processor (CEP). It is the rule engine, which analyzes the events, generated by the business process execution. Several rule engines can be used for this task like Drools Fusion, VisiRule, RuleML. Our instance is realized using Drools Fusion [24], that is able to detect patterns and monitor the business process performance metrics.
- BPMN explorer. It is in charge to explore and save all the possible entities (Activity Entity, Sequence Flow Entity, Path Entity) reachable on a BPMN. Specifically, the extracted paths will be provided to the Rules Manager that through the Rules Generator will create, using the templates of rules stored into the Template Manager, a set of rules that aims to check the KPI defined on the business process.
- Rules Generator. It is the component in charge to generate the rules needed for the monitoring of the business process execution and the assessment of the performance metrics. It uses the templates stored into the Rules Template Manager. These rules are generated according to the specific performance metrics to be assessed. A generic rule consists of two main parts: in the first part the events to be matched are specified; the second part includes the events/actions to be notified after the rules evaluation.
- Rules Template Manager. It is an archive of predetermined rules templates that will be instantiated by the Rules Generator. A rule template is a rule skeleton, the specification of which has to be completed by instantiating a set

of template-dependent placeholders. The instantiation will refer to appropriate values inferred from the specific performance metrics to be assessed. Once the synthesis of the new set of rules is completed, the new rules are loaded by the Rule Generator into the Rules Template Manager.

– Rules Manager. The complex event detection process depends directly from the operation done by the Rules Manager component which is in charge to load and unload a set of rules into the complex event processor and fire it when needed.

– Response Dispatcher. It is a registry that keeps track of the requests for monitoring sent to the monitoring infrastructure.

In this section a refined and complete design of the monitoring infrastructure is presented as depicted in Fig. 2. It includes three new components (shown in pink in Fig. 2) that are:

– DBController. This component has been introduced to satisfy the Learn PAd requirements of having storage of simulation executions data. Specifically, the DB Controller manages the updating of the civil servant score during a simulation or the retrieval of historical data concerning the assessment level of the civil servants. The DB Controller interacts with the Learner Assessment Manager to get the different evaluation scores that will be defined in Sect. 3.2.

– Learner Assessment Manager. It evaluates the learner activities and it is in charge to calculate the different scores. More details about this component are in Sect. 3.2.

– Monitoring Manager component. It is the orchestrator of the overall Monitoring Infrastructure. It interacts with the Learn PAd Core Platform through the REST interfaces (core facade and bridge interface) and is in charge to query the Rules Manager. It also interacts with the BPMN Explorer and the Rules Generator. This component initializes the overall monitoring infrastructure allocating resources, instantiating the Complex Event Processor and instrumenting channel on which events coming from the simulation engine will flow.

Learner Assessment Manager. During learning simulation, it is important to asses learning activities as well as to visualize to the civil servants their success incrementally by displaying the achieved evaluation scores. To this end, the proposed simulation and monitoring component integrates a scoring mechanism in order to generate ranking of the civil servants and data useful for rewarding. The Learner Assessment Manager component evaluates the learner activities and is in charge to calculate different scores useful for the civil servant assessment. In addition, independently from any ongoing simulation, this component is in charge of retrieving the data necessary for the score evaluation and updating them on a database. Data collected during monitoring of business process execution can be used for providing feedback for the continuous tracking of the process behavior and measurement of learning-specific goals. All scores computed by the Learner Assessment Manager are then stored in the DB by the interaction with the DB Controller component. The evaluation scores computed by the Learner Assessment Manager relate both to the simulation of a session of the business process (*session score(s)*) and to the simulation of the overall business process (*Business Process scores*). Specifically, we define the *session score(s)* and *Business Process score(s)* as detailed below.

Session Scores. The civil servant may simulate different learning sessions on the same business process, each one referring to a (different) path. During a simulation session the Learner Assessment Manager computes the following scores:

- The session score (called *session_score*), i.e. the ongoing session score of each participating civil servant.
- An assessment value (called *absolute_session_score*) useful as boundary value for the session score.

Specifically, the session score is calculated using a weighted sum of scores attributed to the civil servant for each task of the Business Process realized during the simulation. Considering n the number of tasks executed by the civil servant during the learning session simulation and P the weight of the task, the session score is computed as follows:

$$session\_score = \sum_{i=1}^{n} task\_score_i P_i$$

Each task of the Business Process is associated with a weight specified as a metadata. These metadata are attributed in the Business Process definition and defined by the modeler. The calculation of the score's task is based on several criteria, namely number of attempts, Success/Fail and finally some predefined performance indicators named KPI (e.g. response time). The formula below allows calculating this score:

$$task\_score = success * (\frac{1}{nb\_attempts} +$$
$$\sum_{i=1}^{k} \frac{expected\_KPI\_value_i}{observed\_KPI\_value_i})$$

where k is the number of KPI considered in the evaluation of the civil servants performances and success is a Boolean. For what concerns the boundary values useful for the learning assessment, the Learner Assessment Manager can provide the *absolute_session_score*, which represents the maximum score that could be assigned to the civil servant during a simulation session. Supposing that the maximum obtained value of the *task_score* is equal to $k+1$, *the absolute_session_score* is computed as:

$$absolute\_session\_score = \sum_{i=1}^{n} (k+1)P_i$$

This *absolute_session_score* computes an accuracy measure of the session_score. A *session_score* value closer to the *absolute_session_score* represents a better performance of the civil servant for the considered simulation session.

Business Process Scores. During the learning simulation, the civil servant can execute different learning sessions on the same Business Process, each one referring to a different path. Therefore, the cumulative score obtained by the civil servant on the executed sessions is a good indicator of the knowledge of the civil servant about the overall Business Process. The learner assessment manager is able to compute the following scores related to the business process:

- Business Process Score (called *bp_score*), i.e. the cumulative score obtained by the civil servant after the execution of different simulation sessions on the same business process. It represents the degree of acquired knowledge of the Business Process activities obtained by the civil servant.
- Two assessment values (called *relative_bp_score* and *absolute_bp_score*) used as boundary values for the *bp_score* to evaluate the acquired civil servant competency on the executed business process. Specifically, the *relative_bp_score* is the maximum score that the civil servant can obtain on the set of simulated paths whereas the *absolute_bp_score* is the maximum score that the civil servant can obtain on all the possible paths of the business process.
- A business process coverage percentage (called *bp_coverage*), i.e. the percentage of different learning sessions (paths) executed by the civil servant during the simulation of a business process. It represents the completeness of the civil servant knowledge about the overall business process.

In the following we provide more details about the above-mentioned scores. The *bp_score* is computed as the sum of the maximum values of *session_score(s)* obtained by the civil servant during the simulation of a set of different k paths (over the overall number of paths) on a business process, according to the following formula:

$$bp\_score = \sum_{i=1}^{k} \max(session\_score_i)$$

Considering a *bp_score* and the set of k paths to which the *bp_score* is related to, the *relative_bp_score* is the boundary value representing the maximum score that the civil servant can obtain on the set of k paths. It is computed as the sum of the *absolute_session_score* according to the following formula:

$$relative\_bp\_score = \sum_{i=1}^{k} absolute\_session\_score_i$$

Considering all paths of a business process to which a *bp_score* is related to, the *absolute_bp_score* is an additional boundary value representing the maximum score that the civil servant can reach. It is computed as the sum of the *absolute_bp_score* for all the paths of the business process according to the following formula:

$$absolute\_bp\_score = \sum_{i=1}^{\#path} absolute\_session\_score_i$$

The more the *bp_score* is close to the *relative_bp_score* the more the civil servant reaches the maximum cumulative learning performance on the different simulated sessions. The more the values of *bp_score* are close to the *absolute_bp_score* the more the civil servant knowledge about the overall business process is complete.

Finally, the *bp_coverage* value is an additional measure for evaluating the completeness of the civil servant knowledge about the overall business process. It is computed as the percentage of different paths *(k)*, executed by the civil servant during the simulation of a business process, over the paths cardinality as in the following:

$$bp\_coverage = \frac{k}{\#path}$$

When the civil servant executes all paths of the business process, the computed *bp_coverage* is 1. A *bp_coverage* value closer to 1 represents a better performance of the civil servant for the considered business process simulation.

4 Functional Specification of the Learning Simulation and Monitoring Framework

The Simulation and Monitoring framework provides the subsystem where learners can simulate the business process interactively and is used by one or multiple civil servant(s) in order to learn processes. As mentioned in Sect. 3, the Simulation and Monitoring framework distinguishes between the two following actors: the civil servant coordinator who is in charge of starting a simulation session and the civil servant who represents a generic participant to a simulation session. In particular, the civil servant coordinator can request to start a new simulation execution of a Public Administration business process or he/she can manage an ongoing one by for instance inviting/cancelling other civil servants. The civil servant coordinator can also restart/stop a current simulation session and redefine a new coordinator. On its turn, each civil servant has different possibilities like for instance joining, disconnecting or pausing a simulation session, chatting, asking for evaluation/help, or managing his/her own profile.

The Simulation and Monitoring framework functionalities have been split into three different phases: (i) *Initialization* in which the simulation framework is set up; (ii) *Activation* in which the participants to the simulation are invited; (iii) *Execution* in which the participants effectively collaborate each other during a learning session. During the Activation phase, the civil servant can select the type of simulation he/she wants to execute. Specifically, three different types of simulation are provided:

Individual Simulation. The civil servant decides to execute the simulation without interacting with other human participants. In this case the other participants are emulated by means of *Robots* (see Sect. 3 for more details). The creation of robots instances is performed before the simulation execution.

Collaborative Simulation. This option of simulation involves the collaboration of several human participants (no robots instances are involved).

During the collaborative simulation, users can interact between them using chat instruments. This will improve performances of the overall learning session due to the possibility to rapidly share experience between human participants. This kind of simulation can be considered the most interesting from the learning point of view, because cooperation can make learning procedures more intensive and productive. Diversities will raise up and the opportunity to reflect upon encountered issues will help learners to improve their knowledge and better understand the problem. For activating a simulation, the system requires that all the civil servants involved have joined the session in order to provide an online collaborative environment. Moreover, the Simulation and Monitoring framework also supports asynchronous tasks execution among simulation participants. If a civil servant does not satisfy the simulation requirements or time constraints, the civil servant coordinator may decide either to kick the civil servant, or to swap him with another one among those available, or replace him with a *Robot*.

Mixed Simulation. This type of simulation requires the participation of both humans and robots. This usually happens when there are not enough civil servants to cover all the necessary roles to execute a BP or if one or more civil servants leave the ongoing simulation (disconnection or kick). The activation of a mixed simulation can be done only if the following two constraints are met: (i) the required instances of robots are ready; (ii) all the invited civil servants have completed the connection procedures.

Both gamification and serious game concepts are also included in the proposed Simulation and Monitoring framework so to engage civil servants during training tasks and activities to be learned. Specifically, two main gamification elements are included in the proposed simulation and monitoring framework for educational purposes: (i) progression that allows the learner to see success visualized incrementally by the achieved evaluation scores; (ii) virtual rewards that allow learner who satisfies some conditions to be automatically awarded by the platform with a specific certificate that gives to him/her additional rights. For more details about the gamification model used in the proposed simulation and monitoring framework we refer to [25]. During the different types of simulation, the monitoring component checks if execution patterns will be respected during the simulation of a business process. In order to do that, the simulation engine interacts with the monitoring component through a pre-fixed set of messages specifying the set of events, detected failures and time values useful for evaluating the learner's competency and assessing non-functional properties such as the overall simulation time completion.

5   Learn PAd Simulation and Monitoring Framework: The Application to Learn PAd Case Study

In this section, we show the application of the proposed Simulation and Monitoring framework to a case study developed inside the Learn PAd project with the collaboration of SUAP (Sportello Unico per le Attività produttive) officers from both Public Administrations Senigallia and Monti Azzurri. The scenario refers to the activities that the Italian Public Administrations have to put in place in order to permit to entrepreneurs to set up a new company. In particular, the case study is focused on the Titolo Unico process, i.e. the standard Italian procedure to be applied so to start a business activity [1].

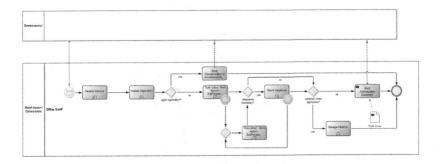

Fig. 3. Titolo Unico Business Process.

In this case, the entrepreneur notifies to the municipality and third parties organizations the starting of a commercial business activity and self-certifies all the required documentation. Then the entrepreneur has to wait for a decision taken by the SUAP office before to really start the activity. If necessary, SUAP office could require document integration or organize specific conference, called *Service Conference*, for critical decisions. In this case the participants (municipality offices, third parties administrations, and entrepreneur) discuss about the specific situation and decide if the application is acceptable or not. In general, the whole process has to be performed within 60 days: within 30 days the regularity of the application must be verified and in the remaining 30 days the decision must be prepared. If a conference has to be conducted, process duration is extended to 120 days. That is after the 30 days for verifying the regularity of the application, 60 more days are available for activating and performing the conference and for reaching a common decision. A simplified BPM representation of the described process is depicted in Fig. 3, in which sub-processes are not presented.

Using the proposed Simulation and Monitoring framework, the Marche Region personnel has the possibility to learn the steps necessary to organize a *Service Conference* and practice with the documentations and several criticalities and exceptions that could be encountered during the Titolo Unico process.

In the Learn PAd project the Simulation and Monitoring framework has been integrated in the more complex project platform as depicted in Fig. 4; however it can also be executed independently. It is out of the scope of this paper to provide a complete description of the Learn PAd platform; however in this specific case the Simulation and Monitoring framework interacts with the other components of the platform by sending through the *Learn PAd Core* component the simulation events and basic KPI evaluations using a REST event API.

---

[1] Italian law D.P.R. 160/2010 in the article 7.

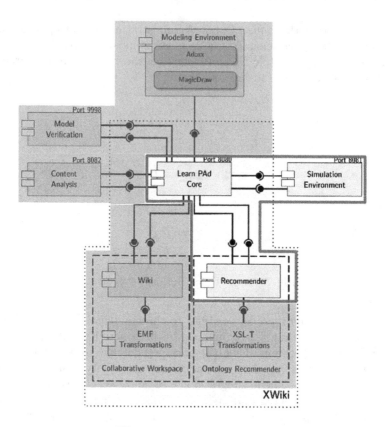

Fig. 4. LearnPAd Platform.

In particular, the simulator interacts through the *Learn PAd Core* with the *Recommender* component which is in charge of providing recommendations for individual learners, suggesting learning material or activities to improve bad learner's performance scores. Moreover, recommendations can also be made for entire organizational units like the SUAP office or the whole Public Administration. They may refer to organizational activities recommended for improving a bad KPI value. In this case study, because the Simulation and Monitoring framework is integrated in Lean PAd, it is automatically instantiated as soon as the platform is executed without requiring additional actions.

In the Titolo Unico process considered in this case study the main actors involved in the simulation process are: (i) the learner, i.e. a Regione Marche employee, who would practice on this BP; (ii) an expert called *Expert1* who is a Regione Marche domain expert employee who can provide suggestions or recommendations trough the *Recommender*; (iii) a second expert called *Expert2* who is again a Regione Marche domain expert employee and who actively participates to the simulation.

ModelSet - SUAP Titolo Unico

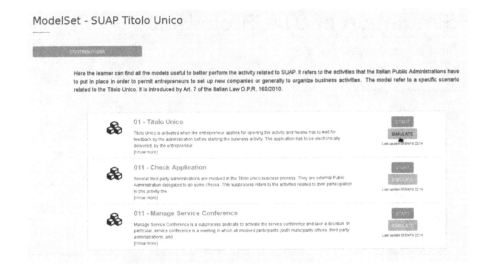

Fig. 5. Create a simulation session of a process.

Interacting with the GUI the learner who wants to start a learning activity, can create a new simulation session of selected BP process (see Fig. 5). In this case, the Titolo Unico BP is by construction a single-user process, however collaborative and mixed simulation can also be executed by selecting other available BPs. Thus the learner logs into the Learn PAd platform and starts running a stand-alone simulation. For aim of simplicity the duration time of each task has been reduced in proportion so to make the overall simulation completion time within the range of minutes. The learner by a browsing mode decides to start a new simulation session by clicking on the "simulate" button shown in the process landing page (i.e. the summary page of a BPMN, where a picture of a process is also shown). In particular, the user can configure the simulation session selection setting the different parameters of the process (see Fig. 6). Depending on the selected BP, the framework is also configured with a set of test application forms, along with their associated metadata info, which are completely separated from the data of the historical cases provided to the *Recommender*.

When a simulation starts, the Simulator and Monitoring framework sends "simulation session start" event with the associated metadata to the Learn PAd platform. Then the learner can execute all tasks of the business process. In particular, the monitoring sub-component collects data of interest (as detailed in Sect. 3.2) and updates the internal database accordingly. Once a task is completed, the associated scores are computed and updated. If all the inputs provided by the user during the task simulation have been evaluated correct, the framework indicates that the task has been validated, and will display new tasks corresponding to the continuation of the process (Fig. 7). Otherwise, the simulator will indicate that the submission is incorrect. In such a way the Simulation and Monitoring framework drives the learner through the process and assesses

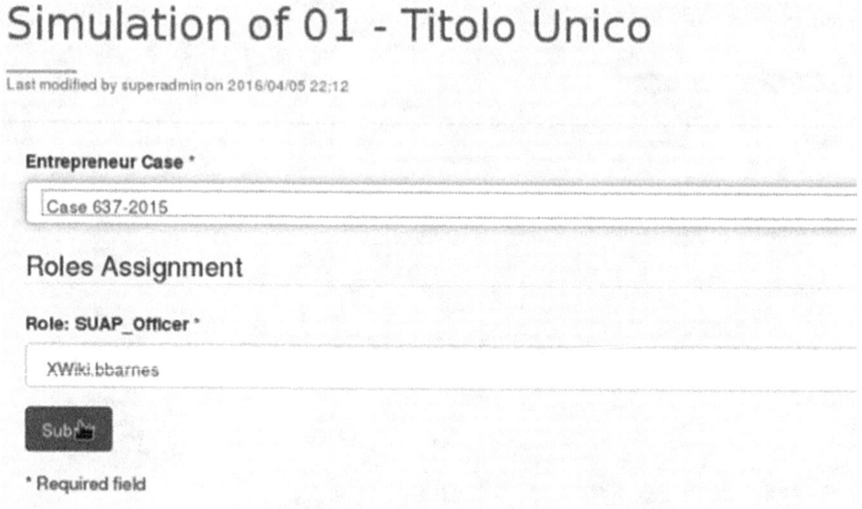

Simulation of 01 - Titolo Unico

Last modified by superadmin on 2016/04/05 22:12

Entrepreneur Case *

Case 637-2015

Roles Assignment

Role: SUAP_Officer *

XWiki.bbarnes

Sub⬛

* Required field

Fig. 6. Configuration of a simulation session.

his/her activities with respect to what it is expected (possibly using previous correct runs of the same activities).

Once the simulation session is terminated, the final scores are shown through the interface as reported in Fig. 8.

In the following, referring to Fig. 3, we describe in detail which are the tasks of the business process executed by the learner during the simulation and for each task the input and output data. When the simulation starts, the task "Receive Instance" is executed using the available robots and metadata because it is not in charge of learner. It passes directly to the execution of the task "Assess Application". The input data for this task is the pdf file with the application data. The output of this task is a statement saying whether the application is accepted or not, the values of relevant KPIs for this task, and in case the application is not accepted, a motivation for rejecting the application. In this task, the learner can ask to the *Recommender* which provides feedbacks according to use-case formatted data.

The learner executes then the task "Send Communications of non-admissible Instance to Third Parties". The input data for this task is the pdf file with the application data. The output of this task consists of the list of the third parties involved and for each third party a referent person and a text message. During the execution of this task the learner can ask the *Recommender* which gives feedbacks about similar cases and third parties involved.

The learner executes the "Check Integration" task. The input data for this task is the pdf file with the application data. The output of this task is a report on the application data and decision about whether arrange or not the conference

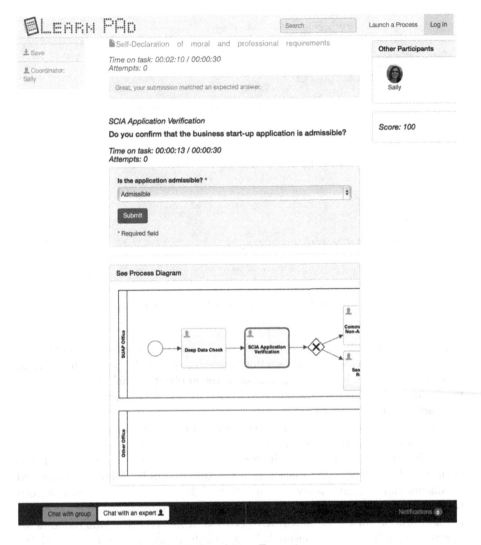

Fig. 7. Simulation Execution.

of services, and if yes the motivation. Also in this case the learner can ask the *Recommender* which gives feedbacks about similar cases.

The learner executes the task "Active Service Conference" that is included in the sub-process, the input data for this task is again the pdf file with the application data. The output of the execution of this task is a list of involved third parties. Also in this case the learner can ask the *Recommender* which gives feedbacks about similar case. Note that ranking of similar cases may change.

The learner then executes the task "Send Authorization Document". In this case, the input data for this task consists of the pdf file with the application data and a document containing the minutes of the service conference.

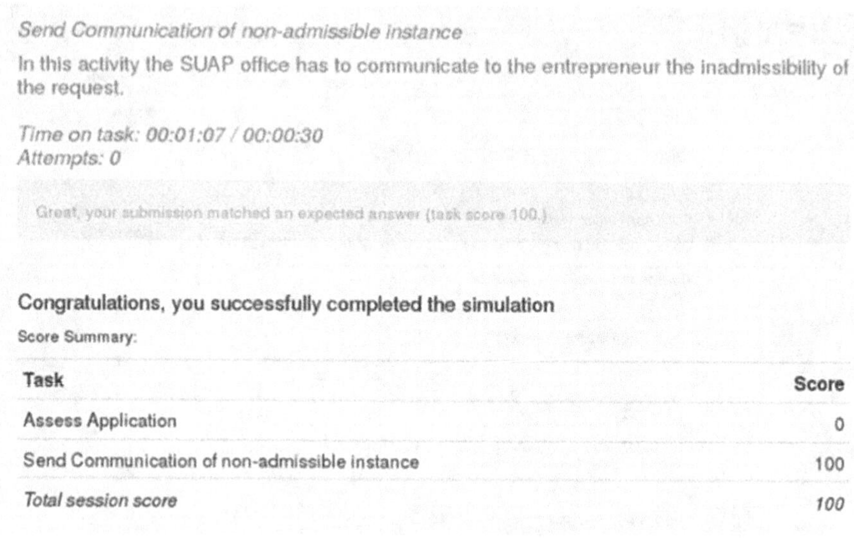

Send Communication of non-admissible instance

In this activity the SUAP office has to communicate to the entrepreneur the inadmissibility of the request.

Time on task: 00:01:07 / 00:00:30
Attempts: 0

Great, your submission matched an expected answer (task score 100.)

Congratulations, you successfully completed the simulation

Score Summary:

Task	Score
Assess Application	0
Send Communication of non-admissible instance	100
Total session score	*100*

Fig. 8. Simulation session completion.

The output of the execution of this task is a summary of the service conference, a document specifying if an integration is needed or not. In case an integration is needed a message is sent to the sender of the application including integration requirement. Also in this case, the learner can ask the *Recommender* which gives feedbacks about similar cases.

At the end of each task and of the overall simulation the associated scores are shown to the learner and the validation of the performed activity provided.

During this first validation, the Simulation and Monitoring framework has been used by different end-users inside the Italian Public Administration and comments and suggestions have been collected. If from one side all users agreed that the framework represents a very good means for improving the understanding and practice of the administrative process, from the other side requests for improvements have been collected. This meanly concerns the usability of the framework especially in case of collaborative simulation as well as score visualization and management. This validation provides a positive assessment of the Simulation and Monitoring framework and a very important starting point for the next release of the learning system.

6 Conclusions

The paper presented a simulation and monitoring framework for assessing the acquired competencies during a learning activity as well as simulating difficult situations or scenarios. In particular a detailed description of the framework components and main functionalities is provided. Differently from the other simulation environment the proposal of this paper supports collaboration and social interactions, as well as process visualization, monitoring of learning activities and assessment. Specific attention has been devoted to the possibility of gamification during the simulation of the business process to be learned, so to engage more users while training them and improve their knowledge. A set of evaluation scores for assessing the leaning activity has also been proposed. They refer to both the simulation sessions and the overall business process simulation; relative values are automatically computed and updated by the proposed simulation and monitoring framework during each execution.

A version of the proposed framework, integrated into the generic architecture of the Learn PAd project, has been presented and used for the learning assessment activity of a case study developed inside the context of Marche Region Public administration. Preliminary results collected evidenced its importance in improving the understanding and practice of the administrative process, as well as the possibility of executing collaborative simulation and providing learners assessment. Moreover, this real case study also provided important feedbacks for the improvement and extension of the framework itself during the project duration. Future works include: (i) improvement of some parts of the architecture, such as the Test Data Repository and Robot; (ii) integration of usability concepts as well as the improvement of evaluation score visualization and management; (iii) enriching the set of learner's evaluation scores considering for instance the number of errors made during the execution of a path; and finally (iv) evaluation of the industrial significance and benefits of the proposed framework in different application areas of technology enhanced learning.

Acknowledgements. This work has been partially funded by the Model-Based Social Learning for Public Administrations project (EU FP7-ICT-2013-11/619583).

References

1. vom Brocke, J., Rosemann, M.: Handbook on Business Process Management 1: Introduction, Methods, and Information Systems (2014)
2. Blumschein, P., Hung, W., Jonassen, D.H.: Model-based approaches to learning: using systems models and simulations to improve understanding and problem solving in complex domains. Sense Publishers (2009)
3. Kapp, K.M.: The gamification of learning and instruction: game-based methods and strategies for training and education. Wiley (2012)
4. LearnPAd: (Model-Based Social Learning for Public Administrations European Project (EU FP7-ICT-2013-11/619583)). http://www.learnpad.eu/
5. Mature Project mature. http://mature-ip.eu/
6. Mirror Project mirror. http://www.mirror-project.eu/
7. Target Project target. http://www.reachyourtarget.org/moodle/
8. Prolix Project prolix. http://www.prolixproject.org/
9. Anderson, P.H., Lawton, L.: Business simulations and cognitive learning: developments, desires, and future directions. Simulation & Gaming (2008)
10. Clark, R.C., Mayer, R.E.: E-learning and the science of instruction: proven guidelines for consumers and designers of multimedia learning. Wiley (2011)

11. Jansen-Vullers, M., Netjes, M.: Business process simulation-a tool survey. In: Workshop and Tutorial on Practical Use of Coloured Petri Nets and the CPN Tools, Aarhus, Denmark, vol. 38 (2006)
12. Crookall, D.: Serious games, debriefing, and simulation/gaming as a discipline. Simulation & Gaming **41**, 898–920 (2010)
13. Bertoli, P., Dragoni, M., Ghidini, C., Martufi, E., Nori, M., Pistore, M., Francescomarino, C.: Modeling and monitoring business process execution. In: Basu, S., Pautasso, C., Zhang, L., Fu, X. (eds.) ICSOC 2013. LNCS, vol. 8274, pp. 683–687. Springer, Heidelberg (2013). doi:10.1007/978-3-642-45005-1_60
14. Maggi, F.M., Montali, M., Westergaard, M., Aalst, W.M.P.: Monitoring business constraints with linear temporal logic: an approach based on colored automata. In: Rinderle-Ma, S., Toumani, F., Wolf, K. (eds.) BPM 2011. LNCS, vol. 6896, pp. 132–147. Springer, Heidelberg (2011). doi:10.1007/978-3-642-23059-2_13
15. Adesina, A., Molloy, D.: Capturing and monitoring of learning process through a business process management (BPM) framework. In: Proceedings of 3rd International Symposium for Engineering Education (2010)
16. Ali, L., Hatala, M., Gašević, D., Jovanović, J.: A qualitative evaluation of evolution of a learning analytics tool. Comput. Educ. **58**, 470–489 (2012)
17. Calabrò, A., Lonetti, F., Marchetti, E.: Monitoring of business process execution based on performance indicators. In: Proceedings of 41st Euromicro-SEAA, pp. 255–258 (2015)
18. Calabrò, A., Lonetti, F., Marchetti, E.: KPI evaluation of the business process execution through event monitoring activity. In: Proceedings of Third International Conference on Enterprise Systems (2015)
19. Calabrò, A., Lonetti, F., Marchetti, E., Zribi, S., Jorquera, T.: Model-based learning assessment management. In: Proceedings of the 4th International Conference on Model-Driven Engineering and Software Development (MODELSWARD 2016) (2016)
20. Zribi, S., Calabrò, A., Lonetti, F., Marchetti, E., Jorquera, T., Lorré, J.P.: Design of a simulation framework for model-based learning. In: Proceedings of the 4th International Conference on Model-Driven Engineering and Software Development (MODELSWARD 2016) (2016)
21. Activiti BPM Platform (2015). http://activiti.org/
22. Camunda (2015). http://camunda.org/
23. jBPM (2015). http://www.jbpm.org
24. Drools Fusion Complex Event Processor (2015). http://www.jboss.org/drools/drools-fusion.html
25. Zribi, S., Jorquera, T., Lorré, J.P.: Towards a flexible gamification model for an interoperable e-learning business process simulation platform. In: Proceedings of I-ESA (2016)

An Ontology-Based and Case-Based Reasoning Supported Workplace Learning Approach

Sandro Emmenegger[1], Knut Hinkelmann[1,2],
Emanuele Laurenzi[1,2,3(✉)], Andreas Martin[1,4], Barbara Thönssen[1],
Hans Friedrich Witschel[1], and Congyu Zhang[1]

[1] University of Applied Sciences and Arts Northwestern Switzerland,
Riggenbachstr. 16, 4600 Olten, Switzerland
{sandro.emmenegger, knut.hinkelmann, emanuele.laurenzi,
andreas.martin, barbara.thoenssen,
hansfriedrich.witschel, congyu.zhang}@fhnw.ch
[2] Department of Informatics, University of Pretoria, Pretoria, South Africa
[3] University of Applied Sciences St. Gallen,
Rosenbergstr. 59, 9001 St. Gallen, Switzerland
[4] School of Computing, University of South Africa,
Roodepoort, Johannesburg, South Africa

Abstract. The support of workplace learning is increasingly relevant as the change in every form determines today's working world in the industry and public administrations alike. Adapting quickly to a new job, a new task or a new team is a significant challenge that must be dealt with ever faster. Workplace learning differs significantly from school learning as it is aligned with business goals. Our approach supports workplace learning by suggesting historical cases and providing recommendations of experts and learning resources. We utilize users' workplace environment, we consider their learning preferences, provide them with useful prior lessons, and compare required and acquired competencies to issue the best-suited recommendations. Our research work follows a Design Science Research strategy and is part of the European funded project Learn PAd. The recommender system introduced here is evaluated in an iterative manner, first by comparing it to previously elicited user requirements and then through practical application in a test process conducted by the project application partner.

Keywords: Workplace learning · Ontology supported learning · Personalized learning · Recommender system · Case-based reasoning · Public administration · Ontology-based Case-based reasoning

1 Introduction

Change is given and an employee's working environment, his/her tasks and duties changes quickly and ever often. According to the US Bureau of Labour Statistics [1], "the median number of years that wage and salary workers had been with their current employer was 4.6 years in January 2014". Already in 2012, Forbes has reported that according to a survey ninety-one percent of Millennials (born between 1977–1997) expect to stay in a job even for less than three years [2]. However, not only 'job

S. Hammoudi et al. (Eds): MODELSWARD 2016, CCIS 692, pp. 333–354, 2017.
DOI: 10.1007/978-3-319-66302-9_17

hobbing' requires (workplace) learning but also taking over new responsibilities within an organisation. In a survey conducted by Accenture [3] 91 percent of the respondents consider the most successful employees to be those who can adapt to the changing workplace. As pointed out by Tynjälä [4] workplace learning is different to school learning as it is mostly informal in nature, as - for example - usually no formal curriculum or prescribed outcomes exist, the emphasis is on work and experiences, it is often performed collaboratively, and no distinction is made between knowledge and skills. In our approach, we aim to formalize workplace learning by defining learning goals that are related to business goals, objectives, and strategies. Competencies required to reach the learning goals and hence, the business goals, are determined and described in the job profiles respectively role profiles. From this, an employee's competence profile is derived in which the level of acquired competencies is reported, for example in an objective agreement. Collaborative learning is supported by using a wiki as a learning platform.

For implementation, we use a model driven approach [5]. That is, we extended existing meta models, e.g. standard notations like Business Process Model and Notation (BPMN) [6] and Business Motivation Model (BMM) [7] or created new ones, based on standards (for example, the Competency Meta Model is deduced from the European Qualifications Framework (EQF) [8]) to model collaborative workplace learning centred on business processes and their context. We then transformed the models and relations between them into an ontological representation for machine execution. We also transformed these models and relations into wiki pages and links.

With this approach we can integrate workplace learning deeply into daily business, i.e. we consider a learner's context regarding tasks he/she has to perform in business processes combined with organizational knowledge about his/her position in the organisation and his/her working experience. Based on this context information, appropriate learning objects and learning material are determined and recommended to the learner according to his/her learning preferences.

Additionally, we complemented our approach with ontology-based case-based reasoning to identify and recommend the content of similar case from a case repository. The application domain is Public Administration (PA) as this sector must support extremely complex processes to provide services to citizens and companies. According to our business partner, today it needs up to two years of learning to become fully operational. These highly complex or knowledge-intensive processes demand the utilisation of an approach the do not require a prior generalisation of training data and previous acquisition of rules. Since such a rule acquisition task is difficult to manage for knowledge-intensive processes, we suggest in this paper the use of case-based reasoning, which requires a later manual or semi-automatic generalisation.

Workplaces in the industry and public administrations lack effective and not too expensive approaches that support workers in learning how to perform daily tasks at best. Unfortunately, no significant attention has been paid in the literature concerning integrated learning approaches in public administrations. Therefore, an ontology-based and case-based reasoning approach is needed that supports a collaborative workplace learning platform. This work is part of the European funded project Learn PAd (cf. http://www.learnpad.eu). The applied research method is Design Science Research [9] complemented by the approach of Grüninger & Fox [10] for ontology design and evaluation. In Learn PAd a learning platform is created to support Public Administration (PA) with workplace learning. PA's can access the platform via a wiki interface (see Xwiki, http://www.xwiki.com/en/). The interface consists of two parts: left and right (see Fig. 1). The left part contains the properties of a process task as well as data input and output. The right part is what we call the recommendation panel where context-related and personalized recommendations are provided.

We assess our approach in an iterative process in the context of the overall Learn PAd project evaluation. A first evaluation was accomplished recently.

The paper at hand is structured as follows: In Sect. 2 we give an overview of related work. Then we introduce an application scenario to illustrate our approach (Sect. 3). In Sect. 4 we provide a specification of the recommender system, followed by a description of its implementation (Sect. 5). First iterations of evaluation are described in Sect. 6. We conclude in Sect. 7.

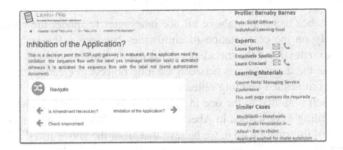

Fig. 1. Recommender interface.

2 Literature Review

In our literature review we consider research on five aspects that are most relevant to our work: recommenders, competency frameworks, imparting knowledge, learning styles and ontology-based case-based reasoning.

2.1 Recommenders

There is today a broad agreement among researchers that e-learning content should adapt to the learner's context and that learners should be guided through learning content based on such context. The recommendation of learning objects can be regarded as a special case of business-process oriented knowledge management. A wide array of recommenders have been proposed, all of which aim at recommending the next learning activity – very often interaction with a learning object – to a learner who is currently engaged with an e-learning system.

Such recommendations can be based purely on a history of the learner activities within the same or previous sessions. Some approaches use content-based filtering; they recommended learning items that have a content similar to that of learning objects in the learner's current session [11, 12]. Others are based on collaborative filtering or association rule mining [12, 13], i.e. they recommend objects that other learners (with similar interests) used together with the objects from the current history. A survey of further approaches of this kind can be found in Sikka et al. [14].

Other researchers claim that – besides the current activities of the learner – additional information is needed to make useful recommendations:

- A profile of the learner including existing knowledge or skill levels, preferred learning style, and current learning goal to enable proper personalization of recommendations [15, 16].
- Meta information about the learning objects including required previous knowledge, content type and interactivity level to match them against the learner [15, 16].
- Information about the role of the learner and his/her position in the organization [15, 17, 18].
- Explicit information about the work context of the learner regarding a currently e.g. executed task or business process [15, 17, 18].

The approaches mentioned above all use ontologies to model the required information and rely on the computation of similarities between a learner's profile (and possibly work context) and the metadata provided with learning objects. Yu et al. [16] additionally use the dependencies between learning objects to create a "learning path" through all recommended learning objects.

Our approach is similar to the one in Schmidt & Winterhalter [15], which relies on semantic modelling as described in Abecker et al. [18]. We propose to model and use the same kind of information – i.e. we believe that all of the above-listed information is indeed necessary to make didactically useful recommendations. We take that approach further by concretising the meta models and ontologies required for modelling that information and by proposing concrete matching procedures.

2.2 Competency Frameworks

In order to develop an appropriate competency model we carefully studied frameworks related to competency, like the RDCEO (The Reusable Definition of Competency or Educational Objective), TRACE (TRAnsparent Competences in Europe), DeSeCo (The Definition and Selection of Competencies) [19], DIGCOMP (Developing and Understanding Digital Competence in Europe) [20], e-CF [21], Bloom's Taxonomy [22] and EQF (The European Qualifications Framework) [8].

Since our application partner in the Learn PAd project already uses the EQF framework, we decided to base the competency model on it. The European Qualifications Framework (EQF) is envisaged as a meta-framework that allows positioning and comparing qualifications. It consists of eight reference levels which are described regarding learning outcomes: knowledge, skills, and competences. For instance EQF level 4 for knowledge is "Factual and theoretical knowledge in broad contexts within a field of work or study"; for skill is "A range of cognitive and practical skills required to generate solutions to specific problems in a field of work or study"; and finally for competence is "Exercise self-management within the guidelines of work or study contexts that are usually predictable, but are subject to change; supervise the routine work of others, taking some responsibility for the evaluation and improvement of work or study activities" [8].

2.3 Imparting of Knowledge

One of the most important aspects imparting knowledge is the notion of a Zone of Proximal Development (ZPD), introduced by Vygotsky [23]. He defined the zone of proximal development (ZPD) as "the distance between the actual developmental level as determined by independent problem-solving and the level of potential development as determined through problem-solving under adult guidance or in collaboration with more capable peers" [23, p.86]. Vygotsky proofed that when a learner is in the ZPD for a particular task, he can achieve it if appropriate assistance is provided.

Another important aspect imparting knowledge is scaffolding. Scaffolding was coined by Wood et al. [24] whose conceptualization of scaffolding was consistent with Vygotsky's model of instruction and emphasizes the teacher's role as a more knowledgeable learner to help learners to solve problem-oriented tasks [25].

Quintana et al. stated, "the process by which a teacher or more knowledgeable peer provides assistance that enables learners to succeed in problems that would otherwise be too difficult" [26]. However, in workplace learning experts' involvement is not always feasible. As shown by Billett [27, p.53] one limitation of workplaces as learning environments is the "reluctance by experts to guide and provide close interactions with learners". Hence, other learning aids - i.e. learning material created with certain didactic considerations in mind, is to be recommended to support learners.

A rather young learning theory that also builds on the ZPD idea and that takes into account the role of technology for learning is the so-called connectivism [28]. Connectivism postulates that learning occurs when connections are made between nodes in a learner's network - where a node can be anything ranging from a piece of knowledge in the learner's mind to a digital artefact or another person. This implies that new knowledge must be connected to existing knowledge or experiences – which can be understood as a concretization of the ZPD and that such connection can be mediated by links in the digital environment.

2.4 Learning Styles

The theory of learning styles describes ways in which learning can be different between individuals and claims that hence different ways of supporting individual learning must be developed and adapted to a learner's individual preferences.

The Dunn & Dunn learning style model [29] describes several elements of learning styles: the environmental domain, the emotional domain, the sociological domain, the physiological domain and the psychological domain. People deal with information and ideas in different ways because of their preference. These learning styles influence the achievement of the learners. Using the right combination of learning preferences will help the learners to achieve their learning goals.

2.5   Case-Based Reasoning

According to Leake [30], case-based reasoning (CBR) can be seen as "reasoning by remembering". It is a technology-independent methodology [31] for humans and information systems. CBR is "[...] the ways people use cases to solve problems and the ways [people] can make machines use them" [32, p.27].

With the use of CBR, one can utilise the experience (a lesson or case content) of previously situations by characterising the current situation and by using this characterisation to retrieve prior similar situations (former cases comprising of characterisation and content) from a case repository [33–35]. The retrieve phase is the first of the four major phases of the CBR cycle of Aamodt and Plaza [33], which comprises of the following four *Rs*:

1. *Retrieve* similar case(s) from the case repository.
2. *Reuse* the lesson from the retrieved case(s) as the suggested solution for the current situation.
3. *Revise* the current case after evaluating it in the current situation.
4. *Retain* the current case in the case repository.

In structural CBR, which is one of three major CBR approaches [36], the cases are described using a certain vocabulary or domain model [34]. However, such a model needs to be acquired ex-ante and can lead to an acquisition bottleneck. Several approaches, therefore, suggest the use of ontologies [37–39] or, more specific, the use of enterprise ontologies, which provide a CBR system with enterprise-specific knowledge [35, 40]. "The more knowledge is embedded into the system, the more effective [it] is expected to be" [41, p.54]. However, enterprise ontologies need to be created beforehand, and this can root in a knowledge bottleneck too. Therefore, several approaches [35, 40, 42–44] suggest the reuse of enterprise architecture descriptions when creating an enterprise ontology. Since architecture descriptions are descriptions of "[...] enterprise's organisational structure, business processes, information systems, and infrastructure" [45, p.3], the architecture descriptions are a solid source of enterprise-specific models and vocabulary. CBR systems that are utilising an ontology-based knowledge container, called ontology-based case-based reasoning (OBCBR) systems, "[...] can take advantage of this domain knowledge and obtain more accurate results" [41, p.54]. Several approaches, such as jCOLIBRI [46], myCBR [47], COBRA [48] and ICEBERG [35] and other [49, 50] combine ontologies and CBR.

3   Application Scenario

The application scenario was developed based on a real case and as a result of several interviews and workshops conducted with representatives of our application partner in Italy, the Marche Region. The application scenario provides all information needed to instantiate all kinds of meta model relevant for workplace learning, i.e. process models, business motivation model, organisational model, document model and competency model. We also introduced two personas: Barnaby, a PA officer who joined the Public

Administration of Monti Azzurri not long ago; and Susan, an entrepreneur who requests a service from the PA.

Our illustration focusses on complex business process tasks that Barnaby performs and will show what Barnaby should learn and how our approach supports him.

The business process in question is called "Titolo Unico" and aims at providing permissions to activity requests of citizens, e.g. start a business, restructuring or extending a commercial location. Depending on the case, the related process can get rather complex. The most challenging tasks are as follows:

1. Assessing citizen's application form of an activity request. This includes the aspect of dealing with mistakes occurring in a form (e.g. declarations that are in contrast to each other or missing documents that require further material from the citizen, leading to time delays).
2. Involving appropriate organizational units (i.e. PA offices and/or private parties) for providing consensus on the activity request.
3. Arranging a service-conference meeting. This is a meeting held if the involved organizational units (a.k.a. third parties) do not reach a common agreement, or someone does not respond to the opinion request. It includes the behaviour of involved parties (e.g. did or did not attend the service conference and did or did not reply to a PA officer request within a given time).

Performing these activities while complying with related time constraints and taking right follow-up decisions is of crucial importance for successfully delivering the service. The two ingredients that enable the PA officer coping with such complexity are a comprehensive knowledge of the Italian law (i.e. national, regional, provincial and municipal norms and regulations) and deep work experience in the field. The latter applies mainly to the second activity on the above list, i.e. involving the appropriate organizational units. In fact, in this task the PA officer deals with various PAs that differ from the number of organizational units and the degree of specialization, i.e. PAs of the major cities (e.g. Rome or Florence) embeds many more organizational units and more ramified specializations than smaller cities (e.g. Ancona or Macerata). Additionally, in small realities (e.g. towns like Amandola, Sarnano and San Ginesio) a PA spans several municipalities, providing services together. Addressing the appropriate organisational units would be a mission impossible for an unexperienced PA officer. Conversely, a skilled PA officer knows the Italian law, the structure of the PA to be involved and the responsible officers in the related organisational units. Additionally, establishing a direct contact with responsible officers speeds up the execution of tasks (e.g. quicker responses to requests and less bureaucracy). Therefore, we consider this knowledge - although informal - highly relevant.

Finally, both accepted activity requests and reasons for the rejected ones help to improve the acceptance rate of next activity requests. Hence, this knowledge is also taken into account.

In the follow subsections we are going to introduce the three kinds of learning support Barnaby receives to overcome the described complexity, i.e. recommending experts, recommending learning resources and recommending historical cases.

3.1 Learning Support

In our application scenario, the entrepreneur Susan requests approval of building a chalet on the lake of Caccamo, which belongs to the municipality of Serrapetrona, which is in the province of Macerata, Italy. Susan uses the application form provided at the web-site of the PA, and we assume that she filled it out correctly.

By submitting the form, the business process at the PA of Monti Azzurri was started. The PA officer Barnaby took over the task to assess the form. Due to his little experience, Barnaby needs support to identify all the possible mistakes and/or missing documents. The LearnPAd system supports Barnaby using *historical cases*.

Recommending Historical Cases

The LearnPAd system applies the Case-Based-Reasoning approach to retrieve the most similar historical cases managed in all PAs. The specification of the approach will be described in the next section. Barnaby looks at the recommendation panel (see right-hand side of Fig. 1), which shows the case entitled *"Building a chalet in a beach area of Senigallia"* as the most similar case successfully managed from the PA Senigallia. Among other aspects, the retrieved case contains the "lesson learned" section from which Barnaby learns how to avoid potential missing documents and misinterpretation of law articles. Barnaby applies this useful information to accomplish the assessment of the current application form.

Next, based on the type of request specific actions are to be taken. In our case the type of request is "receptive tourism" and Barnaby knows this type always requires the authorization of the municipality according to the Italian law (norm 9 of 2006). However, Barnaby does not know the municipality of Serrapetrona and he is not sure of which organisational units should be involved. He needs an expert to advise him.

Recommending Experts

Barnaby enters the Learn PAd system, moves to the task "Identify Organisational Units" he has to perform and checks on the recommendation panel for help (see the right-hand side of Fig. 1). In the panel contact details of two experts – Sarah Brown and Laura Cruciani - are displayed. Sarah is a former PA officer of Monti Azzurri who now works for the municipality of Sarnano. The recommendation system still considers Sarah as an expert as she dealt with many cases concerning the municipality of Serrapetrona. Laura, is the boss of Barnaby, working for the PA of Monti Azzurri for many years.

Instead of searching internal phone books, asking around or applying the trial-and-error method Barnaby can contact one of the experts, who will suggest which organisational units to involve and to which law article it may refer. Additionally, the contact details of the personnel could also be provided to start establishing a not too formal business relationship.

Recommending Learning Resources

After Barnaby got advice which organisational units to involve, he sends requests to obtain the opinion on the case of the involved parties. Responses are expected within 30 days.

However, Barnaby receives answers in time from all but one of the parties. Now he needs help in how dealing with this situation. The Learn PAd system has a section in the recommendation panel that refers to learning objects and learning material (see Fig. 1). All models represented in the wiki are considered learning objects since the learner needs to get familiar not only with a process, its structure and tasks but also with the involved roles, organizational units, business documents, IT systems and so on. For differentiation we call dedicated technical books, tutorials, learning audio and video file and 'learning material'.

Thus, Barnaby checks on the learning material provided by the Learn PAd system. As recommendations in Learn PAd are context-sensitive and personalized the ZPD of a learner is considered. More in detail, Barnaby has an acquired competency EQF level of 3 in "Manage Specific Admin Procedure". Learning material recommended in Learn PAd is also related to competencies it fosters.

In our example the book "Regulation of Titolo Unico" - is related to the same competence ("Manage Specific Admin Procedure") but classified with level 4. The difference of 1 between the competency levels is considered conform to the ZPD of the learner. Since reading books falls within Barnaby's preferences (preferences of PA officers are also made explicit in the model), in the book "Regulation of Titolo Unico", Barnaby learns that if an organisational unit does respond, the "Silence and Consensus" procedure can be applied, i.e. it is assumed that the not responding partner approves the request of the entrepreneur. Since no further challenge comes to light, Barnaby finishes the assessment of the application and finally sends the approval to Susan for realizing her chalet on the lake of Caccamo.

4   Recommender System Specification

We learned from Vygotsky [23] and others that mentoring is very successful in supporting individual learning. However, particularly in workplace learning, experts might be too busy to provide the wishful support and spending their time with mentoring is simply too costly. Hence, an efficient solution is needed that provides a) alternatives, and b) guides to experts most capable of giving advice with respect to expert knowledge but also regarding the Zone of Proximal Development (ZPD) of the learner.

In our approach for recommending relevant information supporting the user in learning we consider three modes of learning: simulation (in a simulation environment a learner can simulate to perform a business process task), browsing (a user can view and navigate through wiki pages, represent his/her business environment like business process, tasks, organisational charts, related documents, etc.), and *execution* mode (using the wiki as a front end to perform a business service; often called learning by doing).

Furthermore, we differentiate between learning objects, learning material, experts and historical cases. As all Wiki articles correlate one-to-one to model elements, they are regarded as learning objects related to these model elements. Learning material is information dedicated to learning, for example (training) books, audio, and video files. Simulation and browsing are considered as interactive learning material.

Besides the characteristics of the wiki content (derived from the meta-model and the models), the recommender ontology also represents characteristics of the learning material as the EQF level of knowledge that is addressed. Furthermore, the ontology contains profiles of the learner, i.e. the workers in the PA, including his/her EQF specification, learning preferences and individual learning goals. With this holistic view on learners, their working environment, and organizational network it is possible to identify relevant learning objects, learning material and experts, appropriate for the ZPD of the learner and according to her learning style.

Most recommendations rely on rules. The left side of these rules (precondition) is defined regarding the learner's context - i.e. his/her required and acquired competencies (including levels) and learning style, as well as the context and application data of the currently executed business process. The right side of rules (consequence) contains the recommended material.

4.1   Basis for Recommendations

We start from the premise that in an organisation business goals and objectives are defined. They can be modelled in a Business Motivation Model BMM [7]. We extended the BMM meta model by introducing learning goals as new Course of Action. Learning goals can be related to business goals and strategies that support them. To achieve a learning goal certain competencies are needed. Note, that we use the term competency to summarize the three learning outcomes (knowledge, skill, competence) defined in EQF. Hence, learning goals defined in the BMM are related to the Competency Model in which competencies are described according to EQF including their levels (1–8).

We further assume that competency profiles are set-up for organisational units or roles to specify a set of competencies *required* by this entity. We also maintain competency profiles of employees which contain the acquired set of competencies. The difference between the required competencies, of a role and the acquired competencies of a person who has this role, determines the individual learning goal.

In addition, we can model specific competencies needed for example to perform certain tasks and hence, related to an extended process model. In this manner we can identify the knowledge gap, a learner has, the learning goals he/she is supposed to meet and his/her learning preference that is also captured in the learner's competency profile.

We finally assume that while a knowledge worker is handling a certain case (i.e. an instance of a business process), we have information about the task-related and case-related context. This comprises information about the current task the user is working on and decisions that have been taken in previous tasks. In addition, it implies that we have knowledge about the case and the application data that define it – in the case of the Titolo Unico process introduced in Sect. 2.5, this refers to the filled-in forms that the applicants submit to the SUAP office and on which Barnaby needs to decide.

Depending on the learning mode, recommendations differ in range. The more is known about the learner's working context, the better (filtered) the recommendations. Thus, most valuable recommendations can be provided in the execution mode. Here the recommender system knows exactly what task a learner is about to perform, what tasks are already done, what decisions have been taken during the business process so far and what application data is relevant. In best case within the simulation, such context information can be 'faked', i.e. instead of real data fictional data is used but the same kind of recommendations can be provided. A less accurate recommendation can be made within the browsing mode as the learner is free to navigate within one or more processes. Hence, no information is available about former actions and application data.

In the following, we are going to introduce three examples of how recommendations are determined with respect to experts, learning material and historical cases.

4.2 Recommending Experts

The difficulty in recommending experts lies in identifying the appropriate expert. Obviously, the choice of an expert depends on the work situation - and hence the knowledge required - as well as on the level of knowledge of the learner and possibly existing relationships between the learner and the expert. We consider three ways to determine experts:

1. line managers from the same organisation the learner belongs to
2. colleagues having (had) the same role as the learner but having executed the very task several times
3. persons having the same role as the learner but belonging to another PA

In the following the recommendation of an experienced colleague is described in detail. As mentioned above for building the recommender we follow the approach of Grüninger & Fox [10] for ontology design and evaluation.

Thus, in the following the informal competency question (CQ) is provided first, followed then by its transformation into an SPARQL query.

Informal Competency Question

Given a user logged into the Learn PAd system and the role this user has in a task and some constraints regarding task (e.g. the task a performer is about to execute) and work experience (e.g. a performer's work experience), what internal experts can be recommended?

- *rationale*: the answer is used to recommend experts from the same organisation that executed the tasks most often.
- *decomposition*: the name of the user, the user is an actor, an actor has a role in the task, the role is assigned to more than one performer, the performer has task log.

Formal competency question (SPARQL query)

```
SELECT  ?experiencedPerformerName ?email WHERE
  { { SELECT  ?experiencedPerformer (COUNT(?executedTaskInstance) AS ?count)
      WHERE
      { ?taskInstance rdf:type bpmn:Task .
        ?executedTaskInstance rdf:type ?taskInstance .
        ?executedTaskInstance emo:activityIsPerformedByPerformer ?experiencedPerformer .
        ?currentPerformer emo:performerHasEmailAddress "barnaby.barnes@fhnw.ch"
        FILTER ( ?currentPerformer != ?experiencedPerformer )
      }
      GROUP BY ?experiencedPerformer
  }
  ?experiencedPerformer rdfs:label ?experiencedPerformerName .
  ?experiencedPerformer emo:performerRepresentsPerson ?experiencedPerformerBusinessActor
  OPTIONAL
  { ?experiencedPerformerBusinessActor foaf:mbox ?email}
} ORDER BY DESC(?count) LIMIT 1
```

The result of the query is a colleague of the performer, working in the same organisation, having the same role and great work experience in the tasks the performer is about to execute. In the recommendation panel, the name and contact details are provided.

4.3   Recommending Learning Material

For recommending appropriate learning materials, the zone of proximal development of a learner must be considered. That is, the level of competency that the learning material fosters should be reasonably higher than the learner's current level of this competency (cf. application scenario described above). Furthermore, the learning material should support the learner's preferred style as, for example, the learning material that matches his/her preferred learning style is listed on top of the list and the link to it is presented in bold characters. It is also possible to completely filter out learning material that doesn't meet a learner's learning style.

Informal Competency Question
Given a user logged into the Learn PAd system and her learning style and some constraints regarding competencies (e.g. acquired and required, i.e. fostered competencies and their level), what information material is recommended?

- *rationale*: the answer is used to provide learning material (i.e. links to documents, video files, simulation) that are relevant to the learner, i.e. fosters one or more competencies she has to improve and the level of the fostered competency is exactly one level higher than the level of the acquired competency.
- *decomposition*: the name of the user, the user is an actor, an actor has a profile, the profile contains acquired competencies and their level and the user's learning style, learning the material, learning material fosters one or more competency at a certain level suitable for a certain learning style.

Formal competency question (SPARQL query)

```
SELECT ?learningMaterialTitle ?learningMaterialType ?learningMaterialURI WHERE
{ { SELECT ?nextCompetencyLevelNumber ?aquiredCompetencyLabel ?learningStyle
    WHERE
    { ?competencyProfile emo:competencyProfileIsAquiredByPerformer ?performer .
      ?competencyProfile cmm:competencyProfileContainsCompetencySet ?aquiredCompetencySet .
      ?aquiredCompetency cmm:competencyBelongsToCompetencySet ?aquiredCompetencySet .
      ?aquiredCompetency cmm:competencyHasLevel ?competencyLevelNumber .
      ?aquiredCompetency rdfs:label ?aquiredCompetencyLabel .
      BIND(( ?competencyLevelNumber + 1 ) AS ?nextCompetencyLevelNumber)
      ?competencyProfile lpd:competencyProfilePrefersLearningStyle ?learningStyle
    }
  }
  ?nextCompetency cmm:competencyHasLevel ?nextCompetencyLevelNumber .
  ?nextCompetency rdfs:label ?aquiredCompetencyLabel .
  ?nextCompetency lpd:proposedLearningDocument ?learningDocument .
  ?learningDocument elements:documentHasType ?documentType .
  ?learningStyle lpd:learningStyleBelongsToDocumentType ?documentType .
  ?learningDocument emo:documentRepresentsdocument ?foafDocument .
  ?foafDocument elements:documentHasTitle ?learningMaterialTitle .
  ?foafDocument eo:documentHasStorage ?documentNode
  OPTIONAL
  { ?documentNode lpd:xwikiPageRepresentsNode ?learningMaterialURI}
  OPTIONAL
  { NOT EXISTS
    { ?documentNode lpd:xwikiPageRepresentsNode ?learningMaterialURI .
      ?foafDocument elements:documentHasSource ?learningMaterialURI
    }
  }
}
```

After giving two detailed examples of how we build recommendations we describe the technical implementation of our approach.

4.4 Recommending Historical Cases

As already mentioned, the LearnPad system platform retrieves similar historical cases by implementing the CBR approach. As we saw in Sect. 2.5, this approach draws upon existing research, in particular on the approach by Martin et al. [35]. The adopted CBR approach makes use of ontology for case retrieval and similarity determination, i.e. OBCBR (see the second part of Sect. 2.5). Our already existing LearnPAd ontology was extended with concepts representing characterisation of cases. For space reasons, we show a limited number of both case characterisation concepts in Table 1 and case content elements in Table 2.

While case characterizations are metadata that describe cases, case content relates to information used to process a case, e.g. documents or links to external information sources. Table 2 provides the content element and its manifestation, i.e. the case folder as a pool containing information produced during case execution.

Extending the LearnPAd ontology with the case characterization concepts allows inferring similar cases. This reflects the first phase of the CBR cycle in which a query case is compared to historical cases (see Fig. 2) [35].

Table 1. Case characterisation.

Concepts	Descriptions
Applicant	A person who submitted the application.
Application type	Application type can relate to new productive systems (i.e. realization, (de) localization) or modification of existing ones (i.e. restructuring, transformation, reconversion, expansion, or quitting an activity).
ATECO	ATECO is an Italian standard classification of economic activities issued by the National Institute of Statistics (ISTAT) – http://www.istat.it/it/archivio/17888 available in Italian only)
Zone	A zone can span one or more cities, provinces and regions, e.g. the National Park of Monti Sibillini located across the two regions Marche and Umbria, encompassing several provinces and cities.
...	...

Table 2. Case content.

Content element	Content manifestation
Case Folder	Documents created, used and/or updated throughout the Titolo Unico process
	Reports/notes about decisions, i.e. accepted or rejected application and explanation
	Descriptions of a lesson learned, i.e. missing documents and misinterpretation of law articles.
	...

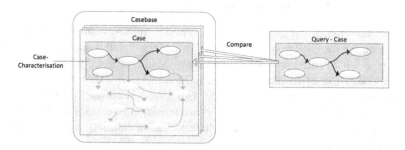

Fig. 2. Comparison of a query case with historical cases [35].

Similarity Model

To retrieve similar cases, similarity measures were applied. We consider two types of measures: global similarity measures, which are defined on the level of cases, and local similarity measures, which are defined on the level of attributes. The global similarity measure provides a way to aggregate all the local similarity values into one value. For our application scenario, case characterizations are mostly simple attribute-value pairs – hence, the global similarity measure can be a simple weighted average of local similarities. However, for other scenarios where case characterizations are more complex, more sophisticated functions can be used [51].

Regarding local similarity, applied functions depend on the attribute type. For string attributes (i.e. free text to be entered by the user), we adopted string similarity measures such as the *Levenshtein* string edit distance (which is the minimal number of edit operations when transforming one string to another) or SOFTFIDF*JaroWinkler* similarity [52]. The latter works well with names or text fields that consist of several words, which might be syntactically arranged in different ways without impacting semantic similarity. For categorical attributes where possible values are taken from the predefined list, but not structured in a particular way, we used a simple equality (corresponding to a similarity of 1) or inequality (similarity 0) of attribute values. Our application scenario addressed two additional relevant attribute types - *Categorical attributes with taxonomic value range* and *Categorical attributes which can take more than one value.*

- *Categorical attributes with taxonomic value range:* those attribute values structured hierarchically, e.g. via a taxonomy like in a tree structure. Among the existing approaches that define local similarity measures, we followed the reasoning of Bergmann [34]. Bergmann proposed to manually assign a similarity value to each inner node of the tree-based on expert experience. This approach overcomes the disadvantage of commonly adopted path length methods where nodes in deeper tree branches are more dissimilar to other branches. In Bergmann approach, the similarity of two leaf nodes is the value that is assigned to the lowest common parent node of the two leaves – or 1 if the values are equal. As an example, let's consider the taxonomic structure of the attribute "Application Type" and its value range, represented in Fig. 3. The rationale is that e.g. the introduction of a new business – even if it is not the same sub-type – is more similar to another new business than to a modification of an existing business. Hence, we defined:

  - sim(Localization, Realization) = 0.8 > 0 = sim(Localization, Restructuring).

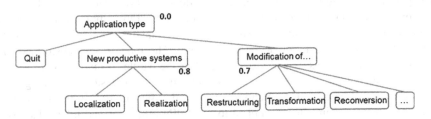

Fig. 3. Taxonomy with similarity values assigned to inner nodes.

Categorical attributes which can take more than one value: there exists a *1:n* relationship between a case and the attribute, i.e. the case can be associated with more than one value of the attribute. We rely on our research [51], which is inspired by retrieval functions in information retrieval. The main idea is that a historical case should not be "punished" for having attribute values that are not shared with the new case (which we call the "query case"). As long as the values of the historical case match values of the query case, its additional values are neglected. For example, consider the two historical cases C1 and C2 and its attribute "zone". Value for "zone" in C1 is "beach area", and in C2 "Beach area" and "national park". If a civil servant wants to find cases that are similar to a new business which is located in a "beach area" (Q1), we argue that both C1 and C2 should be equally similar to Q1 because both share the value of the zone attribute ("beach area"). However, in case a civil servant wants to find cases in which a new business is located in a "beach area" and in a "national park" (Q2), only C2 should be provided as it covers more relevant aspects than C1.

The property of asymmetry of similarity is useful especially in cases where initial case characterisations (queries) are incomplete. In our application domain, the PA officer enters attribute values while performing the process. At the beginning of the process, only a few attribute values might be available whereas in the end all might be entered. Hence, asymmetry is useful for that domain, but not ensured by most similarity measures that are traditionally used in CBR.

5 Recommender System Implementation

The recommender system is an integrated part of the Learn PAd system platform and incorporates mainly the modelling environments, the transformation component, the learning platform's Wiki frontend and the ontology recommender component, which includes a CBR component.

The core of the recommender system is the ontology and recommender (OR) component. The platform independent meta-models and the conceptual meta-models are represented in OWL [53] and loaded at runtime by the OR component. The component is written in Java and uses the open source library Jena [54] which provides an API to work with ontologies.

A new set of models published via the modelling environment is exported in a proprietary XML format. These exported models are transformed in a generic way into Wiki page representations based on the Eclipse Modelling Framework (EMF) [55]. The transformation into the ontology instances is using XSLT [56] templates and an XSLT Engine. This approach enables a straightforward transformation directly into the specific target model and format of the ontology. The models are transformed into RDFS [57] conform classes and are formatted in the Turtle format for a convenient work with text -based version control systems. In a second step, a more generic meta-meta model-based transformation is evaluated. After the transformation into the ontology, an inferencing step is applied to run SPIN [58] rules and infer relations to corresponding conceptual model classes and eventually already existing instance. Examples of such existing instances might be an organisation's employee directory received from a human resource system. The combination of the platform independent and conceptual models, as well as the transformed model objects, build the upper two levels in our OR component knowledge base shown in Fig. 4.

Valuable recommendation rules require context information besides the information from the enterprise models. Application data and logging information from process executions can provide such information. This extended information is made available for reasoning together with the ontology and model instances. However, here, we face the problem of the missing support of multilayer ontologies by the ontology description standards, like OWL. If we add execution data to our ontology, we have an instance of an instance problem, i.e. the execution data represents one layer, the process, and other model instance the next higher layer and our PIMM/LCMM meta-models the highest layer. Fanesi et al. [59, 60] propose an approach with RDFS-FA respectively OWL-FA to overcome that problem and still keep it decidable by reasoners. Executed processes and tasks in our example are added as instances of the process instances. This allows applying a counting rule which suggests a performer as an expert if the performer has executed the task most often.

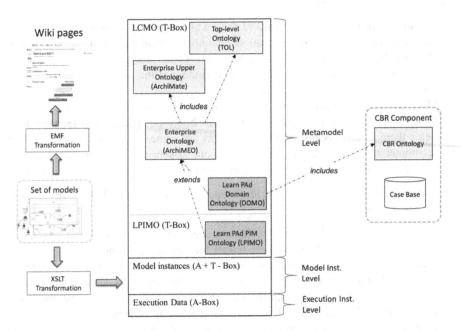

Fig. 4. Ontology levels and transformations.

Another set of learning recommendations relies on a case base with historical cases. The integrated CBR component allows retrieving historical cases of the public administration stored in the case base. The case base and the similarity calculations are all based on ontologies. The cases are stored as instances of the case ontology, and the case characterizations are defined by applied annotations from the CBR ontology.

6 Evaluation

Before proposing the design of our recommender, we compiled requirements based on literature (see Sect. 2) and the results of a questionnaire that was filled in by 52 civil servants. In this section, we present a summary of how our recommender design satisfies these requirements. This is followed by a summary of results from a qualitative evaluation. The results presented here cover only the recommendations of experts and learning materials – recommendations of historical cases are more complex to evaluate and will be validated as part of the final validation of the entire Learn PAd approach.

6.1 Requirements Met

Regarding the interplay of the recommender with the platform that handles the execution of the business process and the necessary context awareness, the following requirements were satisfied:

- Questionnaire respondents had stated that, while receiving recommendations on a particular task, these recommendations should be detailed, but at the same time, they would like to keep an overview of the whole process. This is satisfied by presenting a process overview in the main window of the prototype and displaying recommendations within a sidebar.
- Civil servants emphasized that they often not know where the information contained in existing or new (learning) material should be applied. The recommender helps them in this because recommendations are context-specific (i.e. they get the recommendation where they need it). Context-sensitive recommendations are enabled by rules whose conditions are matched to the learner's current work context

Furthermore, requirements regarding the competence-awareness of the recommender are satisfied as follows:

- The choice to use EQF for the definition of learners' competence levels resulted in the adoption of an EQF-based meta-model for modelling learner profiles
- Based on the definition of the zone of proximal development (ZPD) in Vygotsky [23], we formulated the requirement that the recommender should recommend learning objects aiming to teach the learner competencies at a level just above her current level. This is satisfied by describing learning objects with intended outcomes regarding EQF competency levels and making sure that this level is just above the learner's current EQF competence level for each recommended learning object.

Another category of satisfied requirements concerned the adaptation of recommendations to the learner's learning style:

- Since questionnaire participants expressed the desire to get recommendations for a diverse range of content types, the recommender is able to suggest not only documents or multimedia learning objects but also experts (see below) and historical cases.

– Based on the concepts proposed by connectionist learning [28] which imply the need to make connections with a learner's existing knowledge, the recommender creates such connections e.g. by proposing historical cases.

Finally, requirements regarding expert guidance are satisfied as follows:

– Since questionnaire participants stated the need to have quick access to recommended experts, the recommendations include contact information
– Based on the notion of ZPD [23] and scaffolding learning [24], we ensured that recommended experts have a more advanced level of knowledge than the learner by making rules dependent on experts' EQF competence levels.

6.2 Qualitative Evaluation

The qualitative evaluation consisted of a workshop where civil servants interacted with a prototype of the Learn PAd collaborative platform, which included – among other functionalities – the features of the recommender. The interaction was performed along the application scenario described in Sect. 2.5, and the corresponding application data and learner context were known to the system. The recommender was integrated into the prototype in the form of a sidebar where context-dependent suggestions were displayed. Most of the participants' feedback revolved around aspects of the recommender that were not yet implemented in the prototype. Thus, participants commented that there should be:

– a registration form where a user's competencies can be assessed and then stored in a profile
– more recommendations of multimedia content
– recommendations also on the level of the whole process.

We consider this feedback as a confirmation that these features will be perceived as useful when implemented later.

7   Conclusion & Future Work

With our approach, we could show how workplace learning can be improved by providing context-sensitive and personalized recommendations for learning in a collaborative environment. In the future, we plan to work on key performance indicators for learning goals to assess learning progress. We intend to develop a cockpit to identify for example goals that are not satisfied and the reasons that cause this effect.

Acknowledgements. This work is supported by the European Union FP7 ICT objective, through the Learn PAd Project with Contract No. 619583.

References

1. US Bureau of Labor Statistics: Employee Tenure in 2014. Washington, USA (2014) http://www.bls.gov/news.release/pdf/tenure.pdf
2. Meister, J.: Job Hopping Is the 'New Normal' for Millennials: Three Ways to Prevent a Human Resource Nightmare
3. Accenture: Career Capital 2014 Global Research Results (2014)
4. Tynjälä, P.: Perspectives into learning at the workplace. Educ. Res. Rev. 3, 130–154 (2008)
5. De Angelis, G., Pierantonio, A., Polini, A., Re, B., Thönssen, B., Woitsch, R.: Modelling for Learning in Public Administrations – The Learn PAd approach. In: Karagiannis D., Mayr H., Mylopoulos J. (eds.) Domain-Specific Conceptual Modelling: Concepts, Methods, and Tools. Springer, Cham (2015)
6. OMG: Business Process Model and Notation (BPMN) Version 2.0. Object Management Group (2013) http://www.omg.org/spec/BPMN/2.0.2/
7. OMG: Business Motivation Model (BMM) Version 1.2. Object Management Group (2014) http://www.omg.org/spec/BMM/1.2
8. European Comission: Descriptors defining levels in the European Qualifications Framework (EQF) (2016) https://ec.europa.eu/ploteus/content/descriptors-page
9. Hevner, A., Chatterjee, S.: Design Research in Information Systems. Springer, Boston (2010)
10. Grüninger, M., Fox, M.S.: Methodology for the design and evaluation of ontologies. In: Workshop on Basic Ontological Issues in Knowledge Sharing, IJCAI-1995, Montreal, pp. 1–10 (1995)
11. Ghauth, K.I., Abdullah, N.A.: The Effect of incorporating good learners' ratings in e-learning content-based recommender system. Educ. Technol. Soc. 14, 248–257 (2010)
12. Khribi, M.K., Jemni, M., Nasraoui, O.: Automatic recommendations for e-learning personalization based on web usage mining techniques and information retrieval. Educ. Technol. Soc. 12, 30–42 (2009)
13. Zaíane, O.R.: Building a recommender agent for e-learning systems. In: Proceedings of the International Conference on Computers in Education, p. 55. IEEE Computer Society (2002)
14. Sikka, R., Dhankhar, A., Rana, C.: A survey paper on e-learning recommender system. Int. J. Comput. Appl. 47, 27–30 (2012)
15. Schmidt, A., Winterhalter, C.: User context aware delivery of e-learning material: Approach and architecture. J. Univers. Comput. Sci. 10, 28–36 (2004)
16. Yu, Z., Nakamura, Y., Jang, S., Kajita, S., Mase, K.: Ontology-Based Semantic Recommendation for Context-Aware E-Learning. In: Indulska, J., Ma, J., Yang, Laurence T., Ungerer, T., Cao, J. (eds.) UIC 2007. LNCS, vol. 4611, pp. 898–907. Springer, Heidelberg (2007). doi:10.1007/978-3-540-73549-6_88
17. Abecker, A., Bernardi, A., Hinkelmann, K., Kühn, O., Sintek, M.: Toward a well-founded technology for organizational memories. IEEE Intell. Syst. Appl. 13, 40–48 (1998)
18. Abecker, A., Bernardi, A., Hinkelmann, K., Ku"hn, O., Sintek, M.: Context-aware, proactive delivery of task-specific information: the knowmore project. Inf. Syst. Front. 2, 253–276 (2000)
19. Rychen, D.S., Salganik, L.H.: Key competencies for a successful life and a well-functioning society. OECD Defin. Sel. Competencies Final report. 1–20 (2003)
20. Ferrari, A.: DIGCOMP: A Framework For Developing And Understanding Digital Competence in Europe. (2013)
21. European e-Competence Framework (e-CF), Version 3.0 (2016) http://www.ecompetences.eu/

22. Forehand, M.: Bloom's Taxonomy. Emerg. Perspect. Learn. Teaching Technol. 12 (2012)
23. Vygotsky, L.S.: Mind in Society: The Development of Higher Psychological Processes, p. 159. Harvard university press, Cambridge (1978)
24. Wood, D., Bruner, J.S., Ross, G.: The role of tutoring in problem solving. J. Child Psychol. Psychiatry 17, 89–100 (1976)
25. Kim, M.C., Hannafin, M.J.: Scaffolding problem solving in technology-enhanced learning environments (TELEs): bridging research and theory with practice. Comput. Educ. 56, 403–417 (2011)
26. Quintana, C., Reiser, B.J., Davis, E.A., Krajcik, J., Fretz, E., Duncan, R.G.: A scaffolding design framework for software to support science inquiry. J. Learn. Sci. 13, 37–41 (2004)
27. Boud, D.: Current Issues and New Agendas in Workplace Learning, p. 163. National Centre for Vocational Education Research, Leabrook (1998)
28. Siemens, G.: Connectivism: a learning theory for the digital age. Int. J. Instr. Technol. Distance Learn. 2, 3–10 (2005)
29. Dunn, R., Dunn, K.J.: Teaching Students Through Their Individual Learning Styles: A Practical Approach. Reston Pub. Co., Reston (1978)
30. Leake, D.B.: CBR in context: the present and future. In: Leake, D.B. (ed.) Case-Based Reasoning: Experiences, Lessons, and Future Directions. pp. 1–35. AAAI Press/MIT Press, Menlo Park (1996)
31. Watson, I.: Case-based reasoning is a methodology not a technology. Knowl.-Based Syst. 12, 303–308 (1999)
32. Kolodner, J.L.: Case-based reasoning. Morgan Kaufmann Publishers, San Mateo (1993)
33. Aamodt, A., Plaza, E.: Case-based reasoning: foundational issues, methodological variations, and system approaches. AI Commun. 7, 39–59 (1994)
34. Bergmann, R.: Experience Management: Foundations, Development Methodology, and Internet-Based Applications. Springer, Berlin Heidelberg, Berlin, Heidelberg (2002)
35. Martin, A., Emmenegger, S., Hinkelmann, K., Thönssen, B.: A viewpoint-based case-based reasoning approach utilising an enterprise architecture ontology for experience management. Enterp. Inf. Syst. 11, 1–25 (2016)
36. Bergmann, R., Althoff, K.-D., Breen, S., Göker, M., Manago, M., Traphöner, R., Wess, S.: Developing Industrial Case-Based Reasoning Applications. Springer, Berlin Heidelberg, Berlin, Heidelberg (2003)
37. Díaz-Agudo, B., González-Calero, P.A.: An Architecture for Knowledge Intensive CBR Systems. In: Blanzieri, E., Portinale, L. (eds.) Advances in Case-Based Reasoning, pp. 37–48. Springer, Berlin / Heidelberg, Berlin, Heidelberg (2000)
38. Recio-Garía, J.A., Díaz-Agudo, B.: Ontology based CBR with jCOLIBRI. In: Ellis, R., Allen, T., and Tuson, A. (eds.) Proceedings of AI-2006, The Twenty-sixth SGAI International Conference on Innovative Techniques and Applications of Artificial Intelligence, pp. 149–162. Springer, London (2007)
39. Gao, J., Deng, G.: Semi-automatic construction of ontology-based cbr system for knowledge integration. Int. J. Electr. Electron. Eng. 4, 297–303 (2010)
40. Martin, A., Emmenegger, S., Wilke, G.: Integrating an enterprise architecture ontology in a case-based reasoning approach for project knowledge. In: Proceedings of the First International Conference on Enterprise Systems: ES 2013. pp. 1–12. IEEE, Cape Town (2013)
41. Recio-García, J.A., Díaz-Agudo, B., González-Calero, P.: jCOLIBRI2 Tutorial, Group of Artificial Intelligence Application (GAIA). University Complutense of Madrid. Document Version 1.2 (2008)
42. Kang, D., Lee, J., Choi, S., Kim, K.: An ontology-based enterprise architecture. Expert Syst. Appl. 37, 1456–1464 (2010)

43. Feldkamp, D., Hinkelmann, K., Thönssen, B.: KISS – Knowledge-Intensive Service Support: An Approach for Agile Process Management. In: Paschke, A., Biletskiy, Y. (eds.) RuleML 2007. LNCS, vol. 4824, pp. 25–38. Springer, Heidelberg (2007). doi:10.1007/978-3-540-75975-1_3

44. Thönssen, B.: An Enterprise Ontology Building the Bases for Automatic Metadata Generation. In: Sánchez-Alonso, S., Athanasiadis, Ioannis N. (eds.) MTSR 2010. CCIS, vol. 108, pp. 195–210. Springer, Heidelberg (2010). doi:10.1007/978-3-642-16552-8_19

45. Lankhorst, M.: Enterprise Architecture at Work. Springer, Heidelberg (2009)

46. Bello-Tomás, J.J., González-Calero, P.A., Díaz-Agudo, B.: JColibri: An object-oriented framework for building CBR systems. In: Funk, P., González Calero, P. (eds.) Advances in Case-Based Reasoning SE - 4, pp. 32–46. Springer, Berlin Heidelberg (2004)

47. Roth-Berghofer, T., Bahls, D.: Explanation capabilities of the open source case-based reasoning tool myCBR. In: Petridis, M. and Wiratunga, N. (eds.) UK Workshop on Case-Based Reasoning UKCBR 2008, pp. 23–34 (2008)

48. Assali, A.A., Lenne, D., Debray, B.: Heterogeneity in Ontological CBR Systems. In: Montani, S., Jain, L. (eds.) Successful Case-based Reasoning Applications-I SE-5, pp. 97–116. Springer, Berlin Heidelberg (2010)

49. Díaz-Agudo, B., González-Calero, P.: Knowledge intensive CBR made affordable. In: Weber, R., Gresse von Wangenheim, C. (eds.) Proceedings of the Workshop Program at the Fourth International Conference on Case-Based Reasoning. Navy Center for Applied Research in Artificial Intelligence Washington, DC, USA (2001)

50. Wang, Y., Hu, T., Zhang, S.: Ontology-based reconfigurable case-based reasoning system for knowledge integration. In: SMC 2003 Conference Proceedings. 2003 IEEE International Conference on Systems, Man and Cybernetics. Conference Theme - System Security and Assurance (Cat. No.03CH37483), pp. 4878–4883. IEEE, New York(2003)

51. Witschel, H.F., Martin, A., Emmenegger, S., Lutz, J.: A new retrieval function for ontology-based complex case descriptions. In: International Workshop Case-Based Reasoning CBR-MD 2015. ibai-publishing, Hamburg (2015)

52. Cohen, W.W., Ravikumar, P.D., Fienberg, S.E.: A comparison of string distance metrics for name-matching tasks. In: Kambhampati, S., Knoblock, C.A. (eds.) Proceedings of IJCAI-03 Workshop on Information Integration on the Web, Acapulco, Mexico, pp. 73–78 (2003)

53. Bechhofer, S., Harmelen, F., Hendler, J., Horrocks, I., McGuiness, D.L., Patel-Schneider, P. F., Stein, L.A.: OWL Web Ontology Language Reference

54. Dickinson, I.: Jena Ontology API (2009) http://jena.sourceforge.net/ontology/

55. Eclipse Foundation: Eclipse Modeling Framework (EMF) (2016) https://eclipse.org/modeling/emf/

56. W3C: XSL Transformations (XSLT) Version 1.0, World Wide Web Consortium (1999) https://www.w3.org/TR/xslt

57. W3C: RDF Schema 1.1, World Wide Web Consortium (2014) http://www.w3.org/TR/rdf-schema/

58. W3C: SPIN SPARQL Inferencing Notation, World Wide Web Consortium (2011) http://spinrdf.org/

59. Fanesi, D.: A Multilayer ontology to represent business process models and execution data, Master's thesis, University of Applied Sciences and Arts Northwestern Switzerland and University of Camerino (2015)

60. Fanesi, D., Cacciagrano, D.R., Hinkelmann, K.: Semantic business process representation to enhance the degree of BPM mechanization-an ontology. In: ES2015 Conference Proceedings, International Conference on Enterprise Systems, pp. 21–32. IEEE (2015)

Author Index

Printed in the United States
By Bookmasters